CHILLI... ...N

Prosecutor D... ...ght: This would b... ...eady were laboring ... ...blind alleys and down dead ends. Could the monster who violated this former cheerleader in broad daylight elude the best efforts of some of the craftiest detectives the Midwest had to offer?

As the investigation pushed on, Weber would find himself going to unprecedented lengths, learning about the criminal psyche in dark and frightening ways he never dreamed. Fate would deliver Weber and the police to Special Agent John Douglas of the FBI, well before his amazing abilities became the stuff of legend. Armed with only the most basic facts about the crime, Douglas would create a psychological profile of the killer that gave the cops a bold plan to crack this seemingly unsolvable case. But even if it worked, Don Weber still had to face a jury with a formidable array of evidence and witnesses to try to prove an unimaginable story of criminal behavior and depravity.

Don Weber vowed he would not rest until the pretty girl in the grave could rest in peace....

SILENT WITNESS

Silent Witness

The Karla Brown Murder Case

Don W. Weber
and
Charles Bosworth, Jr.

AN ONYX BOOK

To our wives:

Virginia Weber and Connie Bosworth

ONYX
Published by the Penguin Group
Penguin Books USA Inc., 375 Hudson Street,
New York, New York 10014, U.S.A.
Penguin Books Ltd, 27 Wrights Lane,
London W8 5TZ, England
Penguin Books Australia Ltd, Ringwood,
Victoria, Australia
Penguin Books Canada Ltd, 10 Alcorn Avenue,
Toronto, Ontario, Canada M4V 3B2
Penguin Books (N.Z.) Ltd, 182-190 Wairau Road,
Auckland 10, New Zealand

Penguin Books Ltd, Registered Offices:
Harmondsworth, Middlesex, England

First published by Onyx, an imprint of New American Library,
a division of Penguin Books USA Inc.

First Printing, September, 1993
10 9 8 7 6 5 4 3 2 1

Foreword

This is a factual account of a brutal murder and the long investigation that followed, accurately and painstakingly recounted using the official transcripts, records, and documents, and the carefully reported memories of the people who knew the case inside and out. All of the events are true; a few names have been changed to spare anyone embarrassment. Pseudonyms used are David Hart, Dwayne Conway, Patty Conway, Jack Meyers, Tony Garza, Lee Barns, Annie Tweed, Carolyn Thompson, Susan Andrews, Meg Haller, and Bobby Knoll.

The authors wish to thank everyone who shared their time and memories so freely in detailed interviews.

We owe special recognition and gratitude to Special Agent John Douglas of the FBI, whose amazing abilities were so critical to the case and to the writing of this book.

The authors also wish to express their continuing gratitude to the agents of the Division of Criminal Investigation of the Illinois State Police—especially Captain Randy Rushing, Captain Larry Trent, and Lieutenant Wayne Watson, and Crime Scene Technician Alva W. Busch. Special thanks go to Major Tom O'Connor of the Maryland Heights, Missouri, Police Department; Sergeant Eldon McEuen (Ret.), Commander Ralph Skinner, Detective Rick White, Chief Chuck Nunn, and former crime scene analyst Bill Redfern of the Wood River Police Department; Chief Don Greer of the Crestwood, Missouri, Police Department; and citizen-hero Spencer Bond.

Dr. Mary Case of the St. Louis County Medical Examiner's Office again has earned our thanks for her expertise.

Our editor, Michaela Hamilton, and her staff at Penguin USA once again have given us invaluable guidance and excellent advice on making our work the best it can be. We also wish to thank them for the constant encouragement needed to get through to the end.

And, finally, the authors acknowledge their indebtedness and appreciation to the relatives of Karla Brown for their courage and assistance—and grace—in the preparation of this book: Jo Ellen Brown, Donna and Terry Judson, and Connie and Ralph Dykstra.

Prologue

The young prosecutor could feel a deathly chill in the air as he walked through the house. It had been a week since the vicious crime there, and the heat of those acts was gone now. Left behind, amid the brutally interrupted clutter of what had been a happy time—a special and loving time—were only the thoughts of the horror that visited this small home and claimed the life of the beautiful young woman who had lived there so briefly.

In the five years that Don W. Weber had been in the Madison County state's attorney's office in southern Illinois, he had learned that a visit to the crime scene was mandatory for anyone who really wanted to understand what had happened there. It was especially important for the prosecutor who would have to understand so well that he could convince a jury beyond a reasonable doubt.

But there was another reason to visit the scene. Weber had discovered that some investigators could detect—through what he believed was a sixth sense—whether the heat from the spirit of the crime remained behind. It was difficult to describe to others that sensation, that electricity that moved along your skin; only someone with the passion for delving into such frightening mysteries would understand. But for those who could feel it, it provided a special spark that powered their efforts to find out who had committed the terrible deeds.

There was no such heat there that day in 1978 for Don Weber. As he walked through the little rooms and then ventured into the basement, he felt only a shudder; that was not a good omen. To Don Weber, it meant almost literally that the trail of this killer was as cold as the bite in the air. And in this place, Weber thought, that shiver felt like the devil's cold breath.

The prosecutor's instincts would prove to be right; this would be a tough case, indeed. But he already was drawn irresistibly to it, and would not be able to rest until it was solved. That was a vow others involved in the case would make, too. But it was one that would seem for years to have been made in vain.

The police already were laboring with a slow, plodding search that would take them up blind alleys and down dead ends. Could the monster who violated this former cheerleader in broad daylight elude the best efforts of Don Weber and some of the craftiest detectives Illinois had to offer?

As the investigation lurched on, Weber would find himself going to any length, applying new investigative techniques and forensic technologies he hadn't even known existed. He would probe deeply into the minds of experts from coast to coast, and learn about the criminal psyche in dark and frightening ways he never dreamed. Fate would deliver Weber and the police to Special Agent John Douglas of the FBI, well before his reputation and amazing abilities became the stuff of new legends and celebrity. He was in the earliest stages of developing a tactic called psychological profiling that would become an extraordinary method of analyzing violent crime and violent criminals. Armed with only the most basic facts about the crime and the victim, John Douglas would rattle off a detailed description of the killer, a verbal composite so revealing that the cops shuddered. Douglas even understood the rage that led to the apocalypse in that basement that morning. And, even more chilling, he gave the cops a bold plan he believed would draw the killer irresistibly into the open.

Such extreme measures carried risks, of course, especially for the prosecutor who would have to put them into action at the peril of his own reputation and political career. And, even if they worked, Don Weber still would have to face a jury with a startling array of evidence and witnesses to try to prove an unimaginable story of criminal behavior and depravity.

For reasons even the young prosecutor didn't fully understand, he had vowed he would not rest until the pretty girl in the grave could rest in peace. If he had to drag crime fighting in Madison County into the twentieth century, or even propel it into the twenty-first, so be it.

PART ONE

More Questions Than Answers

Chapter 1

Tuesday June 20, 1978

The little house was unremarkable by most standards—one story and covered by plain, white siding. The two huge trees in front almost dwarfed the small structure, providing ample shade for the yard on the quiet street in Wood River, Illinois. The lot was narrow and the neighboring houses seemed so close—especially the tiny place on the right, just across the sidewalk that led to the backyard.

But the house at 979 Acton Avenue was a dream home for David Hart and Karla Brown—a symbol of David's promise that, finally, they would get married. David's reluctance to take that final step, despite living with Karla in an apartment in nearby East Alton, had caused much of the friction during the five years of their on-again, off-again relationship. She was sure he loved her, but he had been unwilling or unable to give up the nights out with the boys and, Karla suspected, the use of his little black book. But now, he promised, they would get married after they settled into the new place they were buying.

David and Karla made a great couple, everyone agreed. At twenty-two, Karla Lou Brown was a blond beauty with a knock out figure, heavily endowed on top for a girl only four feet ten and maybe 100 pounds. She never failed to turn men's heads, and the former cheerleader loved being the center of attention. She had enjoyed more than her share of boyfriends, after all, and often seemed a little too flirty. Other girls sometimes had problems

dealing with that, especially because of the way men reacted to Karla. But her friends realized that the sexy, free-
and-easy image Karla cultivated was not the real Karla
they knew.

David Hart was a strikingly handsome man of twenty-
seven with sandy, curly hair and fine, classic features. He
was trim and tall, about six feet one. It was easy to picture him on a beach in southern California, launching a
surfboard into the waves.

David and Karla were almost ecstatic during the two
weeks they spent working on the house in preparation for
the move. Karla was taking some time off from classes at
a nearby college, and was at the house constantly, cleaning and decorating. She put a coat of light tan paint on
the basement floor where they set up the couch and tables
for a small TV room. David was working as an apprentice
electrician, but he spent his off hours at the new house,
too. His friends could tell he was excited as he talked
about his plans for remodeling and decorating each of the
rooms.

Many from their large group of old friends turned out
to help Karla and David move in that Tuesday night. The
boxes and bags and barrels arrived in several pickup
trucks and cars, and were distributed quickly throughout
the house. Although most of the rooms still were cluttered with cartons and assorted items, the bedroom was
set up so Karla and David could spend their first night in
their new home.

And when the work was done that evening, the group
swung easily into an impromptu celebration. There was
plenty of beer and music—an especially good and happy
time for a group that knew how to party.

On Wednesday the twenty-first, David went back to
work for the electrical contractor and Karla planned to
spend the day getting more done at the house. After David got off at 4:30, he stopped by the home of an old
friend, Tom Fiegenbaum, to enlist him and his pickup
truck to help move a big doghouse to the new place on

Acton. The doghouse was at the home of David's parents—in a perfect example of small-town coincidences—just two doors from Tom's house on Whitelaw Avenue. Tom was glad to help and they loaded the doghouse into his truck. David followed in his car while Tom drove the truck to the house on Acton. As Tom backed into the driveway, David made a quick trip into the house. When he came out, he mentioned that Karla was gone and that she had left the back door unlocked. That seemed to irritate him a little.

After they carried the doghouse into the yard, David invited Tom in to see the new place. After they toured the main floor, David led Tom down the stairs from the kitchen to the basement. As they reached the bottom of the stairs, Tom saw a concerned look cross David's face as he glanced around the room. He started toward the coffee table that sat in front of the couch; some TV trays and their stand were overturned near one end of the sofa, and there were some small dark spots on the floor.

"What's happening here?" David mumbled. "Karla?"

At the same instant, both men looked to the right, through the open swinging doors into the laundry room. Tom Fiegenbaum recoiled in horror at the scene.

Just a few feet away, Karla Brown was on her knees, doubled over at the waist, with her head submerged in water that filled one of the short, ten-gallon lard barrels the couple had used to move clothes. Her hands were tied behind her back and she was naked from the waist down.

"Karla!" David screamed. "Oh, my God! Karla!"

He ran to her and quickly pulled her from the barrel, lowering her gently back onto the floor. What had been a lovely face now was puffy and a sickly blue-gray color; it bore two deep, ugly gashes across the center of the forehead and the side of the chin. Tom Fiegenbaum saw something dark, probably a man's sock, tied tightly around her neck just above the brightly colored sweater that was all she wore. The sparkling, blond hair now was matted in dark, wet strands across her face. Her eyes were open just slightly, staring blankly at the ceiling.

Even through his shock, Fiegenbaum was certain that Karla Brown was dead.

"Oh God," David moaned as he rocked back and forth on his knees. Karla's head was cradled in his arms and tears were rolling down his face. "They killed her. Oh God, Karla. Karla."

Both men looked quickly around the room, as if they might find something of great importance. Someone hiding in the shadows. Some clue. Maybe even some way to end this nightmare and bring her back.

David looked down at her body again, her knees still bent up stiffly and slightly apart—revealing.

"Tom, get something to cover her. Please."

Fiegenbaum grabbed a nearby red blanket and pulled it over the lower half of her body. He knew he and David had to be sharing the same burning thoughts about what else must have been done to Karla, what other violations had accompanied her murder.

David looked up. "We have to call the police."

Tom dashed up the steps and used the phone in the kitchen to call an ambulance first, and then the police.

Dispatcher Bill Redfern was alone at the police station when the call came in; he sent all three officers on patrol—Sergeant Dick Morris and Officers David George and Jim Stewart. Officer George pulled up first, at 5:49, and saw two men standing in the front doorway. As he got close the porch, he could see that one of them was wild-eyed and hysterical. George hated situations like that; a cop never knew what he could be walking into. The men kept repeating that there was a body in the basement and were almost sweeping the officer in that direction. As they swung through the basement doorway into the room just to the right of the stairway, George saw the body covered with the blanket. There was water all over the floor; the scene was a mess.

Tom Fiegenbaum had gone back upstairs after hearing someone call for Officer George. Fiegenbaum was startled as he reached the living room and was confronted by

Sergeant Dick Morris, who leveled his pistol at Fiegen-baum and ordered him to halt.

"There's no need for that," Tom said quickly as he raised his hands in front of him. He told Morris the other officer was in the basement and then led Morris down-stairs.

David Hart was crying. "Why'd they have to beat her like that?" he asked angrily. He looked at the officers and then back at the body. "She's naked from the waist down. Her head was in that bucket of water."

Sergeant Morris told Officer George to take the two men upstairs. As the officer escorted David toward the stairs, the anger and hurt finally exploded. David wheeled and slammed his fist into the wall, blasting a hole through the paneling.

Officer Jim Stewart—his pistol drawn, too—arrived af-ter Morris, just long enough to find Hart and Fiegenbaum back in the living room. Hart was inconsolable—pacing the room, first sitting on the couch and then hopping up to pace some more. He kept rubbing his face with his hands. "Oh my God," he kept saying. "Someone's killed her. They killed Karla."

Stewart looked at Morris as he came back upstairs. Morris was maintaining his professional composure, but Stewart knew him well enough to see through it. Morris was shocked by what he had seen.

Ralph Skinner's four years as police chief in little Wood River had been fairly uneventful. The wiry, rugged, thirty-nine-year-old cop had been on the force for more than thirteen years, and there hadn't been many major cases—only two murders in all that time. It was mostly routine stuff and an occasional nasty fight or assault. Wood River was just across the Mississippi River from St. Louis; big-city crime was not so shocking as it was unusual. Wood River was in Madison County, had a pop-ulation of almost 250,000, and the area shared TV sta-tions and major daily newspapers with St. Louis. One of the aspects of Wood River that many people liked was its location in a major metropolitan area while it retained a small-town atmosphere.

But for the last few months, Ralph Skinner's job and the city of Wood River had been plagued by a series of bizarre sexual attacks by a very disturbed pervert. Although the public knew little about the actual details or the number of attacks, the chief was feeling substantial pressure from politicians and the public to get the frightening crimes solved.

He hadn't been home long from work on June 21 when the telephone rang at 5:52 P.M. with word of a murder on Acton Avenue, a few blocks from the chief's home.

A small crowd had gathered in front of the little white house by the time Skinner arrived—standard reaction in such a neighborhood. On the screened-in porch of the house next door, two scruffy-looking guys were watching the events. They weren't mingling with the rest of the crowd, and seemed to stand out a little, Skinner thought. He filed it mentally.

As he walked up the sidewalk, the chief could hear a young man's voice roll achingly out of the house.

"Why her?" There were loud sobs. "Why did they do it? Oh God!"

Skinner was met at the door by Officer George, who motioned toward the grieving young man in the living room, and said the victim was his girlfriend; it had been hard to keep him from going back downstairs. Skinner recognized David Hart; they had met around town a couple of times.

The chief was surprised by how clean the basement was; it wasn't the bloody murder scene he expected. He turned and saw the body under the blanket, and winced at the bare feet protruding from the end of the cover. But the sight under the blanket sickened him. His eyes were drawn to the sock cinched around the girl's throat; the knot had cut deeply into the skin. The sweater seemed bunched up around her middle. Nasty cuts on a pretty face. A lot to take in all at once. Grisly.

It was too early to make assumptions. But the evidence

so far suggested two things—a rape/murder case and a scene that had been cleaned up. If the scene was altered, this could be a tough one.

Skinner told Morris to call out Sergeant Eldon McEuen and Detective Chuck Nunn. The chief had promoted both men to detective, and he was confident they could handle any major case. They arrived from their homes within minutes, McEuen slightly ahead of Nunn. By then, it was 6 o'clock.

Sergeant McEuen—a gruff, thick-middled veteran of forty-six with wispy auburn hair—was met by Skinner in the living room. McEuen had heard David's grief from outside, too.

"Why does something like this happen?" David was asking Tom Fiegenbaum. The anger still was there amid the tears. "Who the hell could do something like this?"

Skinner escorted his sergeant toward the basement. "It's pretty brutal, Eldon. A young woman, a blonde. David Hart's fiancée. They were fixing up the house to move in. She's in the basement. Come on down; you have to see it. It's pretty gross."

When the blanket was lifted, McEuen was stunned. He had never seen anything like it. He had seen stabbings and shootings, but nothing approached this. He felt it in his belly.

He looked at Skinner. "My God. Somebody beat the hell out of her. She's been brutalized out of this world."

The chief described how she had been found bent over into the can, and the image flashed through McEuen's mind. God, had she been alive then?

Working through the shock, McEuen began to categorize his observations. Cuts on the face, on the jaw, apparently from some kind of weapon. Lips slightly swollen, some blood collected under her nose. Hands tied behind her back, the cords cutting deeply into her wrists—she had struggled, straining against the cords. She had been conscious, at least long enough to resist what was being done and to try to free herself. The body told McEuen it was a sexual assault; she had resisted sex, struggled, and was killed. That much seemed obvious.

Detective Chuck Nunn arrived in the basement, and someone lifted the blanket again. He grimaced and shook his head. He always tried to remove the humanity from a case like this, to build some immunity against the shock while he was on the job. He would hold that later for thoughts alone, maybe while he nursed a beer.

Then someone mentioned the victim's name. Nunn's eyes widened and he did a double take. "Karla Brown? That's Karla Brown? I went to school with her sisters. I've known her for years. My God, that's Karla? I didn't even recognize her. What a shame."

It was harder to distance yourself from the humanity under the blanket when it was someone you knew, Nunn thought.

He was told about the barrel of water; he grimaced again. God, he thought. This is a pretty good neighborhood for this kind of thing. We've got someone here who has some pretty serious problems to do something like that.

Nunn knew Karla Brown was an athletic girl, active in sports and a former cheerleader. Spunky; she would have fought. She was small, but lithe and well built. She probably would have put up a hell of a fight.

Eldon McEuen glanced around the room: the overturned TV trays; one of the cushions on the couch shoved over, sticking up over one end of the couch; the bucket of water.

He turned to Skinner. "This is as far out as anything I've ever seen. We need the most professional person we can get to handle this crime scene. I think we ought to call Alva Busch."

Inspector Alva W. Busch was only thirty years old and had been a crime-scene technician for the Illinois State Police for almost a year. But that was long enough to develop a reputation as a methodical and tenacious investigator with sharp eyes and great instincts. He had done a tour in Vietnam and was working at a steel mill when a veteran deputy sheriff from Busch's hometown suggested he think about law enforcement. That led to five years as a city cop in nearby Collinsville and another fourteen months on loan as an undercover "narc" with the area's Metropolitan Enforcement Group, the agency that used local cops to infiltrate drug traffic throughout the region. He finished that assignment with a contract on his life by a drug dealer. He had leaped at the chance to become a crime-scene "tech" for the State Police, even though he was about to make detective in Collinsville.

He was a bear of a man with a ruddy complexion that matched his red-blond hair and beard. But he was so soft-spoken—most of the time—that his voice belied his size. He could trade snappy street-talk with anyone—more residue from undercover drug work—and he could be painfully blunt. Calling him colorful was understatement; he was a bona fide member of a dying breed of real characters. And he reveled in it.

He still was at the crime lab in Fairview Heights about 6:30 when he got the call on this murder—perhaps his fiftieth in the last year. It took him some time to get ready to leave for the twenty-mile drive north to Wood River.

In the meantime, Dispatcher Bill Redfern had been relieved at the communications desk so he could take the crime-scene photos for the department. Photography was his hobby and, although he wasn't the official department photographer, he functioned as if he were. Redfern—a tall, lanky man with brown hair and pointed features—took a quick look around before getting some photos. He had known David Hart and Karla Brown slightly, and had gone to school with Tom Fiegenbaum. But Redfern couldn't let that intrude on his work that night. He already had shifted into his "methodical mode," shutting out the emotional and looking only for the useful.

The house and basement were so cluttered with items being moved in that Redfern wondered how any meaningful evidence could be collected. The basement, especially the disheveled couch, suggested a struggle. But had the

TV trays been knocked over during the struggle, or were they part of the clutter among the boxes and other items stacked just behind them? He didn't approach the body, knowing Alva Busch would want as few people as possible disturbing the scene.

Redfern glanced up at the basement window once, and saw David's big brown dog looking in. As almost every officer at the scene would say that night, Redfern mused, "If only that dog could talk."

It seemed to be an extraordinarily long time before Alva Busch arrived. After Skinner gave him a briefing, Busch decided a tour of the outside was the first order of business, even before a visit to the basement. He found no sign of forced entry at the front and rear doors. Nothing struck him about the yard or the neighborhood. He went back inside and made a note of the floor plan upstairs before going downstairs to begin the heavy stuff.

As he reached the bottom of the stairs, his first glance to the right caught sight of the body. The blanket had been removed, and Busch could see that the girl wore only a sweater. Probably a sexual homicide. There was a pair of wet blue jeans between the body and the barrel. But a pair of panties and perhaps some other clothing still were missing, Busch thought. He made a quick return upstairs and glanced through the rooms. Nothing caught his attention amid the disorder of a house in transition. He found a pair of denim shorts and panties on the bathroom floor, almost in front of the sink. Someone told them they thought the victim had worn those the night before; not what he was looking for. The question of the clothes would have to wait. He returned to the basement. He wanted to get to know the rest of that room first.

As soon as he saw the couch against the far wall, with the left cushion shoved away from the middle and sticking up on the far end, he got a mental image of a life-and-death struggle there. She probably had been lying on her back with her head at the right end. She tried to brace her feet, digging in her heels to get traction to strain against her attacker, and her feet pushed the cushion away from her, toward the left end of the sofa.

He walked over and looked into the cup sitting on the coffee table. There was a little dark liquid—coffee, maybe tea. But curiously, the cup also held a dental bridge with two teeth. That was out of place and made no sense unless it had been knocked from her mouth by force of the attack. It might be important, or it could be one of those little loose ends that never get tied up.

Near the cup on the table was another telling, even more personal piece of evidence—a used tampon. That reinforced the sexual motive.

But there, on the floor near the right end of the couch, was the first bit of evidence that Busch knew could be extremely valuable—a few little droplets of what surely was blood. He could tell a lot from those.

It was time to take control. Alva Busch turned to the other officers in the basement and invoked his characteristically, purposefully tactless style. "Everybody out. Upstairs. I don't want anybody else down here right now."

Alva Busch needed absolute control of a scene when he worked. He couldn't afford to have even well-intentioned officers distracting him with their comments and conversations. He didn't want any deputy coroners standing around, impatient for him to get finished with the body so they could haul it off; that made him furious.

This was serious business, and he got only one chance to get everything there was. There had been cases made on shoe prints around the body or other tiny bits of evidence he couldn't afford to miss or allow to be destroyed. Yes, he collected evidence in bags. But this was not like being a bag boy at a grocery store. You didn't just grab things and stuff them into sacks.

Alva Busch thought of himself more as a computer. He digested all the information at the scene and filed it so he could call it up and compute the meaning later.

A crime-scene "tech" was more than a collector of evidence. He had to understand serology—the study of body fluids and blood. He had to know blood types and enzyme types. He had to know how to interpret blood drops or splatter patterns from harder blows. He had to know how to package blood samples from the scene and how to mark which vials he had set up to coagulate and not coagulate. He had to get a proper blood sample at the autopsy. He had to understand saliva and semen.

A "tech" had to know how to collect hair samples— plucked with the follicle, never clipped with scissors. Fifty to 100 samples were needed for testing.

A "tech" had to understand firearms. He had to know which parts of shotgun shells were blown out with the BBs and how to recognize them at the scene. He had to understand tool marks, so he could look for ways to match impressions with objects that might have left them. He had to know how to match broken pieces that used to be part of the same item.

A "tech" had to know about footprints and shoe prints. He had to be alert for tiny nicks or marks on a shoe sole that made it as individual as a fingerprint.

A "tech" had to know enough about physiology, and what happened to the human body during the process of death, to interpret the evidence available from the remains.

And while he was applying all of that, Alva Busch needed time to study the scene, to get a feel for what had happened. He had to reenact the crime in his mind, and find a way to get into the killer's mind. What had he done first? What had happened last? What did the bits of evidence mean and how did they all fit together? Most of all, whom did they incriminate?

Armed with everything there was to know from the scene, Busch always could tell later whether a suspect really knew what he was talking about if he claimed he had been there.

As he applied that training, he began a search for more blood by the couch. It bothered him when there was none; there should have been blood there from the struggle that shoved the cushion over. He looked back at the drops. Some of them had small teardrop tails at one end, indicating they were moving at an angle when they hit the floor. To Busch, they suggested movement toward the laundry room.

It was time to study the body. As he looked down into Karla Brown's face for the first time, her eyes stared back; that bothered him. She was a pretty girl. The cops said she was moving into this house with her fiancée, and they planned to be married.

Alva Busch began to feel the remorse, the emotions that were luxuries he could not afford as a true professional. This lovely girl had been savagely murdered in her own home, her new home, just when her life seemed to be starting. She was unpacking her own stuff, minding her own business, and some lowlife had barged in and violated her.

Busch knew it was time to shift into gear—to channel that righteous anger toward catching the bad guy. It was time for the forensic scientist to kick in.

While Busch was at work downstairs, Sergeant Eldon McEuen took David Hart and Tom Fiegenbaum to the police station for formal interviews and written statements. David didn't want to leave, but Tom assured him it was for the best. On the way out of the house, McEuen sent some of the other officers out to canvass the neighborhood. Surely, on this quiet street of houses crowded tightly together, somebody had seen something during this murder in broad daylight. A strange man on the street, a new car on the block. Someone hurrying down the sidewalk. Any little thing could break this case, and missing it could lead to years of frustration.

McEuen took Fiegenbaum into the interview room first, leaving Officer Stewart to keep David calmed down in the hallway. McEuen started asking general questions about 6:20 P.M., and it took only fifteen minutes for Fiegenbaum to provide a straightforward account of what had happened. He willingly agreed to be fingerprinted so the police could eliminate his prints if they were found.

But then the sergeant startled Tom Fiegenbaum.

"Do you think David could have done it?"

Tom replied defensively, emphatically, "Absolutely not. He was with me. He couldn't have done it. Absolutely not."

McEuen nodded. "Okay." The cop thought David's emotional and angry reaction to his fiancée's murder had been perfectly normal; there was no hint of anything suspicious. And it didn't make sense to McEuen that a man who had been living with a woman and planned to marry her would commit such a brutal, sexually oriented crime. McEuen would check David out completely, of course, and already was wondering if the job where David worked that day was too far away for a round trip—and a murder—on his lunch hour. But McEuen hoped his hunch was right, and David was not Karla's killer.

Chief Skinner, however, was very worried about David. Karla probably was killed by someone she knew, someone she let into the house. Although still a mess from the moving process, the house had not been ransacked, and nothing appeared to have been stolen. Skinner knew they would have to take a very close look at David.

Skinner had seen a picture of Karla upstairs, and was shocked by how different the face on the body downstairs looked. This is extreme enough, Skinner thought, that someone had to be awfully damned mad at her to do that much damage to her face. Could a stranger summon such outrage? Or would it come from someone closer?

While McEuen was questioning Fiegenbaum, David's parents arrived at the station. Robert and Evelyn Hart, both of them badly shaken, were consoling their son when Fiegenbaum and McEuen came out of the interview room. McEuen was touched by the emotional scene in the hallway. He knew the family—good, solid people.

McEuen interviewed David for thirty minutes. The young man's composure faded in and out, and the tears flowed. His story was simple and direct, and so painful for McEuen to hear. It was hard to watch someone who appeared to be hurting that badly. The cop had seen David's beautiful fiancée on that laundry room floor, and he could only imagine how it felt for that to be someone you loved, someone you had held and caressed. As he took David's statement, McEuen was vowing to himself that this was one case they would solve, and one killer who would be found and punished.

David could offer no motive or suspects, other than to suggest the police check out Jack Meyers, a local tough and a suspected drug dealer who was well known to the cops. He had "hit" on Karla repeatedly and insistently for a date, and she had disliked him intensely, David told McEuen.

David didn't know anyone in the new neighborhood. He and Karla had introduced themselves briefly to the neighbors on each side of the house while they had been working there, but David couldn't even remember their names.

But then he passed along one important bit of news. Evelyn Hart had called Karla that morning to chat about the house. During their conversation, at about 11 o'clock, Karla said someone was at the door. She said she would call back but never did. When Evelyn called about 1 o'clock, no one answered.

Our first break, McEuen thought. Maybe they had the time of the murder now, and maybe someone had seen the murderer at the door. Maybe his men covering the neighborhood already had a line on something hot. Maybes.

The detective already was assuming the scene would yield little, if anything, that pointed directly to the killer. That meant interviewing everyone in the circle of friends around Karla and David, especially those who attended the party the night before. Had something happened then?

McEuen and the other cops had heard occasional mentions of David, Karla, and some of their friends in connection with drugs. Nothing heavy; just recreational use, and mostly just marijuana. Some of them might be what Officer Chuck Nunn called "pooches"—small-time couriers for drugs. All of that territory would have to be covered closely for motive and suspects.

McEuen also knew Karla's reputation as a "good-lookin' gal" who was well known among the guys in town and dated a lot. Lord only knew where that could lead.

My God, McEuen said to himself. We've got a hell of a lot of work to do. A lot of questions and very few answers.

He didn't think this was connected to the other sexual assaults in town. None of those included any violent injuries, even when the pervert broke in and forced the women to perform odd sex acts while he held a butcher knife. And those attacks all had happened at night. A link couldn't be ruled out, but it didn't seem likely.

McEuen did know one thing for sure, however. The killing of Karla Brown would send shock waves through little Wood River like nothing that had happened in decades. And the pressure on the local police department would increase dramatically.

Alva Busch was staring at Karla Brown. He looked at her for a long time, waiting for her to tell him about what had happened. He already had concluded that she was dead when her body was thrust into the barrel. The water had only the slightest red tint; she had not bled much in the barrel. The postmortem lividity—the settling of the blood in the lowest portion of the body after death—was on the front of Karla's upper body, also confirming the doubled-over, facedown position after death.

He looked at the deep semicircular ridge around her left hip. After death, skin retained such marks very well.

Busch rejected the obvious conclusion of drowning suggested by the froth around her nose. That occurred, Busch believed, when David Hart pulled her body out of the water, forcing out the air that was trapped in her lungs and windpipe when she was bent over the edge of the barrel. If she had been alive when plunged into the water, there should have been evidence of a struggle to hold her under. Nothing in the laundry room suggested the kind of battle he thought had happened on that couch.

Busch concentrated on the cuts on Karla's face. Why

two cuts? And why were they so strangely parallel? Had one object made both cuts at the same time? What could do that?

Something else about the cuts bothered him. He knew a gash that deep across someone's pumpkin—his irreverent term for a victim's head—meant lots of blood. Under the force that inflicted those wounds, the blood would have spurted out of those cuts, splattering everything nearby. She hadn't been beaten in the laundry room because there was no blood in that confined space. Busch glanced back at the couch; that had to be where she died.

He looked into the cuts to examine the skin-bridging— the slivers of skin still spanning the wounds. That suggested an object with a sharp edge that had been applied with significant force.

He moved next to Karla's neck. Two men's socks—one black, the other dark blue—had been tied tightly around her neck with two very neat knots. The socks were tied toe-to-toe, top-to-top. That was damned neat for a killer struggling with his victim—way too neat. Alva would find the mate to the black sock under the couch later, and the other blue sock in David's dresser upstairs.

On to the blouse—a short-sleeved, multicolored sweater that seemed too heavy for summer wear by a woman working around the house. But what bothered Alva more was the single barrel-shaped button at the top of the V-neck. It still was buttoned, held by a thin fabric loop. Amid a ferocious struggle, could that loop have held? Not very likely.

On Karla's abdomen, just below the bottom of her blouse, and on her left arm, Busch noticed what appeared to be some fluid that had dried—semen perhaps. He scraped it gently and put the material carefully into a small tin container.

Karla's right hand and arm were pinned under her body. Her left arm was bent up at the elbow, her hand death-frozen well above the floor. The white cord binding her apparently had been a double-strand electrical cord split down the middle. It was tied around her wrists in several loops. It ran under the body and still connected the hands. But again, something was wrong. There was too much cord between the wrists. That would have allowed Karla enough movement to grab at a rapist who had forced himself on top of her. No rapist would tie up a victim like that; it defeated the purpose.

Busch looked for broken fingernails. Oddly, given what he thought must have been a desperate struggle, they were intact. He slipped plastic bags over her hands and secured them at the wrists, just in case there were some skin scrapings under the nails.

Busch stepped back and snapped the first of what should have been dozens of photographs. But his flash attachment refused to cycle for the next photo. He checked and rechecked, but couldn't figure out what was wrong. He was standing in a dark basement, knee-deep in one of the worst murders he had handled, and he had no flash.

"Son of a bitch," Busch fumed as his temper boiled over. "I can't believe this."

Bill Redfern, the only officer Busch had allowed to return to the basement, offered to take the pictures. It wasn't the way Busch worked, but he had no choice. He didn't ask, but he assumed Redfern's camera was loaded with color film. That assumption would haunt Busch later.

As Redfern snapped away, Busch returned to his analysis of the scene. The blood drops. The socks and the sweater. The loose bindings. The dental bridge and the tampon. The body dumped in the water.

This crime didn't happen the way this scene looks, Alva Busch thought. This guy was doing something other than what we see right now. This guy is playing games with us.

Busch decided Karla Brown had told him all she could. Redfern and Chuck Nunn helped Busch lift the body onto a sheet and then wrap it to preserve any fibers or other evidence still on the body. The men then lifted the remains onto a stretcher and covered them with another sheet.

Busch turned to the deputy coroner, who would transport the body to the hospital for full X-rays and then to nearby Marks Funeral Home where the autopsy would be done the next day.

"I don't want the body, the clothing, or anything disturbed before I get to the hospital," Busch said. "I don't want the clothing or the cords around her hands touched. Have them X-ray it through the sheets. Don't even unwrap them. I'll be there as soon as I finish with the scene, and I don't want anyone messing with the body before that."

Officer Stewart was helping to control the crowd outside when the stretcher was carried out. He could hear the gasps and the whispers rippling through the crowd. The 1968 Cadillac hearse, escorted by a police car, headed for the hospital at 9:47 P.M.

While Busch worked in the basement, a telephone call and a knock at the door upstairs had provided some helpful information.

Jamie Hale, an old friend of Karla's, called to report that she had talked to Karla on the phone between 9 and 9:30 that morning. They made plans for Jamie to stop by Karla's house that afternoon, but she was to call first to make sure Karla was there. When Jamie called about 2:30, there was no answer.

Another friend stopped by with a similar story. Debbie Davis had talked to Karla on the phone about 10 o'clock, making arrangements to stop by later. When Debra arrived at 11, no one answered her knock on the door.

Another face in the crowd outside Karla's house that night was Joe Sheppard, Sr., her former stepfather. He was so insistent with his questions that he attracted attention from Chief Skinner and Sergeant McEuen. Sergeant Dick Morris was sent over to calm him down, and he eventually faded back into the crowd. But the police would hear about him later, more than once.

The cops' quick canvass of the neighborhood produced nothing useful. The men on each side of Karla's house had been home all day, but had seen nothing. The neighbor on the west, Artie McMillian, had seen David leave for work about 7:30 and arrive home with a friend about 5:30. The young man on the east, Dwayne C. Conway, said he had spent the early afternoon sitting on his front porch with a friend, John Prante of nearby Bethalto. They had noticed nothing unusual between noon and 3, when Prante left and Conway returned to his job painting on a house on the corner.

Chief Skinner arrived at the police station about 8 o'clock, shortly after McEuen had fingerprinted David Hart and Tom Fiegenbaum and sent them home. McEuen's gut feeling that David was not a suspect eased Skinner's mind a bit. And he felt even better after McEuen's calls to David's boss at the electrical company and the electrician David had worked with that day. They confirmed David's alibi and said he seemed perfectly normal all day. He had been on a job in north Alton, some ten miles from Acton Avenue.

McEuen and Skinner headed back for Acton Avenue; there still was much to do before wrapping up for the night.

It would be a long night, too, for Tom Fiegenbaum. He told his gruesome story to his stunned wife, Suzanne, who had worked with Karla Brown the year before and knew her well. They had gone to the same high school, although Karla was a little younger. Suzanne couldn't believe that the happy, outgoing Karla was gone, taken in such a brutal way.

For the rest of the night, flashbacks from those God-awful scenes and sounds at 979 Acton haunted Tom. No one could go through that without feeling their insides twisted into knots. When he finally went to bed, sleep was a long time coming.

One of McEuen's first activities back at the scene was to interview Edna Vancil, who lived directly across the street from Karla's house. Mrs. Vancil had seen an old red car with a white roof in front of 979 Acton that morning. A slim man carrying an attaché case got out of the car, but she didn't watch him after that. McEuen drove her to some drive-in restaurants nearby to see if she could find a similar car; she picked out a 1964 Ford.

McEuen and Skinner were anxious to see what Alva Busch was coming up with in the basement. What they got, instead, was a list of questions the evidence raised for the crime-scene tech. McEuen and Busch decided to check the back door again for signs of forced entry. They found nothing to suggest a break-in, but Busch caught something he missed before. A couple tiny smears of what appeared to be blood still were on the door frame. Later, Busch found more little blood spots on the gatepost in the backyard.

The killer probably had left by the back door and slipped through the gate, with some of Karla's blood still on him, Busch knew now.

Busch returned to the blood drops in the basement. He hoped he could retrace them, perhaps figuring out how and when the body was moved into the laundry room.

There were no drops near the barrel, nor anywhere else in the laundry room. Perhaps too much water had been splashed around when Karla's body was pulled from the barrel. He backpedaled toward the doorway and picked up the trail there. He found drops along the floor, a few splashed on boxes, and some more on a rumpled sheet. The drops led across the room to the couch, reconfirming it to Busch as the place of death for Karla Lou Brown.

His eyes were pulled to a puddle of water under the sofa. As he crouched down, he was shocked to see a pint or more of water forming an irregular shape almost thirty-six inches across. From the puddle, the water trailed off under the couch and along the edge of the wall behind it. The water had a slight red tint.

Busch looked at the couch and found a few small traces of blood on the cushion where he believed Karla's head had been during the struggle. But that still wasn't right. With the cuts she suffered, the couch should have been covered with blood. He touched the cushion and found it soaked with water. The water under the couch had dripped through from the cushion.

The killer had indeed tried to change the scene. He had tried to clean it up and misdirect the attention from the place where the girl had died.

Alva Busch glanced around the room again. What had been used to carry the water from the laundry room to the couch? Nothing in sight seemed likely. The cup on the table still held some other liquid, and it would have taken a lot of trips a cupful at a time.

Busch turned back to the couch. He lifted the cushion and made a discovery that would become an obsession. There lay two small lengths of white electrical cord like that used to tie Karla's hands. The first piece was about five inches long, probably cut with a knife. The ends were blunt, not tapered as if pinched while being cut with scissors or snips. The second length was a little longer, cut on both ends and knotted in the center with a single, simple loop. A single, maddening loop that would torment Alva Busch for years.

He looked around the room again. No appliance or other obvious source for the cord.

He turned back to Redfern and Nunn.

"This scene is . . . screwed . . . up," he said, emphasizing the last two words. "This scene has been staged. This guy was here for a while. This was no 'Wham, bam, thank you ma'am.' "

It was the kind of comment Nunn had come to expect from Busch. From their time together on the Metropolitan Enforcement Group, Nunn had learned that Busch was very serious about his work, but never too serious for an off-the-wall quip that could be shockingly funny under the dark circumstances. Now, the "Buschmaster" had struck again. Another grabber from the guy whose favorite question led to his nickname of "What's the Scam Al Busch."

But even the ever-inquiring Busch had never raised so many questions about a crime scene in such a short time span. And that many questions popping up so quickly meant someone was playing some heavy games with what had happened in that basement.

Busch listed his questions for Nunn and Redfern, so the Wood River cops could be looking for the important evidence and making the right inquiries with suspects. How did this guy get Karla into the position that he could tie her up so poorly and have enough time to strangle her with such neatly tied socks? How did that fight happen on that couch without turning over that coffee table? Why was that dental bridge in the cup?

How could that button on the blouse still be intact? Where was the knife used on the cord, and where did the cord come from? If it was an electrical cord, where were the ends? Where were the rest of her clothes? Why had he doused the couch with water, and what did he use to carry the water?

It was time to finish his work with the body, and Al Busch headed for the hospital.

The sound of the car pulling up in the driveway in the Richmond Heights area of St. Louis, just across the Mississippi from Wood River, caught Jo Ellen Brown's attention inside the house. It was dusk on a summer evening, but there still was enough light to recognize her daughter's boyfriend, David Hart, hurrying toward the house as his mother got out of the car behind him.

That same foreboding Jo Ellen recognized from eleven years earlier clutched at her throat. When they called in 1967 to tell her there had been an accident at work, she knew instinctively that her husband already was dead.

This time, as David hurried toward the door, Jo Ellen knew again. Her beautiful, troubled, rebellious daughter was dead.

Jo Ellen—whose tiny stature marked her obviously as the mother of the three girls who resembled each other and their mother so strikingly—had just talked to Karla on the telephone the day before. Karla was so happy; she was just about to get everything she ever wanted. After all this time, the dreams in Karla's deepest heart were within reach. Those secret desires would have surprised all but Karla's best friends. They weren't the things she talked about to most people; they weren't the things that seemed to go with party-loving Karla.

But deep inside, her friends and mother knew, Karla Brown wanted the real stuff. She wanted what a little girl's memory had clung to so tightly—what had been taken away so cruelly when her father died. She wanted the things that made a real home. A husband she would love forever. The sounds of happy children. A real family, secure in a pretty house on a quiet street.

Jo Ellen knew that those dreams seemed to be coming true for Karla as she carried her possessions into the little white house at 979 Acton that seemed so perfect. It was almost like going home; a few years earlier, Karla and Jo Ellen lived in a duplex unit on the corner, just across the street. Karla felt as if she knew the quiet neighborhood well.

Jo Ellen Brown didn't really hear David's words as he broke the news. There weren't many details, just that Karla had been murdered.

Jo Ellen quickly called the oldest of her three daughters, Connie Dykstra. Connie was another slim, pretty woman with hair just a slightly darker blond than her younger sisters'. Connie was thirty and lived in Connecticut with her husband, Ralph, their seven-year-old daughter, and four-year-old son. Jo Ellen couldn't find the strength in that husky, gravel-coated voice her family knew so well to break the news to Connie, so she tried to tell Ralph. But she still couldn't get out the words. She handed the phone to Evelyn Hart.

When Ralph relayed the brief message, Connie felt the predictable disbelief. She felt it so deeply that she was immobilized; she couldn't absorb this news. Karla had just spent more than a month visiting the Dykstras in Connecticut, and had watched the kids for two weeks while Connie and Ralph went to Europe. Karla couldn't have been back home more than three weeks. How could this have happened so soon?

Evelyn Hart had provided few details to Ralph, and Connie somehow imagined that Karla had been shot by someone who just showed up at her door. Maybe such a random act of violence was easier to accept than the thought that someone who knew Karla could take her life. It was a strange thought, but it stayed with Connie through the night and on the flight to St. Louis the next morning. Connie was a former flight attendant and Ralph was a pilot for TWA; she got an emergency pass.

She sat quietly on the plane, her mind and feelings numb. A cousin's husband met her at the airport and filled in some of the details of Karla's murder. It was a hard story to accept.

After calling Connie, Jo Ellen tried to reach her second daughter, Donna Judson, who was twenty-nine and living in Austin, Minnesota. But she was traveling with her salesman husband, Terry, and it would be the next day before they could be tracked down in Cedar Rapids, Iowa.

David and his mother stayed at Jo Ellen's for a while that evening, but there wasn't much to say. Jo Ellen was stunned into silence, and David was not doing well, either. The Harts soon left for home.

But Jo Ellen had noticed one thing—David Hart's knuckles were badly skinned.

When she was alone with the tragic news, Jo Ellen Brown took some Valium, had a few drinks, and chain-smoked cigarettes until the anger began to creep in. Why had it taken so long to notify her? What really had happened? Why wasn't somebody telling her something? It was her daughter, after all. Jo Ellen could feel a nasty edge coming on.

By 3 o'clock in the morning, when the anger had not subsided, she called the Richmond Heights police. They sent out an officer who listened with sympathy and genuine concern, even when she wondered aloud if the man sent to tell her about her daughter's murder was the one who had killed her.

Chapter 2

Crime Scene Technician Alva Busch always followed the body. In many cases, it was the most important piece of evidence there was, as insensitive as that sounded to people on the outside.

Busch told the Wood River officers to protect the crime scene; he had many more questions to try to answer there before he could release it. Then Busch, Chuck Nunn, and Bill Redfern drove several blocks to Wood River Township Hospital to complete the examination of Karla Brown's body. The most important discovery was some hair—too dark to be Karla's—collected from Karla's right hand and blouse. That could be important if lab analysis could provide a scientific link between the hair and a suspect, and that could link the suspect directly to the body.

He clipped through the socks wrapped around her neck, cutting them in the middle to make sure the knots were preserved. He wrapped tape around the knots and put his initials on the tape to keep anyone from disturbing what he thought might be an important clue, perhaps even a traceable peculiarity about this killer.

Then Alva quietly packaged the brightly colored sweater with the single button that was baffling him. Some of the other officers quoted David Hart as saying it was Karla's favorite sweater, but she only wore it in the winter. Another piece of evidence that didn't add up.

The lab workers at the hospital took the required blood and urine, as well as swab samples of all body cavities. As Busch had hoped, some skin scrapings were found under Karla's fingernails. Busch took Karla's fingerprints, and all the other medical evidence was given to him to take to the lab for analysis.

The autopsy would be done the next day at a nearby funeral home; Busch would return for that.

There was nothing else to do that night; everyone would start fresh in the morning. Officer David George was left at the house to protect it overnight.

On the drive back to the lab, the impact of this case began to close in on Busch. He felt the sorrow for this victim and her fiancé. In the detached, professional opinion of Crime Scene Technician Alva W. Busch, Karla Brown never had a chance. It was such a senseless murder, and she was violated so brutally, invaded among her own possessions and in her own new house.

Had Busch found everything there was at the scene? Had he missed something—that one clue that would solve the case? He never was satisfied with the evidence he collected. He always worried that he had missed something important.

Busch also was frustrated by what he was hearing from the Wood River officers. They already seemed preoccupied with this Jack Meyers, this tough guy they thought was capable of inflicting such a brutal death on a young woman. Busch feared his warnings that the scene was not really what it appeared weren't being heeded by the people who would have to solve this case.

As the cops from Wood River headed for their homes, their own grief at the death of such a pretty girl was intensified by their mixed feelings about the investigation they now faced.

Sergeant Eldon McEuen knew how much work was ahead. There was an incredible amount of interviewing and alibi-checking to do. From what McEuen knew then, there was nothing to lead in one specific direction. It looked more like a case where everything had to be checked and every lead had to be followed while the cops prayed they would turn up something that cracked it.

Detective Chuck Nunn considered everyone Karla Brown knew—including David Hart—a suspect. But

Nunn was not optimistic about what the cops had to work with so far. We've got a body. We've got a lot of evidence. And we've got a lot of people to talk to, Nunn thought. But we really have nothing.

Chief Ralph Skinner's intuition told him that no one ever would confess to this ruthless killing. And this would be a big case, accompanied by more publicity than the Wood River police were used to. He dreaded the inevitable parade of reporters through his office the next morning, certain they would try to link the murder to the unsolved sexual assaults. He would have to give them some information about this startling murder, without compromising the investigation. It would be a thin line, and he knew how insistent reporters could be.

Sergeant McEuen always went in about 6:30 A.M. to read through the reports from the night before, even though his shift didn't start until 8. In the early hours of Thursday, June 22, as he read the reports on Karla Brown's murder, he decided Day Two had to start with interviews of the people who had been at the moving party—some of the last people to see her alive. McEuen knew that, unless something broke immediately, he would have to find out a lot more about this young woman. Who was she, really? How did she act—around her friends and in private moments? Was there something about her that could drive someone to the rage that could inflict that kind of death on her?

What about her past? Anything over the edge? Anything criminal—drugs maybe? Kinky? What about past boyfriends and lovers? Someone insanely jealous over her impending marriage, perhaps? Any serious grudges against her?

There seemed to be thousands of questions that could be asked, each one a painful prying into the life that ended in a basement the morning before.

It still was early when McEuen called David Hart—too early for the kind of night David must have endured. He met McEuen at the police station at 9 o'clock to provide

a detailed account of the moving party and a list of ten
people who were there. He agreed to help contact them to
ask that they go to the station for interviews.

The other interviews later that day began to give Sergeant McEuen a glimpse of Karla Brown as she was seen
through the eyes of her friends. She was a popular and
admired young woman, genuinely loved by those close to
her. Some of her girlfriends couldn't stop crying as they
talked about her; the young men obviously respected her
and held her in deep affection.

A few tidbits came up as McEuen talked to the people
who had been at the moving party. Bob and Debbie Davis
said Karla mentioned being a little afraid of the old man
next door. He was always drinking and dirty, and Karla
thought he was scary.

Debbie also said Karla had gone out with a guy in Connecticut, when Karla and David broke up briefly and
Karla went to visit her sister, Connie. Karla said later that
the guy was coming to visit.

Debbie had heard that Karla had been raped once at a
swimming party; Debbie gave McEuen a name said to be
Karla's attacker.

But two other, major points jumped out at McEuen
from the interviews with Karla's friends.

Joe Sheppard, Sr., was mentioned with suspicion by
Debbie Davis and Carolyn Thompson, another of Karla's
girlfriends. Debbie Davis said Karla recently went to dinner with Sheppard, a move Debbie thought was dumb because Sheppard treated Karla badly while they lived in
the same house. Karla had shrugged it off, and it was
never discussed again.

Carolyn Thompson, a former roommate of Karla's,
went so far as to tell McEuen, "If anyone killed Karla, I
would suspect Joe Sheppard." Or maybe one of his
"spooky friends," she added. She even charged that
Sheppard had struck Karla while he was married to her
mother. Carolyn said Sheppard was always trying to get
Karla's friends into bed; he once climbed into bed with

Carolyn and tried to rape her when she spent the night with Karla after her high school graduation party. When Carolyn broke loose, Sheppard warned her to keep quiet about it or she would be sorry.

Carolyn also said Sheppard claimed to be connected to organized crime, and had told the girls they could make extra money by working for him as prostitutes at a local nightclub.

The second thing that popped up was an account by some of Karla's friends about her contact the night of the party with someone next door at 989 Acton, where Dwayne Conway lived. Jim Nicosia, an old friend of David and Karla, recognized a man standing in the yard next door as Lee Barns, a guy Karla knew slightly from high school. Nicosia said that made him wonder about the neighbor, since Nicosia suspected that Barns had a drug problem.

Bob Lewis had seen Karla talking to a rough-looking, long-haired guy next door. The man stopped in the yard, pointed at Karla, and called her by name. She answered, "You've got a good memory. It's been a long time." Lewis mentioned it to David Hart later and added that, if his neighbors looked like that, David might want to keep things tied down until he got to know them. David said, "Don't worry. That's Lee Barns. He doesn't live there."

That was worth checking out; McEuen went back to Dwayne Conway's house that day. Conway—a thin, scraggly man of twenty-one with stringy brown hair—said Barns was an acquaintance who had been to his house two or three times, including the night before the murder. Barns said he knew Karla Brown, and was thinking about going to her party to have a beer. But Barns never went over, Conway said.

Conway's visitor on the day of the murder was John Prante, pronounced with a long E at the end. Conway couldn't give McEuen an address for Prante's house near a lake in Bethalto, but Conway did provide a phone number. And then he happily consented to McEuen's request to take fingerprints and a photograph.

The autopsy for Karla Lou Brown was held at the Marks Funeral Home in Wood River. In a sad way, it was fitting. Karla had lived with the Marks family for a while when she was younger. She often had been mistaken for a slightly older sister to Paula Marks, another pretty blonde.

Dr. Harry Parks had performed autopsies for Madison County and many other counties in southwestern Illinois since 1964; he probably had done nearly 2,000 over fourteen years.

He began the autopsy with an external exam, noting that the body carried the assortment of marks indicative of a struggle. Even her knees were bruised and battered, perhaps from being dragged. Her neck and throat were badly bruised, especially in the area where the socks had been tied so tightly.

There were other small marks in that area which, unfortunately, seemed unremarkable. They would become quite remarkable later.

The slightly curved gashes on her forehead and chin each measured about five centimeters—a fraction more than two inches—and appeared to have been made by a blunt object. There was a tiny cut on the side of her nose.

From the description of the crime scene, Dr. Parks concluded that the larger gashes were suffered just before or after death. If they had come much before death, there would have been more blood at the scene because the face bleeds very freely.

The doctor found a severe fracture of the jaw at the point of the chin. His fingers traveled over the rest of the skull, but found no evidence of more fractures. The X-ray report from the hospital also showed no skull fractures.

As he examined the many bruises around the throat and neck, he was reasonably sure the cause of death would be "strangulation by garroting"—the use of the cord or something similar around the throat. Once the body was opened surgically, his assumption was supported by injuries to the soft tissues and muscles of the neck, and the structures in the throat. The injuries caused hemorrhages and leaks of blood through the lining of the larynx, or windpipe. The front of the esophagus, the tube that carries food to the stomach, also showed injuries consistent with strangulation.

That was, indeed, the cause of death, he concluded.

Dr. Parks found some congestion, but no water in the lungs. To him, that eliminated drowning and further supported strangulation. His medical opinion was that she was already dead when she was plunged into the water.

Alva Busch was pleased that his observations at the scene agreed with the doctor's conclusions. Both men felt the froth around the nose and mouth came from air being forced out of Karla's lungs as she was bent over the barrel or removed from it.

But Dr. Parks was less sure about the results of the examination for rape. There were no external injuries—bruising and scrapes—that sometimes accompany a forcible rape. Some sperm was found in the vagina, but the amount was quite small. It could suggest an incomplete sex act, or intercourse as much a two days earlier.

The results of the toxicological tests would come in a week later, showing no drugs or alcohol in Karla's system.

With Alva Busch's camera still out of commission, Bill Redfern was taking the photographs at the autopsy. As Dr. Parks pulled Karla's chin up to expose the injuries to her neck, Redfern moved in low to get a good angle. But his professional Mamiya twin-lens two-and-a-quarter by two-and-a-quarter camera with a pistol grip made the shot hard to get. As the camera moved in for a closeup, the lower area in the frame faded out of view. And he couldn't get too close or too low because the pistol grip held the camera away from the body.

It was an odd angle and a tough shot to get.

And it was a photograph that would become more important than anyone could imagine.

* * *

Another photograph was being seen in the Wood River area that day. This one was a typical shot from a high school yearbook. The girl's wavy blond hair draped perfectly onto her shoulders, contrasting with a dark turtleneck sweater. A small pendant hung across the front of the sweater. The girl smiled sweetly.

But this picture ran under the awkward headline "Woman Apparently Slain" as the *Alton Telegraph* announced the murder of Karla L. Brown. In the story, Chief Ralph Skinner offered few details about the case; the reporters hadn't pushed as hard as he had expected.

The story ended with the predictable, brief biography.

"Miss Brown, an attractive blonde, was a 1974 graduate of Roxana High School and attended Southern Illinois University at Edwardsville.

"Upon learning of her death, a secretary at the high school expressed shock.

"Miss Brown was a cheerleader, member of the student council one year and participated in chorus, dramatics, gymnastics, intramurals, the pep club, the Fine Arts Council and the Thespians at the school.

"Miss Brown started SIUE in 1974 and left during the spring of 1977."

Four short paragraphs. That was all that was allotted to sum up the young life of Karla Lou Brown.

The police returned to 979 Acton on Thursday. Busch, Redfern, and Nunn discovered some marijuana, a few pills, a syringe, and three needles in a dresser drawer in the bedroom, and turned them over to McEuen. He assumed they proved casual, occasional drug use, but contributed nothing to the investigation.

By the time Alva Busch left the house on Thursday, he had collected a dizzying number of evidentiary items during two visits.

He had all the obvious bits—the cord that bound Karla; the socks around her throat; the dental bridge, coffee cup, and tampon; the soaked couch cushion. He had the blouse

she had worn, and the blue jeans found near the barrel.
He had lifted four latent fingerprints from the coffee cup,
and more from the dresser that held David's socks, a beer
can found in the yard, and an ashtray on a box in the
basement. The ashtray also yielded a partly burned, hand-
rolled cigarette—probably marijuana—and a regular cigarette butt.

Busch also took samples of the blood drops he found in
the basement and on the back door. He had spent at least
thirty minutes searching the wall behind the couch for
blood splatters, using a bright light to illuminate the surface; he found nothing.

He had samples of the liquids in the coffee cup, under
the couch, and in the ten-gallon barrel. He had blood
samples, urine samples, and hair samples, and the other
intimate swabs of evidence collected at the hospital.

He had physical evidence that raised more questions
than it answered; he had pieces of a crime that didn't fit
together.

What he didn't have, however, was evidence he felt
would lead to the killer.

A tangled series of calls from home caught up to
Donna Judson and her husband, Terry, early Thursday
morning, amid several days spent traveling across the
northern Midwest as Terry made the rounds of buyers for
the neckwear he sold. Donna—a petite blonde with short
hair and delicate features—had quit teaching school for a
while to go on the road with Terry—a husky man with
dark brown curly hair behind a receding hairline.

Terry and Donna had just walked into a buyer's office
in Cedar Rapids when a call came in from a salesman
friend of Terry in Indianapolis. The friend recounted the
frantic calls from Terry's father, Richard Judson, Sr., back
in Wood River. And then it was time to deliver the tragic
message.

From the look on Terry's face, Donna knew it was bad
news—her mother must have died. She already was back-

ing away when Terry shocked her with, "It's Karla. She's been killed."

Donna was struck with the finality of the announcement. It already was over. There was no hope for a rescue or survival.

She called her older sister, Connie, but there was no answer. Donna made several more calls on the drive back to Wood River before she reached Connie at their mother's home. Connie was not dealing well with the shock. "Please come as fast as you can," Connie implored. "It's worse than you could imagine. Karla was murdered."

Donna kept wondering what had happened. Had Karla been shot? Had it been some twisted and tragic accident? The word "murdered" kept ringing in Donna's ears.

On the fourteen-hour drive—in the midst of the grief and confusion—Terry Judson thought a lot about how this one moment would change the lives of everyone in the family. A year without cigarettes ended when he picked up a pack on a stop for gasoline.

They reached Wood River well after midnight and went to the home of Terry's parents to learn little more than they had known. Terry was amazed that the crime was not solved already, wrapped up in two hours between six commercials, just like on television.

While the Judsons were on the road Thursday afternoon, Jo Ellen Brown and Connie Dykstra drove to Wood River to check on the investigation. Connie still was uncertain how her mother was taking Karla's death, because Jo Ellen was good at hiding what really was going on inside. But Jo Ellen was so distraught that she had been in Wood River for some time before she realized she was wearing the same clothes from the night before. Amid the hurt and confusion, Jo Ellen now felt ashamed because of the way she looked.

They steered clear of Acton Avenue, and met only briefly with the police. They were given minimal information and a promise they would be kept informed.

The women chose a burial plot at Woodland Hill Cemetery in East Alton—less than a mile from Karla's dream house—and made arrangements for a funeral on Saturday afternoon from Marks Funeral Home. Connie didn't want to wait more than another day. The family had delayed the service for Connie's father too long, prolonging the emotional pain, and she vowed never to go through that again. Jo Ellen agreed with the choices, gladly letting Connie make those decisions.

Connie thought she was handling the trauma well until they went to a dress shop to choose an outfit for Karla's burial. They had decided on a beautiful, silky, light blue nightgown and matching robe when a sales clerk approached and asked cheerfully if she could help. Faced with offering an explanation for their purchase, the harsh reality set in and Connie burst into tears.

Sergeant Eldon McEuen knew something hot should have popped up by Thursday, and he was beginning to feel the frustration that would be the hallmark of this investigation. No prime suspect had emerged, but Jack Meyers had to be at the top of the hit parade so far. McEuen was relatively comfortable ruling out David Hart, but it was still early and there was a lot to do.

On Friday morning, Chuck Nunn learned from Connie Dykstra that the man Karla dated in Connecticut in May had bothered her for more dates after they went out a couple of times. But he was eliminated as a suspect when his employer said he had visited a number of his customers in southern New Jersey the day of Karla's death.

But it was Officer Nunn's next interviews that rattled the police department. James Moses of East Alton, who lived in the house on Acton before selling it to David and Karla, said his mother had been driving his six-year-old son to the dentist on Wednesday morning when they saw a woman they believed was Karla Brown talking to a man in the driveway.

The grandmother, Edna Moses, told McEuen she had missed the street for the dentist's office, turned onto Acton, and then did a turn-around in the driveway of her son's former residence about 10:45. She saw a big man, six feet to six feet five, with a full face and a heavy build, wearing a white shirt and dark pants; he may have had some facial hair. He was talking to a small blond woman who turned and walked away as Mrs. Moses pulled up. The man also turned, so she did not get a good look at him. She scoured three books of mug shots without finding a familiar face.

She suggested that the police talk to her grandson, Eric. Although he was only six, he had a good memory and might be able to identify a photograph.

The Brown family gathered on Friday in Wood River at the home of Terry Judson's father. Donna and Terry Judson knew it would be up to them to take charge. Jo Ellen said little and asked few questions, content to let others make the decisions. Perhaps this was one of the times her heart attack in 1973 had taught her to handle as evenly as possible.

Connie was waiting for her husband to fly in to join the family later Friday, and wanted little to do with the details of the crime. After arranging the funeral, she wanted to withdraw from the brutal realities. She never liked cop shows on television or graphic news accounts of killings; even her sister's murder did not bring out a driving curiosity about such things. Karla was dead, but there was no burning need to know all the details.

Connie did accompany Donna and Terry on Friday morning to speak to Chief Ralph Skinner at his office. The chief's rough-hewn, craggy looks were tempered with a comfortable and soft smile. He was friendly and sympathetic, and vowed to the relatives that the police were doing everything possible to solve the brutal murder. He couldn't disclose much about their efforts yet, but he told them what he could.

Connie's heart broke when the chief described the sweater on Karla's body. Fancy vertical designs of red and green and white. Connie pictured it perfectly in her mind; she had chosen it specially as a Christmas gift for Karla just six months earlier. Connie could see Karla wearing it with a red turtleneck underneath. But now the image of that sweater changed horribly, too painfully for Connie to think of Karla wearing it for the last time.

The hometown paper, the *Alton Telegraph*, already was speculating about a possible link to the other sexual assaults: "Reports of the strangling caused some anxiety in the community. The Telegraph has received several phone calls from persons saying there have been a number of unreported rapes in Wood River recently. One man said he fears for the safety of his daughters when he is away at work. The man claims all of the rape victims were blonde women in their early 20's."

In the story, Chief Skinner explained there had been three incidents in which a man broke into homes and sexually assaulted women. The police were looking into the possibility that those attacks were connected to Karla's death, but Skinner denied that the women looked similar.

Those reports marked the beginning of a turning point for Ralph Skinner.

Karla's sisters returned to Marks Funeral Home on Friday afternoon to make a painful decision. Accompanied by their husbands, Donna and Connie stood beside a blue steel casket and looked down at Karla's body. Although the funeral home had done a good job preparing the body, the relatives agreed no one would be served by a memory of Karla as she .looked in that casket. They decided it would be best for everyone to close it, and set the photograph from Karla's high school yearbook atop it in her memory.

Connie and Ralph, and Donna and Terry watched silently as the casket was closed for what the four grieving relatives thought surely would be the last time.

Visitation for Karla Lou Brown at Marks Funeral Home began at 4 o'clock Friday and the crowds continued throughout the evening. Nearly 300 people signed the register, and so many calls for flowers came in to the nearby florist that the shop was forced to stop accepting orders.

The evening was painful for everyone. How do you say good-bye to such a vibrant, beautiful young woman? A daughter, a sister, a sister-in-law. A fiancée and lover. An old friend. It was wrenching for those who assembled before the blue casket adorned by the photograph of the smiling young woman. How could someone so full of life be gone so suddenly? How could something so barbaric happen to such a special person?

It was the first time Karla's sisters and their husbands had seen David Hart since the killing. He was so close to joining their family as another brother-in-law, another young man wed to one of the Brown girls. Donna and Terry Judson felt especially close to David; he had visited them in Minnesota with Karla and, although they had welcomed him, the visit gave Donna some difficulty as she adjusted to the idea that her younger sister was sleeping with her boyfriend in Donna's house.

But it was a different David Hart at the funeral home this night. Still an emotional wreck, he spent much of the evening collapsed and crying in a chair, often sorting through newly developed photographs of a recent trip with Karla.

Donna and Terry knew David was beating himself up with useless regrets. Why hadn't he married Karla long ago? Why hadn't he avoided the many fights and hurt feelings and separations? Worse than those unanswerable questions, however, was the guilt and feeling of responsibility David shouldered for Karla's death. He asked why he hadn't gone home for lunch that day, even though he never ate lunch at home. There was no consoling him.

And Debbie Davis, who had been like a sister to Karla since the seventh grade, couldn't stop crying. She had spoken to Karla on the phone Wednesday morning, and had stopped by the house at the time the killer may have been ending Karla's life in that basement. She had called Karla all day long, but never got an answer. Debbie had clutched her little son in her arms and stood on Karla's

porch and cried Wednesday night, wondering how she
would cope with the loss of the best friend she ever had.

Kathi Hawkins, who had been Kathi Goode when she
and Karla met in high school and became lifelong friends,
entered the funeral home almost in a daze. She had driven
almost 115 miles to be there, and could hear the ripple of
whispers of "Kathi's here, Kathi's here" as she signed the
register and walked into the parlor. Kathi greeted Jo Ellen
Brown and they walked arm-in-arm to the casket.

When Kathi looked back toward the crowd, the faces
of several girls who had treated Karla badly only a few
years before leaped out at her. Some particularly cruel incidents came to mind, and Kathi remembered the hateful,
jealous things that had hurt Karla so deeply. Kathi felt a
pulse of anger at the hypocrisy of those girls now seated
among the mourners. Kathi's stomach tightened, and the
nausea began. She turned and walked out.

But something else even more discomforting was present that night for Donna and Terry Judson and Ralph
Dykstra. As they scanned the crowded room, they wondered if Karla's killer was there. Had the person who viciously took Karla's life just offered condolences to the
family for the terrible loss?

That thought hadn't struck Connie. But the other three
couldn't help but wonder if a face in the crowd was the
last one Karla saw. Everyone was a suspect; no one was
a suspect. Donna, Terry, and Ralph even wondered if they
were suspects to the others in the crowd. As the people
came and went in front of the casket, offering sympathy
and kind words, Donna and Terry pondered whether there
was a proper funeral protocol for dealing with relatives,
friends—and suspects. The Judsons were convinced that
Karla had been killed by someone she knew, someone
from her circle of friends. Would the killer brazenly come
to pay his—or her—last respects, just to keep from being
conspicuously absent?

Although no one in the family seriously suspected David, he could not be ruled out yet. Was he the distraught

boyfriend, or a man who could brutally kill a woman who loved him so deeply?

Even the man named most often in rumors—Jack Meyers—came to the funeral home that night. Another friend in mourning, or a bold killer come to gloat?

The Brown family went back to the Judsons' house after the heart-wrenching visitation was over. It was the first time the relatives really had a chance to talk about their feelings, and they stayed up nearly all night grieving, looking for a way to deal with the sorrow and shock. They decided they wanted a special epitaph for Karla's headstone. David wanted to write it, since he would have to live with it the rest of his life. But when he offered some fourteen or sixteen lines, everyone knew it was too long—and Donna thought much too intimate—for inscription on stone. Donna finally offered the words everyone agreed were perfect in remembrance of Karla.

"So Lovely. So Loving. So Loved."

One of the jobs that fell to Chief Skinner on Saturday was to double-check the story from one of Karla's scraggly neighbors, Dwayne Conway. Skinner drove to nearby Bethalto to talk to John Prante, who Conway said was at his house the night of the moving party and returned to sit on the porch from noon to 3 o'clock the next day.

Prante—a dark, husky man of thirty with frizzy hair, a thick mustache, and several days' growth of beard—was as scruffy looking as his friend. As Skinner sat with Prante and his father at their kitchen table, Prante backed up Conway's story with calm and thoughtful answers to the chief's questions. The night before the murder, the men were joined on Conway's porch by Lee Barns as they watched Karla and her friends move in. A loud party followed, and Barns mentioned that he might go over because he knew some of the girls. The three men were disappointed that they weren't invited. After a while, as the party wound down, Prante gave Barns a ride home.

Skinner was not surprised that Karla Brown had not extended an invitation to these yokels vegetating on the porch next door. Karla and David may have run with a pretty fast crowd, but they were several rungs above Conway and Prante on the social ladder.

Prante's account of the day of the murder varied somewhat from Conway's version. Prante said he stopped by Conway's house about 8:30 that morning, just after filing a job application at the Shell Oil Company's refinery in nearby Roxana. Prante asked if Conway wanted to ride along and put in job applications at some other industries. But Conway declined because he was painting the house on the corner; Prante left a few minutes later.

He said he first learned about the woman's death about 6 o'clock that evening while visiting a friend on Hamilton Street in Wood River. Dwayne Conway stopped by to tell them that the girl next door—Conway's new neighbor—had been murdered. Conway told his friends he didn't know any of the details, but there were police cars all over the place.

The chief thought Prante's story could be checked out with the personnel offices where he applied for jobs. But his account of the events seemed relatively sound; it varied only slightly from Dwayne Conway's and seemed within the tolerance for differences among the memories of people involved in any event, especially if they had been smoking and drinking all day.

Karla's family had agreed to talk to Sergeant Eldon McEuen at the police station before the funeral. McEuen sat down first with her former stepfather Joe Sheppard, who said he last saw Karla two or three weeks earlier at a vegetable stand. She told him about the new house and her marriage plans. He was pleased, partly because he had not approved of her living with David. Sheppard suspected David was using Karla and never intended to marry her.

McEuen didn't like Sheppard, and was convinced he was massaging his story to make himself look good. McEuen wasn't impressed with the "concerned father" bit.

Sheppard denied having any real trouble with Karla while he was married to Jo Ellen; and he certainly never struck Karla or came on sexually to her or her friends. He denied having dinner recently with Karla, as Debbie Davis reported. But he said he had given Karla money occasionally, including $200 to help pay for the dental bridge that replaced her two missing incisor teeth.

Sheppard had heard the rumors about the attempt to rape Karla at a swimming party. He said he considered finding out who attacked her and having the man beaten up. But it had been some time ago, and Sheppard had forgotten about it until Karla's murder.

Sheppard agreed to be fingerprinted by McEuen and signed a consent form for a polygraph test later if the police desired.

McEuen then ushered in Jo Ellen, her daughters, and their husbands for a group session. Jo Ellen did most of the talking as she recounted the years of the unsettled relationship between Karla and David. Jo Ellen did not suspect physical violence between them, but she knew they argued. In Jo Ellen's estimation, the couple's problems stemmed from David's reluctance to marry Karla. They would break up for a while, and Karla would date other men; but she always returned to David. He meant too much to Karla to lose.

The sergeant asked the sisters and their husbands to wait in the lobby while he talked to Jo Ellen alone; he wanted to know about Joe Sheppard. Jo Ellen said Karla claimed that Sheppard raped one of her friends during a party Karla was hosting about four years ago. Jo Ellen did not know if that was true, but she was convinced Sheppard was not having sex with Karla. Jo Ellen believed Sheppard gave Karla money just to be nice to her.

The Judsons and the Dykstras talked to McEuen privately, but knew little of value to him. Connie and Ralph were able to pass along only reports about a couple of men Karla had gone out with while she was staying with them in Connecticut. McEuen told them those reports already had been checked out.

* * *

The funeral service at 1 o'clock Saturday went much the same as visitation the evening before. While the family members tried to squeeze onto two small settees at the front of the parlor, Donna and Terry saw David Hart standing in the doorway, alone and crying. It was as if he did not feel he was part of the family, or that he would be welcome among the grieving mother, sisters, and other relatives. Donna and Terry escorted him to a seat with the family—another heartbreaking moment for all of them. This last time, David was part of the family.

Seated among the mourners, Debbie Davis sobbed uncontrollably. She was sure everyone wished she would leave. She had never lost control like that, but she couldn't help herself. She couldn't leave before saying that final good-bye to Karla.

David had chosen the pallbearers, and his decision to have Karla carried to her grave by six of her former boyfriends had bewildered Donna and Terry Judson. It seemed a most peculiar decision for a wounded fiancé. But it had been his choice, and they respected it.

David continued to cry in the limousine as the family members rode to the cemetery. He put his hands over his face and leaned his head against the car window. Ralph Dykstra glanced at David, and his eyes were drawn to the scratches along David's right wrist and hand. Ralph motioned silently to Terry Judson with his eyes and a nod toward David; Terry saw the injuries. They later discussed Ralph's suspicions but decided only that they hoped the scrapes would not turn out to be evidence that David had killed their lovely sister-in-law.

About 1 o'clock Sunday afternoon, David Hart met Chief Skinner and Detective Nunn at 979 Acton. It was a difficult return for the first time, and David asked Terry Judson to come along for support. The cops wanted David to see if anything was missing, or if he spotted something the police had overlooked.

In a closet in the northeast corner of the basement, op-

posite the laundry room where Karla was found, David
showed the cops a ten-gallon lard can identical to the one
that so grotesquely held her body. Both barrels had been
filled with Karla's clothes when she put them into the
closet. David was sure the clothes piled outside the closet
door had been in the barrel, and he thought the sweater on
Karla's body had been among them. The metal lid to the
can sat on the floor next to the clothes.

It was painful for the men to imagine the killer—
glancing around for something to apply to his perverted
and perplexing purposes—spying the cans, popping open
the lid, and dumping out the contents. The image of the
killer filling the barrel with water and plunging in Karla's
body was disgusting.

Skinner knew it was time to ask David one of the more
difficult questions he would have to pose to anyone. Because of all the rumors, the cops had to know about
Karla's sex life. It was a tough question for a man whose
fiancée had been murdered in such a sexually suggestive
way. But David understood. He considered their sexual
activity completely normal; Karla never had been interested in anything weird or kinky. The last time he and
Karla had sex was the Monday night before she was
killed. Skinner realized that could account for the small
amount of sperm found during the autopsy, and might
mean that Karla was not raped.

David admitted that he and Karla had occasional arguments, usually over her desire for marriage. Sometimes
he would leave for a while to cool off, and sometimes she
would leave. She seldom stayed away overnight. After an
argument a few months ago, she spent a week with her
mother in St. Louis. But David went over and talked her
into coming back to their apartment. Shortly after that,
they decided to buy the house and get married.

After the police left, Terry Judson realized how spooky
it was to be in the house. He also was aware of mixed
feelings about being there with David, and about David
himself. Did Terry know David as well as he had

thought? What was he capable of doing under extreme passion?

Terry allowed himself the secret hope that he was astute enough to spot the murder-solving clue that the police had neglected. When they went to the basement the first time, Terry followed with a combination of trepidation and excitement. His first impression, however, was surprise at how clean it was. Nothing marked it as the scene of such mayhem amid the scattered remnants of Karla's worldly belongings. Those bits and pieces reminded Terry that Karla had been there so briefly, and had died there so horribly. It was eerie and chilling, and Terry was glad to leave, even without the evidence he had hoped for.

When David took Terry back to his parents' house, the two men stood in the driveway and talked for a long time. Terry thought David seemed reluctant to leave, as if this good-bye severed his ties to Karla's family and took from him one of the small parts of Karla he had left. Terry used the chance to tell David that the family did not hold him responsible in any way for Karla's death. It was almost the truth; it just ignored, out of compassion, that tiny sliver of suspicion everyone hoped was only natural and would be erased when—or if—the real killer was caught.

Chapter 3

Larry Trent would realize later that this murder had been the cruelest blow in a long and horrible siege against what had seemed to be a nearly perfect, Ozzie-and-Harriet family. The killing struck him that way from his perspective and new maturity as a detective with the Illinois State Police. But the real outrage he felt was swept in on his memory, recalling through the eyes of a sixteen-year-old with a crisp new driver's license and a crush on a beautiful girl. Not the victim of this murder; at least, not directly. But a girl remembered as equally beautiful.

What a great family, the young Larry Trent thought on the occasions when he had summoned up enough courage for a visit to the house. The father of the three beautiful girls there had been very pleasant to the young suitor, not intimidating as Larry Trent himself would be years later when the boys began to call on his teen-aged daughter. Of course, the mother had been very nice, too, but the girls' mothers usually were nicer than their fathers.

The family had a nice house in Kendall Hills, one of the nicer subdivisions in the Roxana-Wood River area. The mom and dad, the three girls—they all seemed so happy, so . . . nice.

Larry Trent had known the family since he was in junior high school. The oldest daughter, Connie, a year younger than he was, appeared suddenly in school when her family moved to town. Larry and Connie played the leads in their high school production of *Stage Door,* and there had been a stage kiss. In 1966, the year after Larry graduated, the class play was *The Sound of Music* and

Connie's little sister, Karla—only ten years old then—played the youngest Von Trapp daughter, the one in pigtails.

Larry had visited Connie during those high school years to see if the attraction he felt was returned. There was, he was sure, something there for her, too. But romance had not blossomed; just a warm friendship and an abiding admiration for her family.

And then the dreadful assault began. The nice father was killed so unexpectedly—so tragically young—in a bizarre accident at work. The family was devastated. The nice mother was crushed by the loss and smothered by the weight of her grief. The two older daughters went away to college, married, and moved to far-flung parts of the country. The mother and the youngest daughter couldn't seem to get along, even though it was obvious they loved each other. There were fights and separations in times when they should have been clinging so tightly to each other. It had been painful to watch the crumbling of an ideal family.

And now, Larry Trent knew, he had seen the cruelest blow. The youngest daughter, Karla Lou Brown, had been murdered viciously in the sanctity of her own home.

Trent felt the repercussions from the murder twice—one as an admirer of the stricken family, and again as Special Agent Larry Trent of the Illinois Division of Criminal Investigation. He had been a detective only two months, moving out of the uniformed section of the Illinois State Police to its investigative squad, called the DCI. He always wanted to be a homicide investigator, but he took the first opening, in the fraud unit. While he waited for his chance to solve murders, he worked on welfare cheats, bad checks, insurance scams, and other mundane, white-collar crimes.

On Thursday, June 22, Larry Trent left his home at 656 Acton Avenue in Wood River and, as usual on the way to work, drove two blocks east on Acton before turning onto Central Avenue. As he passed 979 Acton, he was surprised to see yellow crime-scene tape strung across the yard and the Wood River police officer posted in front, obviously guarding the little white house.

I wonder if something big has happened, he thought. He shook his head. No, nothing big ever happens in Wood River.

When he arrived at the office, however, he learned that there was something big, indeed, behind the yellow tape. He was stunned to learn that the victim of a vicious murder two blocks from his home had been Karla Brown, the girl he recalled in pigtails.

He felt the rush. He wanted in on this case, and he wanted in bad. For the first time, he felt a personal stake in exactly the kind of case he always had wanted to take on. He would do almost anything to get in on it. DCI had no jurisdiction in Wood River without an official request from the local cops. But Trent figured there was no foul in fishing for the invitation. After all, the Wood River police handled a murder once very few years; DCI agents handled them daily. Once invited, DCI could provide the manpower and expertise for the best shot at breaking a case in those all-important, first twenty-four hours when witnesses and clues were fresh, and when murder cases usually took a dramatic turn—toward a quick solution, or a long, slow investigation.

Chief Ralph Skinner was courteous when Trent called, thanking him for the offer and promising to get back to him; but it was apparent Skinner wasn't too interested. He hadn't said no, and he hadn't bristled with resentment. But Trent thought the odds were against DCI getting the invitation.

The next day—Friday—Trent swallowed hard and called Skinner again. Trent would follow protocol, but he wanted in. He walked on eggshells again, hoping his subtle hints would convey to the chief that the full force of the DCI was standing by anxiously, ready to pounce on even a reluctant invitation. But it didn't come during that second, equally polite conversation, either.

* * *

On Monday, June 26, in an early-morning meeting with Chief Skinner, Sergeant McEuen explained that the case was bogged down with interviewing and reinterviewing. It seemed that Karla Brown knew everyone in the Midwest, if not the entire world, and the cops were spending hours and hours tracking her huge circle of friends. Each time they talked to someone new, several questions popped up that had to be checked with someone already interviewed.

Some bizarre theories were emerging. Checking out each hypothesis consumed more precious time, even though some were so off-the-wall they probably could be rejected without much review.

At the top of that list was the "organized crime" theory, which went like this: Joe Sheppard claimed ties to organized crime and reportedly boasted about Karla and some of her friends working for him as prostitutes. Had Karla, as beautiful as she was, caught the eyes of some heavy hitters in organized crime? Could she have seen something she shouldn't have, or learned too much for her own good? Was she eliminated—maybe "rubbed out" was the proper term under this theory—to keep her from talking? Little Karla Brown—a gun moll or a high-class hooker?

Joe Sheppard was on McEuen's short list of suspects. From the statements by almost everyone who knew Karla, there was good reason to believe Sheppard was, as McEuen indelicately put it, trying to "nail" Karla. There were the unsupported, but very believable, stories about Sheppard's attempt to rape Karla and one of her friends, and his transparent efforts to come on to them with the suggestions that they would make big money as prostitutes for him. That wasn't hard to believe, since Sheppard had been one of three men arrested in 1973 on a pandering charge for arranging for a woman to work as a prostitute. One of the men pleaded guilty, but the charges against Sheppard and the third man were dropped.

McEuen found Joe Sheppard to be one of the most offensive and simply disgusting human beings he knew.

Next on the list was the "lesbian" theory, fueled by

Karla's membership on a bowling team whose members were thought to be lesbians. In fact, one of Karla's good friends would confirm a few days later to Detective Nunn that she was gay; Carolyn Thompson said she and her roommate, Susan Andrews, were in love. But Carolyn stressed that she did not believe Karla was homosexual or bisexual, and certainly never had sex with Carolyn or Susan. Karla was so comfortable with her own heterosexuality, Carolyn said, that she once draped herself sensually across Carolyn's lap as a joke when David walked into the room; he didn't think it was funny.

Nunn interviewed Susan Andrews the same day, and she agreed with Carolyn; Susan never knew of Karla being involved in any gay relationship. And Susan added that she could think of no one who would want to hurt Karla, although a number of women might be jealous because she was so friendly with everyone.

Although the lesbian theory was thought by most cops to be too far out for serious consideration, there were some who thought it bore careful examination. Could Karla have been killed by a jealous woman lover?

The least unlikely theory concerned drugs. Karla and David, as well as many of their friends, were known to use a little marijuana. David had admitted that much to the cops and, after all, the police had found some pot and a few pills in his dresser drawer. But he was adamant that he and Karla were not involved in selling drugs in any way.

Had Karla been killed so ruthlessly over a bad drug deal? Was the brutality of the attack really a warning to other drug dealers? Was the killer someone she knew whose normal personality was jacked up by drugs?

Another speculative scenario that popped into McEuen's mind was that someone had come on to Karla the night of her moving party and confused her friendly reaction for interest. Had he come back the next day expecting a rendezvous, perhaps bringing the marijuana joint found in the ashtray? Was he provoked into murder by a humiliating rejection? There was no evidence to support any of that, either, but it might fit the circumstances.

Sergeant McEuen counted off the theories for the chief. He wasn't endorsing them, just explaining the quagmire that seemed to be dragging down the investigators. McEuen also was eating up some time setting up a series of polygraph tests for anyone remotely considered a suspect. The tests could never be used as evidence in a trial, of course; even their mention was prohibited in state courts. But they could be of some value to investigators wading through a confusing assortment of suspects. David Hart and Joe Sheppard, Sr., would be the first ones hooked up to the box, scheduled for the next day.

But in short, McEuen told Skinner bluntly, he didn't have enough men for this investigation and he wasn't happy with the lack of substantial leads from all the legwork and paperwork. The investigation was four days old, and there was no prime suspect. McEuen concluded it was time to ask for help.

About 10 o'clock, Skinner made the return call to the DCI. He got an enthusiastic reception and was told that agents would be in his office by 1 o'clock to begin their review.

In the meantime, Skinner, McEuen, and Nunn went back to Acton to give Alva Busch the information from David Hart about the barrel and lid. Busch decided to take the lid to the lab, but was sure he already had collected everything of use from the barrel. Any other evidence surely had been washed away in the water.

Busch rooted around in the closet for a while, going through several cardboard boxes on the shelves. He was disappointed when no more white electrical cord showed up. Skinner already had ordered a check on the cord taken off the body. The manufacturer listed on the plastic coating said the cord was sold as standard extension cords available at most hardware and discount stores. There was no way to trace it and no individual characteristics of use to the investigation.

As Busch drove away, Skinner took another look around

upstairs. Standing in the kitchen, scanning the scene with a careful eye, he noticed a Mr. Coffee coffee maker on the counter. In the sink was the brown plastic lid from a glass carafe. Where was the carafe? Skinner and Nunn began an all-out search, ending up back in the basement laundry room. Skinner was startled when he glanced up and spotted the carafe wedged into the X-shaped supports of the floor joists above the furnace.

"Well, I'll be damned," he muttered. "Why would someone put a coffeepot there?"

Busch was called back; he grinned widely and shook his head as he looked into the rafters and mused about the weird things he had witnessed. He put the carafe and plastic lid into evidence bags for the lab.

The cops were pleased that they had solved at least one of the irritating puzzles at this bizarre crime scene. They finally knew how the killer carried the water to the couch to pour on the dying, perhaps already dead, Karla Brown; the water soaked through the couch and pooled on the floor beneath. That probably was a panicked attempt to revive Karla after the heat of the attack inflicted such unintended and grave injuries. Or, it may have been done simply and coldly to wash away the blood left on the couch.

But to the cops, the irrational, illogical hiding of the carafe in the rafters certainly confirmed its use in the crime.

Larry Trent was thrilled; the DCI finally was on the Karla Brown case. It hurt that he wouldn't be involved personally. But he was glad the assignment went to Special Agents Randy Rushing and Fred Donini. Rushing and Trent were close; Trent thought of Rushing more like a brother than just a coworker. They were almost the same size—about five ten, trim, and athletic. Rushing was huskier and a bit darker with a heavy, drooping mustache and longer hair. Trent's neat appearance and shorter hair easily could have pegged him as a business executive.

They had gone through the State Police Academy in Springfield together and had been assigned to District 15 in the Chicago area as new troopers. They patrolled the highways during the day and attended classes at night to complete their bachelor's degrees. They later taught criminal law together at the academy, and everyone kidded them about being together so often they were interchangeable. Rushing moved into DCI before Trent, but now they were together again in the Collinsville office. If Trent couldn't be in on the Karla Brown case, having alter ego Randy Rushing there was the next best thing.

Rushing had been working the streets in Wood River and nearby cities for some time. He knew the area pretty well, and had developed a good relationship with a detective in adjacent East Alton, Mike Urban. They had worked well together on several cases and respected each other.

Rushing was glad to get the call from Wood River on Monday, June 26. He was used to a bit of reluctance from some smaller police departments to ask for help. There was a tendency to protect territorial rights in major cases, with the locals sometimes resenting the state cops. Often, DCI was called only after several days of work failed to turn up anything substantial.

Still, Rushing was only too happy to accept the assignment for him and Fred Donini to go to Wood River. Donini—another slim, dark-haired cop with a heavy mustache—had spent years becoming one of the best undercover narcotics investigators in the territory, and had just been rotated into general assignment work. And he had a good rapport with Wood River Detective Chuck Nunn from their service together in the regional drug unit.

The agents arrived at Chief Skinner's office about 1 o'clock and got a warm reception with their first briefing. Jack Meyers was the most-mentioned suspect, but a few less memorable names came up when officers engaged in speculation. It was a slow start to what would be a long, frustrating, and in some cases, tense relationship between the Wood River cops and the state agents. But to Rushing, it appeared the city police had done everything they could. They wanted desperately to solve the case and would go to any lengths. He sensed the tension among them, and was aware of the other sexual assaults casting a shadow across this case.

Karla's murder was so unique that Rushing was fascinated from the start. It wasn't one of the standard barfight killings, so common and uncomplicated that they were often called "misdemeanor murders" by the more jaded veterans in the system. No, this case was different. The victim was different; such a special person who seemed to be getting everything she wanted, only to be killed so cruelly in her own home. Every aspect of the case made it more special, more sensitive, and more challenging to solve.

Rushing also got a briefing on the evidence from his pal, Alva Busch, whose resolve to find the killer was growing as days without an arrest passed. Rushing and Busch worked well together, and they hoped that would give them the extra edge that would make the difference.

Later Monday afternoon, Sergeant Eldon McEuen conducted an interview that helped shape his thoughts about Karla Brown. What he heard captured the essence of the young woman he thought he was getting to know. He avoided moral judgments, but he was finding a definite generation gap between the victim and the cop.

At 4 o'clock, McEuen was visited at the station by Jamie Hale, the old friend who talked to Karla on the phone shortly before her murder. The police had questioned Jamie before, mostly about the timing of the call. McEuen was probing for more personal, even intimate, information that might help the police understand Karla better. The more they knew about her personal life, her friends, her quirks, her habits—even the most secret, revealing details—the better chance they had to learn what had brought victim and perpetrator together for the moment that some killers described as the most intimate of all experiences.

McEuen already had heard much of what Jamie Hale

told him about Karla's bubbly personality, her friends, and her separations from David. The only people Jamie knew that Karla ever had trouble with were her former stepfather, Joe Sheppard, and the guy who tried to rape her at the pool party; Jamie even gave the same name provided for the would-be rapist by everyone else.

McEuen asked about Karla's sex life; the question didn't shock Jamie Hale and she was frank in her response. Later, as McEuen wrote his report, he thought again about the differences between the generations. At forty-six, McEuen was more than twice as old as Karla. But he wasn't all that old, or even old-fashioned. It was just that, in his day, sex was rarely talked about openly in mixed company, and there were damned few young women willing to admit to a series of sexual encounters. As he wrote his report, it seemed to confirm some significant changes in society.

"Jamie advised that Karla was very friendly and that most likely she had sex with all the boys she went out with," McEuen wrote as he echoed the assumption made by some of Karla's friends about her sex life. Those who knew her best would dispute that rather flippant allegation about Karla's sexual scorecard. They believed her to be much more reserved than her friendly, almost flirty nature would indicate. But they could understand how those who knew her less well could jump to a conclusion about jumping into bed.

McEuen's report reached farther into the darkness he sought to illuminate. "I then asked Jamie about how Karla felt about sex with girls. Jamie advised that Karla had friends who were called lesbians, and that she did not feel one way or the other about them. Jamie advised that, sometimes when David and Karla would have a disagreement, she would go to Carolyn Thompson's to stay, and that another time she stayed with Meg Haller. Jamie advised that, if Karla had sex with girls, it was never mentioned. Jamie advised that Karla was, or seemed to be, very open-minded. If she wanted to perform sexual acts with girls, she would."

McEuen shrugged. They were from different worlds, all right. The openness about sexual activity just seemed to be the way they were in Karla's group; they all seemed more open about it. McEuen could accept it. Hell, he had no choice. And, if he was going to solve this case, he had to work with things as they were in this world, in Karla's world.

He concluded that Karla would have had sex with any of her dates if she wanted to; she was independent enough and liberated enough for that. But McEuen was even more convinced that no one could touch Karla Brown if she didn't want them to. Everything he had learned about the diminutive beauty so far proved she also was independent and liberated enough to fight like hell if attacked.

Early on the morning of Tuesday, June 27—a week after Karla's murder—prosecutor Don W. Weber visited the house, and felt the shiver up his spine. The house radiated the frustration generated by this case, and it already was pulling him in. This kind of active approach was becoming the hallmark of this twenty-nine-year-old prosecutor. He had spent five years as an assistant state's attorney, starting while he was a senior in law school. He did his time in the juvenile division and advanced to felonies in 1976, facing some of the worst criminals the busy courts had to offer. He learned trial strategy from his older brother, Philip, and others who exhibited the kind of legal skills he wanted to acquire and practiced the philosophy akin to his own. He drank in their methods and learned from their victories. By 1978, his aggressive style already had earned him a nickname among the members of the defense bar—Mad Dog Weber.

He would need all the tenacity he could muster for this case.

Sergeant Eldon McEuen was somewhat surprised by how cooperative the suspects were when it came time for polygraph tests. They were not only accommodating, but willing. It was almost disappointing to have the only people on the discouragingly lean list of suspects march in voluntarily for a test that might suggest they were lying about their innocence. Even though the results weren't evidence, tests by a skilled examiner could be helpful in pointing the police in the right direction or negotiating with a suspect.

On Tuesday, June 27, McEuen drove David Hart and Joe Sheppard twenty-five miles southeast to the State Police crime lab in Fairview Heights. Each man was asked four questions probing into whether they knew anything about Karla's murder or participated in it. They denied any involvement, and examiner Mike Musto later wrote on both reports, "It is the opinion of this examiner, based upon this subject's polygraph records, that he is being truthful when he answered the above listed questions."

The same procedure would be followed with eight more men by the end of August.

"People who used to leave doors unlocked in a friendly, small-town atmosphere now bolt them nervously as the result of the murder of Karla L. Brown."

That was the lead under the headline, "Murder Shocks W.R.," in the *Wood River Journal* on Wednesday, June 28. The weekly was one of dozens of shoppers distributed free in the St. Louis area by the same company; they were long on advertisements and short on experienced journalists. But in this case, the story hit the nail on the head. Wood River's residents were frightened, indeed.

Sales of heavy-duty locks were soaring and, more ominously, so were sales of handguns. Chief Skinner and his men fielded dozens of calls from scared citizens worried that a homicidal maniac was roaming their streets. They weren't comforted much by the cops' reassurances that they were safe in their homes and neighborhoods. Other callers demanded a solution to the murder. The cops couldn't blame them, and promised their best efforts.

The pressure was building in Wood River, basically a quiet town of 12,000 residents who ran the gamut from blue-collar factory workers to executives for local companies. The city was part of a string of small towns that sprouted up along the riverfront in Illinois across the Mississippi from St. Louis. The towns were anchored by steel mills, a brass foundry, and several refineries for companies including Shell, Amoco, and Clark. Wood River sat at the confluence of the Mississippi and Missouri rivers, and prided itself on being the site of a winter camp for the Lewis and Clark expedition before the explorers paddled up the Missouri in 1804 on their journey to the Pacific Ocean.

The population in the two counties around Wood River was more than 500,000; the region called itself Metro East. That identity was coined in the 1960s as a way to shun the pejorative label of "east side" that had been used for decades to connote the stepchild relationship with St. Louis, and recall a slightly exaggerated history of bootlegging and dangerous racketeering during Prohibition. Some folks on the St. Louis side still grew up thinking they needed an armed escort if they ventured across the eastbound bridges. And the tag on the "east side" was thought by most residents to be a slam against the deteriorating city of East St. Louis, another reason a lot of the people in Metro East had looked for a new nickname.

Although there were few taverns actually located in Wood River, the towns that ringed it offered a wide selection of drinking establishments with a fair number of honky-tonks catering to the rougher crowd. Hard-knock characters who worked in the steel mills, refineries, or construction trades had been known to settle many arguments with fists and chairs.

Wood River was not unaccustomed to violent crime. But the killing of Karla Brown was something that struck hard in the heart and shook the notion of safe harbor at home.

The *Journal*'s short front-page story, accompanied by Karla's high school photo and a shot of the little house, also mentioned an aspect of the town's worry that soon would erupt. Saving it for the end of the story, the article stated, "A number of rumors have spread as a result of the murder. Skinner discredited stories that a rash of rapes have taken place in the area, as well as those of a second murder in Wood River. He did say that three rapes, of the home break-in type, have occurred in the city since the first of the year, but added that there are no similarities to the present case, although that is not being ruled out."

Awkward and ungrammatical, but oh so prophetic in an unexpected way.

As the newspaper was being distributed that day, the cops were getting around to interviewing two vaguely suspicious men.

The first was Lee Barns, the high school acquaintance of Karla's who was visiting her new neighbor, Dwayne Conway, the night before the murder. Another thin, crusty-looking character with long brown hair, Barns gave Detective Chuck Nunn essentially the same story already told by Conway. Barns hadn't seen Karla for at least two years before that night. They exchanged some pleasant general conversation before he went on to Conway's to drink and shoot the bull with Conway and another man, John Prante. Barns thought about going to Karla's party for a beer, but never did. The evening ended uneventfully, and Prante gave Barns a ride home.

Sergeant Eldon McEuen, meanwhile, was taking a look at a man Karla had found "scary." That was how she described the man who lived on the other side of her home. Karla had found sixty-seven-year-old Artie McMillian a little threatening and felt uneasy when he and his friends were sitting around in his backyard. But McMillian could not imagine why Karla reacted that way. No one said anything to her that was "out of the way," and he was nothing but friendly to her. He even remembered when she lived in the duplex on the corner with her mother years before.

When McMillian took a polygraph two months later, examiner Michael Musto gave him a qualified rating as truthful when denying involvement in Karla's death;

qualified, Musto said, because McMillian consumed alcohol before the test.

DCI Agents Randy Rushing and Fred Donini were headlong into the chase as the second week of the investigation neared an end. Rushing was pleased that there still were leads to follow, but the case didn't feel good. At Sergeant McEuen's request, the agents had gone over some of the ground already covered by the city's cops—interviewing some people again—and had found nothing new. As the legwork was done, Rushing couldn't avoid the feeling that nothing important was turning up. The big break just hadn't come.

Even the guy accused of trying to rape Karla at the pool party checked out. He admitted making unwelcome advances to Karla, and getting the crap kicked out of him by some other guys for his transgression. Her reaction—and the thumping he got—changed his way of thinking about things.

That was the pattern as the police followed every trail. They washed out the reports of cars and strangers in the neighborhood, tracking down one man who only had been peddling knives.

A half-dozen former boyfriends were located. Some hardly qualified as boyfriends as they told similar accounts of dating her once or twice while she and David were separated. They thought Karla truly loved David; they all spoke highly of her, and never noticed anything unusual or suspicious about her. And not one of them registered as a suspect.

The cops took seriously, however, a tip that came in on Friday, June 30, about a former mental patient—Bobby Knoll—who was overheard talking about Karla's murder. He denied knowing anything about it. But, when McEuen learned that Knoll was absent from his job at a hair salon the day Karla died, the sergeant arranged a polygraph. There was an open appointment at the state crime lab that day because McEuen had canceled a test for John Prante. When McEuen picked up Prante earlier that afternoon, he was so wasted, probably on marijuana, that a lie-detector test would have been corrupted beyond use.

The test of Knoll brought a qualified opinion of "truthful" from examiner Michael Musto—qualified because Knoll was under a doctor's care and could have been medicated. The investigation of Knoll ended, however, when his doctor said Knoll was psychologically unable to lie and pass a polygraph, and was not the kind of person who could kill someone.

Another example of fast, smart police work on a hot trail that led directly to a dead end.

McEuen had scheduled John Prante for a polygraph after noticing a slight contradiction between his account of the day of the murder and the information from his pal, Dwayne Conway. They agreed they sat on Conway's porch Tuesday night and watched Karla's moving party. But, according to Conway, Prante returned on Wednesday, June 21, and the pair sat on the porch again from noon until 3 or 4 o'clock, when Prante left and Conway returned to his job painting the house on the corner.

Prante, on the other hand, said he stopped by Conway's about 8:30 that morning after putting in a job application at the nearby Shell Oil refinery. Prante asked if Conway wanted to accompany him on an application-filing tour of St. Louis; Conway took a pass in favor of painting the house. In Prante's account, he then left on his quest for a job and never went back that day.

The discrepancies could, of course, be simple mistakes in the memories of two guys who obviously were something less than Rhodes scholars. Dwayne Conway and John Prante had no criminal records and didn't seem threatening or dangerous, unlike Jack Meyers and others on the fringes of this case. But the conflict in the stories nagged at McEuen. It was a loose end, and no cop likes loose ends dangling from the edges of a murder case. Having failed to get Prante to the polygraph test clean and sober the week before, McEuen decided to pay Prante a visit on Wednesday, July 5—two weeks after Karla was killed.

McEuen sat with Prante and his father at the kitchen table in their home, just as Chief Skinner had ten days earlier. McEuen was sure Prante had been smoking marijuana again—"smoked up" in the slang McEuen applied so eloquently.

McEuen could see why Dwayne Conway and John Prante would be friends—a couple of potheads dedicating their lives to nothing more ambitious than drinking and smoking. Prante was in better shape than he had been the day of the aborted polygraph. But McEuen still could see the occasional vacant stare into space through heavy-lidded eyes; it was a look some might interpret as calm, or serenity, or inner peace. McEuen knew it to be something else—another symptom of the social revolution of the 1960s and 1970s that had swept in free love and the search for enlightenment through heavy drug use. Prante was another product of the times, his senses dulled and his mind clouded with a lot of pot.

The sergeant explained why he wanted Prante to go over his account of that morning again. Prante stared back blankly at McEuen, and then surprised him by agreeing that Conway's version could be correct. Prante may have been at his buddy's house as Conway had said, maybe even from noon until 3 or 4. Prante looked directly into McEuen's eyes and spoke quietly.

"I may not have been recalling my whereabouts that day accurately. Dwayne may be right; I just don't remember it that clearly. Sometimes, I have problems remembering things. A lot of times, I can't remember things that happened the day before, you know."

McEuen knew. He had no trouble believing Prante might have trouble remembering what happened the day before. In fact, McEuen doubted John Prante and Dwayne Conway would be sure what month it was most of the time, let alone remember exactly what time they had done what on a particular date.

But Prante did remember the events of the night before

Karla Brown was murdered. He had hoped to be invited
to the noisy party that Conway's new neighbors were
throwing next door.

"They were playing the stereo pretty loud, and there
was beer and good-looking gals," Prante remembered.
The recollection drew out a smile. "The gal that was
moving in there was really beautiful."

"Did you invite you guys over?" McEuen asked.

Prante was staring past McEuen's shoulder.

"John, did Karla Brown and the others at the party invite you guys over?"

"No," Prante said quietly. "Pretty soon, they closed the
door. They didn't invite us over. We hoped they would,
but they didn't."

McEuen detected no anger, not even any resentment in
the memory—just a kind of resignation to a fact of life
for guys like Prante and Conway and Lee Barns. Prante
still seemed disappointed as he recalled that he eventually
just went home. He couldn't remember what time that
would have been.

But he was sure he had gone to the Shell refinery early
the next morning to put in a job application before stopping by Conway's house. Conway didn't want to join him
on the trip to the other personnel offices, so Prante went
alone. He put in applications at the McDonnell-Douglas
aircraft plant, Rockwell International, and Airco Industrial Gases. Prante couldn't remember what time he finished the job search that day.

McEuen asked again, "Did you go back to Conway's
house after that?"

Prante's hollow gaze veered off into space.

"John, could you have gone back to Conway's again,
after you put in the job applications?"

"I'm not sure," Prante said slowly and softly. "I don't
think so. I may have; I'm just not sure. But I do remember later that evening—about 6 o'clock—when I was at a
friend's house on Hamilton Avenue, that Dwayne came
over and told me that good-looking gal next door to him

had been killed. It was the first I heard of it. I was really shocked."

McEuen nodded, "Okay, John. Thanks." That was all he was going to pull out of that fogged memory.

"But listen, John, would you let me take your picture and fingerprints? And would you agree to take a polygraph test later?"

Prante squinted and seemed a little concerned. "Well, I don't mind taking a polygraph, but I have a thing about having my picture taken. I just don't allow anyone to photograph me. I just don't like it."

A little drug-induced paranoia? McEuen wondered.

"Well, John," McEuen began patiently, "I just want the photograph so I can eliminate you as one of the people who was seen on the street, in the neighborhood, the day of the killing. Two people have said they saw a male on the street that day. And I need your fingerprints to eliminate you as someone who could have left fingerprints in the house, at the scene of the murder."

Prante thought on it for a moment, his gaze off in the distance. "Okay," he finally nodded.

McEuen snapped the photograph and inked a set of fingerprints quickly before leaving. As he started out the door, Prante said again, "You know, I just don't remember whether I went back to Dwayne's or not that day. I may have been there at the times he says, but I'm just not sure. I just don't remember."

Eldon McEuen could believe that.

Back at the station, while McEuen was scheduling Prante's polygraph for a week and half later, Chief Skinner was on the phone, double-checking Prante's story. The personnel departments at Shell, McDonnell-Douglas, and Rockwell had applications from John Prante dated on the morning of June 21, just as Prante had said. Airco said its application was dated June 19.

Another dead end. Two pot-fogged porch-dwellers had given slightly different accounts—a little worrisome but not evidence of murder. Prante's version seemed to square more closely with the facts, despite his admission that his muddled memory was not quite up to total recall. The evidence suggested that Conway's recollection probably was faulty. After all, in a contest between these two giants of memory, Conway could have just as easily confused the days and times as his buddy.

Prante would pop into McEuen's mind again on Friday when he showed the photographs collected during the investigation to the woman and her grandson who turned their car around in Karla's driveway that morning. Edna Moses and six-year-old Eric Moses were unable to identify any of the photos as the man they saw standing with Karla in the driveway, near the front of the garage. The boy said the man was heavier and a little taller than McEuen's 195 pounds and five eleven and a half. The man wore glasses and a cap, which caused his dark curly hair to stand out on the sides. He had a mustache and a beard.

That sounds close to Prante, except for the beard, McEuen thought. He double-checked with the boy, and Eric was pretty sure about the beard.

McEuen thought Eric Moses probably had seen the killer standing with Karla. But Eric's young age made it nearly impossible to get a definite identification. His description would be slightly suspect, anyway. The man had been big, but everyone looked big to a six-year-old. So what had he really seen?

The chance to question the suspect at the top of the list came the next day, July 6, when Agent Randy Rushing and Sergeant Mike Urban sat down with Jack Meyers at his small apartment in Roxana. If reputation and suspicion counted, twenty-five-year-old Meyers came in first. He had no felony arrests, but had been in minor trouble off and on for years and was suspected of being a midlevel drug dealer by most cops. The muscled, hardlooking man stood five feet ten and was about as tough as they came in the Wood River area. With his black hair piled in a pseudo-Elvis pompadour and the "go-to-hell" look on his face, it was obvious he considered himself a lady-killer. Could he be one, literally?

A couple of his girlfriends claimed he beat them; one was convinced he was capable of murder. When one of them was being shoved around by one of the guys in their group, Meyers got the guy to push her head into a bathtub of water. Meyers still talked about Karla and became angry if anyone mentioned her plans to marry David Hart. Meyers claimed he and Karla had been very close, but she would not settle down with him because she was bisexual. Meyers seemed to know a lot about Karla's death, claiming she was badly beaten and dumped into water. He also knew that some hairs had been found.

But one girlfriend offered kinder words. Meyers dropped by her house the night Karla's body was found. She asked him to drive her by Karla's, but he would have missed the turn onto Acton if she had not alerted him; she concluded Meyers was not even sure where Karla lived. The woman could not believe he would have harmed Karla; it was obvious he really liked her.

With all of that background in mind, the police were surprised when Meyers seemed anxious to talk. He was hearing the same rumors linking him to Karla's murder; he wanted to set the record, and the cops, straight. He had known Karla for some time—well for the last year. He even took her out for drinks a few times, and considered her a good friend. But there was no sexual relationship, and he never would have done anything to hurt her.

He saw Karla for the last time on June 13 at a discotheque. He accompanied her and a large group of her friends, and they danced and drank their way to a good time. But Karla seemed more interested in getting home than partying; must have been the new house and all that, Meyers guessed.

He knew Karla and David would smoke a joint occasionally, but he was sure they weren't involved in anything heavier. He didn't believe Karla's murder was drug-related.

He said he learned of the murder from Karla's old

friend, Debbie Davis. She called him at home about 8:30 that night, and he was so shocked that he called Karla's house to confirm her death with the cop who answered the phone. Meyers said he couldn't believe that could happen to Karla.

He couldn't remember where he had been earlier the day Karla died. But he was willing to take a polygraph.

Rushing wasn't too impressed with Meyers's story or his adamant denials. When the two men ran into each other at the Madison County Jail later, Rushing used the opportunity to make sure Meyers knew the score.

"You know, Jack, it's just a matter of time until we get this guy," Randy said softly. "We will get him. It's just a matter of time."

The meaning wasn't lost on Meyers.

"It wasn't me. I didn't do it. I liked Karla and I wouldn't do anything like that to her."

"Yeah, we'll see."

On Monday, July 11, the state lab filed its report on the evidence. All of the blood samples came back as Type A—Karla's type—or insufficient for analysis. The crusty material scraped off Karla's abdomen was not semen or any other body fluid, and remained unidentified. Tests for sexual assault were inconclusive. The scrapings from under Karla's fingernails were too small to analyze. The hair found in Karla's hand was animal hair, probably the dog's.

Tests on the four pieces of electrical wire that had bound Karla's hands or were found on the couch showed that they had once been a single, continuous length of wire. But tests on the clipped ends failed to match them to the snips or knife found at the house.

Crime Scene Technician Alva Busch had been back to Wood River several times to discuss the case with the cops; nothing new had come up. Busch was disappointed, but not surprised, with the lab results. He had been handling a lot of murders in those few weeks, but he had squeezed hard to find some extra time to go back over his findings in the Karla Brown case. He kept seeing the pitiful body of that beautiful young woman. This case would not let go of him; he would crack it or else.

On July 14 and 17, polygraphs were given to three more on the list of "possibles" in this increasingly frustrating case.

Only Dwayne Conway's was extraordinary. He denied seeing anyone enter Karla's house, choking Karla, or knowing who killed her. And he said John Prante had been with him on the afternoon Karla was killed. But examiner Michael Musto was unable to render a definite opinion because of Conway's "erratic and emotional disturbances" throughout the test.

For Sergeant McEuen, the uncertain result confirmed Conway's place on the short list of suspects. But McEuen also knew there was a long list of possible explanations for Conway's shaky performance. Drugs or alcohol certainly could skew the results. Just taking the test could have rattled this man of limited intelligence and stability if he realized he was under suspicion in a nasty murder. But, as with most of the evidence in this case, McEuen wasn't sure what this test really meant.

John Prante and Jack Meyers passed their polygraphs three days later, denying any involvement in the killing.

Assistant State's Attorney Joseph Brown got an unexpected visit at his office in Edwardsville on July 21 from three of Karla Brown's friends—three of the prettiest young women he had ever seen. Named in his report only as A, B, and C, they politely but firmly inquired why Karla's death was unsolved, and offered to explain why they believed Jack Meyers was the prime suspect—if the prosecutor would protect their identities.

Kathi Hawkins and the other two who wanted to remain anonymous had decided on Meyers because of his obvious sexual desire for Karla, his reported criminal activity, his suspected ability to beat a polygraph, his history of beating women, and his openly hostile relationship with David Hart.

The normally quiet and demure Kathi Hawkins, still outraged and grieving for Karla, shocked her friends as she described confronting Meyers at his apartment. She stood face to face with him and asked, "Did you murder Karla?" Meyers was flabbergasted, but his shock turned quickly to anger. He stuttered, "No, I did not. I can't believe you asked me that." Kathi shot back, "I just wanted to see your face," and stalked out.

All three women had heard about a violent confrontation between Meyers and Karla Brown when he drove her home one night, made a pass at her in the car, and ripped her blouse when she resisted; Karla fled into the house. She was scared by Meyers's strength, and was angry because she had not protected herself better. Karla liked to think she could handle any situation.

After the women left, a still bedazzled Joe Brown floated into Don Weber's office; Brown was more impressed by their beauty than their information. Meyers was a convenient suspect, but there was not enough for the prosecutors to elevate him beyond that status.

Chapter 4

In the last week of July, the police finally got a break in the series of sex offenses haunting Wood River. Just after 12:30 A.M. on Monday, the twenty-fourth, Tony Garza—a scraggly, bearded, twenty-one-year-old—was arrested as he climbed into his car a few blocks from a house where a woman had just reported that a man had climbed into her bed and tried to rape her; her screams had scared him off. She promptly identified Garza as the would-be rapist.

That brought a collective, albeit slight, sigh of relief from Sergeant Eldon McEuen and Chief Skinner, confident they had their pervert. That took off some of the pressure from politicians, the media, and the citizens. And there was more; Garza lived barely six blocks from the little white house where Karla Brown was murdered a month earlier. That put Garza low on the list of suspects. But none of the sex crimes carried the kind of violence inflicted on Karla Brown.

Skinner announced Garza's arrest to the newspapers that morning, adding that he was a suspect in Karla's murder because he fit the general description of a bushy-haired man—six feet tall, weighing about 200 pounds—who was seen in the area that day. Skinner didn't divulge that the source for that was little Eric Moses.

Prosecutor Don Weber, who still remembered the eerie chill in Karla Brown's house, volunteered for the Garza case and immediately issued charges of deviate sexual assault, armed violence, and burglary. Garza became a guest at the county jail in Edwardsville.

Don Weber joined Sergeant McEuen for the follow-up

investigation. The cop was glad to work with the energetic young attorney who was developing a reputation as one of the most aggressive prosecutors in years. McEuen also thought Weber was a cop's prosecutor, backing up the police while pushing relentlessly for convictions.

Tony Garza quickly admitted two sexual assaults, apparently in a circuitous attempt to dispel suspicion that he had killed Karla, too. "I did some of the others, but I didn't have anything to do with her murder," he protested. He was, in fact, sick and tired of the allegations. He agreed readily to a polygraph.

That was fine with McEuen and Weber. On Tuesday, July 25, a different examiner ran the polygraph. The result was the same as the others; Garza's claims of innocence registered as true.

The arrest in the sexual assaults drew more interest from the press than Chief Skinner had expected. Under intense pressure from the newspapers, Skinner admitted that he had, indeed, buried some reports to protect the investigation into fourteen attacks in fifteen months. In the press, Skinner looked like a public official keeping the public in the dark amid a frightening wave of sex crimes. The *Journal* even ran a chronological list of the attacks. One victim was seventy-three; the rest were between nineteen and thirty-five. In most cases, a man awoke the women in their bedrooms. Sometimes armed with a knife, he often molested them or, in some cases, raped them. Other times, he made them watch while he masturbated. All in all, it was pretty sick stuff, and the public had been kept in the dark.

Barely a week after Garza was arrested, the police department's small triumph wilted. The city council, which had been just as uninformed as the citizens, was miffed. Skinner came in for some unkind words from some officials, and he feared that the reflection on the police department was unfair. At the city council meeting on

August 7, Ralph Skinner unexpectedly resigned as chief and asked to be returned to his former rank of sergeant. Karla Brown's murder and the series of sex crimes had claimed another victim. Skinner had tired of the politics, back stabbing, and bureaucratic wrangling. He would rather just be a good cop.

A national search for a new chief began immediately.

The afternoon before Ralph Skinner stepped down, he got a call from the Madison County sheriff's department about Tony Garza's cellmate, Jerry Gibson. The "cellie," awaiting trial on marijuana charges, told Sergeant McEuen that Garza not only talked freely about committing the sexual assaults, but claimed to have killed Karla Brown. Garza said he climbed through a window, performed an unspecified "deviate" sex act with Karla, and then strangled her with a scarf or pantyhose—Gibson couldn't remember which.

McEuen didn't trust confessions reported by cellies who could be looking for breaks on their own cases. But Gibson had enough information to justify putting him on the box. Examiner Michael Musto administered the test, but said it would take some time to evaluate the results; they might be affected by Gibson's cold.

On the trip back to jail, Gibson told McEuen that any reaction during the test probably was due to a case of nerves about informing to the police. Gibson said, "I'll get my head stomped off" if anyone learned he was snitching on Garza.

Musto's report weeks later concluded that erratic and inconsistent emotional disturbances prevented a definite opinion on Gibson's claim that Tony Garza admitted killing Karla.

By then, McEuen also had interviewed another Garza cellie who had even more details. Tom Lawson, a rape suspect, quoted Garza as admitting he killed Karla Brown after he climbed into her home through a window. He intended to make her watch him masturbate, but she became frightened and tried to escape. Garza choked her and shook her, but had not meant to kill her. Lawson was polygraphed on August 31, and Musto said Lawson's account of Garza's claims was truthful.

McEuen and Prosecutor Weber still couldn't see Garza as the killer. The cellies' versions of the murder were well wide of the facts. And Garza's "method of operating" didn't jibe with a violent murder in broad daylight; Weber knew a criminal's "M.O." usually didn't vary that much from his established pattern.

But Weber took a hard line in plea negotiations with Garza's attorney, Ralph Mendelsohn. On November 14, Garza pleaded guilty to charges of attempted rape, deviate sexual assault, armed violence, and burglary in two of the incidents. Weber asked Circuit Judge Harold Clark to give Garza twenty-two years; Mendelsohn pleaded for a lighter sentence since no one was injured in the cases before the judge. In a statement to the court, Garza claimed a jail-house conversion and said his life was in the Lord's hands. Judge Clark, however, placed twenty-two years of Garza's life in the hands of the Department of Corrections—in prison.

It was a satisfactory sentence in Don Weber's eyes—actually quite a slam-dunk. Weber knew his tough stand on the sentence may have been influenced by that slight chance that Tony Garza was Karla Brown's killer. That hard-nosed attitude wasn't lost on Garza's lawyer. As Ralph Mendelsohn left the courtroom, he walked over to the grinning Sergeant McEuen and growled, "This case is worth no more than fifteen years and Weber knows it. And he's a no-good, son of a bitch for insisting on twenty-two."

McEuen kept grinning.

And the hunt for Karla's killer went on.

As chief, Ralph Skinner provided regular updates to Karla Brown's family. Donna and Terry Judson stayed closest to the case; Jo Ellen Brown decided to leave that to them. When Jo Ellen once talked to a Wood River cop, she angrily and bluntly accused the department of blowing the case. The Judsons were more tactful and understanding, but it was clear that they, too, wondered why no prime suspect had emerged. After a while, they suspected that the police knew something they weren't disclosing, probably to keep it from getting out and interfering with the investigation. In reality, the police would have been thrilled if that were true.

The Judsons kept up by telephone from their home in Minnesota, usually talking directly to Skinner or his successor. And they made the nine-hour drive to Wood River every six weeks to two months for a face-to-face visit with the police.

They lived with Karla's murder every day for months, talking about it for hours in the evenings. They even considered posting a $10,000 reward for information leading to the killer's conviction; the police rejected that as unnecessary.

The Judsons realized that they, too, were victims, and they started listening to crime stories with different ears. They had great empathy for the families of murder victims interviewed on television. They listened more closely to friends' stories about such losses. They suffered anew with every violent death they heard about, even when it was a fictional character on television.

Donna even wondered how to answer when asked how many sisters she had. How many did she have? One, or two? And now, for the first time since she was seven, she was the youngest in the family.

The Judsons lived that way for the first year before deciding, reluctantly and painfully, that they had to move on with their lives. Karla was dead, and putting their future on perpetual hold would not bring her back or solve her murder. Donna and Terry began to work at letting go— not of their love and memories of Karla—but at least of the investigation.

That was hard for the young couple, who had been so close and loving with Karla. Donna was aware that Terry, with the quiet resolve and strength she knew was below the cool surface, may have exacted revenge in his own way—eye for eye—if he had learned who killed his sister-in-law. Donna realized he was the male in the family who felt the traditional rage at being helpless while a beloved woman was violated sexually and then murdered.

That dedication to Karla probably had placed Terry somewhere low on the suspect list, the Judsons assumed. The police were a little surprised to hear that Terry had offered to let Karla live with the Judsons in Minnesota, and bought Karla a new coat once and a set of tires another time. The police had misinterpreted those acts. Terry did, indeed, love Karla; but it was brother-sister, and the family knew there was nothing improper involved.

McEuen also had encountered impatience with the investigation from David Hart. He, too, found it hard to believe that the brutal murder of his fiancée in broad daylight could go unsolved for so long. McEuen wished he had a better answer. But in his heart, he knew he and his men had done the best they could.

When the city fathers in Wood River appointed a new police chief in November, they chose a former Green Beret lieutenant with the nickname of "Duke" and a record as a tough, aggressive leader. Melbourne E. Gorris, thirty-three, promised to transform the police into a progressive, well-trained force. He was a graduate of the FBI Academy and had spent eight years climbing the ranks in departments in the St. Louis area. He presented himself like a hard-nosed drill sergeant, complete with close-cropped hair, prominent chin and stiff-backed, six-foot frame. But he had eased on a little paunch around the middle.

Duke Gorris surprised McEuen by offering him the job as assistant chief. McEuen turned it down because he would have had to leave his post as union shop steward, which he figured was part of the motivation behind the offer. Within a couple of months, Gorris moved McEuen

back to patrol, ending his involvement in the Karla
Brown investigation.

Gorris took personal charge of the case; he and Officer
Don Greer, who was moving up quickly through the
ranks, were guarded and secretive about it. They never
discussed it with McEuen or sought his advice. The man
who knew the most about it heard only bits and pieces
about it. But, by then it was at a standstill.

In late November, in hopes of jolting the case back to
life, Don Weber arranged another polygraph for Tony
Garza. Weber had required it as part of the plea-bargain,
agreeing not to use anything from the test unless it solved
Karla's murder. Weber hoped for a more definite opinion
than in previous tests, so another assistant prosecutor, the
venerable and veteran Robert E. Lee Trone, brought in re-
tired but respected polygraph examiner Dwight Whitlock.
After a two-hour session in which Garza cried and dissolved into emotional wreckage, Whitlock concluded
Garza was truthful when he denied involvement in
Karla's death.

To some, that seemed like the end of the investigation.
But in reality, a new start was about to arrive with the
natural emergence of the political genes in Don Weber's
lineage. His father, Norman, had been a city commissioner and mayor of Collinsville, Illinois, in the 1950s
and 1960s. Norman Weber's father, John, was president
of the school board there in the 1930s.

In early 1979, Don Weber decided it was time to step
into his legacy and unleash his conservative Republican
philosophy on local politics. He ran for city commissioner in Collinsville. He won, but it was a costly victory.
He was fired by his Democratic boss, Nick Byron, who
said the posts of commissioner and assistant state's attorney were incompatible. Weber opened a private practice
and decided to pursue one of his original goals, becoming
a patent attorney.

But politics intervened again; Weber decided to run for
state's attorney against Byron. Weber mapped out a hard-

hitting campaign for the general election in November and went to work.

Little did he know that other events about to occur over the summer would chart a course to an unbelievable climax in a murder case that, somehow, still held him and several cops in its mysterious clutches.

Chapter 5

The murder of Karla Lou Brown ended a life that had been an exuberant mix of joy and tragedy, love and disappointment, tenderness and rebellion, promise and pain. Those she left behind remembered a fire that burned so brightly, lighting up the room with warmth, and then leaving such cold, deep darkness when it was extinguished. Almost fifteen years after she was taken from them, her family and friends still could hear her laughter and see her smile. They still missed her desperately.

"She's my baby," her mother still would say with a smile.

Karla Brown touched people in special and different ways. Jim Nicosia, one of David Hart's best friends since kindergarten, always felt so good just being around Karla. He became a little boy again when he heard that tiny, high voice that came from that wonderful face. It was impossible to describe to someone who never experienced it. Jim got giddy whenever he heard that sound. At only five feet four, Jim Nicosia took a lot of kidding about being short. But Karla, almost six inches shorter, would lean her shoulder against him and coo, "Oh, Jim, you're not little." She made him feel ten feet tall.

Jim didn't think Karla was classically beautiful, but he found her very striking—a rare combination of a fabulous figure, a lovely face, and a great personality. She was bubbly and friendly, so much fun. She was so confident; others could see it, sense it, in the way she carried herself. Some girls thought she was too flirty, and perhaps some guys interpreted her friendliness the wrong way at first. She was affectionate, but not "easy." She was open to everyone, but wouldn't hesitate to tell a guy to buzz off if he got out of line. Even the guys who were just friends with Karla, maybe even good friends of David's, realized that they were at least a little attracted to her. They couldn't help but react that way when someone who looked like Karla touched them softly on the arm, paid them such nice compliments, or built up their egos with kind words. That was just Karla's way, and Jim and the other guys always were aware that she was David's girlfriend.

Girls who knew Karla well also realized that she really was no threat to their boyfriends, despite the sexy image. Once they understood that, they could become close friends with Karla. Few knew that better than Kathi Goode, who met Karla in the high school chorus. The girls hit it off immediately, realizing they were the perfect complements and supplements for each other—both pretty blondes who handled their looks in distinctly different ways.

Kathi—willowy at five feet ten with her hair worn long—always held back a little. Her reticence often was interpreted as being stuck up. Little Karla—about a foot shorter with her perky, short hair—reached out to others with an unusual intensity that sometimes put them off. But the girls understood each other.

Karla could help draw Kathi out of her shell. The shorter one always asked the taller one why she let others walk on her, why she was a "doormat" when she was big enough to handle anyone. Karla often defended Kathi against the insults when Kathi would have let them pass. Over the years, Kathi learned how to take care of herself through the example of her diminutive friend.

On the other side of the coin, Kathi often helped hold Karla back a bit when she needed some restraint. With the energy and mischief behind Karla's eyes, that was a frequent necessity.

The two Ks called themselves Mutt and Jeff.

Karla Brown knew how to connect with people. Once the connection was made, no one could forget her.

The all-American promise of the Brown family that had impressed the young Larry Trent began in a bar in Cape Girardeau, Missouri, at the end of World War II. An eighteen-year-old named Jo Ellen VanGilder was fixed up by her sister on a blind date with Floyd Brown, a trim, young Navy pilot who flew training missions at Lambert Field in St. Louis. Romance blossomed, and Jo Ellen had just turned nineteen when she married Floyd in October 1946.

Floyd Brown became a welder and supervisor for the Chicago Bridge & Iron Co., making huge, steel tanks and vessels for industrial use. The Browns' first daughter, Connie, was born in 1948, while they still lived in a mobile home in Cape Girardeau. They moved several times because of Floyd's job and were living in Lima, Ohio, when their third daughter, Karla, was born on February 28, 1956. In 1960, Floyd's job took the family to the St. Louis area, where Jo Ellen had relatives. The Browns settled in a mobile home court in the Illinois suburb of East Alton. Two years later, they bought their first house in a pleasant subdivision in Wood River.

The family spent the next five years building the happy and satisfying life that could be a legacy for generations. Jo Ellen was amazed that she had found the ideal marriage. Floyd was a good husband and father, a good provider who worked hard every day.

Connie and Donna Brown were every parent's dream daughters—cheerleaders and excellent students headed for college, promising careers, and the good life. Little Karla, a perilously cute and precocious pixie of a girl, showed all the same promise spiced with a twinkle of mischief that attended being the spoiled baby of the family. Since her sisters were so much older, Karla enjoyed a special niche in the family and learned early how to manipulate that position to the best advantage. She always seemed older than her years, picking up the ways and mannerisms of her sisters. Mom always thought Karla seemed to be trying to grow up too fast.

She reveled in being the center of attention and had a flair for performing to gain the spotlight. She would sing or dance, the obvious beginnings of an extroverted personality. When she was three and the family lived in Idaho, she developed her own rock 'n' roll version of the "Idaho Stomp," which she danced to entertain her fawning audience. When she was thirteen, she attended a dance at a military school and was bored out of her mind by the ballroom music. But when the rock music began, Karla moved onto the floor—swinging her long white gloves—and showed everyone how to dance. She could move so well that black girls at a cheerleader camp Karla attended one summer wouldn't believe she was from an all-white high school. White girls never danced that well, they said.

Karla was demanding of perfection in all things. Even as a toddler, she would wear nothing but the best shoes. She became so picky that her parents eventually shopped nowhere but Stix, Baer & Fuller, the most expensive department store in St. Louis. She once made such a fuss while picking out shoes that her embarrassed sisters vowed never to go shopping with her again.

By the time she was thirteen, she had developed such unusually large breasts for a petite young girl that she was embarrassed and even more self-conscious about her appearance. As her maturity caught up with her figure, it seemed to her mother that Karla learned to deal with being big-busted—and the attention that drew from boys. It was a fact, and Karla dealt with it.

She seemed to be a happy child, but the mother's instinct in Jo Ellen was not so sure. Karla's normal exuberance could fade rapidly, and the emotional valleys could be bottomless.

But the real challenges for the family began in 1967, when Karla was only eleven years old. Jo Ellen's handsome Navy pilot was killed at just forty-six in a freak accident; Floyd was asphyxiated while welding in a storage tank. When the numb Jo Ellen and her minister broke the news to Karla, the tiny girl doubled over as if she had been slammed across the belly. Jo Ellen never saw anyone take bad news so hard, so directly to heart.

Years later, close friends would wonder if the loss of a father's love at such an early age in Karla's emotional development had shaped her outgoing, loving, and love-seeking nature. Was she always reaching out, offering and searching for the love that had been stolen from her?

Jo Ellen Brown's father had died just six years earlier, and she had learned the difficult lesson of going on with life in the face of death; the only alternative was to die, too. With three daughters—two in college and one still in grade school—Jo Ellen knew she had to apply that lesson now. So she sucked up the pain and panic from the most difficult time of her life, and carried on.

Floyd's death left his wife and youngest daughter with only each other at home. Jo Ellen and Karla clung tightly to each other; they even slept together in Jo Ellen's bed. But, as Karla moved through adolescence, her independent and outgoing nature conflicted with Jo Ellen's attempts to establish some discipline and structure. The clashes intensified as Jo Ellen was having her own problems adjusting to single life after twenty-one years of marriage. She was a waitress and barmaid, drinking more than she should. Her return to the dating scene upset Karla, who disapproved of the men Jo Ellen selected.

Jo Ellen began to feel that everything she did was a "bummer" for Karla. She became rebellious, and mother and daughter soon were unable to discuss even simple things. The two older girls could tell their mother was having a hard time coping with Karla's emerging wild and aggressive side. Jo Ellen was sure that, by the time Karla was fifteen or sixteen, she was using marijuana, probably exposed by the people she met dancing at a club called the Coliseum in a nearby town. Jo Ellen once came home to find Karla and Debbie LaTempt drinking beer in the kitchen. When Jo Ellen began to raise hell, Karla responded flatly, "You know, we don't have to be here. Everyone else is on the levee drinking and probably getting into worse trouble. We're trying to stay home and be good about this." Karla always had an answer.

When Jo Ellen began dating Joe Sheppard, Sr.—a tall, slim man of fifty-five with a full head of dark hair— Karla threw a tantrum. She had become possessive about her mother, and she didn't like the way Jo Ellen was treated by this man she met at a bar. Her marriage to Sheppard in 1970 after a courtship of just two months upset Karla even more. Jo Ellen thought her new husband tried to be good to Karla, but they just didn't hit it off. It rapidly became a very bad scene, driving the wedge between mother and daughter even deeper.

When Karla and Joe Sheppard once quarreled over some minor point, she leaned defiantly into his face as she fiercely defended her position. Jo Ellen was as surprised as her daughter when Sheppard slapped Karla in the face. That was the beginning of the end. Even Jo Ellen was becoming disenchanted with Sheppard and she lived with him only a few months. She knew nothing about this shadowy figure's background, other than he often worked for a contractor and was active in union affairs. She knew a lot of people didn't like him, and she began to find out why. He didn't know the truth from a lie, but he lied so smoothly that even a transparent prevarication seemed fun and exciting.

During the summer of 1970, Karla spent several weeks with her sister, Donna, to get away for a while. Donna was a counselor at a science camp at MacMurray College in Jacksonville, Illinois, and a senior on her way to becoming a teacher. Donna ran the recreational program and Karla joined in the activities. Donna decided her energetic sister would benefit from the structured program at a residential Catholic girls' school in Springfield, Illinois. Donna convinced her mother to agree, and they enrolled the unwilling Karla there in the fall. Karla lasted only two months before bailing out and returning to Roxana High School.

Despite all the disturbances and distractions, Karla kept

up her grades. Jo Ellen always was amazed at how Karla's performance came without much effort. She was lazy about her schoolwork, preferring to spend time lolling on the couch or goofing off instead of studying. She missed a lot of school, staying home on days when the effort to attend classes seemed too much.

Most of the kids who knew Karla Brown at school never guessed that she had a troubled home life. Some of them knew, however, and Karla spent short periods of time living with the families of a few close friends. Karla was like another daughter in the home of Debbie LaTempt, who felt Karla had adopted Debbie's father as her own. Debbie thought Karla enjoyed the stability of the LaTempt family and its firm footing in the Roman Catholic faith. Karla surprised her family by taking instructions in the church and announcing her conversion later. Karla also spent some time with the large family of Bill Marks, who owned the funeral home where Karla would return finally one night in June 1978.

Few friends were allowed to see the unhappy side. Karla developed an upbeat personality and a reputation as friendly and outgoing, even vivacious. With those traits, she also brought a candor and outspokenness her friends respected. She had an intelligent, informed opinion about everything and could voice it articulately and unabashedly, without being overbearing. If someone crossed her or a friend, however, she could shred them mercilessly. Few people wanted to get into an argument with Karla Brown. It was a trait that may have been fatal.

The girls she chose as pals became trusted friends for life. They spent nights at pajama parties and hours at Karla's, where she played favorite Cat Stevens albums over and over, or strummed the guitar while they harmonized on songs from Simon and Garfunkel, or Peter, Paul and Mary. Routine events at school became great times, transformed by the fun and force of Karla's personality.

She followed her sisters as a cheerleader in junior and senior high with Debbie LaTempt, who was two years older but still one of her very best friends. When Karla failed to make the squad as a freshman, it was Debbie who felt horrible. Karla bounced back onto the squad as a sophomore and junior. Her athletic nature served her well on the gymnastics team and while playing other intramural sports; everyone agreed she was strong and athletic for such a little girl. She served on the student council and sang in the chorus; her love of the spotlight led to the thespian club and school plays. She and Kathi Goode were the only ones who felt no embarrassment at singing and dancing with abandon in the chorus for performances of *Carnival.*

She had her choice among the boys in school. Jo Ellen always knew there would be a steady stream of suitors appearing at the house. She dated a lot of different boys, but only one at a time. Jo Ellen respected that.

Although some girls resented Karla's popularity among the boys, her close friends knew she was not a threat to their dates. For Kathi Goode, there was no competition with Karla because they fell for completely different kinds of boys. Kathi looked for the quieter type; Karla went for the hunks. In most cases, neither one could figure out what the other saw in her current beau.

But other girls envied and feared Karla, and that occasionally turned to harassment. Some of them would follow Karla down the hallway at school, stepping up close behind her to clip the heel of her shoe and make her stumble. And it could be nastier than that. When Karla arrived at a party with her date, Bob Davis, some of the other girls plastered her—and the new coat she wore so proudly—with a shaving-cream pie. Debbie LaTempt could see that Karla was devastated, much more hurt than angry. Karla's escort—later to become Debbie's husband—returned to the party after he took Karla home and exacted his own retribution with cans of shaving cream sprayed on the girls who perpetrated the cruel joke.

Some of those girls gathered in the funeral home years later, and their hypocrisy was too much for Kathi to bear. Karla's sister, Donna, always feared that some of the abuse Karla suffered at school was a legacy from the first two Brown girls. Donna wondered whether some people had tired of hearing about the "Brown sisters." Connie's striking looks had won her the Miss Alton title for 1967–68 and an appearance in the Miss Illinois pageant. She was a cheerleader and excellent student, as was the second, pretty Brown girl, Donna, following just one year later. Donna speculated that, when the unique Karla came along a few years later, her popularity triggered lingering resentment that made things more difficult for the third Brown girl.

Perhaps that and other jealousies were behind some of the slights Karla endured, such as being passed over for candidate for homecoming queen. Kathi Goode knew Karla was hurt, even though she wouldn't let it show.

But Karla always seemed more than capable of meeting the challenges. Her efforts to get Kathi Goode to stand up for herself included instructive demonstrations. When one of Kathi's boyfriends went out with another girl while Kathi was recovering from gallbladder surgery, Karla was outraged and urged Kathi to tell the girl how terrible her conduct was. Kathi refused, so Karla made the call, pretended to be Kathi, and told the girl to stay away from her boyfriend. The act was purely for Kathi's sake; Karla never liked the guy. Kathi's marriage to him later lasted only ten months. Karla was not above noting then, "I told you so."

Karla's courage was matched only by her ability to make almost any moment fun. When Kathi and Karla tried to visit Kathi's injured boyfriend in the hospital, they were turned away because Karla was barefooted. The girls stepped outside, where Karla borrowed one of Kathi's shoes before they hopped—each one on their single, shod foot—back into the hospital. The ploy failed, but it made the moment memorable.

When Karla and Kathi went shopping, Karla sometimes would pretend to be blind. She loved to draw the sales clerks into the charade as they tried to describe the clothes to their customer and she felt the fabric to try to "see" what it was like.

Karla also could be counted on when she was needed. Despite being sick—noticeably green, in fact—she spent the night in the hospital room with Kathi Goode after her surgery. When a snowstorm canceled their party plans on New Year's Eve in 1973, Karla strapped garbage bags to her feet and carried soda pop six blocks to Kathi's for their own celebration. When Debbie LaTempt Davis delivered her first baby in 1976, the first flower delivered—a yellow rose—came from Karla.

Karla's dental problems surfaced while she was in high school. She wore braces for some time, and eventually suffered the removal of her two upper canine teeth—the pointed ones on each side of her front teeth. The dentist replaced them with artificial teeth on a removable bridge; her family and friends knew Karla never allowed anyone to see her without that dental appliance.

Karla had enough credits—despite her less than dedicated academic habits—to graduate from high school early, in January 1973. She was unsure what she wanted to do and, to buy some time to think, went to work as a waitress at a popular restaurant in Wood River called the Pancake Ranch.

During the fall of 1973, after Karla started attending Southern Illinois University at Edwardsville, she met David Hart. He was tall and handsome, and had just returned from service as a military police officer in Vietnam. Karla and Kathi were at a nightclub in Alton when David was introduced to them. Karla was struck immediately, and that was it from that day on. David was Karla's first serious romance, and Kathi wondered if the attraction wasn't party because David did not fall all over Karla the way the other boys always had. For the first time, Karla met someone who held her at some distance, much as she handled the other boys.

Even Karla's mother would make the same observation over the years. David's reluctance to commit to Karla seemed to keep her enthralled. There were stories that

David shied away from promises because he was jilted by a girlfriend who married someone else while he was in Vietnam. Whatever the reason, David's desire not to be tied down caused repeated problems with Karla. But no matter what happened between them, no matter how many times she left him or he walked away, Karla always went back to him. Everyone knew there was no doubt she loved him deeply.

The Brown family got another shock in October 1973, when Jo Ellen suffered a heart attack. She never had been sick, but she needed thirty days in the hospital to recover from the attack caused by blockage of some arteries. Karla was a constant visitor, but Jo Ellen always suspected there was serious partying going on in the Brown duplex while she was hospitalized.

Kathi Goode may have been the only one who knew how Jo Ellen's illness affected Karla. Karla stayed with Kathi's family then, and those first days were the only time Kathi had ever seen Karla Brown afraid of anything; she was terrified. "I don't have a dad. I can't lose my mom, too," Karla cried. "There are too many things I haven't said to her." Kathi understood; there always were things like that between mothers and daughters.

By that time, Jo Ellen had been trying for months to get rid of Joe Sheppard. She decided to run away from home, a rather desperate move for a grown woman. She accepted an invitation to visit a friend in Texas, and stayed for four years. During that time, she had her marriage to Sheppard annulled.

Karla was stunned by her mother's decision to stay in Texas, but she understood her desire to get away from Sheppard. Jo Ellen let Karla keep their apartment in Wood River. Karla was getting a couple hundred dollars a month from the Veteran's Administration as a dependent of a deceased war veteran. Between the check and the salary and good tips she was earning from her waitressing job, she made out pretty well. She bought a blue Volkswagen Beetle and her friends often saw her zipping around town in the cute car.

Karla moved through a series of apartments and room-mates over the next few years; many of those roommates would be questioned intensely by the police a few years later. Although she was dating David more often than not, Karla also saw a number of other young men when she and David were separated; she never went out on David when they were together. Debbie LaTempt, who had mar-ried and become Debbie LaTempt Davis, thought Karla had developed a real "love 'em and leave 'em" philoso-phy. It was a side of Karla that Debbie and older friends hadn't seen before.

While she was attending college, Karla also worked as a lifeguard at the university lake and at a nearby private lake. Kathi Goode visited Karla often at the guard's shack at Tower Lake, where they would play cards during Karla's breaks; Karla was a hell of a bluffer. A photo-graph taken by the university news service in 1975 and distributed to area newspapers to promote activities at the lake caused Karla some unforseen problems. The photo showed a tanned Karla, wearing a straw hat and a tiny bi-kini decorated with giraffes, splashing along the edge of the lake. She was gazing off to her left and smiling, if anyone could force their attention to her face for very long. The figure that had drawn so much attention over the years was amply displayed. The *Wood River Journal* ran the picture, identified Karla by name, and mentioned that she lived on Acton Avenue—ironically in a duplex on the opposite corner from the house she would move into three years later. That was enough information to make Karla a target for obscene callers. She got so many heavy breathers and nasty mumblers that she had to have a new, unlisted number.

By 1977, Karla had changed jobs several times and was working as a secretary in the customer-service de-partment for an airplane parts company at the small air-port near Wood River. One of her friends at the office, Jamie Hale, had lunch with Karla daily. Sometimes they sunned themselves in a nearby park while drinking a beer. Other times, they locked the office door and gave each other back and neck massages to ease the tension from the job.

Jamie once saw David and Karla wresting playfully in the floor, and thought it was hysterical when Karla's dental bridge popped out of her mouth. The sight would come back to Jamie's memory barely a year later.

Karla visited her mother at South Padre Island in Texas in 1977 after another argument with David. Karla complained that he was spending too much time with his friends, sometimes claiming to play cards when she suspected something else was going on.

Karla also spent a month that summer visiting her sister, Connie, in Connecticut. The family spent three weeks on their thirty-foot sailboat anchored off Martha's Vineyard. The close quarters—for Connie, her husband, their two children, and Karla—reminded the girls of the old days in the Brown family trailer.

Connie learned then about Karla's interest in some unusual things, such as Ouija boards, oriental philosophy, and the art of massage. Karla even claimed to have had an out-of-body experience while on the boat. She dreamed she had been ashore overnight, and awoke to find her shoes muddy. They were anchored offshore, and no one had left the boat that night.

Their sister, Donna, knew of the incident, and years later would believe she shared a similar supernatural moment with Karla.

Not long after Karla's visit to Jo Ellen in 1977, Karla told her mother that David finally had agreed that they should live together, an idea he had resisted. They moved into an apartment on Harper Court in East Alton around Labor Day; Karla was thrilled.

Jo Ellen finally tired of Texas and moved back to St. Louis in November of 1977. She bought a house in the Richmond Heights area in St. Louis, staying across the Mississippi from Wood River just to keep a comfortable distance from Joe Sheppard.

Karla and David invited their parents over and they all enjoyed a barbecue. It was the start of a good time for mother and daughter, a time that turned out to be much too short. Jo Ellen and Karla's friends marveled at her as she worked so hard to become domestic. She cooked; she baked; she talked about recipes.

The problems between David and Karla continued, however. In early June, Karla told Debbie LaTempt Davis that she and David had quarreled over his suspected interest in another woman. "I just want someone to love," Karla cried to Debbie. "I want a husband and kids and a house. I've done all the partying and running around. I want what you have."

By the spring of the next year, David had decided to buy the little house on Acton Avenue, and everyone who knew Karla could see how overjoyed she was. She was sure that, finally, she was on the verge of getting the things she wanted. As moving day neared, she spent hours there cleaning and painting, and talked to anyone who would listen about the plans she and David had for the house.

Jo Ellen stopped by the house one afternoon in mid June to drop off some things of Karla's, hoping to catch her working there. But no one was home, so Jo Ellen left the packages on the porch. She never would see the inside of Karla's dream home.

On Wednesday, June 21, Jamie Hale got a call from Karla sometime after 9 A.M.; the telephone company had just connected the phone and Karla was trying it out. Jamie told Karla that she would drop by that afternoon, and Karla suggested calling first to be sure she was home. Jamie never got an answer when she called back later. She dropped by Karla's house just before 3 o'clock, but it was closed up tight and no one answered the door.

Debbie LaTempt Davis was lying in the sun that morning, watching her eighteen-month-old son play in the yard, when Karla called about 10 o'clock. Debbie stood in the kitchen and chatted with Karla about all the work she was doing at the new house. Debbie was trying to keep one eye on her little boy in the yard and listen to

Karla at the same time; it wasn't working, so Debbie suggested she stop by Karla's after a trip to the bank. When Debbie arrived at the house about 11 o'clock, Karla's car was in the driveway, but no one answered the front or rear doors. Debbie thought about stepping in, but decided against it. She drove away.

The news that evening arrived in different ways to different people. But it left all of Karla's family and friends stunned and shattered. Debbie and Jamie second-guessed themselves, wondering if they should have gone into the house. Could they have saved her? Or would they have been murdered, too?

Debbie was terrified. Had the killer seen her through the window? Was he looking for her next? She wouldn't be able to stay home alone for months, and even took a job to get out of the house during the day.

Jamie Hale was so shaken she was afraid to take a shower. It required hours of therapy before she could recover.

Kathi Goode Hawkins was living in Clinton, Illinois, when she heard the news. She had talked to Karla on the phone just a week earlier. Karla was so alive, so happy with David; she deserved that.

In the months after Karla's death, Kathi would suffer a breakdown and three years of the same desperate dream—she would get the news of Karla's death, but then Karla would appear and explain that the report was just part of the police investigation; she really was alive. Then Kathi would awaken to reality.

Kathi suffered excruciating back pain, until a doctor diagnosed its origin. "It's Karla's pain," he said. "You're feeling Karla's pain." Shortly after that, the pain stopped.

Two months after Karla's death, Kathi got pregnant. Her daughter would be named Karly. Naming her Karla would have been too much; Karly was just right.

* * *

Jo Ellen Brown was propelled into a period of depression and confusion, regret and anger. She was thankful, however, that she had moved back for those months before Karla's murder; the two of them had become good friends again, after all the years of conflict. Right after the funeral, Jo Ellen went to Connecticut to spend a few weeks with Connie and her family. They didn't talk much about the killing. When Jo Ellen came home, she found herself drinking a lot, talking a lot, and bitching a lot. For some time, she was sure the Wood River police would catch the killer. When her hopes faded and she lost confidence in the police, she didn't hesitate to tell others how stupid she thought the cops were.

A couple months after the killing, David Hart took Jo Ellen to dinner; it was a downbeat, sad evening. Both of them were depressed, and Jo Ellen still hadn't completely shaken the nagging suspicion that David was a suspect. They talked about Karla a lot that night and it was painful for them both.

Donna and Terry Judson stayed deeply involved in the investigation for some time. Connie Dykstra kept informed, but she preferred that her sister handle the details. For a long time, Connie didn't even feel safe in her home in Connecticut. She would break out in a sweat if the doorbell rang unexpectedly. She wondered if someone had it in for the Brown family and might track down all the members. She talked to an FBI agent who lived in her neighborhood, and he assured her that the police eventually would find the killer. But after six months or so, when nothing had happened, Connie's confidence in law enforcement flagged and she lost hope. She was frustrated and angry that someone did that to her little sister and got away with it.

Jim Nicosia was at work when he heard the shocking news. Who would want to do something like that to Karla? he wondered. No one disliked her. No one could have anything against her.

He and other friends of Karla and David would resent what they felt was the repetitive, accusatory questioning by the police, and the inescapable inference that the police suspected one of them had killed Karla. One cop—Jim wasn't sure which one—seemed to push him to point the finger at David; that was even more ridiculous. Jim had known David since kindergarten. David was incapable of that. He had been an MP in Vietnam and nothing intimidated him. But he was incapable of that, for God's sake.

And Jim knew that David was angry about the questioning, too. David loved Karla. Why would he kill her? How could they suspect he had done that to her? He had moved in with Jim shortly after Karla was murdered. Jim's big house offered them plenty of room, and David certainly couldn't go back to the house on Acton.

A couple of weeks later, when David mentioned selling the house, he broke down and cried in front of Jim for the first time. They were sipping a couple of beers when thoughts about the house triggered it, and David fell apart. He described for the first time to Jim—in painful, graphic terms—how he found Karla's body. David's words would ring in Jim's ears forever. "It was so horrible. They tied her up and stuck her head in that bucket. Naked. She was naked. I can't believe she's dead," David repeated over and over.

Jim remembered the cans from the moving party, and seeing one of them in David's garage at the apartment, filled with towels to wash his car. What a depraved use for those cans had been found.

Jim knew that David would let it out one day, when he was ready. He wept bitterly as he talked. So did Jim Nicosia. It would be hard for Jim to put those thoughts out of his mind later, but he would do it. He would protect his memory of that last night. The smiles, the little girl. That would be his last memory of Karla, and he would protect it forever.

Chapter 6

Alva W. Busch tied the lengths of white electrical cord into knots again, for what had to be at least the hundredth time. Scattered across the table in front of him were several pieces of the cord in different shapes. These strands had bound him almost obsessively to the Karla Brown case, and he had spent many hours trying to discover what they meant. They were, literally and figuratively, loose ends in this horrible crime. And the detective in Alva Busch's soul couldn't allow those ends to dangle in front of him; he had to tie them up. He had to figure out how the cords came to be in those shapes, and what that told him about what had happened in the basement at 979 Acton Avenue almost a year earlier.

The bits of cord on the table were identical to those recovered at the scene. Two were tied in the same kind of knots found around Karla's wrists; Navy knots, Busch had learned. A straight length was about five inches long, like the one under the couch cushion. The last one was a little longer with a simple loop in the middle.

He bought identical white cord and spent hours and hours tying and untying the strands, struggling to recreate the evidence. The smaller pieces had to be the results of cutting the cord. Maybe the killer had retied Karla at some point, for some reason Busch couldn't fathom. He would tie knots and loops, and then cut them, trying to find the explanation only the killer knew.

Finally, as he cut through the cords late one evening, the pieces literally fell into place. If he tied the cord as someone might tie a woman's hands together, and then cut through it with a knife between the wire and the woman's wrist, Busch could re-create the single loop and straight length, each section cut on the ends. He didn't know if he had proved anything other than the way Karla probably had been tied up, cut free, and then retied. But the modest victory made him feel great. It was a step forward, no matter how small.

The search for an answer to the electrical-cord quandary was symbolic of Alva Busch's obsession with the Brown case. Most cases, even murders, came and went. Busch did the crime scenes; they got solved, or they didn't, and Busch moved on to the next one. But it was not that way with Karla Brown. Whenever he had a few minutes, he went back to the file and the evidence. Surely there was something there, between the lines. A lovely young woman, so alive and so promising, couldn't die so tragically without getting justice. Alva Busch wasn't going to let that happen.

In the spring of 1979, Busch met with Inspector Don Greer of the Wood River police. The new chief, Duke Gorris, had made Greer a detective and given him the rank equivalent to assistant chief. Greer—a stout, broadshouldered man with receding light brown hair and a thick mustache—was assigned to the Karla Brown case to reorganize its paperwork chaos and look for any angles to pursue. He and Busch went over the evidence, including the barrel with "David" written on the side; that bothered Greer terribly. He had been friends with David Hart for years, even double-dating while they were seeing girls who were close friends. Despite that, Greer had been unable to shake his suspicion that David could be the killer. This kind of murder usually was committed by someone the victim trusted enough to allow into very close range.

Greer also met with Randy Rushing, and they made a list of the most likely suspects: Jack Meyers, Tony Garza, Artie McMillian, and David Hart. There wasn't much to suggest a new direction, but the officers agreed to look for ways, at least, to eliminate some of the men from consideration.

Alva Busch had begun researching a new application of lasers in forensic science, using green lasers to detect fingerprints not suitable for lifting with standard powder. Busch wondered if the laser could be used on the glass coffee carafe that surely had been used by the killer to pour water on Karla.

But, while Busch worked on the electrical cord and other ideas, the regular assignments went on. One case he handled a year or so after Karla's death was the processing of a stolen car abandoned in East St. Louis. The car belonged to an important figure from New Mexico who was murdered—burned horribly in his own bed. Busch gave thought to passing on the request to interrupt murder cases to check out a stolen car; hardly a good use of time. But he decided to take the call anyway.

It would be a momentous decision, especially since it had been made on a "what the hell" basis.

In late June of 1980, Busch flew to Albuquerque to testify in the trial of the man charged with murdering the owner of the car. Although there was a delay of perhaps a week while the lawyers argued a series of motions, the prosecutor asked Busch to hang around until they were ready for him. Since Busch knew absolutely no one in town, he wandered over to the sheriff's department and checked in with the crime-scene technicians. He soon was trading war stories with some new colleagues.

During the conversations, one of them mentioned getting good results analyzing photographs with a new technique called computer image enhancement. The computer transformed the image in a picture from one-dimensional to three-dimensional, and then turned it on different planes to provide different views and perspectives. That offered a lot of new information about items as diverse as body wounds and tool marks.

Busch was fascinated and asked to hear more; his timing was excellent. A leading expert in the field, Dr. Homer Campbell of the University of Arizona, was about to present a program in the sheriff's department on the emerging forensic sciences of image enhancement and bite marks. Busch was honored to be allowed into a program designed mostly for pathologists. The presentation was complete with a slide show, and Busch was awed by Dr. Campbell, a forensic dentist or, as the specialty was known in the scientific community, a forensic odontologist.

Campbell's explanations of the new sciences, especially image enhancement, held Busch's attention like a vise. He already was wondering if this new technique could identify the object that made the nasty cuts and other injuries to Karla Brown's face.

At the end of the program, Busch took Dr. Campbell aside and asked if he could spare a few minutes. "Hey, Doc, have I got a case for you." Busch smiled with his normal, casual irreverence.

Busch explained about an unsolved case back in Illinois, and described the injuries to the beautiful young woman. Could Dr. Campbell's image-enhancement technique provide new leads about what had been used to batter Karla Brown? Dr. Campbell agreed to study some photographs if Busch would send them to him later.

Busch was ecstatic. A series of fortunate events halfway across the country from Acton Avenue—lucky breaks or a divine design—had combined to lead Busch to an expert who could apply emerging technology to the mystery of who killed Karla. Busch couldn't wait to get back to Illinois to talk to "Chico," Busch's nickname for the dark-haired and mustached Agent Randy Rushing. Rushing would have to approve supplying photos to Dr. Campbell. During the flight home a week later, Busch ignored the scenery, spending his time running again through the evidence and fantasizing about the possibilities that had just opened up.

Busch called Randy Rushing about 10:30 that night, as soon as he arrived home from the airport. Busch's energetic and rapid-fire delivery almost blew Rushing off the phone.

"Chico, we've got to send the pictures to this dude in Arizona. He's going to look at them and use this computer image-enhancement thing to see if he can figure out what made the cuts."

"Busch, what the hell are you talking about?" Rushing knew which case Busch was talking about; it was the case they always talked about. But who was the dude and what was he going to do?

"I talked to this expert in Arizona, Dr. Campbell. He's going to look at the pictures of Karla Brown. We've got to get enlargements and mail them to him. He might be able to tell us what made the marks on her face. He's going to use computer enhancement of the pictures."

Computer enhancement was a term new to Rushing, and he was anxious to hear more. He could tell Busch was pumped up and running at full bore. The two agents had spent hours and hours discussing the case over the last two years; both of the men were held firmly in its grasp. Rushing still drove past the house every time he was in Wood River. They had kicked around the evidence and theories so much they thought there was nothing else to say. But every time they got together, there was another discussion about Karla Brown. The case was unique—a real whodunit. Rushing knew only one or two cases would stay with a cop throughout his life. This would be one of them for him.

Busch's enthusiasm was contagious and Rushing was breathing it in. As Busch explained the enhancement process, Rushing agreed it certainly was worth the trouble of making up a set of photographs and mailing them to Arizona. He gave Busch the go-ahead to contact the Wood River police and arrange it.

It took several weeks of juggling schedules before Busch could get together with Chief Duke Gorris in Wood River. On August 15, they met to talk about the new techniques and look at the coffee carafe from Karla's house. Busch's evidence tag on the plastic handle still covered the fingerprint that was inadequate for comparison by the state crime lab; perhaps a green laser could pull more detail from it. The officers agreed to hold an official meeting on August 21 to take another close look at the case.

For the big conference, Randy Rushing prepared a chart laying out the various lines the investigation had followed and explaining the evidence on each person regarded as even a low-level suspect. Rushing accompanied Busch to the meeting with Chief Gorris, who called in Don Greer and Bill Redfern, the dispatcher and unofficial photographer when the investigation began. He had become the department's crime-scene analyst under Gorris.

Busch explained the image-enhancement procedure and the use of green lasers. Although he could barely contain his enthusiasm, he warned there was a chance nothing would come of the ideas. He also demonstrated his discovery about the electrical cord, tying up a chair and clipping through the strands to produce pieces of wire identical to those collected at the scene.

The Wood River police were pleased with the new ideas and optimistic about their application. Gorris agreed to file an official request for the FBI to use the green laser on the coffeepot. And he agreed to provide Busch and Rushing with the negatives to make photos to send to Dr. Campbell. But Gorris made it clear that he would insist on retaining control of the investigation.

Randy Rushing was a little concerned by that attitude; this wasn't the time to be playing control games. But it was too soon for Rushing to make any harsh judgments about Gorris. Rushing would wait and see how things worked out.

The conversation at the meeting then turned to other evidence, and the cops began to discuss an issue that was ringing a bell with all of them. Greer had been struck by the contradictions between the stories of Dwayne Conway and John Prante, the two mopes who sat on the porch next door to Karla's house the night before and, depending on which story was believed, perhaps part of the day of the murder. Rushing's chart also noted the discrepancies. Greer's casual check on the streets had turned up reports that Prante had left the area and perhaps was on a shrimp boat in Louisiana. Conway still was around, so they probably could find him.

The conversation rang a strange cord with Al Busch. He remembered being watched by someone on the neighbor's porch as he loaded evidence into his van the night of the murder. He shuddered; had he been under the watchful eyes of the killer at that very moment, without realizing he was only a few feet from the solution to the case?

As the cops discussed the divergent stories by Conway and Prante, a consensus developed that Conway's version of the events was looking a little more suspicious than the first time around. Greer had found a report by Sergeant Eldon McEuen that said the polygraph examiner had concluded that Conway was truthful on the test, and had not been involved in the homicide. McEuen had used the polygraph to all but eliminate Conway as a suspect.

As Greer continued to look through the file, however, he found the examiner's actual report, and it was far from exculpatory; there must have been some breakdown in communication between the examiner and McEuen. According to the examiner, Conway gave the shakiest performance among the whole bunch that was polygraphed. He exhibited "erratic and inconsistent emotional disturbances" so substantial that the examiner was unable to render an opinion on the truthfulness of Conway's denials.

It was John Prante who passed his polygraph without any doubt from the examiner.

Gorris also noted that Conway, by both men's accounts, never left home on the day of the murder. He was right next door to Karla the whole time. He had tried to place his buddy, Prante, there during the most likely hours of the murder, giving Conway an alibi and a witness.

John Prante, on the other hand, thought he was at Conway's for only a short time in the morning. If he returned later, as Conway claimed, Prante couldn't remember it. Prante's account of visiting some local industries to file job applications that morning seemed to check out, and Prante was relatively sure he had not seen Dwayne Conway again until 6 o'clock that evening when they met at a friend's house on Hamilton Avenue. It had been Dwayne Conway who announced then that the girl next door had been killed; that was the first Prante had heard about it and it was shortly after Karla's body was found.

The cops all nodded in agreement. Dwayne Conway deserved another very close look.

The next day, Busch and Rushing had the photos printed to send to Dr. Campbell. They chose several close-ups of the wounds to Karla's face, showing the injuries from different perspectives to give Campbell as much as possible to work with. Among the shots was the one Redfern took from such a difficult angle during the autopsy, as Karla's chin was pulled back to display the strangulation injuries to her neck.

The cops also included some general views of the scene in the basement, in case anything pictured there would be of any use.

Don Greer boarded a plane to Albuquerque with the photos on August 22, and Rushing and Busch crossed their fingers. Greer spent the night at Campbell's home, dined on pizza, and learned more about the doctor's technique he developed to study the wounds suffered by the victims in the violent prison riots in New Mexico.

The next morning, Greer accompanied Campbell to his office at the university to get a look at the image-enhancement computer. The photo was placed on a table lighted from below and a video camera above it relayed the image into the computer. It interpreted the image by measuring the density of the shading of the various surfaces in the picture. That information was used to create a more detailed, three-dimensional image on another computer screen.

Dr. Campbell showed Greer an example using a photo of a head wound. As Greer looked at the enhanced image, the computer reversed the plane, in effect turning the wound inside out. A negative became a positive—a valley became a mountain—and Greer marveled as what had been the depth of a wound became the shape of the weapon that made it. The claws of a hammer emerged from the new image. Unbelievable, Greer thought.

He headed back to Wood River with new hope.

Alva Busch was surprised on August 26, when Dr. Campbell called. That was awfully quick, Busch thought. What did that mean?

"Al, there's a set of television trays and a stand in one of the photos taken near the couch. Would you be able to get them and send them to me?"

Now Busch knew what the call meant, and he realized immediately what the doctor was getting at. Could the wheels on the bottom of the stand have made those strangely parallel, slightly curved cuts spaced several inches apart on Karla's forehead and chin? Busch felt a throb of anger that he had missed something so obvious now.

"Well, I can check, but I'm not sure of the status on them, Doc. It's been a long time. I don't have any idea where they are."

"Okay, but we're really interested in them. I think they might be what we're looking for."

Busch promised to check and let Campbell know ASAP.

The damned stand for the TV trays, Busch thought. Why hadn't he seized them as evidence? They were scattered across the floor right there, damn it, only inches from the couch where Busch was convinced the death struggle had occurred and so near several big drops of Karla Brown's blood. How could he have missed something so obvious that Dr. Campbell could pick it up from a photo two years later? Oh, well. Busch couldn't be a hundred percent right every time. He couldn't see into the future and hindsight didn't count for squat. If this helped solve the case, Busch didn't care who found the clue.

* * *

And then Campbell dropped an atomic bomb in Alva Busch's lap.

"What about the bite marks? Do you guys have any suspects in the bite marks on her neck?"

Busch was flabbergasted. His mind started racing, remembering what he learned about bite-mark evidence in the seminar in New Mexico from Dr. Campbell, the man who was now telling him there were bite marks on Karla Brown's neck.

"W-what bite marks?" Busch stuttered. "We don't know anything about bite marks?"

"Oh, it's definitely a bite mark."

Busch almost gasped. "But, Doctor, is it a good bite mark? Does it qualify to be used to identify a suspect?"

"Oh yes, it qualifies. It's not real good and I've got some more work to do on it with the computer. But it can be identified. You give me a suspect and I think I can make a good comparison with the teeth."

Busch had already jumped to his feet and started pacing.

"Doc, this is fabulous. Please let me know anything else you find out."

Busch realized that, if he had taken the easy way out and refused to process that stolen car so long ago, or if he had just hung around his hotel in New Mexico, none of this would have happened. This case wanted to be solved, Busch knew. Too much had fallen into place by sheer happenstance. There was a force at work that wanted Karla Brown's killer found.

"Whoever did this" Busch grinned to himself "just got his butt kicked by fate. We're going to get some boy out there unless he pulls out all of his teeth."

A similar call to the Wood River police from Campbell had sent Chief Duke Gorris bounding down the hall, yelling for Don Greer.

"She was bit! She was bit!"

"What are you talking about?" Greer asked, trying to ignore the ungrammatical aspect of the exclamation.

"Karla Brown was bit. There are bite marks on her that the doctor thinks he can use to identify a suspect."

Greer had some idea how devastating evidence on bite marks could be from reading of a book on the case of Ted Bundy, the famous serial killer convicted and sentenced to death in Florida in the slayings of two women at a college in 1978 and the killing of a little girl three weeks later. Bite marks, on the girls' buttocks if Greer remembered correctly, had played a major role in the trial and convictions. Bundy still was a suspect in dozens of other killings across the country, and was well on his way to becoming a media celebrity—one of the most famous and frightening serial murderers in history.

This is really exciting stuff, Greer thought as he reflected on the new evidence. This is the real thing; what really counts.

Chief Gorris and Campbell decided to have Gorris fly to Albuquerque with the trays and TV stand as soon as he could get them.

Busch called Bill Redfern about the trays and the stand, and told him the rest of Campbell's news; Redfern was stunned. He remembered how difficult it had been to take the photo using the two-and-a-quarter camera mounted on a pistol grip. It had been so awkward when he tried to get a good shot of the marks around Karla's neck. Apparently, that picture was worth well more than the thousands of words written about this case so far.

But he was depressed that he had not included a ruler or scale beside the wound. He had not known about that technique then, of course. That was part of the training he received since becoming a crime-scene technician. A ruler provides a way to measure the wounds portrayed and, in the case of a bite mark, to check the size of the teeth and the spacing between them. No one had suspected there were bite marks when he took the photos. How could so many people, so many experts, miss that potentially crucial evidence?

Redfern thought about the stand to the TV trays, and slapped his palm against his forehead in disgust. Of course it was the stand that made those cuts. Redfern checked the evidence list and learned that the stand and TV trays never were collected. That meant Gorris had to call David Hart to inquire about them without divulging too much about the new developments, especially the bite marks. Letting that slip out now could be disastrous.

David was surprised by the chief's request for the trays. It had been so long since David had heard anything new that he had given up hope. But, surprisingly, he still had the trays and stand packed away. He gladly delivered them to Gorris's home, and wished the police good luck in their new efforts.

Gorris boarded a plane for New Mexico on September 5. Busch thought flying out there was a little excessive, but with everything that was beginning to pop, who could blame Gorris?

Randy Rushing was fired up, too. He couldn't believe that everyone had missed the bite marks originally, and he was glad Dr. Campbell had been drawn in to find them— Alva Busch scores again. Rushing's only exposure to bite marks as evidence was through news accounts of the Ted Bundy trial. After Dr. Campbell's discovery, Rushing read everything he could find on the Bundy case, looking particularly for the role played by the bite marks.

When Gorris delivered the TV trays and stand, Dr. Campbell studied and measured the wheels and bottom of the stand carefully. Remarkably, he discovered a blond hair and traces of dried blood still present on one wheel. With that evidence and analysis, Campbell had no doubt the stand was the weapon that caused the cuts on Karla Brown's forehead and chin.

Campbell showed Gorris at least two bite marks on the right side of Karla's neck and collarbone. The marks were clear enough in the photograph Campbell enhanced with the computer that he believed they could be linked scientifically to the teeth of the person who inflicted them. One of the bites, in particular, would be useful because it was not overlapped by other marks.

Campbell described the teeth that made the mark by

squeezing his fingertips together and rotating his hand back and forth to illustrate—"a small mouth with crooked teeth." All he needed for a comparison was a mold of a suspect's teeth.

With the renewed suspicion on Dwayne Conway, Gorris and the DCI agents agreed that the next step was to get a cast of Conway's teeth. Don Greer arranged for a local dentist to make the dental impression.

Gorris and Greer also decided that Conway was a good candidate for a procedure Greer had been specially trained to administer. Psychological stress evaluation, called PSE, was something akin to a polygraph and applied a special machine to detect the stress in a person's voice. A recording of an interview was slowed down until it was unintelligible, and the machine printed out a graph charting the stress it detected in the voice. Greer probably had used the technique 200 times and decided it was about seventy-five percent accurate in pointing out what the stress indicated about a person's responses.

The PSE had been used on John Dean's testimony during the Watergate hearings, but still was considered an experimental technique. Greer thought Dwayne Conway would be a most interesting subject.

But finding Conway after that much time was a challenge. As they called his relatives and friends, the cops pretended to be insurance agents with a sizable check for Conway. They even used the name of the insurance company that previously occupied the building where the detectives were quartered, just across the parking lot from the police station. In fact, the front window still bore the name "Emmett Howard Insurance Company."

The ruse worked when a relative suggested the payment must be from Dwayne's injury in a barge accident, and told the callers he was staying at a YMCA in Granite City, about fifteen miles south of Wood River. On September 30, the cops called on Conway and explained that they would like to talk to him about the Karla Brown case. Reluctantly, he agreed to go to Wood River to be interviewed and given the PSE test. As the officers escorted

Conway into the detectives' building, they noticed him glance at the name on the front window. They assumed he had figured out their little subterfuge; ten minutes later Redfern scraped off the sign.

Conway was seated in a small room with Don Greer and Randy Rushing. The cops explained the PSE to him and recorded his answers as they questioned him closely about Karla's murder, even asking if he had killed her. The still scrawny Conway trembled almost violently throughout the interview. At times, the cops sensed that Conway might be on the edge of some breakthrough, perhaps even a confession. But he held firm, steadfastly denying that he knew anything more than he had seen from his own front porch as the authorities arrived.

Greer ran the tape through the machine, and Conway seemed somewhat intimidated as Greer marked certain areas on the graph as it was printed out. Although Conway couldn't begin to understand the results, Greer was seeing patterns in Conway's responses indicating severe stress with the series of questions abbreviated as the "S-K-Y block" for the key words in the questions. The person tested was asked, "Do you SUSPECT someone in particular of having committed this crime? Do you KNOW for sure who committed this crime? Did YOU commit this crime?"

The pattern that indicated the most severe stress was called a "block," because of its square shape. On the S-K-Y series, Dwayne Conway had sent up a beautiful block. Greer's interpretation was that if Conway didn't do it, he knew who did.

When Greer and Rushing left Conway for a few minutes to confer on the test results, the telephone rang at the front desk where Bill Redfern was seated.

"Investigations."

"Hi. Uh, this is Dwayne Conway. Do I still get the insurance check?"

Redfern quickly glanced down the hall and there, looking back at him through the open doorway to the interview room, sat Conway, holding the telephone. As the men stared at each other, Redfern realized that Conway, despite being ferried to the police station and grilled by the cops, still thought he was in line for an insurance check from the Emmett Howard Insurance Company. Conway had dialed the number displayed on the phone he was using, and it rang through to Redfern.

Redfern squelched the grin he felt coming on.

"No, there's no check. Sorry."

"Oh. Okay," was the disappointed reply.

In another room, an intense conversation was underway after Greer explained the results of Conway's test to Gorris and Rushing. Now, they were more convinced than ever that the mousey, unkempt man down the hall could be the killer. They had examined his crooked teeth closely, and they seemed to fit the description given by Dr. Campbell. Conway's account of the events around the murder didn't check out with John Prante's version. Conway had been "erratic and inconsistent" on the polygraph two years earlier, and he really had hit the wall during the stress test.

The three cops even kicked around the idea of charging Conway with something minor right then to hold him over, hoping he might come clean under the pressure. But they decided the best course was to push ahead with the dental impressions that night and see if more solid evidence could be developed.

Meanwhile, Conway was siting with Redfern, watching television and discussing science-fiction stories and *Star Trek*. It all struck Redfern as a very weird experience. Greer and Rushing interrupted the spacey conversation to present Conway with the request for impressions of his teeth, adding that it was a way to clear him of suspicion. They were disappointed when his reaction was somewhat cautious, but still very cooperative.

"If I do it, will you guys believe me?"

Greer nodded. "This will clear you."

"Okay. I'll do it."

Conway seemed happy and disturbingly confident as

the dentist filled his mouth with the gooey mixture prescribed by Campbell.

The next day, the cops sent the ugly set of crooked choppers by Federal Express to Dr. Campbell. As they waited anxiously for the verdict, there was an air of anticipated celebration. They were sure they would be breaking out the champagne soon. The nastiest murder in the town's history was about to be solved by a stunning combination of good police work and modern technology. They dreamed of slapping the cuffs on the killer, who had escaped by hiding right next door. Every time the phone rang, the cops hoped it was Albuquerque calling.

It was several long days before the stunning call.

"I can't make them match," Campbell said quietly.

Greer was jolted, as if he had been kicked in his own teeth.

Alva Busch felt the blow in a much lower part of his anatomy.

The police had no direction left. If they couldn't pin it on Conway with the bite marks, where could they go? John Prante still couldn't be located, and he might be the only guy who could incriminate Conway.

Later in October, the former prosecutor and current candidate for state's attorney, Don Weber, was entering the courthouse in Edwardsville when he was hailed by lawyer Eddie Unsell. Unsell had known Karla for about five years, and had been friends with David Hart since high school. Unsell and Hart had become even better friends since Karla's death.

Unsell was close to a number of powerful Democrats in the legal profession and politics, but he had played softball with Weber. Unsell liked the aggressive prosecutor, even if he was a Republican. Unsell offered his support to Weber in the election that was only a few weeks away, on November 5.

And then he jarred Weber by recalling the unsolved murder of Karla, not that Weber could have forgotten it.

Unsell offered a nod toward Weber's reputation for tenacity.

"Maybe you can get something done on the Karla Brown case. You may be the only guy who can prosecute it now. If ever there was a person put on this Earth who was full of life, it was her. She was a wonderful girl, and she didn't deserve to die that way."

Weber wondered if anything was happening with that case; but thoughts of that would have to await the outcome of what should be a close election.

PART TWO

"We're Going to Get This Guy"

Chapter 7

The hallway ran the length of the old office, about sixty feet of dark and dank, dusty and shabby corridor marked by doorways every dozen feet or so. It smelled of yellowed paper and aged wood. The faded green tile on the floor sounded the tap of leather or the squeak of rubber from the heels of secretaries and lawyers hurrying back and forth, going about the business of the Madison County state's attorney's office.

It was a path Don Weber had followed many times as an assistant prosecutor. He usually went out of his office, down the passageway, and around the corner to the door at the stairs. Sometimes the trip was interrupted by a stop in the corner at the boss's office—slightly larger but just as worn and battered as the assistants' quarters down the hall.

But this trip was unlike any of those before it. Now Don Weber was the boss; the sounds of a party filtered down the hallway from the celebration for the new state's attorney. Weber had just taken the oath of office and was enjoying his day—December 1, 1980.

But he had a special trip to make down the hall. There was unfinished business from a long time ago.

The old file was in another assistant's office, near the bottom of a stack of unsolved and now inactive cases; Weber knew exactly where it was. He pulled it out of the stack and looked at it briefly before turning and making the short trip back to the boss's office in the corner of the hallway.

It was Don Weber's office now; he had wrested it from

Nick Byron, the man who had fired him twenty months ago. Weber had won the November 5 election in a stunning upset by a Republican in an overwhelmingly Democratic county. He was the first official from the GOP elected county-wide in almost twenty years. He had campaigned hard on his record of tough prosecution, and had promised he would do his job in the courtroom, not at a desk. As Ronald Reagan was swept into the White House, Don Weber won a whisker-thin victory by 614 votes out of 97,000 ballots.

And his first official act was to retrieve the Karla Brown file and put it back on the state's attorney's desk—his desk. That case wasn't inactive any longer. He didn't know when it would be solved, or even if it could be. But he knew he had to try. A strange compulsion had seized him in the little house on Acton Avenue more than two years ago, and he had made a silent promise to himself that he would not rest until the man who had brutalized the pretty blonde was brought to justice. He couldn't quite explain why the case haunted him. But he never could get out of his mind the picture of Karla Brown that had run in the newspapers—the image of the cute, smiling high school senior.

And now, the case that had stuck with him so long was reopened officially. The file was only an inch thick. It was obvious that not many of the police reports had been forwarded to the state's attorney's office. The information was sketchy and incomplete, certainly not enough to give Weber much direction. He was unaware of the efforts and discoveries the summer before by Alva Busch and the others. He didn't know about the bite marks and Dr. Homer Campbell in New Mexico. He hadn't seen the crooked dental impression taken from Dwayne Conway's mouth.

Weber just knew the case was on his desk and it was reopened.

Weber got detailed updates on the new evidence in subsequent meetings with Agent Randy Rushing. But the optimism of August and September had faded. After the pulse of hope offered by the bite marks and the identification of the TV-tray stand as the weapon, the police were disappointed to run out of ways to follow up on the new leads. Dr. Campbell's conclusion that seemed to eliminate Dwayne Conway from the bite marks had taken a lot of the wind out of the cops' sails.

Weber spent the first several months in office on the details of starting a new administration, as well as personally prosecuting a number of major criminal cases. Four months into his term, he kept his promise to restore capital punishment in Madison County when a jury imposed the death sentence on Girvies Davis, probably the worst serial killer to prowl the Metro East area in decades. He was convicted in four robbery-killings and was suspected in a number of others.

Weber began assembling a young staff led by him and the "dean" of prosecutors in the county, Bob Trone. Weber was looking for aggressive and competent trial experts who could use every weapon in the crime-fighting arsenal. That required special training, and Weber arranged as much as possible. In July 1981, he planned to take four assistants to a seminar at New York University on forensic science in criminal investigations. One of the demonstrations would examine bullet trajectories in the fatal shooting of Dr. Herman Tarnower, author of the Scarsdale Diet book. Other speakers would address child abuse, child murder cases, blood-spatter evidence, and the use of bite marks as evidence.

The last topic would be handled by Dr. Lowell Levine, a forensic odontologist who, like Dr. Campbell, had been a prosecution witness in the Ted Bundy trial. Levine was one of the leading experts on bite marks, and Dr. Campbell suggested that Weber take the Karla Brown photographs to Levine to see if he could offer any more assistance.

Weber had followed the Ted Bundy case closely, devouring Ann Rule's book, *The Stranger Beside Me*. It was the second true-crime book he had read, after *Helter Skel-*

ter by the prosecutor he admired tremendously, Vincent Bugliosi. Weber found Bundy's evil genius as fascinating as the way he was brought to justice. Weber even checked the timing and geographic pattern of Bundy's victims, just in case he had made a quick trip through Wood River in June 1978. After all, Bundy had beaten and strangled two sorority sisters at Florida State University in January 1978, and killed a twelve-year-old girl in Florida three weeks later. There was no evidence linking Bundy to Karla Brown, of course. But, by the time Bundy finished talking to police just before his electrocution in 1989, he admitted killing twenty-three women and was linked to as many as fifty victims. Some investigators estimated the number was closer to 100.

Weber knew of Dr. Levine from his role in the Bundy trial. The use of bite marks had intrigued Weber then, and he hoped Levine could provide more direction on how to use those found on Karla.

But before Weber could tap into that expertise, he needed a set of the photos. That gave him a good reason to start a new dialogue with the Wood River police, who also had undergone some changes. Duke Gorris had left town two months earlier to take a job in northern Illinois. He had been brought in to shake up things in the department; he did it, moved on, and was succeeded by Don Greer.

Weber had an assistant, Keith Jensen, call the new chief to set up a meeting to discuss the case and get the photos. Jensen asked Chief Greer to set aside some time, but wouldn't tell him why; Greer was puzzled, but agreed. Jensen called back later to cancel the meeting, and then again after that to ask Greer for a set of photos in the Karla Brown case. Continuing what Greer thought was a rather mysterious approach, Jensen said he couldn't tell Greer why the photos were needed. Greer's answer was characteristically blunt for the husky and pugnacious cop. "If you won't tell me why you need them, you don't get them."

When Weber heard that Greer refused to provide the

photos, the prosecutor exploded and placed an angry call to Greer.

"Look, I'm the state's attorney of this county and I need those photos."

"Well, I'm the chief of police of this city and, unless you tell me what you're doing, you don't get them."

"You're withholding evidence, you know. That's illegal."

"You're interfering in a police investigation. That's illegal, too. You ain't getting the pictures until I get an explanation."

When the extremely loud conversation was over, Greer was about half-convinced he would see a deputy at his door with an arrest warrant. Instead, the chief got a call from a calmer Don Weber. "Let's talk about this. Why don't you meet me in my office?"

Greer arrived with Detective Rick White, who would serve as the chief's witness if the conversation reverted to the tone of the first phone call. The strategy was for White to stay cool so he could develop a working relationship with the prosecutor, no matter what happened. Greer, on the other hand, would be free to express his view of Weber's approach in candid and, if necessary, loud style.

Weber and Jensen welcomed the cops into the office, and the meeting went downhill quickly. Weber said some problems with the Karla Brown case had developed because the Wood River police had not shared all of their photographs and reports. Rick White said he knew for a fact that the prosecutors and state agents had everything. Weber said that was a lie, and White threatened to throw the prosecutor out of his office window.

As White went downstairs to cool off, Weber filled in Greer on the recent developments and explained that they needed the photos to show to a bite-mark expert at a seminar in New York. Greer said he wished he had known that earlier. He had White retrieve the photos from their car, where they had been conveniently just out of reach.

The chief was, in fact, delighted that the case would benefit from the vast resources available to agents of the state of Illinois. He thought the Wood River police had stumbled badly in the beginning, especially by failing to bring in the DCI early enough for effective assistance.

Shortly after becoming chief, Greer had met with Donna and Terry Judson to discuss the status of the investigation. Greer was shocked and embarrassed to learn that Karla's relatives had been told virtually nothing for some time; they certainly deserved better than that. Without being too specific and, after swearing the Judsons to secrecy, Greer told them about the bite marks and other developments. He could not predict the case would be solved, but he tried to answer Donna's questions completely and candidly. It was the first of many meetings between them, and the start of a long relationship they all felt was built on honesty, respect, and ultimately, concern for each other.

Greer agreed to cooperate with Weber and DCI as long Wood River retained its fair share of responsibilities. He wasn't going to surrender the case—it still should be Wood River's bust when the time came. But he was more than willing to cooperate with the other authorities to get someone in prison for this murder. Greer assigned Rick · White to the case; although the short, trim, dark-haired cop with the earnest face behind the glasses was only twenty-six and a rookie detective, Greer trusted him.

Weber decided not to confront Greer about who was in charge of what; if that became necessary, it could be done later.

The forensic seminar in New York, held amid another legendary garbage-collectors' strike, was as exciting as Weber hoped. Dr. Lowell Levine reviewed the photos Weber had brought, but was reluctant to offer much of an opinion on the spot. He confirmed, however, that the shadows in the pictures were indeed bite marks, probably good enough to identify a suspect's teeth. In fact, Levine detected an unusual pattern in the teeth that made the marks; the teeth were spread out, oddly spaced. Nothing like the earlier "small mouth, crooked teeth" report.

Weber wondered if there was any way, after all the effort last summer, that the marks could be matched to the gnarled teeth of Dwayne Conway.

The prosecutor filled in Levine on the details, explaining that the bite marks were not detected; Dr. Campbell identified them more than two years after the killing. In what Weber would learn was a typically macabre comment for a forensic expert, Levine offered an almost shocking suggestion on how to improve the quality of the bite-mark evidence.

"You know, of course, that a casket is really just cold storage for evidence."

"What do you mean?"

"I mean you could exhume the body and you probably would find out that the bite marks were well preserved. Human skin is an excellent medium for retaining bite marks. And if they occurred near the time of death, they probably still would be good enough to yield valuable evidence. Once the heart stops pumping blood through the body, bruises don't heal; they are preserved in the skin. We could examine the bite marks on the body, and we might be able to link them to a suspect with much more scientific certainty than we can by working from the crime-scene photographs."

The thought sent a shiver down Weber's spine. As grisly as it sounded, an exhumation could advance the case. Karla's murder had just become a bite-mark case, and Weber would do anything necessary to solve it. Would Karla have to come back from her tomb to identify her killer? Would the most important witness in the case be a silent witness?

In early 1982, Randy Rushing and Keith Jensen quietly decided to try something slightly unusual for Madison County. They paid a visit to Greta Alexander, a well-known psychic from Illinois whom Jensen had consulted on an earlier case. It was not something they did very often, but they saw no harm in finding out if she could come up with something interesting. Rushing and Jensen knew better, however, than to mention their plan to Don

Weber. They were well aware of Weber's religious and professional objections to psychics.

Greta Alexander knew nothing more than Karla's name and age. But the psychic's first words stunned Rushing and Jensen; with a strange expression on her face, she said, "I hear water dripping." That sent a shiver up the investigators' spines.

The psychic offered several other ambiguous details that were generally related to the facts. She also said she believed the killer lived near railroad tracks. That meant nothing to the cops—then. And since Madison County is matted with railroad tracks, it didn't help much, either.

A series of major cases kept Weber from concentrating on Karla's murder for a while. But in March 1982, Weber attended the annual training session for the St. Louis Metropolitan Major Case Squad with Agents Randy Rushing and Larry Trent, who finally had moved to the homicide division. The squad was the regional agency that used officers from different departments in the St. Louis area and the adjacent Metro East area in Illinois to investigate the worst crimes.

Weber, in fact, was one of the speakers at the seminar. But the presentation that hypnotized him and the state detectives was given by FBI Agent John Douglas, who was pioneering the bureau's study of serial killers. Douglas and the six agents who worked with him in the Behavioral Sciences Unit at the FBI Academy at Quantico, Virginia, were learning to analyze crime scenes by concentrating on what the evidence revealed about the criminal. There had to be patterns in the killer's life that showed up in his criminal conduct. If those clues could be interpreted, perhaps the secret to the killer's identity could be revealed.

Douglas was interviewing the worst multiple killers— people like Charles Manson and Richard Speck—to learn how their minds worked. He would go to the prisons around the country, usually finding the killers surprisingly cooperative. With that kind of insight into the criminal mind, and the techniques he was developing for interpreting crime scenes, Douglas was performing what he called "psychological profiles" of killers. He was beginning to learn how to extrapolate facts from the crime scene into descriptions of the criminals—their appearances, their habits, their occupations, their thought patterns, their obsessions, sometimes even the kinds of cars they would drive. Douglas was the only agent in the bureau drawing such profiles, and he was fathering a new force in criminology.

Weber and the detectives were amazed and intrigued. Could that be applied to the Karla Brown case? Could Douglas interpret the bizarre evidence from that basement to tell the police something new about the killer?

The trio from Madison County made it a point to meet Douglas and ask if his new techniques could be used in their case. He said he would be glad to discuss any difficult investigation with them if they could contact him later at his office at Quantico.

In a case already powered by bite-mark evidence and computer enhancement of photographs, Weber figured the use of psychological profiling was an appropriate step. He already was pulling out all the stops. Why not take this extra chance?

Weber and Rushing approached Chief Greer, and learned that Rick White had attended the seminar, too. White had thought Agent Douglas seemed to be describing the perfect plan of attack for the Karla Brown case. Greer assigned White to set up a meeting with Douglas. The FBI agent suggested the investigators drive out to see him, let him review the crime-scene photographs on the spot, and tape-record his reactions. White jumped at the idea.

Weber wanted Alva Busch on the trip because no one knew the scene in the basement at 979 Acton the way he did. Rushing agreed, but supervisors for the State Police rejected the request. Busch had been bucking efforts to replace current crime-scene technicians with state troopers. His characteristic bluntness about the idea was not appreciated up the line, and he was in the doghouse.

Weber made a quick call to State Police headquarters in

the capitol and threatened to use his Republican contacts to make a call directly to the governor. For Weber, this was too important to be scuttled by bureaucratic politics; he was willing to call in markers, make threats, and pull rank on anyone to get it done.

The tactic worked, and Busch was approved for the trip. But the state wouldn't pick up the cost of his meals. Weber shook his head. "How petty. All right, I'll pay for his meals myself."

The trip was arranged hastily for Monday, May 17, 1982. As much as Weber wanted to go, he couldn't spare the time from the pretrial work in other cases. He assigned Keith Jensen to go with Rushing, Busch, and White, and to bring back a recording of Douglas's insights into who killed Karla Brown and how it was done.

Chief Greer was vacationing in Daytona Beach, Florida, when White called about the plans. Greer booked a flight to Washington so he could attend the session, too. The four investigators would pick him up at the Washington airport before driving on to Quantico.

The arrangements left no room in the car for Larry Trent. Knowing this was a once-in-a-lifetime experience, Weber and Trent were dying inside as the others departed for a straight-through drive of 800 miles in White's unmarked Chevrolet Malibu. It was quite a trip. Busch's appetite kept the men constantly on the lookout for restaurants along Interstate 64; he said, simply, that if he was going to work like a horse, he was going to eat like one.

Some of the time on the road was spent planning what the investigators would say to Agent Douglas—how they would describe the case, present the evidence, and discuss the various theories. Who would say what and in which order to be sure Douglas got the complete picture of this complicated and diabolical murder.

They agreed that Jack Meyers had faded from serious consideration, and John Prante might be a low-level suspect. But Dwayne Conway was still the most likely candidate, despite the results of the dental comparison two years earlier. Such a review led to a myriad of theories among the foursome. Rushing enjoyed the insightful discussion; these guys knew their stuff pretty well.

As the Chevy sputtered through the mountains of Virginia, Don Greer was fuming outside the locked doors of Washington National Airport. Who would have expected the place to close at 10 o'clock? Still wearing a pair of "Florida vacation" shorts, he shivered as he waited for his ride. Finally, a local cop asked if Greer had a problem and, upon learning the identify of the apparent tourist and his mission, offered Greer a ride to Quantico. The chief arrived at FBI headquarters sometime before the rest of the group, and still was doing a slow burn when the others pulled in about 2 A.M.

The weary group was billeted at the academy for the rest of the short night. After a few hours of sleep and a shower, the eager investigators were ushered into a conference room and seated around the large table with Douglas. He was a tall, slim man with what Rushing throught was typically "good hair," the kind all top FBI agents seemed to have. He was quite handsome and distinguished, dressed in a dapper vest and tie. He struck the group as pleasant, articulate, and approachable. He wasn't intimidating, and Busch felt an immediate kinship with him. When Rushing mentioned that Busch always was in trouble with the bosses, Douglas noted that he often drew the ire of bureau administrators for his less than regulation approach to things.

And Douglas soon knocked all of the investigators' careful plans into a cocked hat. He asked for the photos from the scene, but didn't even inquire about the cops' theories. Rushing wondered what Douglas possibly could see in the photographs that the others hadn't noticed in the thousand times they had looked through them.

After asking some basic questions about the case, Douglas looked up at the expectant faces and smiled slightly.

"Are you ready? You might want to record this."

As the recorder whirred away, Douglas proceeded to blow the investigators' minds with a portrait so intricate and insightful that it seemed as if he had been in that basement on June 21, 1978—as if he had known the killer personally for years and spent hours talking intimately with him. The investigators had never witnessed anything like it, and they were awestruck. Each word was an amazing new revelation, each point a new and exciting way of looking at little bits of evidence they had seen so many times before, but had never "seen" that way. Rushing glanced over at Busch, who was mesmerized. Don Greer wondered where all of this was coming from. How could this guy know this stuff?

Douglas first tossed off a couple of quick observations. Experience had taught him that, in cases where the victim ended up in water—a shower or bathtub or other container—the killer was not so much trying to destroy evidence as he was trying to stage the crime scene to reflect how he believed a certain kind of crime would look. If he wanted the crime to look sexually motivated, he would include bondage or some other unusual act. The use of the water was an easy way to portray something bizarre and kinky.

And, Douglas added, the police had already interviewed this killer. He knew Karla somehow and interviewing him had been a logical step. He would have been overly cooperative to reduce suspicion on him. If he took a polygraph, he may have shown signs of deception. But he may have passed it if he felt no guilt or anxiety. If he was satisfied with the killing, he might not show an emotional response—no remorse—that would register on the test. Douglas had seen too many cases where killers passed the polygraph, only to be convicted later.

What could that mean in a case where a whole list of suspects had passed polygraphs?

But the cops were nodding; so far, the expert was confirming with a new clarity some things they had suspected intuitively.

Then Douglas dissected the crime in microscopic detail. He seemed to slip into the killer's role—not quite in a trance—but almost assuming the identity of the man the police wanted so badly to find. If John Douglas could become the man for a while—before the cops' very eyes—and tell them everything he could draw from his special knowledge, he might be able to expose the killer for what he was. He might be able to give the authorities, finally, those special clues and a new advantage in their search. If he could unlock the killer's mind, John Douglas might be able to open the door to the man's identity.

The five men from Madison County listened spellbound to every word the agent offered.

"The day he went into this residence, he didn't plan on killing this victim at all. The killing of the victim was an afterthought. If he had planned on doing this, he would have brought a kit with him—a murder kit or a rape kit . . . He did not plan on killing the victim, because of the things he did to revive her.

"The idea of manual strangulation and the blunt-forced trauma to the facial characteristics tells us initially that he did not plan on killing the victim. It was a confrontation with the victim. Anger. What the reason was—rejection. The killing was a spontaneous thing, to strike out. The place you go for when you strike out is the face, the throat; manual strangulation, facing the victim.

"This type of crime is generally either a neighborhood crime, with the killer from close proximity to the crime scene, or it's someone within the household. We don't generally see these kinds of cases where a guy drives long distances and breaks into a place and does his thing. You just don't see that.

"This crime scene reflects comfort on the part of the killer. He is very familiar with the house—he has been there before or he lives in the immediate area . . ."

The investigators wondered if Agent John Douglas had just fingered Dwayne Conway, the next-door neighbor.

"If he got blood on him . . . there is no way in hell that, by hitting her, he is not going to get blood on himself. Even carrying her, chances are, some blood may have dripped on him. And if there was no blood on the door, that is an indication he may have cleaned up inside the house. But if there is blood on the door, he is going to go someplace close to finish cleaning up."

There was blood on the door, Douglas and the cops knew. How much closer could he go to clean up than to the house right next door, they wondered.

"But you've got him coming out of there and it is broad daylight, which is another thing that tells you it's very unorganized. It's somewhat careless and, like I said, he cannot have planned on killing this girl. He did not plan it at all.

"He may know the person through surveillance on his part or through information given to him just in conversation. He knows no one is going to be there for a period of time. He visually saw them leaving the area."

Alva Busch marveled at the degree of sophistication to which Douglas had brought the job Busch tried so hard to do. Now THIS was crime-scene interpretation on an astronomical scale. And Douglas was just warming up.

"The crime scene also reflects, to me, age on the part of the killer. You rarely see someone in their teens, even late teens, doing something like this—not even early twenties. Usually mid-twenties, as a minimum age, to late twenties.

"This is the type of case, too, where you are not going to find a person who is a professional killer, or who has killed before. This person, however, would have to have a history as an explosive personality. There would be rejection in the past, like he may also be recently divorced or separated, or there would be some marital discord.

"He is not a winner. He has a poor self-image. He may come across as being, at times with you, very confident. But deep down, he may be an extremely inadequate type of personality . . . He is just one hell of a loser.

"You are not going to find a guy who necessarily has a history of assaultive behavior, because if you did, he would have gotten better at this in the school of hard knocks, in jail. He would have done a better job of staging his crime. We would expect him to do a lot more things.

"Education-wise, he is going to be very average intelligence, normal IQ. High school education—tops. I think what is interesting is the use of some of the wire there. He may have used it in his occupation. Or in his past he may have taken some courses in school that lean toward the vocational trades, to plumbing or electricity—not necessarily college preparatory type courses.

"As far as post-offense behavior. First, he would have changed residences and he would have changed employment. We find them turning toward drugs or alcohol, heavily involved. If he was with a female, he was having problems with her, just breaking up or whatever. His personal sexual life—he could be having problems, perhaps even becoming impotent. He would become extremely nocturnal. He has difficulty sleeping at night. He has absenteeism from his job, particularly post-offense.

"He may have left the area after the crime. He had trouble leaving. He really wanted to go. He didn't want to stick around. He felt forced to leave because of your investigation that focused in on him. But you really forced him to stay in the area because, if he would leave, it would show that he was the guilty one. That's why he went overboard in cooperating with you.

"But it also was reflected in his personality. He would have become extremely rigid in his personality. By rigid, I mean you may have noticed a change in his hairstyle, the way he trimmed his hair. If he had a beard, shaving the beard. The way he would keep himself would be very rigid, tight, too orderly.

"That is not the way he was, because the crime scene is not an orderly crime. It's a very disorganized crime. I expect initially for him to have been some kind of a shaggy guy, kind of scruffy looking. The person is not going to be a spit-and-shine type of person. He's going to drive a beat-up, old car—something like an old red or orange Volkswagen or a Datsun, a car like that. What I am saying is, it is not going to be a highly maintained type of individual. Not very neat, orderly, shined up, and that sort of thing. Basically, a slob.

"They have a poor self-image. Some have speech defects, a stutter or a stammer. They have an inadequate style with women. That's why a man commits a crime like this. It has to be some kind of buildup. You don't just do it overnight. This is not a serial or multiple murderer.

"Because of the inadequacies, sometimes you may find that they keep a scrapbook or diaries. With an investigative search warrant, you want to be looking for things like that—newspaper clippings. If he took something, it would not be money. But it could be a pendant, a driver's license, a picture—her picture.

"After the crime, he will begin to over-control. After a while, he becomes mentally and physically exhausted. I don't know what your media coverage was back then. But if the full force of your investigation was very, very positive—developing new leads and using different investigative techniques—you would have driven him crazy. However, if the press was negative—with the chief of police saying, 'No leads, dead end. We don't know if this case ever will be solved'—you would have, in essence, allowed the individual to cope with the crime. He is relieved. You've taken the heat off this individual and he is clearly able to cope."

Rushing and the others felt they had a whole new feel for the guy they were looking for, a more solid perspective on the man who killed Karla Brown. But what, they asked, could be done now to nail the guy? How could they prove who did it and affect an arrest?

Douglas agreed with the idea of exhuming Karla's body—not only to improve the bite-mark evidence, but to renew the investigation in a dramatic and, for the killer, frightening way. The investigation would be, symbolically, resurrected when Karla was brought back from the grave to try to name her killer. The killer's fears of capture also would be brought back to the surface after years of comfortable hibernation. The image of bringing Karla back from her grave would be real to the killer because, Douglas was sure, he had visited Karla's grave on many occasions, probably talking to her as he stood there. He probably had sent flowers a few times. He wanted to talk to someone else about it, but couldn't. So he talked to the only one who would understand what had happened—Karla. He could confess to her without fear of retribution; she was the only other soul who knew what really happened that day. He would talk to her, and convince himself she understood why it happened.

Douglas said there had been one case in which the police wired a microphone into flowers on a headstone and captured the killer's confession when he was talking to his victim's grave.

During the exhumation, Douglas added, someone should photograph everybody in attendance. There was a good chance the killer would be unable to stay away when his victim was brought back from her tomb. He might even call the medical examiner or reporters later and see if he could get information on the condition of the body. That question would be driving him crazy.

The killer experienced intense stress at certain times of the year that reminded him of the killing, such as the anniversary date or Karla's birthday. He might become severely depressed, even suicidal on those dates; that is when he would be most vulnerable. Using one of those dates—such as scheduling the exhumation near the anniversary of the murder—could increase the stress and perhaps force the killer into a revealing mistake.

"What do you think his reaction is going to be when you dig the body up? That's going to be stress where he is going to be overly concerned. He is going to be inquisitive.

"He may even call you up! It will draw him out. It will draw him to you."

The cops couldn't imagine a murderer being so brazen.

Douglas urged that the exhumation be accompanied by a relentless series of public statements from the police and prosecutors playing up the new bite-mark evidence and all the technological advances being employed in the renewed investigation. Tell the public about the use of psychological profiling and green lasers and computer image enhancement. Disclosing that information would not damage the investigation because the psychological effects on the killer would be irresistible to him.

Use catchy phrases full of optimistic predictions about breaking the case immediately and anticipating an arrest soon. That would tear down the comfortable insulation the guy had built around himself, the cocoon of confidence he felt protecting him all these years.

Someone should become the visible spokesman for the new investigation—the authority figure with a very high profile behind the new drive. The spokesman's picture should appear regularly in the newspapers and on television, and he should be the person making the upbeat and optimistic statements about the impending solution of the crime.

As Douglas began to launch into another series of suggestions, he grinned and said that many prosecutors would leave the meeting at this point. He was about to suggest that, even in cases where a defense lawyer was hired and instructed the authorities not to talk to the suspect, the spokesman for the investigation still could be "visible." He could show up at locations where the suspect would be—not a "bumper-lock" surveillance—but a signal to the suspect in a restaurant or even church that he had been identified and would be watched. That would put even more stress on him. Have the spokesman on the street, interviewing the suspect's neighbors, so the guy could watch as the authorities closed in on him.

About the time the investigators were reeling from those suggestions, Douglas added an even more bizarre idea. He said chilling phone calls to the suspect from his dead victim—the woman's sobbing voice softly asking, "Why? Why? Why?" before hanging up—might spook the suspect, too. The calls should come about the time the press is publishing accounts of what an all-American girl the victim was and how tragic her murder was.

The killer must get copies of the stories, even if someone has to drop the newspapers on his porch or mail him photocopies. He has to be reminded that he was the one who did this brutal thing to this wonderful girl.

At the exhumation, the spokesman for the group should say the police were uncertain about the condition of the body and whether the evidence they wanted still would be there. Draw the killer in; pique his curiosity. But after the exhumation, the leader should stress what good condition the body was in and how optimistic he was about the results of the tests—exaggerating if necessary.

The campaign should take seven to ten days before the killer would crack, break down under the stress. That was true even in the series of child murders in Atlanta, where Douglas's advice helped lead to the arrest and conviction of Wayne Williams.

When Douglas was advised that the police had two primary suspects, he said the same tactics could be used on both of them while the police watched to see which one was responding in the manner consistent with guilt. Which one was losing sleep, staying up late, becoming more isolated and distant from his friends? Which one was becoming even more of a loner than before?

When that kind of behavior was observed, the police might use informants, sending them in to the suspect's favorite tavern to try to draw comments from him while he was having a drink.

But an arrest should be delayed as long as possible to make sure the strategy had left the killer vulnerable to interrogation—less able to resist or mislead the authorities. If the suspect should approach the authorities amid the full-court press and defiantly ask if they want to talk to him, the proper response would be, "When the time comes, we'll talk with you." They should control the situation to choose a time when he was weak, not when he was rigid and confident.

Douglas offered special suggestions on how and when to conduct interviews with the suspect, before and after he finally was arrested. How to arrange the room, how to light it, how to set some props from the murder scene to be visible while the suspect was trying to answer questions. How to avoid verbal mistakes that would reinforce him, strengthen him in his battle of words with the authorities. The police don't want him thinking, You guys don't have nothing.

Use only details known for sure. Avoid mentioning the uncertain staging of the scene. But use the other factors.

"We know you tried to revive her. You used water on her. You didn't plan to kill her. You carried her. She got blood on you—your hands, your clothes. You don't feel good about what you did."

With those insights and tactics, John Douglas suggested, they might find and break down the man who killed Karla Brown.

Randy Rushing was overwhelmed. As Douglas finished, Rushing and the others just stared at each other in silence. Douglas had drawn a map that could lead directly to the killer, and he had done it after looking at some crime-scene photos for a few minutes. He had gone through an incredible list of factors and scenarios that fit with what Rushing had learned in years of experience investigating homicides. But Douglas had pulled those things together in an innovative strategy that could be used to crack the toughest case Rushing had encountered.

Even after giving the investigators so much of his time, Douglas graciously led them on a tour of the FBI Academy before saying good-bye. They thanked Douglas profusely, and he responded in character.

"You'll thank me by getting this guy in jail. If you need anything else, just call. I'll do anything I can to help."

The drive home was different than before, and the four men came alive with a rapid-fire discussion of the new possibilities opened up by their time with Douglas. Busch laughed as he thought about the prosecutor waiting in Edwardsville. "Weber is gonna' go nuts when he hears all this stuff, man."

Rushing sensed fresh confidence from the new avenues opened by this FBI agent with such amazing powers of observation and insight. Rushing suddenly realized that the field of suspects had been reduced scientifically from "almost anyone" to pretty much just one or two guys who seemed to fit John Douglas's descriptions so well— Dwayne Conway and, perhaps, John Prante.

Most of the cops had focused on Conway since they began discussing the contradictions in the stories from him and Prante. Conway could be the killer, Rushing thought. But he wasn't comfortable with the idea; Conway just didn't seem strong enough by himself.

Despite the animated conversations going on in the car during the drive back, the trip seemed endless to Rushing. He and the others couldn't wait to get back and resume the investigation. The thought was bittersweet for Alva Busch. He knew his role in the case had ended. From now on, the detectives would take over. The crime scene had been put to use and Busch's work had been critical— the night of the murder and every day since while the case nagged at him so mercilessly that it dragged him all the way to New Mexico. He knew his pals on the team were going to have a field day with the rest of it, especially when it came time for the pinch. He was out of it. But, man, it still felt good.

After they arrived back at their offices, and before going home, the groggy and unshaved Rushing and Busch stopped in Trent's office to fill him in. Trent was almost speechless, and he could sense the excitement the meeting had generated for the other two cops. Trent decided then that he was in on this case, no matter what. After four years of being on the outside looking in, Trent was inside now. He had enough authority to assign himself to work with Rushing, and he would do it. The only one who could complain officially was Rushing, and he welcomed his pal.

Although Don Greer was alone, he was just as excited as his colleagues as he flew back to his family and vacation in Florida. He was so pumped he even prattled on and on to the woman sitting next to him. She probably thought he was nuts, but he had to talk about it to someone.

Greer wasn't worried about the big media campaign Douglas suggested. Despite the occasional friction between Greer and Don Weber, the chief respected the prosecutor's abilities. Weber knew what he was doing, and could handle the program described by Douglas. Greer even winced, thinking he wouldn't want Weber coming after him in a case like this.

Don Weber read the transcript of the interview with John Douglas, and then he read it again. He had never seen anything like it, and he wished he had taken the time to make that trip; he had missed something very special.

As Weber read Douglas's analysis, the prosecutor realized he was looking at something that could revolutionize criminal investigations. This was the cutting edge of criminology, and Weber was about to add psychological profiling to bite marks, computer image enhancement, and green lasers he already was using as tools in this case. If there was a chance that something would work, Weber would use it.

He had never seen a road map to a murder arrest before. But there it was, courtesy of John Douglas. What to do; when to do it. What to say, how to say it, and when to say it. It almost seemed like instructions on how to put a murder investigation on autopilot. Chart the course, set the controls, punch the right buttons, sit back, and wait for touchdown.

Of course, it would not be that simple. In fact, it would be a challenge the likes of which Weber had never envisioned before. Another whole new chapter in criminal prosecution was about to be written in Madison County, and there would be no room for mistakes by an elected official whose fate would rest in the hands of the voters later.

Even so, he couldn't wait to get started.

The exhumation was the first order of business, and it was no easy matter to arrange. Dr. Lowell Levine agreed to fly in and examine the bite marks after Karla's body was unearthed; Levine's schedule was open for June 2, a Wednesday barely two weeks away. But it was enough time to do what had to be done. The exhumation would be done on Tuesday, June 1, and Levine would arrive the next day.

June 2 also was close enough to the anniversary of Karla's murder that Weber thought it would be a stressful, vulnerable time for the killer. If things went right, perhaps the police could be ready for an arrest by June 21—four years to the day. Wouldn't that be justice?

Next, Weber had to line up the most expert pathologist he could find to perform a second autopsy and assist Levine with the bite marks. Dr. George Gantner, medical examiner for the City of St. Louis, recommended his assistant, Dr. Mary Case. She was one of the most respected and capable pathologists in the country, and she and Levine knew each other. That would be a bonus when it came time for them to cooperate on the critical work facing them.

Weber dreaded the next step. Karla's relatives had to be consulted; he prayed they would be able to handle the emotional stress of an exhumation after all those years. It was bound to be an excruciating event for them to contemplate. Would they rather she be left to rest in peace? Weber could get a court order for it, of course, whether the family agreed or not. He was prepared to do that, but hoped he wouldn't have to.

Don Greer called Donna Judson to tell her about the plan. After a few moments of silence, she said she would approve anything that might solve her sister's murder. Greer also talked to Jo Ellen Brown, who was shaken by the suggestion that left her with a combination of excitement and regret. Greer had Jo Ellen come to his office for a meeting with Weber. Weber was delayed by some last-minute business and was a bit frazzled by the time he arrived in Wood River. He blustered into Greer's office, where Jo Ellen already had been presented with a consent form to sign. Before Weber knew her reaction to the idea, he blurted out, "We don't really need your permission. If we have to, we can get a court order for the exhumation over your objections."

Jo Ellen just looked at him, and Weber realized he had sounded more abrupt—more callous—than he had meant to. He was just trying to explain that she didn't have to give her consent if it made her uncomfortable, and that would not impede the investigation. He planned to get the court order anyway, just to document everything and cover all the bases. But he hadn't meant to put such an edge in his voice.

Jo Ellen shook her head. "That won't be necessary. If it will help solve the case, then do it."

She looked at Weber and thought, What a smartass. She was put off by his "we'll get a court order anyway" attitude. But he was aggressive, and she thought he was the kind of man who would do whatever had to be done to break this case. She also was buoyed by the prospect of new evidence and the optimistic attitudes of the other officers. She hadn't seen that since the beginning, and she felt the hope inside come alive. Jo Ellen was not going to let sentiment stand in the way; if the exhumation was needed, it would be done. After all, it wasn't really Karla who would be subjected to the procedure; the real Karla had been somewhere better for four years. And catching Karla's killer was more important than anything else now.

Don Greer also was left with the task of arranging the work at the cemetery. His uncle had owned a funeral home and Greer had grown up around the business. He knew what was involved in "opening" a grave, as they say. He talked to the cemetery director, agreed on a price to be shared by the three jurisdictions handling the case, and made sure everything would be supplied. He also prepared the cemetery official by warning that the exhumation would be a media circus like he had never seen before.

Weber began a series of meetings with Randy Rushing, Larry Trent, Don Greer, and Rick White to map out an investigative strategy to complement the other, less orthodox, methods being applied. Rushing suggested bringing in DCI Agent Tom O'Connor, an expert interrogator who was unknown to Weber. O'Connor, a hard-nosed Irishman, had been hired three years earlier from the St. Louis Police Department, where he had served for years on the homicide and arson division. In addition to murder investigations by the scores, part of his duties had been disarming bombs. He had carefully snipped wires and disabled sensitive switches on a dozen explosive devices; everyone knew that required a cool head and steady nerves. That combination of expertise was rare and DCI figured it could be useful.

O'Connor was known as a brash and aggressive big-city cop. But soon his reputation as a streetwise, tenacious, and dedicated investigator who liked to tackle tough cases won over those who had been skeptical. He became one of the first two agents in the state trained in hostage negotiations. And he earned new respect for his ability as an interrogator, having fine-tuned the techniques required to pry information out of people less than anxious to share it with the cops. O'Connor could talk nonstop and knew what buttons to push to get results. He once interviewed the girlfriend of a murder suspect for ten hours before she admitted what she knew about the killing.

During the planning meetings, Weber kept urging Rushing to step forward as the spokesman. He was the case agent. He was articulate and had a calm, commanding presence. Weber figured Rushing was perfect for the role described by John Douglas. And when it came time for an arrest, Rushing would be the guy leading the charge. The suspect would recognize him as the spokesman, and there would be an immediate relationship that might help Rushing and O'Connor with the interrogation.

But Rushing demurred, and everyone agreed that Weber had to be the front man. He was the prosecutor and he should be responsible for making the statements. He would know, legally, what was right or wrong to say. The cops didn't want something they said during the investigation to haunt the case later, perhaps interfering with the trial. Weber reluctantly agreed; he knew he would get even more criticism than usual for his already high-profile approach to cases.

And there also was a more risky political reality in this case. If these techniques worked, as unorthodox as they were, it would be great. If they fell flat on their face, Weber would be the one who would get bruised—perhaps fatally wounded—for trying such experimental concepts. He thought to himself, I'm the only one here who has to run for election.

He had tried to duck the publicity this time, and it didn't work. Oh well—no guts, no glory.

So, the next step was to begin the publicity campaign recommended by Douglas. Getting the coverage would be simple enough; there was a large pool of aggressive reporters covering Madison County and it was easy to assemble them for a news conference on short notice. That would be a little unusual for Weber, but the full complement of reporters routinely checked in with him every day—often more than once. It had become a habit they cultivated carefully during eighteen months of covering Weber's headline-making term as state's attorney.

Weber had learned that a lot of his time each day would be spent talking to reporters from the local bureaus of the *St. Louis Post-Dispatch* and the *St. Louis Globe-Democrat*, as well as local newspapers such as the *Alton Telegraph*, the *Edwardsville Intelligencer*, the *Belleville News-Democrat*, and an assortment of small independent publications and the weekly Journal outlets.

For this news conference, the word went out quickly and, on Wednesday, May 19, the curious reporters squeezed into Weber's private office for an important announcement. They would get the first of several carefully paced releases designed to pique their interest and curiosity, but keep them hungry for more. They would get other bits later, keeping the story alive and the pressure on.

At this first session, Weber told them he was reopening the Karla Brown murder case, and would seek a court order for an exhumation to conduct unspecified tests with newly developed forensic techniques. As John Douglas's advice kicked in, Weber explained that the results of polygraph tests and other evidence from the original investigation had been reviewed, and one primary suspect had emerged. Weber believed sex had been the motive for the slaying, since the victim was a beautiful young woman. She probably was killed after she rejected the man's sexual advances.

All of that was relatively safe use of the evidence and reasonable inferences by Weber. He didn't want to violate Douglas's warning against factual mistakes the killer would see as weakness.

Although Weber was holding back some details—such as the bite marks—he began to apply more strategies from Douglas. The special message was about to go out that the heat was being turned up, and the guy who killed Karla was about to be slapped onto the grill.

Weber worked hard to sound optimistic and upbeat, but he knew he was crossing the Rubicon with some of his comments.

To reporter Charlie Bosworth from the *Post-Dispatch*, Weber explained, "This is a very active case with a very real suspect. We are going to put in enough money, time, and effort to solve it, and we expect to solve it. Evidence doesn't get any better after it's been buried for four years. But we expect to find what we're looking for, and that will tell us who killed Karla Brown. If we get that, we've got the guy."

To Terry Hillig from the *Alton Telegraph*: "We're not fishing. If we were, we wouldn't disturb Karla Brown's grave. If I were the assailant, I would be very nervous right now."

To Patrick Gauen from the *Globe-Democrat*: "We're going to get this guy. It may take us years still, but we're going to get him."

The prosecutor also explained that nationally known forensic experts who had helped win convictions of Ted Bundy and Wayne Williams were advising the authorities in Madison County, and one from the Bundy case would be in town on June 2 to help with the tests on Karla's body. Weber disclosed that a squad of investigators had visited the FBI Academy on Monday for more assistance.

As the stories hit the papers, Weber grinned with satisfaction. The news was intriguing enough to capture the reporters' interest—even those who had covered dozens of murders and would require something extra to get excited about. They had knocked out dramatic stories filled with tantalizing quotes about the renewed investigation, the exhumation, the forensic advancements, and the experts' assistance. If John Douglas knew his stuff the way Weber and the cops were sure he did, there was some guy out there who was having a very bad day.

And the stress was just starting. Weber began to leak more details to the reporters over the next few days to keep up the pressure. He also explained to some of the reporters that they might be prepared for a call from someone who was unusually interested in what the press knew about the case. If that happened, Weber winked, it could lead to a hell of a story.

On Friday, Weber gave an exclusive to the *Post*'s Bosworth on the bite marks and named Levine as the expert, adding for credibility that Levine was the president of the American Academy of Forensic Odontology. Weber didn't explain that the academy was a small group of forensic dentists formed mostly to promote the specialty and gain acceptance of the new forensic technique; the public didn't need to know that.

The prosecutor did explain, however, that Levine had been an important witness against Ted Bundy, and that videotapes of that trial were being acquired from Florida State University at Tallahassee, which had broadcast the murder trial of the two members of the Chi Omega sorority. The tapes would help Weber prepare for trial, and that bit of information should make a killer in Madison County sweat.

Weber also told Bosworth that the county grand jury would be asked to appoint Agent Randy Rushing as its special investigator on the case the following Monday. Weber didn't explain that the move was more than cosmetic. He feared he might be headed for a showdown with Greer over what Weber thought was the chief's refusal to give the others everything from the department's files. This grand jury appointment would give Rushing unchallenged authority if it came to that.

And then Weber really poured it on, all for that one guy he hoped was reading the newspapers quite closely by now.

"Bite marks are as good as fingerprints. There definitely was a bite mark on Karla Brown. That's what we're going after. If it still can be used after four years, it will tell us who killed her.

"Karla Brown will never rest in peace until this guy is caught, and neither will I. This is a case of 'price is no object and time is no barrier.' I have lived with this case for four years. We will get this guy."

As Weber was letting the details out, he was engaging in his own, one-man "Dr. Jekyll and Mr. Hyde" routine especially for the suspect. Weber wasn't talking to the reading public; he was talking directly to the killer. In his mind's eye, Weber was visualizing tomorrow's newspaper in the hands of yesterday's killer, and the look on the guy's face. Weber had just played the mean Mr. Hyde role; now it was time to bring back a compassionate Dr. Jekyll.

"This guy is not the vicious killer everyone might think. He is a pathetic, frustrated character who didn't go into her home with the intention of killing her. He is probably very remorseful about this. He was acquainted with her, and sex was on his mind. But this was spontaneous. It was not planned, not premeditated. He is not dumb. According to the profile, he is at least of average intelligence. He is between twenty-two and thirty-five, probably on the younger side. The profile fit our suspect so well that it is eerie. The man probably wore a beard and shaved it off after the killing. The profile even predicted what kind of car this guy drives. And both of those points fit our suspect.

"The suspect was among a number of people questioned in 1978 and he was one of them who took a polygraph. But his results were erratic and inconsistent."

Weber wondered if he was painting a bull's-eye on Dwayne Conway's forehead, and if Conway realized he was the target as all of these details were fired at him. Surely, he was beginning to squirm by now. Weber was not yet absolutely certain that it was Conway; Prante remained a suspect, too. The evidence seemed to point to Conway, but Weber was making his statements broad enough to cover both possibilities.

The press was eating it up. On Tuesday, May 25, Pat Gauen of the *Globe* stopped by Weber's office to discuss the case again. Weber and Gauen had gone to high school together in Collinsville, and Weber used their meeting to validate a revelation he believed could explain his dedicated, if not obsessed, vow to solve the killing of Karla Brown.

Weber laid a copy of Karla's high school yearbook photo in front of Gauen.

"Who does that look like?"

Gauen picked it up and grinned. "It's Cairn Beals," he said in amazement.

Weber nodded. That's what he finally had realized. After all this time, it finally had come to him. Karla Brown looked like Cairn Beals, the pretty cheerleader at Collinsville High School when Weber and Gauen were classmates. Weber, Gauen, and almost every other hormone-driven, male teenager had endured something of a crush on her. That attraction may have drawn Weber powerfully to the mystery surrounding the death of another pretty cheerleader who looked so much like her.

Gauen had his story.

"Although he never knew Karla Brown, Madison County State's Attorney Don W. Weber says he is drawn to find her murderer by some barely explainable force that may be rooted in his high school days."

It played very well, indeed.

Weber also reiterated for Gauen many of the details of the profile, such as the shaved beard and the beat-up car. Weber added that the profile had helped the police narrow the list of suspects from the original twenty or so to "a list now not longer than three people, and two of them are not principal suspects."

Weber had in mind Conway, Prante, and Tony Garza.

Then Weber handed Gauen a great line no reporter could resist.

"He was a down-and-outer and a loser with women. When it came to sex, he was a real Rodney Dangerfield."

No respect, indeed.

The next day, May 26, Weber held another strategy session with the cops. During the conversations, Rick White made reference to an old report in the Wood River files that Weber and Rushing complained they never had seen. White and Greer insisted again that they had handed over everything. The old conflict between Weber and Greer resurfaced, and the meeting ended without any resolution of what Weber considered a serious problem. He decided it was time to proceed with a plan he had hoped he wouldn't have to implement. Weber filled out a grand jury subpoena for the entire case file from Wood River and instructed Randy Rushing to serve it as special investigator.

There could be no pretense from that point on; things were moving too quickly to let this prickly situation slow down the decision-making process while Weber tried to maneuver around pride and territorial instincts. This no longer could appear to be Wood River's investigation assisted by Weber and the state. It was time for Weber to take charge by putting Rushing in the lead and serving the subpoena. There could be an angry and resentful response from Greer and the other officers in Wood River, but the case was beyond that. John Douglas had warned Weber not to make any mistakes that would strengthen the killer's suspicion that the cops had little evidence.

The prosecutor had to have all the facts, and that couldn't happen if some members of the team were holding back. He would worry later about repairing the damage to egos.

Appointing Rushing as a special grand jury investigator was unprecedented, as far as Weber knew. He was convinced the grand jury had the authority. A police chief wouldn't hesitate to argue with a state's attorney, Weber had learned. But a grand jury carried an aura of secret power that no one wanted to challenge.

The appointment certainly was a new experience for Rushing, and delivering a subpoena to another police agency for its records went well beyond that. Rushing could become a persona non grata around the Wood River cop shop after this little adventure. He even wondered if it would adversely affect his career somehow.

But he also suspected there was evidence the police in Wood River had held back ever since 1978. Rushing hated that kind of attitude when a team of investigators was moving heaven and earth to solve a nasty case. Professionals should put aside petty differences and jealousies, and work together to solve a case. Territorial disputes served no one. One reason, Rushing believed, that serial killers sometimes escaped apprehension was jealousy between police agencies. If an arrest could be made in a case like Karla Brown's murder, there would be glory enough to go around.

Rick White and Bill Redfern had tried to be helpful to Rushing and Weber. The cops tried several times to provide Weber with information or evidence from their files. But Greer often had canceled the orders, saying the others didn't need whatever it was. Redfern and White tried to remain neutral in the tug-of-war. They wanted to see the case solved, but they could feel Wood River losing control. And they weren't sure they liked that any more than Chief Greer did.

Greer and White had sensed the subpoena was coming. White spent a whole day copying the file, which was kept rather casually in a cardboard box. The new copy was filed in the office, but the original was handed to a secretary with instructions for her to spend the day out of state, in St. Louis. After the subpoena was served, Greer sent White to Weber's office with the file copy, insisting that Weber sign a receipt for the delivery.

Fortunately, the chief and prosecutor refused to blow the incident out of proportion. Weber was perturbed, but the investigation was more important. Greer was insulted and perplexed, wondering what Weber was really up to. But neither of them wanted to derail this train heading for the station.

Agent Tom O'Connor read through the case file at Rushing's request, preparing to join the team. O'Connor closed the folder and sighed. Back in 1978, the Wood River cops could have solved it. They had worked hard and gathered a lot of information, but they had failed to understand the significance of the information they gathered. O'Connor told Rushing flatly, "There were only three suspects—Dwayne Conway, John Prante, and Jack Meyers. Solid interrogation would have brought out useful information on each one of them. This case should have been solved then, and it still can be solved today. It'll be tougher, but it can be done."

As a first step, O'Connor suggested a personal session with Dwayne Conway, already the prime suspect to most cops. O'Connor hoped to get some feel for what Conway was like four years after the killing; Weber liked the idea. O'Connor and Rushing also offered a little ruse to keep from scaring off their target. A new background investigation had shown that, some seven months earlier, Conway had married a woman with three children and they were living in a mobile home in Brighton, a small town in Jersey County just north of Madison County. The family was receiving state public-aid payments of $374 per month, even though Dwayne Conway was working. Under state law, his job probably made the family ineligible for aid. The agents could pretend to be reviewing that, a perfect excuse for dropping by Conway's home.

Rushing called in Agent Wayne Watson from the finan-

cial fraud and forgery unit; he also lived in Brighton.
Watson would conduct the interview with O'Connor
along to observe Conway.

Watson had some reason to be concerned about the situation. His grandmother lived within sight of Conway's
mobile home in the old "Jugtown" area of Brighton. It
was a working-class neighborhood of small homes and
trailers, and still carried the tag that recalled the time
years ago when it was the only part of town where drinking was allowed. Watson was torn between being a good
grandson and warning his family about a neighbor who
just might be involved in a homicide, and keeping his
mouth shut like a good cop.

When Dwayne Conway answered the agents' knock,
they thought the little man looked like a thousand other
pot smokers they had known. His wife, Patty, seemed
pleasant and assured the agents that the state aid was legal because Dwayne had lost his job at a grocery store.
She added that her three children weren't his, so he
wasn't responsible for their support. Dwayne Conway
said he had worked briefly for a freezer company in Louisiana earlier that year, but had lost that job, too.

Watson had Conway list all the jobs he held since
1975, and then asked for every address where he lived
during the same period. Conway listed six residences,
but, curiously, he missed one. He failed to mention the
little house on Acton Avenue in Wood River. Watson had
the perfect opening, and ran for daylight.

"Dwayne, it's evident you're trying to mislead us. You
lived on Acton Avenue. You missed that one, but remembered all of the others. Why did you forget that one?"

Conway's answer was soft and low. "I'm trying to forget that because it brings back so many bad memories."
He stood abruptly, and walked toward the rear of the
trailer.

Watson and O'Connor were startled, and Watson wondered anxiously if Conway was going to get a gun or just
ending the interview. Either way, it was unlikely this con-

versation was going any farther. Watson had hit a very touchy nerve.

Conway returned in a few moments with a cigarette and sat down again.

"The cops hassled me for two years because a neighbor girl got killed," Conway began, slightly irritated.

"Who was she?" Watson asked.

"I don't remember her name."

"Was it Karla Brown?"

"Yeah, that was it. I didn't know her personally, but she was my neighbor. I'd seen her around the house for a couple months before she was killed. Sometimes, I saw her layin' outside in these skimpy bathing suits. Some of the neighbors said she was a prostitute. She was strangled and beaten, and she was drowned in a fifty-gallon barrel. All kinds of things were done to her."

Time for a little test about how much Conway knew, Watson thought. He repeated, "She was shot, strangled, and drowned in a fifty-gallon barrel?"

"No, no. Not shot! Not shot!" Conway responded quickly and emphatically.

It was a pretty forceful, almost bold comment from the man who had been so laid back until then, Watson thought. And it suggested direct knowledge of the crime. If Conway wasn't involved, he should have been less positive about that and, perhaps, even willing to accept the additional information from a cop.

Conway described how the police had questioned him several times about the killing, including once a year or two ago when they lied to him about an insurance payment. Some lingering anger over that episode rose to the surface.

The cops had kept lying to him, trying to get him to confess. "Of course, I couldn't confess. I didn't do it," he insisted.

They had taken his teeth impressions, he remembered, and that was the last straw. If they picked him up again about that case, he was going to sue them for harassment.

Tough talk, Tom O'Connor thought.

One of the goals of the interview was to see if Conway knew what was happening with the new investigation. Watson mentioned that Karla Brown's body was to be "dug up" on June 1.

But Conway already knew about it, and he knew the right word. "I believe they call that 'exhumed,' " Conway corrected his guest.

He had been reading the publicity, all right. "Exhumed" was not a word that fell trippingly off this guy's tongue. He had been reading those details closely.

Weber and Rushing had suggested using some of Douglas's tactics by offering Conway an "out"—a way to minimize the crime if he was the killer. Watson suggested that this girl may have asked for what happened by the way she dressed and acted around men. She may have been a tease, giving the killer the idea she was interested in sex, and then cruelly rejecting the advances she had invited.

Patty Conway agreed that was possible and discussed these theories freely. But her husband had little to say. For the first time, Dwayne Conway had nothing to contribute to the conversation. Watson was surprised Conway didn't bite on that.

To get Conway to open up again, Watson asked about Dwayne's past. In a very matter-of-fact tone, Conway explained that he was six when his father left the family, not returning for ten years. The old man was an alcoholic and was supposed to be in an institution somewhere. Conway admitted some marijuana use between the ages of sixteen and twenty. He still drank a lot of beer, but didn't think he was an alcoholic like his father. Most of his relatives were on drugs or alcohol, and he saw little of any of them.

Although he was a high school dropout, he liked to read, mostly science fiction and articles about spaceships. Often, he volunteered wistfully, he daydreamed about a spaceship picking him up and taking him away. What was the significance of that, Watson asked. "Escaping from reality," was Conway's rather sad answer, an indication he already had done some primitive psychoanalysis of himself.

Sometimes he even dreamed about becoming a millionaire. He read dirty books, too; he thought they had helped him with his sexual activities after he got married.

Watson asked about religion. O'Connor was interested in the answer; his experience with religion among suspects was simple—the guy who showed up with a Bible was the guy who was guilty.

But Conway came down the other way. He and Patty attended the Brighton Methodist Church, but not regularly. And it wasn't as important to him as it seemed to be to his wife.

On the way back to Madison County, O'Connor and Watson were well satisfied with the interview. O'Connor was impressed that Watson, not that long out of a trooper's uniform, had performed as well as he had during the interview. Watson had drawn out some new details about Dwayne Conway, some insight they might be able to use later. They confirmed that Conway was a man of limited intelligence who seemed to be interested in little more than watching space programs on TV and puffing on some weed.

Tuesday, June 1, was bright and sunny. The investigators assembled early at the Woodland Hill Cemetery in East Alton, barely a mile from the house where Karla Brown was murdered just three weeks short of four years ago. With the cops were several other officials, including county Coroner Dallas Burke and her chief deputy, Ralph Baahlmann. Off to one side stood the nervous representatives of the burial vault company. They had come to make sure their guarantee of a watertight seal was good—after all, that guarantee wasn't checked very often.

The scene was being captured by the media. Reporters and photographers from the newspapers were joined by their colleagues from the electronic side. Television had discovered the Karla Brown story, now that there was something visual underway.

Few others knew it, but there was someone else recording the event, too. Bill Redfern was tucked out of sight in
the nearby woods photographing the scene through a tele-
photo lens, just in case Douglas's prediction came true
and the killer was compelled to attend the resurrection of
the evidence. Other officers were jotting down license
numbers as cars cruised by.

By 8:05, the backhoe had rumbled in and was digging
at the site marked by the flat bronze plaque bearing the
words, "So Lovely. So Loving. So Loved."

A somber hush fell over the assembly. Larry Trent
watched the others' faces. Chief Don Greer obviously
was affected deeply by the event. No one was saying
much. Trent realized he, too, felt uncomfortable about the
exhumation. He knew the soul was gone, but bringing a
body back from its resting place was a significant and
disturbing event.

Randy Rushing also felt some personal reactions creep-
ing in. What would come of such an invasion to this
grave? Would they get what they needed? He even sensed
an unwanted curiosity about what the beautiful woman
would look like after four years of dust-to-dust reality.

Shortly after 9:30, the concrete vault was secured by
chains and the 2,500-pound load was winched out of the
grave. When the seal on the vault was broken, an audible
hiss was emitted that suggested an airtight closure.
Though it was a somewhat grisly sound, Weber and the
others hoped it meant the condition of the body might be
the best possible under the circumstances.

A woman from the vault company insisted that the considerable amount of dark fluid in the bottom of the vault
was condensation that did not threaten the body or, more
important to her, the company's warranty. She didn't convince everyone, and some of the cops feared it really
meant something ominous.

By 10:10, the blue casket had been removed from the
vault and loaded into a hearse to be taken to the medical
examiner's office in St. Louis, where the autopsy would
be performed the next day by Doctors Case and Levine.

Karla's pallbearers this time were law enforcement officials. Their history with Karla was different from the boyfriends who had brought her to her resting place the first time. That group had been dedicated to her memory in a special way. This new group was just as dedicated, however, to bringing her killer to justice and bringing final peace to Karla.

Weber obligingly stood before every television camera and microphone pointed his way, answering every question in the terms he had been provided by John Douglas. Upbeat and optimistic—two words Weber was not given to using very often—fell from his lips like they were his personal motto.

Although few realized it at the time, someone else was featured prominently in each TV interview. Tom O'Connor—who the authorities hoped would face off against the killer someday and come away with the full story of what happened in that basement—was tight at Weber's elbow in each scene on television. It was a condition Weber set before he granted interviews, and he made the reporters promise they would use sound bites featuring O'Connor beside Weber. Weber wanted the killer to recognize O'Connor when the face-to-face came.

Another mind game, courtesy of John Douglas.

O'Connor played the pose for all it was worth. With clenched teeth, he hoped he looked every bit the tough, intense interrogator ready to pounce on whatever evidence came from that grave.

The casket arrived in St. Louis about 11 o'clock and was wheeled into the medical examiner's office to await the vital inspection the next day. Chief Deputy Coroner Ralph Baahlmann had ridden along in the hearse to provide official verification that the casket taken from Karla's grave was the one that arrived in St. Louis. Once the coffin was in the storage room, curiosity got the best of Baahlmann. He opened the lid and was surprised to see a body in pretty good shape, under the circumstances. The skin seemed a little pasty, however, and he worried about how much physical testimony was needed to prove that a particular set of teeth left some marks so long ago. Baahlmann was anxious to hear what the experts would say the next day when they took a close look at the sight he had just seen. It was an image he never would forget.

About 11:30 that morning, a volunteer walked into the Wood River police station with a startling revelation that would kick the Karla Brown investigation into overdrive. A young man named Martin Higdon said he went to high school with Karla Brown, and now worked at a home for the developmentally disabled called Beverly Farms in nearby Godfrey. The recent newspaper stories about the new evidence led to some discussion among the employees there. One woman said she knew who killed Karla and another said she was at a party where a man claimed to have been with Karla at her house the day she was murdered. Martin Higdon thought the police should know.

Detective Rick White had a sudden flash of confusion as he recalled John Douglas's prediction that the killer might be driven to contact the police. Was this new character on stage really the killer? White wondered if this young man realized how much attention he had just focused on himself.

White and the others soon realized, however, that Marty Higdon was exactly what he had said he was—someone interested in providing potentially useful information to the police.

O'Connor and White were dispatched to check out the tip. O'Connor was intrigued that this subject had come up among these people so long after the killing. White expected it to be another in a long line of unsubstantiated rumors; no big deal.

By mid-afternoon, the cops arrived at Beverly Farms to learn that only the woman who reported talking to the man at the party was working that day. Over the next few days, the police would learn that the report about the other woman was the result of a misunderstanding. But it wouldn't make any difference by then.

At 3 o'clock, O'Connor and Rick White were interviewing the first worker who, coincidentally, was named White. Vicky White, an aide at the center, told the detectives that she and her husband, Mark, had been at a party thrown by some friends, Spencer and Roxanne Bond, several days or a week after the killing. Vicky said she was chatting with a guy she knew from junior college who had tried often and unsuccessfully to date her.

His name was John Prante.

That certainly got the cops' attention.

When the subject of Karla Brown's murder came up at the party, Prante said he had been at Karla's the day she was murdered, but she was all right when he left. He was supposed to go back later, but didn't. He said Karla's body was found curled up in the basement. He was planning to leave town because he was a prime suspect in the killing and would go to jail for a long time if the police caught him. He was headed for Oklahoma or Texas.

And then John Prante said there were bite marks on Karla Brown's shoulder.

The bells and whistles went off in the cops' heads as they shot a quick glance at each other. O'Connor felt that chill up his spine. In the week after the murder—and for two more years—no one, not even the police, was aware of the bite marks. Not until Dr. Homer Campbell stunned the cops in 1980 was the phrase "bite mark" ever used by any official associated with the investigation. How could Prante have known?

The other information from this pleasant and totally credible witness was important, too. She quoted Prante as putting himself in the home of the victim that day and repeating details about other evidence in the basement. To O'Connor's trained ears, the information came from Vicky White in exactly the right way. It was natural recollection, not forced or artificial. O'Connor thought she would be a devastating witness in front of a jury. As Vicky White gave O'Connor a written statement, she seemed pleased to be helping with something important.

To Tom O'Connor, John Prante had just become "THE" suspect.

O'Connor and Rick White, also reeling from the new revelation, immediately arranged to interview Vicky's husband, Mark, at their home in Godfrey a little later. White called Greer and O'Connor called Rushing with the incredible news. Rushing relayed the information to Weber, who was just as stunned as the others.

"Randy, we've got to get on this right away. Interview all of those people right now."

Rushing almost laughed. "We're already on it, buddy. It's all being done right now."

When O'Connor and Rick White talked to Mark White at 5:45 that afternoon, they were thrilled to learn that his account of the party was similar to his wife's, although he had not heard Prante make any comments about bite marks. That little discrepancy in the statements between the husband and wife gave them even more credibility. And Mark White, who was just as receptive to the interview as his wife, offered other helpful details. While Prante, Spencer Bond, and White were sitting around the kitchen table, Prante claimed to have been the last person to see Karla alive. To Mark White, Prante was implying he was at Karla's house to try to have sex with her. Prante said he was leaving town because he was afraid he would go to jail; Mark White heard later that Prante went to Texas. He had indeed been acting strangely that night, not like his usually relaxed self.

This really was getting good, and the cops didn't want to lose the momentum. They were getting more and more excited, and couldn't wait to hear what the next person had to say. They arranged to meet Spencer and Roxanne Bond, the hosts of the party, at their house in East Alton at 10 o'clock. Spencer Bond agreed to go to the East Alton police station for an interview.

Bond seemed to be a friendly, affable man interested in helping in any way he could. He quickly admitted some marijuana use, and some experience as a "snitch" for the police on small drug cases. O'Connor waved that off; he didn't care about that stuff. What happened at the party?

That relaxed Bond, and he explained that he had known Prante since high school. They became good friends years later after meeting again at Lewis and Clark Community College in Godfrey. Bond had just seen his friend two days ago; Prante was driving a red Volkswagen and living in East Alton.

Bond's recollection of the 1978 party matched the Whites' versions, and he knew even more. Prante mentioned that their mutual friend, Dwayne Conway, lived next door to the victim and Prante had been at her house about 2 or 3 o'clock that day. Karla lived in the basement of her house, and he talked to her on several occasions. Bond remembered that, even before the murder, Prante mentioned that a good-looking girl had moved in next door to Conway. Prante was explicit and emphatic in his comments about wanting to have sex with her, using the most common, vulgar slang.

O'Connor zeroed in on that mentally. Prante had admitted—graphically—his sexual attraction to Karla. The crude comment was the first time the motive for the killing had been mentioned by someone. And for the first time, here was a witness who had more than one conversation with Prante about the victim. Could things be falling into place after all this time?

Bond quoted Prante as saying he was leaving town, probably for Texas, because he and Conway gave the police conflicting stories about the day of the killing, and Prante was afraid the police would "crack" his alibi. He wanted to get together with Conway so they could get their stories straight. Their versions needed to be more believable in case they were questioned again.

Incredibly, Prante realized the importance of those conflicting accounts long before it dawned on the police.

Then Bond gave the cops one extra detail. As he quoted Prante as saying Karla Brown had bite marks on her shoulder, he swung his left hand up to his left collarbone.

White and O'Connor flinched. The marks in the photos had been on the right side. But at least, O'Connor thought, the area of the collarbone was the correct part of the neck; it was damned close. Rick White wondered if that little move had been the clincher.

Bond also remembered talking to Dwayne Conway about six weeks after the killing. Conway described Karla's body as being curled up with her pants pulled down around her ankles. He claimed to have seen that, but he hadn't explained how. Conway also mentioned the bucket of water and how it was positioned in the basement.

Bond knew the killer, Conway told him. Bond asked, "The killer was John Prante, wasn't it?"

Conway nodded and said, "Yes, it was."

"I don't want to hear any more," Bond responded.

O'Connor liked that; it gave Bond terrific credibility.

Conway said he was going to stick around to see what happened. But, if the heat got too bad, he was getting out of town, too.

O'Connor was somewhat shaken by the new information from Dwayne Conway. Did that mean O'Connor had to rethink his decision on Prante as the bad guy? Which one was the killer? Who did what? Was it a two-man operation? Was one a lookout? Had they both abused her sexually? Which one should the cops talk to next?

O'Connor thought Conway's code was almost too easy to crack. His reference to the "heat" obviously meant the police. Conway was wondering if the cops would be smart enough to put the case together.

When Don Greer got the news from White later, he felt something wash over him; the whole thing was changing again, just as it had after the news of the bite marks and John Douglas's analysis. And something else struck Greer, too. He was a year younger than Prante, a year older than Bond, and had gone to high school with both of them. He knew they both had a lot of drug use in their past, and he wondered how reliable any of this information could be. But things were moving now, and the chief could feel this investigation shifting up another gear.

Don Weber got a late call from Rushing with an update on the interview with Spencer Bond. Weber laid awake for a time digesting the stories the cops had heard that day. The investigation, powered by the tactics and publicity campaign recommended by John Douglas, had been catapulted to a new level. At the very least, Weber was now positive that Karla Brown's killer was one of two men sitting on that porch next door. Dwayne Conway— the scraggly, unemployed loser who lived next door to the victim; or John Prante, the husky, shaggy-haired pot smoker who had left the area in his red Volkswagen.

As O'Connor drove home, he realized the case had crossed the threshold of "who did it?" They had a real target—a face in the bull's-eye. But O'Connor wanted physical evidence. The case still wasn't made without that—without some physical corroboration. He thought about the autopsy the next day; if there wasn't anything left in that coffin, there was no case.

"Please God," he prayed, hoping that his prayer would be accepted despite its mixture of earthy realism and cop cynicism.

"Please give us good embalming fluid and a tight casket."

Chapter 8

When Don Weber rolled out of bed on Wednesday, June 2, the first thought that ran through his mind was, This is going to be one hell of a day.

At an early conference with Randy Rushing, Weber learned that most of the cops were convinced that John Noble Prante was the sadistic killer they had been searching for all these years. After the news the day before, most of them had ruled out Dwayne Conway as the lead suspect; it had to be Prante. How else could he have known the details he mentioned to the others, especially the bite marks? For two years after Karla was dead and buried, nobody knew about them, except for the guy who put them on her neck on June 21, 1978.

But Weber held back. The cops were taking the new information at face value; Weber was more skeptical than that.

"I don't know, Randy. There could be a logical explanation. I think we can assume that either John Prante is the killer, or he talked to the killer. But what if Conway was the killer and he just told Prante about it? That could fit with Conway naming Prante as the killer to Spencer Bond. Maybe Conway was covering up, positioning himself to shove it off on Prante later. It still could be Conway."

Weber also was concerned about the results of the polygraphs. Prante had passed; Conway's answers had been "erratic and inconsistent." Yet, Dr. Campbell had concluded that Conway's teeth didn't match up with the bite mark in the photo. Weber knew the cops didn't have the killer yet, but the game was afoot.

Rushing wouldn't back down. He was convinced Conway didn't have the guts or the brains to kill Karla Brown, or to keep quiet about participating in the killing with someone else. With the new information about Prante, Rushing was sure that Conway, at most, had been Prante's lookout. But the killer had to be John Prante.

Despite Weber's caution, he had to admit that he didn't think Dwayne Conway was clever enough to design a cover-up or frame Prante. Conway didn't seem capable of such a sophisticated plan.

Weber's mid-morning trip to the medical examiner's office in St. Louis for the autopsy took on a whole new feel, as if a huge weight had been lifted off his chest. He had climbed far out on a limb with the publicity campaign and the exhumation. And he had been surprised by the intensity of the publicity he had generated, especially from the TV stations in St. Louis. Despite his confidence in John Douglas's advice and the combined expertise of Doctors Levine and Case, Weber still was hanging pretty far out on his own. He had promised a lot in a loud, "optimistic," and "upbeat" voice. If the new triumvirate forged between Weber, the cops, and the experts couldn't pop the case now, Weber's career might be buried along with Karla's body.

The publicity campaign had yielded unexpected but exciting results. It hadn't yet spooked the suspect into some incriminating error. But it had jogged some devastating memories from people who had not realized the importance of what they knew. With the details from the Whites and the Bonds, the cops now had two very solid suspects and some hard evidence—John Prante's own statements to his friends. Even if the autopsy failed to produce what was needed on the bite marks, the cops still could bring in the weaker of the two suspects—probably Conway at this point—lay out the evidence, and try to get him to roll over on his pal.

And the promise from Levine that his analysis of the bite marks would at least eliminate suspects had become even more important. If the authorities had two suspects and Levine could eliminate one of them—bingo—they had the killer.

Weber thought the case now seemed a bit like one of his favorite board games, Clue, in which players draw cards with tips as they try to solve a killing. The clues don't reveal who committed the murder or how it was done. They eliminate suspects and weapons and locations until the remaining facts have to be the answer. If Weber and the cops could begin eliminating the various factors that were incriminating or exculpatory for Conway or Prante, the truth soon should emerge.

As Weber entered the medical examiner's office, he was glad he had worn his "Ronald Reagan" suit that day. Weber had considered it his "Sunday go to meetin' " outfit until he wore it to get his picture taken with Reagan at a fund-raiser in March 1980, when Reagan was running for president and Weber was campaigning for state's attorney and convention delegate. After that, it became Weber's "Reagan" suit, worn for special occasions. Weber was going to get a lot of air time on television today, and he wanted to look his best and most authoritative.

A small crowd of people related to the investigation gathered at the medical examiner's office for this critical, but disturbing, event. Weber had pulled more strings to get Alva Busch there, too, after his supervisors said no. Weber stretched the point as far as possible by claiming Busch was needed to identify the body.

Dr. Mary Case spoke at some length with Weber about the autopsy. She was an imposing woman—slim and attractive even in her green surgical gown—and she spoke with a commanding authority. Weber immediately developed trust and confidence in her.

Dr. Lowell Levine arrived a short time later, greeting Dr. Case warmly and planting a kiss on her cheek. The scene amused Weber—two people about to conduct an autopsy in a four-year-old murder case were greeting each other as if they were at a gala social event. They were thrilled to see each other again and were looking forward to the day's activities. Despite a certain incongruity in that scene, Weber was glad the experts he was counting on were on such good terms.

After a little more conversation, the doctors agreed it was time to get started, and headed off through the swinging doors that led to the autopsy room. It was 12:45 P.M.

Rick White had never seen an autopsy, and this was not going to be his first. He didn't want to see the remains of the special person whose innocence in death was driving this investigation. To White, there were killings, and there were murders. If one punk knifes another one in a bar, that was a killing. But Karla Brown was murdered. She was an innocent victim, minding her own business in her own home. She was murdered, and White didn't need to see the events about to take place to confirm that.

Don Weber was standing with Randy Rushing and Keith Jensen, and the three men glanced at each other. Rushing sighed, resigned to the fact that his position as case agent required him to witness what was about to happen. But Weber decided his position allowed him more leeway. He ordered his assistant to watch the autopsy.

After all this time and all these thoughts—Cairn Beals and all the rest—Weber didn't want to be there for the necessary, but grisly, work. In his mind's eye, Weber had his own vision of Karla Brown; it was part of what kept him going. He didn't want that image destroyed by four years in the grave and an hour on the autopsy table. He didn't want a sorrowful experience in that sterile room haunting him when he tried to be optimistic and upbeat again for the cameras and microphones and notepads. And, after all, he was the boss. He had the right to some perks. Everyone had jobs to do in this investigation, and what would happen next wasn't included in his. He shuddered as he watched the swinging doors close behind the others.

Alva Busch emerged within a few minutes, shaking his

head and wearing a huge grin. "They got me again." he said with a laugh, to Weber. "They had me identify the body, and then they ordered me to get out. I have to go back to the office." Weber wondered why police agencies seemed to waste so much time on petty annoyances.

Inside the room, the procedure was underway. When a bright light was shined on Karla Brown's neck, Don Greer could see the dark spots the killer had left there with his teeth. Oh my God, Greer thought. There they are. It was worth it, after all.

Tom O'Connor wonder if that could be the physical evidence he had demanded, and prayed for.

Two hours later, Doctors Mary Case and Lowell Levine came out of the room, still in their green surgical garb. Levine walked calmly over to Weber, smiled slightly, and gave him the verdict.

"We got what we wanted. We got the bite marks. The body actually was in pretty good condition, considering the time element. The bite pattern is there. We took sections of the bite marks. I'll take them back to New York and look at them in detail. I'm sure I can eliminate people based on what we got."

Levine also explained that he used an unusual method to establish measurements for the bite marks. He measured one of Karla's teeth, and then made sure it could be seen in the photos taken of the bite marks. The measurement of her tooth might be extrapolated to the bite marks in the same photo.

Weber was relieved the evidence had been there, and appreciative of Levine's expertise.

"That's great. Now, the reporters are going to want to talk to you. We need you to be very optimistic and upbeat. Say you're confident you got good evidence. You're confident you can analyze the bite-mark sections and use them to make scientific and medical comparisons to suspects. Keep everything very positive."

Levine didn't disappoint Weber this time, either. The expert sat down at the table in front of the microphones and cameras and delivered a masterful performance. He said everything the right way and went even farther in his optimistic appraisal of the evidence than Weber had expected.

"That's why the guy's an expert. That's why he's the best," Weber mused. Levine's tab for his assistance would be high, but Weber now knew it would be worth it. As John Arbuckle advised on the old TV coffee commercial, "You get what you pay for."

Dr. Mary Case also was encouraged by the condition of the body and tissue samples she had taken. She was confident that microscopic examination would show bruising consistent with bite marks inflicted during the attack. But she also had learned something new, something else missed at the first autopsy. Karla had suffered three injuries to the back of her head, including a skull fracture. They probably were not from direct blows; they more likely were the result of having her head pounded against the concrete floor. They would not have been fatal, but could have caused Karla to lapse into unconsciousness within a couple of minutes. The other blows to her face, even the one that broke her jaw, would not have been enough to knock her out.

Weber's heart sank. Had the struggle been more prolonged than he imagined? Had Karla battled her killer across the room, on the couch, and onto the floor before suffering the head injuries? Had she been awake to suffer through the sexual violation, the removal of her clothes, and even the humiliation of the removal of the tampon? Weber felt an entirely new flush of anger. He wondered if he could have uttered the merciful remarks about the killer not being so vicious if he had known these new details.

And then he realized how many mistakes had been made in the case so far. Not only had the telling discrepancies in the stories of Conway and Prante been overlooked, but the autopsy had failed to find the bite marks and the skull fracture. How could so many errors pile up in one case? Unanswerable questions, Weber thought.

Then he pushed the new disappointment from his mind.

It was his turn before the press, and he had to be able to deliver the proper performance to keep up the psychological stress on the killer. It was even more important now. Weber suddenly felt more like an actor playing a role than a prosecutor discussing the deadly serious business of this investigation. He had memorized his lines, and now he was delivering them dramatically.

The media coverage was bombastic again, and Weber prayed it was having the intended impact on the other end. Surely the suspect was reading and watching, and beginning to worry if all this strange new activity was leading to his door.

As the task force was assembling that afternoon in Weber's office, Don Greer was taking care of a special mission. He followed Karla Brown's body back to the Woodland Hill Cemetery and attended this second burial. Someone should be there from start to finish on this day; Greer wanted to be able to tell the family members, especially those with whom he had grown so close, that Karla was resting peacefully again.

At Weber's office, the electricity in the room was palpable. Each of the savvy investigators was sensing that the beginning of the end had arrived. There no longer way any doubt that an arrest was coming soon. The question was who, and the cops were unanimous that they were closing in on John Prante.

But Weber still was cautious. The cops had the luxury of thinking no farther than the arrest; Weber had to be looking a year down the road to the trial. He had enough evidence to arrest two men right then. But he didn't think he could prove the charges against either of them at trial. He was thinking about their potential defenses, the stories they could tell from the witness stand. He was thinking like a juror, and he wasn't convinced beyond a reasonable doubt on either suspect.

The killer could be John Prante, based on his own statements to his friends. Testimony from four people who heard nearly identical comments from him at the party would be damaging evidence. The police didn't need to look for more corroboration for that. But what if Dwayne Conway was the killer and he told the details to Prante, who repeated them to increase his stature among his friends? That was plausible under the evidence, and would be a tough story to refute if told from the witness stand.

The bite marks could be essential, but their exact value still was undetermined. Conway's teeth had been ruled out once, after all. So, obviously, the next step was to get Prante's dental impressions. If he was excluded, too, this case was in deep, deep trouble again. Weber wanted an answer to that question as soon as possible. Rushing was assigned to make the arrangements.

The other prudent move at this point was to begin locking in Prante with his own words. He already had put himself in a trick box by blabbing at the party. Now, Weber was looking ahead to cross-examination at trial. One of the lessons Weber had learned was the importance of using earlier statements to give suspects absolutely no wiggle room. Get them committed to a story before they realize the importance of the facts or the timing. Make sure they're trapped on the details so they can't forget them conveniently later, or suddenly experience a burst of improved memory down the road.

In this case, the best way to accomplish that was an eavesdrop, a wiretap on John Prante. Weber turned to Tom O'Connor. "Would Spencer Bond be willing to let us wire him and go talk to Prante to try to get him to make the bite-mark statements again?"

"I'm sure he will, Don. He's really interested in helping us. He really wants to do the right thing and I think he's genuine. I think he'd do anything we asked him if he thought it would help."

"Good. Let's start setting it up. Let's do it tonight. Prante has to be really stressed out tonight, like John Douglas said he would while all this is happening. The news on TV about the autopsy will give Bond the natural opening to bring up the case and try to get Prante to admit the earlier statements. If he admits it all, we've nailed him. If he denies knowing anything, we've got him on the contradictions from the party and he can't change his story later."

The meeting ended at 3 o'clock and everyone scattered helter-skelter. O'Connor went to fetch Spencer Bond. Larry Trent was arranging the surveillance and Rushing was calling the DCI's electronics experts to rig the wiretap. Greer was to make sure Prante was located so they knew where to send Bond later.

Shortly after 4 o'clock, O'Connor returned triumphantly with Spencer Bond and ushered him into Weber's office. Bond had agreed without hesitation when O'Connor asked about wearing a wire.

The prosecutor got his first look at this citizen-investigator who was about to play a major role in this case. Bond was slightly bigger than average with unruly brown hair and a thick mustache. His dimensions were expanded by a ten-gallon cowboy hat that sported a small feather on one side. He wore a casual shirt and blue jeans—nice but not new. The look was set off by pointy-toed cowboy boots in snakeskin; not new, either, but comfortable. Weber thought he could tell a lot from a man's shoes, and that was the word he chose for Spencer Bond—comfortable. Weber liked him.

Bond was friendly and outgoing, and showed no sign of being nervous, suspicious, or defensive. And he certainly wasn't intimidated by this high-powered legal and police presence. Weber engaged him in general conversation, learning he was a Vietnam veteran working as a salesman for a construction company. He'd had a few minor brushes with the law, mostly things like drunken driving. Spencer Bond assumed none of the affectations Weber usually noticed when average folks got involved with the authorities. He wasn't playing "super-spy" or James Bond. He was just Spencer—Spencer Bond—being himself.

When the conversation swung to the issue at hand and Bond repeated his story about the party, he refrained from accusing John Prante of murder or offering an opinion that Prante was the man. Weber could tell that Bond was personally offended by the murder of Karla Brown, and genuinely wanted to help. He and Prante were friends, yes, but if Prante had done this thing, he had to pay. A pretty basic, decent sense of justice, Weber thought.

O'Connor explained to the new operative that the goal was just to get Prante talking about the case, not to be confrontational or accusatory. Just two old buddies kicking around old times. Bond would be sent in shortly before the television news at 10:00; when the exhumation was reported, it would provide the perfect opportunity for Bond to bring up memories of Prante's comments from so long ago. Bond was to look for ways to get some emotional response from Prante about the murder.

Weber added that anything Prante said would be useful to nail him down one way or the other, eliminating escape hatches for later. Bond didn't need to worry about fishing for a confession. Bond nodded his understanding. Weber hoped the seemingly cool Bond could get his old pal talking without tipping him off.

While the mechanics of the eavesdrop were set in motion, Weber talked to Bond at length about Prante's statements. The party with Mark and Vicky White took place a few days after the killing, and Prante, an almost daily visitor at the Bond household, walked in on the festivities. The men sat around the kitchen table while the women stood nearby or hurried in and out of the room to attend to the children. As they passed around a marijuana cigarette—standard procedure in those days—Bond brought up the recent murder because he heard the girl lived near their mutual friend, Dwayne Conway. Bond wondered if Prante knew anything about it.

Prante offered his knowledge of the case in a very low-key manner, typical for him. Bond described him as a strange, off-the-wall guy, but pretty laid-back. He loved being the center of attention and usually held himself out to be the intellectual superior to his friends. He probably talked about the case for an hour or so, responding to the group's requests for more information. When Prante referred to himself as the prime suspect, Bond chalked it up to typical "bullshitting" by Prante to try to build himself up for his friends.

When Prante mentioned the bite marks, Bond and the others assumed they were common knowledge. Prante had not made a big deal out of them.

Weber focused in on Prante's knowledge of the bite marks, again with the trial in mind.

"Spencer, think back to that moment and put yourself back in the situation again. Picture what's happening and let your memory work. As Prante mentioned the bite marks, which shoulder did he point to?"

Spencer thought carefully, staring off in the distance. Slowly, he raised his left hand and brought it up, but then crossed over his chest to his right shoulder.

"I'm pretty sure he used his left hand to point to the right side of his neck."

Weber and O'Connor smiled at each other. The right side; the correct side.

Prante did not seem nervous about the killing, but said he probably would leave for Texas because of it. Even though he had nothing to do with it, he didn't want to stay around and be persecuted just because he happened to be next door. Prante and Conway were to get together "to get their stories straight." Their stories needed to be believable so the cops couldn't crack his alibi. Prante prattled on defensively for some time.

He talked about the killing again a couple of weeks later, when he and Conway told Bond that Karla's body had been submerged in a barrel of water. The bite marks were mentioned again, and it seemed that Conway knew all the same details Prante had.

Then Bond offered Weber an interesting insight into Prante's sexuality. Before the murder, Prante had told Bond, "There's a big-boobed blonde moving in next door to Dwayne." And then he said crudely how he would like to have sex with her. The comment was made matter-of-factly and was a normal remark for Prante. Such a reference to a woman was nothing unusual for him, or for that matter, most of the guys Bond knew.

The conversation with Conway about six weeks later had surprised Bond, however. When Conway named Prante as the killer, it came as a revelation to Bond. He never thought Prante capable of anything like that. After Conway left, Bond decided that Prante or Conway had to be the killer. But Bond assumed the police knew everything he did, and he never bothered to report what he had heard.

If only he had, Weber thought.

When Bond's wife called him two days later to tell him the DCI was coming, he knew why. When he opened the door for O'Connor and Rick White that night, Spencer remarked, "I've been expecting you guys; you want to talk about John Prante. What took you so long?"

It was not the last time someone would ask that question after opening a door for the cops.

The eavesdrop process was clicking along and, in fact, seemed to be gathering speed and momentum just as the entire investigation had over the past several days. The procedure took well past quitting time to pull together, and some clerks in Weber's office stayed late to type the paperwork as quickly as it could be drafted. Randy Rushing signed an affidavit of pertinent facts to justify a wiretap, and Spencer Bond signed his consent to the recording of his conversation. Rushing delivered the documents to one of the criminal court judges, Horace L. Calvo, at his home. He signed the order for the eavesdrop at 9:11 P.M., and Rushing called to let the others know they had the judicial green light.

In the meantime, more than a dozen cops had been blanketing the area in a delicate search for John Prante. They couldn't ask if anyone had seen him, because that would tip their hand. So they had to scout carefully and, for a while, they wondered if they were going to run out of luck. He wasn't at his home at 198 Goulding Avenue in East Alton, and he couldn't be located anywhere else.

As things got tense, Rick White thought of all the special efforts underway by this high-powered task force, and mumbled, "All dressed up and no place to go."

Finally, Prante's car was found in front of the Benbow Inn, a tavern in downtown Wood River only three blocks from the police station. The tavern was named for old Benbow City, the area near the refineries that had been populated by hookers and gambling joints years ago before it was annexed into Wood River. The Benbow Inn was a good place for John Prante, thought White.

DCI Agents Bruce Lindstrum and Richard Burwitz, from the technical service section at state headquarters in Springfield, had hurried the ninety miles south to Madison County. They met the task force at Weber's office about mid-evening to equip Spencer Bond for the meeting. They wrapped the protective band around a shirtless Bond's waist to insulate his skin from the heat generated by the tiny recorder and transmitter. Then they secured the units to the band and taped the thin microphone and wire up the middle of Spencer's chest.

When the experts—dubbed "the boys from Brazil" by the rest of the team—recommended that Bond wear a T-shirt over the bugging equipment to help conceal it, Rick White rode to the rescue again. He peeled off his and handed it to the considerably huskier Bond. It was a tight fit, but it served the purpose. Another cop had given the shirt off his back for this case.

The recorder was turned on at 9:43 P.M.—just seventeen minutes before the news started—and the hastily arranged operation was launched. Bond drove to the Benbow Inn as the others fanned out nearby. Weber rode in Rushing's unmarked car with him and O'Connor. They stopped in a parking lot just around the corner from the Benbow, where they would pick up the conversation broadcast over a special, secure channel. Lindstrum and Burwitz were stationed in the electronics van a block away to monitor the transmission. Sergeant Mike Urban was on another nearby street in his car and Detective

Rick White was parked close by. Agent Larry Trent was the rover, assigned to stay on the move around the scene.

Weber and the agents watched Bond park his car and head toward the tavern, losing sight of him as he rounded the corner.

Bond encountered his old friend, a cup of beer in hand, sitting on a bench just outside the tavern door.

"Hi, John."

"What do you know?"

"Oh, not a hell of a lot."

The game was on, and Weber could sense the anticipation. This would be very interesting, no matter what happened.

Bond eased his way onto the bench and into the conversation with no trouble. When a woman acquaintance described wrecking her Pontiac Trans Am, Bond slipped right into character.

"Way to go, Linda."

"Yeah, really," she said.

"Wrecked your Trans Am," Bond drawled mockingly.

He was improvising well, even explaining why he was out without his wife. He and Roxanne were having "a little toot-tee-do," and he decided to get out and cool down. Nice touch. He was just one of the guys dropping by for a beer. They talked about a car that passed by and the noise rolling out of a motorcycle's pipes when it started up. Bond was handling it like a pro. Weber thought, This just might work.

Prante mentioned going to Lewis and Clark Community College to study welding. Weber smiled, remembering Agent Douglas's conclusion that the killer had a background in industrial arts.

Weber listened closely to Prante's voice. It was low and very controlled. Weber thought Prante sounded like most other burned-out potheads he had heard over the years.

Then Prante said he had been out-of-state for a while, living in Louisiana. As the unsuspecting suspect joked that the state bird there was the mosquito and describing eating crawfish by biting off the heads, Weber was thinking, Bingo. Another mark in the column under Douglas's predictions. Prante had been driven out of the area by the investigation.

The conversation drifted along for some time, boring Weber with uninteresting chatter about used cars and old friends. To Bond, Prante seemed to be getting fidgety until the talk turned to women, and he began discussing his frustrated love life. He had been through a series of unsatisfying and brief relationships.

"One-night stands could turn into two or three weeks and then I get tired of it . . . Yeah, I get bored. Time to go out and look for someone else."

Bond knew what Prante meant; he was the same old John.

"Well, you always were the kind of guy to go around chasing women if you could. I hear ya'."

A loser with women, Weber remembered.

Bond was beginning to get antsy; he had found no way to drag Prante into the tavern in time to catch the TV news. That easy entrée to the subject of Karla Brown's murder could be lost, and Bond wondered how he could steer the conversation in the right direction—so far into the past—without being too obvious.

He was only half-listening to Prante's prattle, looking for an opening when the magic words drifted through the open doorway from the television at the bar inside. Karla Brown's name could be heard as the anchorman began a report on the doctors' comments after the autopsy. Bond pounced.

"Dig it, man. Did you see where they're digging up that girl again?"

Prante looked away, and Bond wondered if John had heard him. But before Bond could repeat himself, Prante bit—hard.

"Yeah. I wonder if they're gonna' be callin' on me again," he said in a voice dripping sarcasm.

"I don't know, man."

"Because me and Conway were getting drunk and ornery, you know, right next door, and that crossed my mind when I heard about it. They bothered me three times over that."

At least, Weber thought, Prante had just put himself next door on the day of the killing.

As quickly as the conversation had turned to Karla's murder, it detoured. Weber was lost again amid the chit-chat, but he was impressed even more by Bond's acumen at this new game. He let Prante go for a while, then pulled him back by asking for an update on Dwayne Conway's whereabouts. Prante had heard the house where Conway was living with a woman burned down, and Prante suggested Conway or the woman set the fire, perhaps accidentally. Weber filed that; if there was some evidence of arson, he could use it to impeach Conway at trial. And Weber remembered that serial killers sometimes had arson in their backgrounds.

Prante wandered off again, talking about cable television and satellite dishes. It was obvious that Prante did not want to talk about Karla Brown's murder. Bond was getting lost in his own thoughts, too, remembering that the cops, prosecutors, and probably others would be listening to this tape. That made him a little nervous. And he was worried about getting Prante back onto the subject. As he turned things over in his mind, he was missing some of Prante's conversation. To cover himself, Bond dropped a few universal, all-inclusive "yeahs" at the right moments.

Finally, he dragged Prante back again.

"You know, I saw that on TV tonight. It showed them out there at that cemetery digging that gal up and shit. Man, that's crazy. Why would somebody want to go and do something like that?"

Prante knew the answer. "Bite marks or something," he said calmly. Weber liked that; Prante hadn't missed that tidbit among the news flashes.

Prante immediately and emphatically qualified his knowledge. "They can ask me anything. I didn't bite her. I didn't have nothing to do with it."

"You didn't?"

"Of course not. I was next door and didn't know it."

Prante seemed irritated. He was glancing up and down the street a lot, and Bond wondered if he was beginning to get suspicious and look for surveillance. The operative became self-conscious about the wire taped to his chest. But he forged ahead, using the denial to bring up the specific comments from long ago.

"Well, see, that's a funny thing, man. I was talking to a lot of friends and we seem to remember that, a little bit after that happened, you came over to the house and mentioned to us something about that, about—"

"I didn't even know about it until a few days later in the paper."

Weber imagined a big star by that line in a transcript. Prante had just contradicted his repeated claims that he learned about the killing that night from Conway at the home of a mutual friend.

"Then the third day after that, an officer wanted to talk to me about it ... I never even knew the girl. Some people we know did. I think Harold knew her. I think Flash knew her."

"Well, I thought you mentioned her a couple of times to me before, about the good-looking girl livin' next door to Dwayne."

"Shit. They were still moving in when that happened."

"Who?"

"That girl ... Yeah, they just unloaded a truckful, and me and Dwayne ... and I think someone else was there. I'm not sure."

"With Dwayne?"

"Yeah, we were all sittin' around, drinking easy wine, gettin' high on the porch, and watching the moon. Then three or four cops came around and we said, 'Let's go inside and watch TV. Can't get high out here no more.' "

Prante explained that polygraph tests were given to him, Conway, and several other men. Prante said the police told him he was not a suspect. "I said, 'Okay, fine.' "

Weber realized that passing the polygraph had relaxed

Prante considerably amid the investigation. Coupled with the lack of leads, it would have helped him cope with his guilt and anxiety about getting caught, as Douglas had explained.

Bond tried to pin Prante down about claiming to be at the house and the last one to see Karla alive. Bond was doing a good job of walking a fine line, becoming more aggressive while maintaining a very matter-of-fact and friendly tone of voice. But Prante admitted only that he and Conway had seen Karla outside "puttering around" that day. Prante even threw Bond a curve by claiming the TV news had said two black men were under suspicion.

Weber shook his head. Prante not only was denying his statements to the Whites and Bonds, but he was throwing in a racial factor to shift suspicion. Pretty crafty.

Prante's adamant denials of his earlier statements were leading Bond to the conclusion that his old pal could be guilty. Why else would he lie to old Spencer?

Bond decided to notch up the pressure a bit by adding that he and Roxanne remembered Prante's desire for him and Conway to get their stories straight. Prante had a pretty good response again. If he and Conway differed even on minor details, such as whether they were barbecuing or not, that could cast suspicion on them. He just wanted to be careful.

"Why? You think me and Dwayne did it? Or me?" Prante asked with surprise.

"Hey, I don't know, man."

Bond moved back to the exhumation. "They dug her up and got those teeth marks things out of her."

"Well, I don't know who did it."

"The TV people said they expect to have the guy in about a week or so. They had a pretty good lead on him. And that doctor said that they did get a good enough impression. The body wasn't decayed enough. Before long, man, they're gonna' be comin' round and gettin' your teeth marks, John." Bond was closing in.

In a voice so calm and controlled that Weber was disappointed, Prante said, "I don't care. I'm right here."

It wasn't the response Weber wanted. It was too confident—not stressed or worried enough. "Great. What if his teeth don't match, either?" Weber moaned.

But he also knew that Prante was exhibiting the guilty-man syndrome. He had reached the point where an innocent man would tire of the innuendo and say so loudly. He would demand a halt to this assault on his innocence. But Prante was doing what the guilty person often did. He was sitting there, much too calmly, turning aside insulting suggestions with cool patience.

Prante's confidence continued. "I don't have anything to worry about."

"You think Dwayne would have anything to worry about?"

"No, he was with me. We was both sittin' on the porch when all the cops showed up. That's when we found out something was going on."

Prante added that he saw a guy wearing glasses arrive in a pickup truck, and figured he must be the girl's "old man."

Putting the last comments together, Weber thought Prante just admitted being on the porch when David and Fiegenbaum found Karla's body and the police arrived. That was inconsistent with his claim a few minutes earlier that he knew nothing about the murder for days, and contradicted his statement to the police in 1978. It was difficult to keep the details straight in the middle of a lie.

Then Prante uttered the words that gave Weber a shudder.

"Maybe I'll go talk to an attorney. In any case, I'm getting tired of it."

The reference to an attorney was a potential legal problem, but Weber was confident it did not taint this tape as evidence. Prante wasn't in custody, and making such a comment didn't invalidate the eavesdrop. It just made Weber uncomfortable.

Bond had the same reaction, and even decided to change the subject for a while; it was getting too hot.

They droned on for a while, and Prante even began a discussion of a push in Congress for unilateral disarmament.

Great, Weber thought. I really want to hear a discourse on geopolitics from John Prante.

Bond eventually drew the talk back to the case by feigning concern for Prante and Conway when the exhumation was announced.

"That's what I thought when I heard about it," Prante agreed. "I was even thinking yesterday, when I heard about it on the news again, that I might just go on down to Wood River and say, 'Okay, my name is John. I'm here. What do you want to talk to me about again? Man, I don't even remember it anymore.' "

Weber shook his head again. Just as Douglas had predicted; Prante was so curious about the new investigation that he was considering going directly to the police to see what they knew. He was fitting Douglas's profile in spectacular fashion.

Bond challenged Prante more. "There was something about a bucket of water that was in there."

"Bucket of water?"

"A bucket or pail or something. You don't remember nothing about that, huh?"

Prante dismissed it with a wave of his hand. "Didn't pay any attention to that, not even when it happened. None of my business."

The conversation rambled again, boring until it turned to talk of guns and Prante said casually, "I got me a Thompson."

All the cops' ears perked up then. Great, they all thought in unison. We probably are going to have to arrest this guy, and he has a Thompson machine gun. Just great.

As the discourse rumbled along, Bond decided to push again.

"I feel sorry for you, John."

"Why?"

"Because I can almost bet you ten to one those sons a bitches are gonna' be comin' back talkin' to you."

"Don't worry, man. I don't."

Prante's control was fully engaged, but Weber detected worry in his voice.

Bond kept needling. "What are you gonna' do if they want to take teeth marks off you? Let them have them?"

"Get a lawyer and just do what he advises. I'd readily go ahead with the test, anyway, but I'm just tired of being hassled. Just because I happen to be sitting next door, that don't mean I gotta' be drug in every single time. I'm gonna' claim harassment against them and press charges."

Bond said he heard that Prante had given the police different "reports" about his activities that day. Weber and Rushing flinched; that was Bond's only mistake. He used a word that might sound too official while mentioning something he probably wouldn't know unless he was working for the cops.

But Prante didn't react suspiciously.

"I don't think I did. I don't know ... Shit, I don't even remember it."

Weber decided the next step was to take Prante's dental impressions, just as Bond had suggested. Ted Bundy had filed down his teeth in an attempt to render bite-mark evidence useless, so Weber would move quickly to get a search warrant requiring Prante to submit to the procedure.

There would be one last tidbit among the exchanges between Bond and Prante—Prante mentioned that he had been divorced in 1974. Weber shook his head again; it was the first he had heard of a failed marriage. Another score for Douglas. The suspect had a poor record with women and had been through a divorce.

Bond was trying to close out the conversation, but decided to leave the door open a little by suggesting he might drop around to see Prante, maybe even the next day. Weber grinned. Bond already was thinking like a cop; he quickly was becoming one of the guys.

And, just to keep things normal, Bond asked Prante for a marijuana cigarette. Prante passed him one, and the old friends parted. They had talked for eighty minutes—it was 11 o'clock.

When Bond arrived at the Wood River police station, Chief Don Greer quickly relieved him of the marijuana. Bond grinned. "Sorry, sorry." He had just been trying to keep Prante convinced that the meeting was purely social. Right.

Weber gave Bond a rave review for dragging out of Prante a juicy collection of comments Weber could use to help build a case. Prante contradicted himself too many times for an innocent interpretation. It wasn't conclusive, of course, but it was probing. And the suspect had lined up well with the profile supplied by John Douglas; to Weber, that was perhaps the most exciting aspect of the evening.

Spencer Bond said he would be willing to have another run at Prante if it would help. Weber appreciated his dedication, and said the investigators would get back in touch with him later.

The cops didn't say much, but they didn't think the wiretap had been very productive. Larry Trent had let himself hope for a confession, and he certainly hadn't got that. Rushing, O'Connor, and White agreed they hadn't heard anything helpful.

The end of one hell of a day had come. The autopsy that morning seemed a year ago, and not nearly as crucial as it might have been. Weber wondered what other bizarre turns could be ahead.

Spencer Bond was relieved it was over, but feared he had been a complete failure. He had a long talk with his wife that night, and even jotted down a list of Prante's comments and contradictions. Although Bond was a lot more suspicious of John Prante now, he wasn't convinced his old friend had murdered anyone.

But I know this much, he thought. He was feeding me a line of bullshit all the way around.

Chapter 9

Preparations for another blitz against John Prante consumed most of Thursday, June 3, and Don Weber was anxious to see what would develop next. A court order compelling Prante to submit to dental impressions on Friday was signed by a judge, and another eavesdrop order was prepared so Spencer Bond could be wired and sent in against Prante one more time on Friday night.

Randy Rushing made arrangements for him and Weber to visit Dr. Lowell Levine at his home on Long Island, New York, the next Tuesday so he could compare the cast of Prante's teeth to the bite-mark photos from the second autopsy. Levine had warned Weber that it was unlikely he could make an exact match; that required characteristics from individual teeth, and Levine didn't think the marks on Karla's neck were clear enough for that. But he was sure he could eliminate a suspect's teeth; the distinctive spacing might allow that much. Weber hoped Levine could rule out Conway, even if he couldn't conclude that Prante made the bite mark. Scratching one of the two finalists and adding in the evidence from the Whites and Bonds still left only one conclusion—it was Prante.

Don Greer and Rick White gladly drove to Prante's house about mid-morning Friday to get the dental impressions. Sending the local police was another bit of strategy; they wouldn't alert Prante as much as a visit by state agents. Prante greeted the cops calmly at the door and Greer, his acquaintance from high school, downplayed the need for a model of Prante's teeth; the authorities were just tying up loose ends and marking suspects off the list.

Prante asked if he could call an attorney, and seemed almost disappointed when Greer answered, "Sure, call anyone you want to." Prante shrugged, mumbled he wouldn't know who to call anyway, and agreed to the dental procedure. Greer didn't mention the court order, and was glad it had stayed casual. He hoped to keep Prante as ignorant as possible about the gathering storm around him.

Prante hopped into the backseat of the unmarked police car and began to discuss old times with Greer in a friendly and comfortable tone. But it was obvious Prante was nervous.

"By the way, you'll never guess who I bumped into the other night at the Benbow," Prante offered coyly.

"Yeah? Who was that?"

"Spencer Bond. You remember old Spence?"

"Sure. Boy, I haven't seen him in a long time."

"Yeah, he just popped up. Asked a lot of questions. I kind of got the impression he was working for you guys."

"Spencer, working for us? Not hardly. How would you get that idea?"

"I don't know. Just wondered."

Greer was glad Prante had not pushed any harder.

The suspect relaxed in the chair while the dentist, Dr. Warren Waters, filled the dental plates with the mushy substance for the impression and explained that there would be a slight uncomfortable fullness in the mouth while the mixture hardened. But Prante's reaction to the procedure left no doubt that he felt more than a little discomfort. His arms and legs fidgeted anxiously as he snorted and hacked. After two complete impressions of his upper and lower teeth were made, Prante got out of the chair and spat out, "That was a humiliating experience. It was like drowning."

The cops looked at each other. That was a strange

choice of words, and it made them even more optimistic that they had the right set of teeth.

Greer drove Prante back to his home. Again, Prante seemed almost anxious for the cops to play their roles.

"I guess it's time for the standard line, 'Don't leave town.' "

The officers chuckled, and Greer departed with a casual, "Thanks, John. See ya' later." But Greer thought "sooner."

About noon on Friday, Don Weber and Keith Jensen were discussing strategy for that night's activities when Don's secretary, Denise O'Neill, leaned into his office.

"You have a call."

"We're pretty busy right now. Can it wait?"

"Well, I thought you might want to take it," she said with a mischievous lilt in her voice. "It's John Prante."

Don Weber's mouth dropped open; he felt electrified. His first thought was, Douglas was right. We spooked the killer, and he called. We pressured him, and he cracked. Absolutely, positively incredible. That was it; all doubt was gone. John Prante was the killer. Dwayne Conway may have been there, or Prante may have told him about it. But John Prante was the creep who murdered Karla Brown on June 21, 1978. Amid the flood of thoughts, Weber envisioned the microphone wired to a grave marker in the story told by Douglas. This was almost that good.

Weber racked his brain for the proper strategy; he wasn't prepared for this. What were the details he needed to nail down now that he had the suspect on the line? This would be an intense mind game, and Weber had to be careful not to reveal any details Prante could claim later he had heard from the authorities. Weber had about thirty seconds to collect his thoughts.

He grabbed a pen and a piece of paper to take notes, and then looked at his phone. Talking to Prante could make Weber a witness at trial, and this prosecutor was not about to get thrown off this case later. There wasn't time to tape-record the call, so Weber told Jensen to get on the extension as soon as Weber picked up the phone; that provided another witness.

"Hello."

"Hi, Don. This is John Prante. I wanted to call because the police came by and took my teeth impressions this morning. I just wanted to know what was up."

Weber recognized the voice from the eavesdrop. It was the same drug-dulled tone, but Weber thought he detected a bit more struggle to rein in some nervousness. And this mope had called him "Don," as if they were old pot-smoking buddies.

Weber grimaced as he began the contest. "Well, we're just trying to tie up some loose ends and eliminate some old suspects. Nothing special. But since I've got you on the line, what do you remember about the day of the killing?"

Prante launched into a rambling story about bringing wine to Dwayne Conway's and drinking it on the porch. Prante stayed on the porch, except to go get some more wine, until he left Conway's to go to another party about 6 o'clock or so, after the police arrived at Karla's. Weber liked that; Prante had contradicted his earlier statements about not being at Conway's very long that day, and admitted being there when the cops showed up.

Prante also admitted seeing Karla Brown "puttering around" in the garden in front of her house about 1 o'clock, when Weber believed she was dead or, at least, tied up in her basement.

Prante hadn't talked to her, although he allowed that there may have been a "catcall" at her from Conway. Prante didn't know the girl was dead until two days later, when Conway showed him a newspaper story. Prante had blundered again, Weber thought. This was the third version of how he learned of the killing.

The prosecutor tried a trick question. "Did you see the body brought out?"

"No, I was in the house then."

Another stumble. Prante had contradicted himself again

on when he knew about the murder, and he was admitting that he was at Conway's house much later.

Weber tried to shift Prante to a third-person scenario, hoping the suspect might offer a supposedly speculative theory that would reveal what really happened. Weber asked if Dwayne Conway could have killed Karla Brown; the response was curious and obtuse again.

"I don't know. Dwayne broke down and cried one time when I backhanded him."

"Would you be willing to talk to the police and me again on this case later? Would you be willing to be hypnotized to see if you can remember anything else?"

"Yeah, I'd undergo hypnosis . . ."

Then Prante fulfilled another of John Douglas's predictions.

"I want to cooperate with you guys and assist the police any way I can, as long as that's the end of it. I don't want to be considered a suspect."

Weber shook his head again; this was getting too eerie. How could Douglas have been any more accurate than to predict almost the exact line Prante used about not wanting to be a suspect? Considering his audience, Weber took some license with the facts.

"At most, you're a low-level suspect. We think you might know more than you're telling us. That's why we want to eliminate you from consideration by checking your teeth. We're really looking at Dwayne Conway and maybe Jack Meyers. Meyers was the prime suspect for a long time. He has a history of beating women up and even putting their heads in toilets. And he knew Karla Brown. We took his dental impressions a few days ago."

"Well, the police have been harassing me on this. They've talked to me on a number of occasions and they just took my teeth impressions this morning. Don, do you have the number for the ACLU?"

Weber was taken aback. What did Prante want with the American Civil Liberties Union?

"No."

"Oh. Well, the ACLU is going to check with Dwayne Conway to see if the police took his teeth impressions."

That should have rung an alarm in Weber's head, but it slipped by. It would pop up again later.

The conversation closed on another odd note.

"Sometimes I have trouble remembering things," Prante said. "I was on an aircraft carrier in the Navy. They beat me with a rubber hose and made me do five-hundred pushups. I'd be glad to talk to the police about this case. I can't do it today; I have to go register for classes."

Weber felt his heart thumping as he hung up. Forget Dwayne Conway; the killer was John Prante.

Randy Rushing freaked out when Weber told him about the call. It confirmed Rushing's insistence that Conway was not the killer, and convinced the agent even more that Prante was their man. O'Connor reacted the same way, marveling at how perfectly John Prante fit the profile John Douglas had drawn.

The plan to send Spencer Bond back to Prante that night became even more important. When they called Bond, he informed them that Prante had called his house, nervous and looking for him while he was gone earlier. John Prante really was spooked; he was trying to cover all the bases, and his call gave the cops a perfect excuse for having Bond show up at Prante's door that night.

At 8 o'clock, Tom O'Connor prepped Spencer Bond with a new strategy for this round. Bond was to be aggressive, accusatory, and downright insulting. Prante had some incriminating details about this murder and, by God, Bond wanted to know how.

By 9 o'clock, Spencer Bond was walking in the front door of John Prante's little house in East Alton. The surveillance was tighter this time. Weber, Rushing, and O'Connor joined the boys from Brazil in the stuffy electronics van around the corner. Other cops were parked strategically around the neighborhood.

Larry Trent had a nagging uneasiness about Spencer Bond's safety this time. It wasn't likely he would be in any danger, but this conversation could get hostile and, if Prante was indeed a killer, things could get very ugly, very quickly. Prante had called Weber, so he might be cracking under the pressure. If Bond pushed him over the edge, the anger that killed Karla Brown could emerge again. Prante's comment about owning a machine gun came to mind, too.

Trent was the "eyeball," assigned to confirm that Bond had entered the house at 198 Goulding. After that, Trent parked around the corner where he could watch the side and rear of the house. If anything went wrong, Trent would be the first one through the front door. He couldn't pick up the transmission of the conversation, so he would rely on periodic updates via radio from Rushing.

Thinking this would take a while, Trent popped the tab on a can of soda, tuned his car radio to the Cardinals baseball game, and kicked back in the reclining seat. Then he heard it—the low moan of a whistle and the rumble as the train got closer and closer. On the other side of Prante's house was a set of train tracks. As Trent thought back to Greta Alexander's prediction about train tracks, he shuddered and mumbled, "Oh no. I can't believe this."

Around the corner, the same shiver ran down Rushing's spine.

Inside the house, John Prante was sitting in his easy chair opposite the couch where Bond sat. Prante recounted Greer dropping by for the dental impressions, and even revealed that he asked if Bond was working for the police. With a singsong, "Way to go, John," Bond tried to shrug that off as too ridiculous to contemplate.

Prante said he had been upset by Bond's comments the other night, and Bond shot back that he still was upset, too. Prante recounted a conversation with a lawyer who told him not to talk to the police and offered to seek an injunction if they continued to harass him. As Prante described his call to Don Weber that morning, Bond thought his old friend was visibly more nervous than two nights before. But he seemed to have been reassured by Weber's description of him as a "low-level" suspect. He claimed to be bothered, however, by Weber's suspicion that Dwayne Conway could be the killer. Prante didn't know this Meyers guy that Weber had mentioned. But Prante said Weber seemed "hot to trot" on Meyers as a suspect and had taken his dental impressions, too.

In the middle of the conversation, Prante fell once again into Douglas's profile with a casual question. "Want to get high?" Bond tried to gloss over that, too, with a casual, "Sure." Weber winced, thinking ahead to how that exchange might sound at trial.

Prante set off alarms for the investigators when he said he had been trying to get in touch with Dwayne Conway to see if the police had talked to him again or had taken his dental impressions. Weber looked at Rushing and O'Connor across the small van, and the men knew what had to be done. They would have to find Conway before Prante did, even if it took all night, that night.

Prante then surprised them by referring to the murder and adding, "I don't think Dwayne would do something like that. And, besides, he was with me from, like 10 or 11 in the morning until about 4 o'clock. We was just sittin' there."

Bond set the confrontational tone for the evening.

"Well, let me lay some heavy problems on ya'."

"Go ahead," Prante said, betraying some nervousness.

"You remember telling me somethin' about bite marks?"

Prante engaged his control and answered calmly, "Nope, sure don't."

"I do." Bond leaned forward, hoping some righteous anger would mask the jitters in his belly.

"Well, I don't," Prante responded more emphatically.

"You told me about them."

Prante was getting annoyed. "I sure don't remember."

Bond's response sounded threatening, even to the guys out in the van. "Yeah? Better think hard."

"I'm sure I didn't say something like that, 'cause I didn't even know the girl was raped."

They parried some more, with Bond adding that there was another "dude" who remembered similar comments by Prante. Bond refused to give a name, and Prante finally became defiant.

"Well, if you feel determined about puttin' me in jail, go ahead. What can I say?"

Prante was convinced there was no case against him, adding that innuendo didn't count. Weber wondered if Prante was onto Bond and the guys outside. The suspect almost seemed to be performing for a tape recorder. Words like "case" and "innuendo" seemed strange choices, unless Prante was trying to make specific points for other listeners to protect himself later.

The defiance became a challenge when Spencer Bond asked if Prante would mind answering more questions.

"Ask 'em, 'cause I'm not guilty of anything. Ask away."

"You remember me asking you about the bite marks?"

"No, I don't remember the bite marks, 'cause I'm sure I didn't tell you nothing about it. Because I'm sure I didn't know nothing about it."

In a rapid-fire exchange, Prante denied mentioning a bucket of water, insisting, "I was never in the house; I was never there."

"John, you told me some things that nobody could know except for somebody that was there or somebody that did it, man. I'm serious."

The cops were impressed with Bond again. He was deadly serious and incredibly gutsy with his first direct accusation that his pal could be a killer.

Prante remained defiant. "You seriously got a problem."

"No, you do; you got the problem. You don't remember doin' it, huh?"

"I didn't do it."

Bond was turning in another savvy performance, raising the stakes with precise timing.

"I remember Dwayne saying a few things that was pretty bad about it, too."

Prante was surprised to hear his buddy hadn't backed him up. "What? We were getting high and drunk on the porch all day!"

"Nope. He said, since you and him gave different reports to the police, he was wondering whether you might have done it, too. In fact, he thinks you did it. In fact, I heard him positively say he thought you did it!"

Prante was taken aback. He paused for a long time and, when he spoke, his voice displayed some resignation for the first time.

"So, he is the other person."

"I'm not saying who the other people are, man."

"Well, they'll show up in court, anyway."

Weber thought Prante could see the handwriting on the wall; he realized where all of this was going now. When Bond charged again that Prante had known too many details, Prante's anger and defiance flashed.

"I didn't tell you nothin'."

Bond was just as defiant. "Bullshit."

More denials as Bond repeatedly accused Prante of lying.

"You told me you talked to her that day over at her house."

"Never went to the house."

"You're lyin'."

"I mighta' talked to her from the walkway."

Good, Weber thought. There was the first suggestion of direct contact between the killer and the victim.

"You're lying, John. You're lying."

Amid the increasingly angry exchanges, an old resentment slipped out; Bond asked Prante why he had made a pass at Spencer's wife, Roxanne. Weber suddenly found himself agreeing with Prante when he responded, "What's that have to do with this? Let's talk about Karla Brown."

"Either you know who did it, or you did it, man," Bond charged.

"I don't know who did it, man."

The heat was getting to Prante, and he shifted gears. "Have you ever seen Dwayne in action around women? 'Hey, cutie, how you doin'?' "

"I've seen you the same way."

"Not too often. I think I've changed since then."

"It's drivin' me crazy; it's drivin' Roxanne crazy. We been thinking about it, and we know too much, too much that's not even been let out publicly, man. And we heard it from you."

"No."

Bond's voice rose to a new volume that surprised the eavesdroppers.

"You lyin' sack of shit."

Prante kept his cool, his voice slipping back to a low, controlled tone.

"Don't be calling me names. I'm not calling you names."

"I can't help it, man. I know you're lying to me. You better think hard, brother.

"You better leave, if you can't abide by common courtesy. You oughta' go."

O'Connor was shaking his head. Prante was too controlled to fit the innocent-man profile. Amid the accusations and the anger, an innocent man would have lost patience with a friend who didn't believe him. He would have blown his cool, and screamed, "Get the hell out of my house." The guilty man would restrain himself, fearing that any outburst would seem incriminating. He would take the accusations, as long as no hard evidence of his guilt came along with them. Prante was fitting the guilty profile, just as he was fitting the special profile from John Douglas.

Bond changed his tactics.

"Well, do you think Dwayne might have done it?"

Prante seemed relieved to have the focus off him.

"You know, for the first time in my life—and all this is honest, this is for real—I thought about that all day today. But I still don't think so, 'cause I knew him as a younger brother I never had ... It's possible, but I don't think he went over there. I'm pretty sure he was right on the porch with me."

Prante volunteered that Conway had found Karla attractive, and then added, "Personally, I don't care for short-haired blondes. I never have. I don't like short hair. I like long hair. Ever notice that? Every woman who's got hair down to here or farther, boy, I'm right there. I want to talk to 'em."

Pure baloney, Weber thought.

Prante mentioned calling the ACLU again, fulfilling Douglas's prediction again by explaining that he wanted to get information about the investigation. He wanted to find out what was going on because he was tired of being harassed by the police. The thought of going to jail drove him "completely insane." He had served thirty days in the Navy brig, where he suffered a nervous breakdown and was pushed almost to suicide.

Prante offered some self-analysis; he didn't think he was capable of murder and would have to tell the police if he knew someone else had committed one.

"If I thought that somebody else did it, say, like if I thought that Dwayne went over there and came back with blood up to his elbows or somethin' ..."

Weber leaned forward. Prante had just slipped over the edge and started to discuss his own crime in the third person. John Prante was the one who came back from Karla Brown's "with blood up to his elbows."

The same thought was striking Bond—*You're telling me what you did, and you're putting Dwayne in your place.*

Prante kept going. "... and I consciously knew he had done something bad, I would definitely have to do something about that. You know, I'd call the cops immediately or the ambulance immediately; call the psychiatric ward immediately. To the best of my consciousness, you know, Dwayne wasn't involved. Now, as to whether he was or not, that's something else. I could be totally wrong. If he went to the bathroom for a moment, and ran over there and did a number on her in a matter of minutes and came back ... To the best of my knowledge, the only time he ever left was to go get more wine and go to the head and drop the wine."

Had Prante slipped into the third person again? Had he done his number on her while he was supposed to be getting more wine? Or was he just babbling?

Weber was surprised to hear his own name mentioned once more as Prante suggested he and Bond go to the prosecutor and see if they could be hypnotized to answer Bond's questions. That might be better than waiting until the cops "came down here, bustin' in the door and draggin' me away." That was what would happen if Bond went to the police. It might be easier to undergo interviews and other tests so the authorities could learn what Prante already knew—that he didn't do anything and he didn't know anything. They probably would find out that anything he knew he had heard in casual conversation with a cop or someone else—an exchange so unimportant that Prante had forgotten it over the years.

The conversation was winding down after nearly ninety minutes. Spencer Bond made it clear he didn't believe Prante's denials. Prante didn't know what else to say to his old friend, and bemoaned the change in their relationship that surely would follow this confrontation. Prante dropped another little remark that Weber and the cops caught, however. As he bummed a cigarette from Bond, Prante motioned toward his wastebasket.

"As you can see by my trash can, I'm up to about two or three packs a day, for the last four months or so."

Excessively nervous, as John Douglas said the killer would be.

Prante said he wanted to go to the store to get some more cigarettes. Bond offered him a last chance.

"Sure there's nothin' you want to tell me?"

"No, not a thing. I believe we've about covered that. I can't think of anything else ..."

"Well, you better think hard, man."

"... and what bothered me a little while ago, now it's

starting to bore me." Prante was exhausted and disheartened. Was it fatigue, or foreboding?

Bond accepted a ride from Prante to the store. Bond stepped out of the car and said he hoped visiting Weber could help the men clear up their differences, perhaps under hypnosis.

Prante said, "I've done many things wrong in my life, but I certainly couldn't commit murder. You might have a point there. I might know more than what I really think that I even know."

Bond rounded the corner as the surveillance team began a frantic search for their disappeared informant. Finally, Bond saw Mike Urban's car and hopped in, thinking his duty was done.

Urban smiled as he turned the car toward the parking lot at a store where the team was reassembling.

"We're going to Dwayne Conway's tonight. We want you to record a conversation with him, too."

Weber and the others were worried. Aside from the logistics of a late-night eavesdrop and surveillance on short notice, they needed a good excuse for Spencer Bond to walk back into Dwayne Conway's life at that hour and dredge up this old murder, all without arousing suspicion. Lacking any creative ideas, they told Bond to say he was so upset after talking to Prante that he had to find Conway immediately to see if he could answer the burning questions about Prante's incriminating knowledge.

Would something so thin work? It was all they had.

Meanwhile, the mechanics of the eavesdrop were in motion. Brighton was in Jersey County, so a judge there had been rousted at home to sign an eavesdrop order. Detective Rick White, who had been a patrolman in Brighton before joining the Wood River force, called his former colleague in Brighton, Bill Burton. As it turned out, Dwayne Conway lived right across the street from Burton, and Burton made his driveway available to the surveillance crew.

Weber and the agents stopped at the Brighton police

station and were wiring Bond again when Chief Jerome
"Jay" Wooldridge came roaring into his office. He was
furious that a task force had descended on his town without so much as a courtesy call. Who the hell did they
think they were? Rick White had assumed that Burton
would call his chief and let him know. But Wooldridge
hadn't been notified, and he was well beyond angry about
it.

DCI Agent Wayne Watson and Chief Wooldridge were
close friends, and Watson and Rushing took the chief
aside to explain and apologize. Wooldridge was normally
an easygoing man, and he accepted the agents' explanation. But the scene certainly had been exciting for a few
minutes, as if Weber's crew needed more of that.

On this tape, Weber hoped Conway would confirm his
earlier suspicions that Prante was the killer and, perhaps,
offer the true and complete story of what happened that
day. Had Conway been the lookout or helper when the
scene was staged?

It was nearly 1 o'clock in the morning when Spencer
Bond knocked on the door at the mobile home where one
light showed dimly through the window. Weber and the
others held their breath as they waited for Conway's reaction to this untimely visit. Conway, dressed only in his un-
derwear, opened the door and was shocked to see his old
buddy. It was a pleasant surprise, however, and his cheerful
tone relaxed the agents listening nearby.

"Hey, Spence."

"What's going on?"

"Oh, nothing much, man. Let me put some pants on.
What're you doing way out here? How'd you find out
where I lived?"

"I was talking to John earlier tonight. What you been
up to?"

Conway introduced his wife, Patty, and matter-of-factly
recounted a recent firing from a grocery store for drinking
on the job.

Then he sent laughter rolling through the surveillance
vehicles with a question so predictable it was a bad joke.

"Hey, you wouldn't have any pot to smoke, would ya'?"

It struck Weber so funny that he would remember it forever. He had been so worried about Bond's surprise visit alarming Conway. Instead, Conway welcomed his old friend and immediately asked for a joint. What a different world.

Bond hedged, saying he had smoked his last one in the car. The question had struck Bond as typical for the little guy he remembered mostly as Prante's friend.

Easing through some chitchat, Conway explained he had just signed up to take a welding course at Lewis and Clark Community College; Bond and the others noticed the coincidence. They had just heard the same plan from Prante; it was another throwback to John Douglas's analysis.

Then the operative deftly steered the conversation by asking if Conway had seen the news on TV. To the surprise of Bond and Weber, Conway said he had received a newspaper clipping in the mail recently from some anonymous source. That kind of less-than-subtle hint had been suggested by John Douglas, but no one in the investigation had done it, as far as Weber knew. He would find out differently later.

Conway wondered if Bond was asking about the same thing the newspaper clipping reported.

"What is it, about that chick that got killed?"

"Uh-huh, you betcha', brother."

Conway had been trying to connect the clipping to the visit he had received the week before from some investigators he thought were from the state public aid department. Bond shook off the whole mystifying incident and asked Conway if his wife could hear them from the bedroom.

"No. Why? You think it was John?" Conway asked softly.

"You damn near told me it was," Bond retorted.

"But I don't think it could be John."

Conway would insist for some time that he didn't think

John Prante was capable of murder. That was disappointing to Weber, but it was still early in the game.

Conway's view of his old friend changed somewhat as he described how Prante once pointed a .22-caliber survival rifle at Conway's chest. Prante was angry because Conway and his cousin were horsing around and bickering with each other. Prante assembled the rifle, pointed it at Conway, and ordered the men out of his house. Then Prante fired a shot through the ceiling before pushing Conway off the back porch. Conway took off, only too glad to get out of range. He never learned why Prante got so angry.

It was a telling story about some unexpected violence from the prime suspect, Weber thought.

As the conversation progressed, it became abundantly clear that Conway still was angry at the Wood River police for all the harassment, especially the insurance-check scam the night they took his dental impressions. The cops used some phony test—Conway called it "voice crap"—that they rigged before his very eyes to make it read that he was guilty. Conway answered their questions, took their bogus test, and gave them his teeth impressions.

"I know I ain't guilty, so what the hell I got to worry about, you know?"

"You don't know who did it though, huh?"

"Huh-uh."

"You sure?"

"No. But, since you mentioned that about John, I don't know. You think John's capable of something like that?" Conway was interviewing the interviewer.

"Oh, man, I know John's capable. He pointed a gun at your head, didn't you just say?"

"Yeah."

"What the hell, then. What's to keep him from killing a good-lookin' stranger, especially a girl? Do you remember him going over there or anything, man, because this is really heavy."

"No. He said he knew her, though."

Bond kept up the pace. "Well, I remember him mentioning her name a couple of times. He said there was a good-lookin' blond girl that lived next to you. I remember him saying Karla Brown a couple of times. That was before the girl was even dead. Things are lookin' mighty spooky, you know."

"Yeah. John's been refused sexual intercourse before from women."

"Yeah."

"Why would he kill her in particular? But it's kind of strange that John would mention bite marks before he would even know anything about it."

The seeds of doubt were planted, and Conway was beginning to wonder about his old buddy. Bond fed the growing uncertainty by recalling that Prante was on the front porch all day, ample time to commit the murder. But Conway jumped at that, insisting that Prante was there briefly at 8 in the morning, returned about noon, and stayed only for an hour or so; he hadn't been there when the girl's boyfriend got home or when the police arrived. Conway was on scaffolding painting a neighbor's house when the police arrived. And Prante's claim that they saw Karla in the front yard was wrong, too; they never saw her at all that day.

Weber was certain that Conway was lying about some of the timing. Prante described watching David Hart and Tom Fiegenbaum arrive in the pickup truck, followed soon by the police and the coroner's wagon. Prante had been there then, so Conway had to be lying for some reason.

Bond asked if Prante could have slipped over to Karla's house while he was supposed to be going to get more wine.

"Naw, they said she was killed early in the morning."

Weber's ears perked up. No one had been able to establish the time of death accurately. How would Conway have known? Then Conway really got Weber's attention.

"But you're right about that, pourin' water on her and stuff like that."

Bond was stunned. "Pouring water on her?"

"Yeah. Well, see, they had a bunch of pictures of stuff, and different objects in the living room . . ."

"Oh. Did you see the pictures?"

"Not of the chick. But, see, she had started up the stairs—"

"You said something about pouring water on her, man. John mentioned something to me about a bucket of water or a pail of water, or something about water like that."

"Uh-huh. Well, anyway, from what I understand, they started up the stairs and she was hit in the face with a rack of TV trays . . ."

Weber and Rushing looked at each other. How could Conway know that? There had been no public identification of the TV trays as the weapon. That could confirm one of their fears—that the Wood River police had shown Conway some crime-scene photos or given him other information while interrogating him two years ago. Giving suspects details to try to get more out of them was not the best interrogation technique, and now it could be coming back to haunt the investigation. If Conway saw the pictures, and then talked to Prante, some of the evidence could be slipping away.

But the other tidbit from Conway intrigued Weber. "She had started up the stairs . . ." Was that a detail about the killing no one ever heard before? Had Karla confronted her killer on the stairs, or had she been trying to escape up the stairs when the killer caught her from behind? How did Conway know this, too?

"Have you ever caught John in lies before this?" Conway asked.

"Oh yeah."

"I know he's a woman chaser."

Each time Conway offered some criticism of Prante, he followed it with a disclaimer. "I just can't hardly believe that John is capable of something like that. Damn! It could be possible. You never know."

Weber was more confused than ever. Conway's doubts about Prante's capacity for murder sounded genuine, and the prosecutor feared he was falling for a con game by

Conway that could fool a jury, too. Weber was reassured, however, by the unequivocal rejection of Conway's claims by the two seasoned agents in the car. Rushing and O'Connor were sure they could get the truth out of Conway in an interview later.

Conway sent the weary eavesdroppers into hysterical laughter again when he described going to a Halloween party—as a marijuana plant. The image of this longtime doper dressed in some bizarre costume to look like his favorite substance in the world was too much for the tired, slap-happy investigators to handle with anything less than howls of laughter.

Inside, Bond was hammering at all the details Prante knew, connecting that incriminating evidence to the potential for sudden violence Conway had seen firsthand. That juxtaposition seemed to have an impact on Conway, and he began to draw some new conclusions. "That's what made me suspicious of him in the first place. That's why I said, 'Hey, I wouldn't put it past John, you know.' "

"I wouldn't either. Not now."

"Murder, I mean. He actually murdered this chick, and bit her in the neck and all this other stuff."

Then Conway offered an intriguing suggestion. "What may have happened was, you know, John approached her and made sexual advances and stuff, and she got pissed off and hauled off and kicked him or slapped him around or somethin' like that. And that could have set him off, you know . . ."

"I was thinkin' that, too. Kinda' funny how we both just jumped to the same conclusion."

". . . and then he got pissed off, you know, and went a little too far, you know."

Had Dwayne Conway just repeated a scenario he heard from John Prante, or something he had witnessed? Had Conway offered a true account of the crime, disguised as speculation? The suggestion that the killing followed Karla's rejection of sexual advances was a major point agreed on by everyone, including John Douglas.

Conway followed that scenario quickly with another interesting allegation, suggesting that Prante had "slapped around" his former wife a few times. More violence, this time against a woman.

The conversation petered out after that, and Bond said his good-byes. As he headed out the door, he was ninety-nine percent convinced that John Prante killed Karla Brown. Spencer didn't know how or why; the long conversations he endured with Prante and Conway hadn't been that enlightening. But he was lied to at almost every turn, and there had to be a damned good reason—like murder.

It was 3:13 in the morning. The investigators fired up their engines and turned south for an incredibly late meeting in Weber's office. With the eavesdrops and the meeting with Dr. Levine next week for the final comparison of dental impressions, Weber was confident an arrest was close.

The cops were less sure; they weren't seeing the case with the prosecutor's eye toward locked-in statements and incriminating contradictions. Larry Trent said the tapes hadn't advanced the case; "We didn't get squat." Rushing agreed, and said so with a succinct pun: "We need something more that we can sink our teeth into." That brought a groan from everyone on the exhausted team.

They decided to hit Dwayne Conway again, hard, in a tough, official interview as soon as everyone had a chance to get a few hours sleep. Although they were exhausted, Rushing and O'Connor were anxious to get a crack at Conway on their terms.

It was daybreak when Weber's head hit the pillow. Despite the fog of physical and mental fatigue, Weber still felt good. He was proud of what the team had done, and his role in it. There had been no egos or prima donnas when it got down to the nitty-gritty. Everyone had shown the true spirit of law enforcement—finding the person who really committed the crime and making sure justice was done. But Weber also knew it was time to give credit where it really belonged; he ended an incredible week with a prayer thanking God.

Chapter 10

The first annual—but never to be repeated—picnic sponsored by the nonexistent Madison County Press Association was set for Saturday afternoon, June 5. For some inexplicable reason, several of the veteran reporters covering the county—instigated by Girard Steichen of the *Belleville News-Democrat*—decided it would be a good idea to get together with the news sources with whom they took turns dishing out and receiving abuse. There really was no formal press association. But the sizable and tightly knit corps of reporters had a fairly good relationship with the officials, and everyone agreed it couldn't hurt to share a few laughs over beer and barbecue in a neutral setting. The well-shaded lot at the picturesque old school building on Quercus Grove Road, just outside Edwardsville, was chosen as the spot for this historic event.

The picnic got underway about mid-afternoon and was in full swing when Don Weber arrived a couple of hours late. He still was trying to recover from a very long night, but he wasn't quite ready to explain to the hosts what had occupied him until daylight. Neither would he explain why it was so important for Deputy Sheriff Bob Henke's car to be parked nearby just in case a certain message came over the police radio. After all, the hosts also were reporters, and their news instincts were intact even when clad in shorts and T-shirts. They knew something big was up, but they couldn't quite figure it out.

Weber was content to let them wait. He couldn't explain that he was anxiously awaiting "the word" from

Brighton, where Randy Rushing and Tom O'Connor already were several hours into the interview with Dwayne Conway, laboring mightily to get him to tell them what he knew about Karla Brown's murder.

Dwayne Conway was surprised when Detective Rick White and Brighton Patrolman Darren Carlton knocked on his door about 1 o'clock Saturday afternoon to ask him to accompany them to the police station for yet another interview about the Karla Brown murder. What a coincidence, the cops coming just a few hours after that out-of-the-blue, middle-of-the-night visit from old Spencer Bond. But Conway was agreeable and consented one more time.

He was ushered into the large all-purpose room at the Brighton City Hall where Agents Tom O'Connor and Randy Rushing were waiting. The wooden accordion door that split the room down the middle was pulled, hiding on the other side Chief Jay Wooldridge, Agent Wayne Watson, and Spencer Bond.

Tom O'Connor looked into Dwayne Conway's face as they sat around the corner from each other at the table. Conway looked so much like his voice sounded—kind of slow and dull and flat. O'Connor was about to flex his interrogation skills, and he was thinking, "I want this guy bad."

The agent began with a laid-back approach; the standard, rapid-fire, question-and-answer police technique would not work here. Conway would reject someone with a common police personality. Instead, O'Connor would build a rapport with Conway, make friends with him, establish some trust. It would take at least three hours to get any useful information; in other cases, O'Connor had gone as long as twelve. Cops who want to wrap up an important interview in forty-five minutes never get past the bull.

From what O'Connor had heard during Bond's conversation with Conway, the agent already was expecting a very long and difficult interview. Conway was not too smart, and O'Connor knew it was tough to "interview dumb." It was clear the priority in Conway's life was getting high. He was a throwback to the old 1960s and 1970s drug culture, and dealing with him would be a painstaking operation.

O'Connor would study Conway's verbal pacing, and then speak to him with the same cadence. Conway would be more comfortable talking to someone who used the same number of words per minute as he did and seemed to have the same verbal skills. O'Connor would have to balance two very different personalities to make them compatible.

O'Connor always aimed his interviews at a target with three concentric bulls'-eyes. First, he went for a confession. If he couldn't get a confession, he went for an admission of guilty knowledge. If he couldn't get that, then he wanted to catch the subject lying. A hit in any of those circles was a good score. It was the ultimate game; O'Connor loved every minute of it.

His opening gambit was a quiet explanation that the cops were uninterested in Conway's lifestyle, drug use, or other activities that might make him reluctant to discuss the important facts of the case. "We don't object to any of that and we don't care about any of that," O'Connor said reassuringly. "We just want to know what happened that day."

He even mentioned that he knew things had been tough for Conway financially. He had some job problems; he and his family had not been living as well as they should. With the contacts O'Connor and Rushing had through their state jobs and other sources, maybe they could help get him a real job. They wanted to be friends, and would do what they could to help.

Conway was responding, but it was an even slower process than O'Connor expected. It took about an hour to build a rapport that would withstand any pressure at all. Conway never refused to answer any question, and that was a good sign; he simply resisted by being slow and having a poor memory. It was O'Connor's job to improve that memory.

As Conway told his story of the events on June 21, 1978, his most concrete recollection was the arrival of the coroner's van; O'Connor built on that. He took Conway backward from that point, exploring things that happened right before, and then a little longer before, and then quite some time before. Then he moved forward from the arrival of the van, delving into what had happened just after that, and then after that.

Each bit of information was dragged out slowly. O'Connor led Conway with questions as long as Conway was following with answers. When Conway failed to follow, O'Connor retreated to a comfortable subject until Conway relaxed and was ready to move forward again. Then O'Connor led him with more substantive questions. Back and forth, back and forth.

O'Connor made only brief and cryptic notes to remind him of points to hit harder at the appropriate time. He didn't want to scribble furiously now, telegraphing to Conway what might be important. He would get the details written out later.

Rushing was watching and listening intently. The interview seemed mostly like a battle of wits with an unarmed man, he mused.

Conway's story didn't change appreciably from what O'Connor and Rushing heard before. Conway saw Karla around the house while she and her boyfriend were moving in. She was a "short but very attractive blonde" and he probably said "hi" to her at least once. On the day of the murder, he was painting the other neighbor's house—green and white, in fact. Prante showed up about noon, and Conway took a lunch break to talk to him. Conway drank Pepsi; Prante drank Busch beer from a quart bottle in a paper bag. They smoked a pipe filled with marijuana supplied by Prante.

Prante asked if Conway had seen the girl next door around that morning; Conway said no, and Prante asked if he was sure. Then Prante left, saying he had to go to the Shell refinery to put in a job application. Conway spent the rest of the day painting, until the police cars began arriving at the blonde's house; Conway went back to his porch to watch the activity.

About five minutes later, John Prante suddenly appeared on the porch from inside Conway's house.

O'Connor perked up; something new with good potential.

Conway asked Prante where he had come from; Prante hesitated, and then said, "The Laundromat." Prante, wearing a yellow ball cap, was flushed and out of breath, as if he had been running. Prante sat down next to Conway and they turned their attention to the cops. Prante's face was wet and his orange T-shirt looked as if water had been splashed on it; it was "splotchy." The T-shirt bore the words "Big Bamboo," a brand of cigarette paper for rolling marijuana joints. The brand had been part of a joke in a movie where comedians Cheech and Chong rolled a huge reefer.

The image of Prante's wet face and T-shirt instantly flashed to life for O'Connor and Rushing. The time element had to be out of sequence; that had to be much earlier. But the agents knew they had just heard a description of the way the killer looked after he left Karla Brown's basement, and left Karla Brown in the barrel.

Conway had the feeling Prante had come from the bathroom in Conway's house. Prante looked as if he had been sweating, but said nothing was wrong. After they had watched the activity next door for another twenty minutes, Prante said something about the Wood River cops being stupid. He made some reference to getting out of town, but didn't explain.

When the coroner's van arrived, Prante said, "Here comes the coroner; someone must be dead. Wow, that good-looking chick must be dead."

He suddenly announced, "I gotta' split," and said he had parked his car at a Laundromat across Central Avenue, the street that intersected Acton at the corner. Prante had never parked there before and had never done his laundry there, either. Prante asked if he could leave by Conway's rear door, but Conway explained that it was padlocked. Prante walked off the porch and cut through Conway's backyard to the alley and toward the Laundromat.

O'Connor had just heard quite a few real facts—the details about the color of clothing and other bits proved that. Despite working on just few hours of sleep, O'Connor wasn't the least bit tired anymore. He was hearing about the murder now, and the adrenaline was pumping furiously.

Conway also remembered that Prante claimed earlier to know the girl next door because he went to school with her. O'Connor wondered if that was Prante's code acknowledging his sexual interest in Karla by claiming falsely that he "knew" her.

More details. Prante said he wanted to have sex with the girl; he asked if her husband worked, and Conway answered that he worked days and drove a pickup truck. Prante was stalking Karla.

Conway added that Prante, in fact, was always flirting with other men's wives. He tried to get their attention by seeming to help them. And he sometimes put his hand on the women's "rear ends," which naturally upset many of their husbands.

Conway had come around. He had broken loose with some devastating details about old John Prante, and it was time for the big question.

"Dwayne, with what you've told us, at this point, do you feel John Prante is responsible for Karla Brown's murder?"

"At this time, I do."

Tom O'Connor believed Dwayne Conway. They had spent almost five hours together, and the agent was sure that Conway had bonded well with him; Conway would be trying to tell O'Connor the truth.

Conway agreed to give O'Connor a written, signed statement, and they started the procedure over again. O'Connor asked the questions, and wrote out Conway's answers in longhand. The ten-page statement took another hour and thirty-five minutes to complete. Conway signed each page, as did Rushing and O'Connor.

It had been one of Tom O'Connor's toughest interviews—tougher than getting confessions out of eighteen-year-old gang members from Chicago in prison. Conway forced O'Connor to call on every technique, every trick he had learned. Conway would be a good witness—a goofy witness, O'Connor thought—but a good one.

Rick White assessed O'Connor's performance as playing Conway like a fiddle.

O'Connor figured he had just given prosecutor Don Weber about seventy-five percent of a murder case, between the interrogation of Dwayne Conway and the interviews with the Bonds and the Whites that had pointed so convincingly to Prante just three days ago. Some physical evidence was all that was needed to complete the case, and maybe that would come from Dr. Lowell Levine in a couple of days, O'Connor thought.

Before he left, Conway had another memory to offer. Sometime around noon, while Conway and Prante were on the porch, a young woman drove up in front of Karla Brown's house and knocked on her door. Prante remarked that the girl had "nice legs," and then added, "I don't know why she's knocking. She's not gonna' answer."

When the radio in the police car crackled with a message from Randy Rushing, Don Weber thought, Here we go. Even through the radio, Weber liked the tone in Rushing's voice.

"It took hours and hours, but O'Connor cracked him," Rushing announced. "Conway said Prante was there that day, and had showed up with his face and shirt all wet. Conway even described the clothes Prante was wearing. And get this, Don. Prante told Conway the Wood River cops were really stupid." The line brought chuckles on both ends of the radio transmission. And Weber thought, If the cops are so stupid, John, why are you going to prison?

Weber leaned back in the car and sighed. One of the last few dominoes had fallen. Maybe Levine would knock down another one on Tuesday. Weber felt tired again; really good, but tired. He begged off the press picnic early and went home to collapse.

Wood River Chief Don Greer was finding it difficult to enjoy himself at the annual policemen's dance Saturday evening. Why hadn't he heard something from Rick White about the interview with Conway? Greer perked up when White, looking dead tired, arrived after driving Dwayne Conway home. Greer charged over to him and demanded, "Did we get it?"

White wanted the chief to sweat a little. "Well, we didn't get the smoking gun." The men looked at each other blankly, Greer unsure what to think. Then White smiled, pulled back one side of his jacket, and pointed to the copy of Conway's statement protruding from his inside pocket. "We got him."

Greer grabbed the statement in one hand and White in the other, and pulled him into the men's room. White closed his eyes and leaned back against the wall, feeling the exhaustion tugging at him as Greer read the statement. Finally, the chief looked up and grinned. "Yeah! We got him!"

Greer grabbed White and hugged him, and then kissed him. As they grinned almost foolishly at each other, they couldn't keep the tears from welling up in their eyes. It was the emotional response to what they also were feeling in their bellies. They were sure they had just nailed John Prante. It had taken four years, but it was done, and it felt good.

Greer was so excited that he announced to the crowd, "For those of you who know what we're doing, we got what we wanted." He didn't explain the curious comment that almost no one understood, but Greer and White enjoyed the inside joke.

The team could rest on Sunday, finally. It had been an incredible week, and everybody had gone beyond the call of duty. They deserved a day to relish a job well done, and the prize that would be coming up in the very near future. Before too long, the cuffs would be snapped around the wrists of the man they all truly believed had killed Karla Brown.

But not everyone was resting on the Sabbath.

Karla Brown, age 4.

Jo Ellen Brown and her three daughters, 1958: Karla, age 2, Connie, age 10, and Donna, age 9.

Christmas, 1977: *(from top)* Connie Dykstra, Donna Judson, Karla Brown; *(bottom left)* Jo Ellen Brown; *(bottom right)* Jo Ellen's aunt.

LEFT: The Roxana High School Cheerleaders, 1972: *(top)* Karla Brown; *(center)* Debbie La Tempt. (Delmar Studios)

BELOW LEFT: Karla Brown dressed up for her prom junior year, 1973. (Delmar Studios)

BELOW RIGHT: Karla Brown with friend Kathi Goode Hawkins in South Padre Island, Texas, 1977.

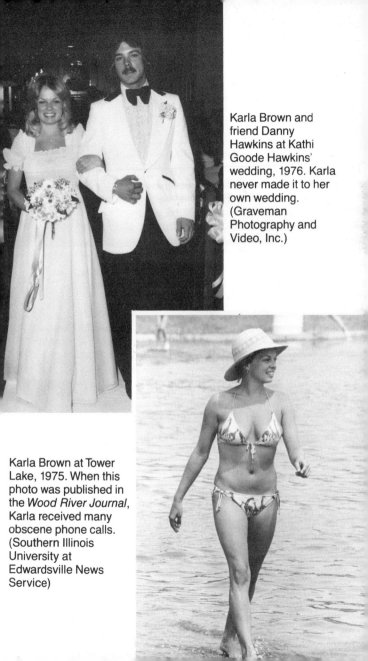

Karla Brown and friend Danny Hawkins at Kathi Goode Hawkins' wedding, 1976. Karla never made it to her own wedding. (Graveman Photography and Video, Inc.)

Karla Brown at Tower Lake, 1975. When this photo was published in the *Wood River Journal*, Karla received many obscene phone calls. (Southern Illinois University at Edwardsville News Service)

Karla Brown and her fiancé David Hart's dream house at 979 Acton Avenue in Wood River, Illinois. Their dream would soon be shattered when Karla was murdered in the basement.

The murder scene in the basement of 979 Acton Avenue. The killer hit Karla Brown in the face with the TV tray stand, leaving an identifiable mark. (Bill Redfern/Wood River Police Dept.)

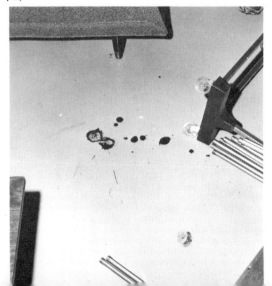

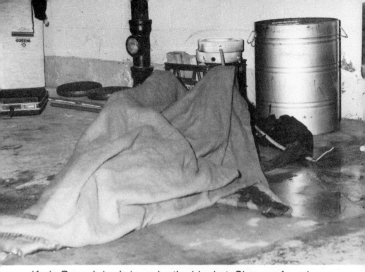

Karla Brown's body is under the blanket. She was found naked from the waist down and her head had been submerged in a barrel of water. (Bill Redfern/Wood River Police Dept.)

Autopsy photo showing bite marks on Karla Brown's right collarbone and neck. Thanks to dramatic breakthroughs in forensic science, these marks contributed to the arrest of the killer. (Bill Redfern/Wood River Police Dept.)

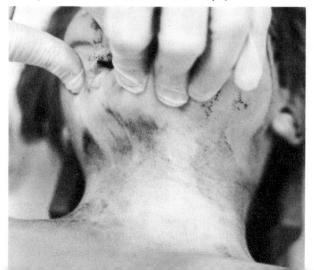

TOP: The Illinois State Police and Wood River Police team: *(front)* Randy Rushing, Tom O'Connor, Alva W. Busch; *(standing)* Detective Rick White, Sergeant Eldon McEuen. BOTTOM LEFT: Prosecutor Don W. Weber. (Alva W. Busch) MIDDLE: The Prante trial was the first Judge Charles V. Romani, Jr., presided over. BOTTOM RIGHT: Madison County Assistant Public Defender Neil Hawkins.

ABOVE LEFT: John Douglas, head of the FBI's Behavioral Science Unit in Quantico, a specialist in psychological profiling and crime scene analysis. ABOVE RIGHT: Alva W. Busch and a crime scene kit. (*St. Louis Post-Dispatch*)

ABOVE LEFT: John Prante in 1978, at the time of the initial investigation, wearing the cap witnesses remember him wearing the day of the murder. (Sergeant Eldon McEuen)
ABOVE RIGHT: Mug shot of John Prante at Madison County Jail, June 1982. (Madison County Sheriff's Department)

John Prante led into court for trial by Deputy Bob Henke. (*St. Louis Post-Dispatch*)

Donna Judson, Karla Brown's sister, (*left*) comforted by her husband Terry just after the verdict. (*St. Louis Post-Dispatch*)

Chapter 11

The flight to New York was to leave Lambert Field at St. Louis late Monday afternoon, June 7. Don Weber liked to travel, but he couldn't remember when he had looked forward to a trip the way he anticipated this one. Sometime within the next twenty-four hours, Weber hoped, Dr. Lowell Levine would give him the physical evidence needed to slam shut the case against John Prante. Either of the two scientific conclusions Levine might offer would be sufficient. Eliminating Dwayne Conway's teeth from suspicion in the bite marks on Karla Brown's neck would be good enough, and would be damaging circumstantial evidence against Prante.

The other possibility—identifying Prante's teeth as the offending dental weapons—would be fabulous, but probably too much to hope for. It might have been done four years ago, within hours after those marks were left in the victim's skin. But such a definitive conclusion was unlikely after time had taken its toll.

Weber and Rushing were passing a few minutes at their favorite Edwardsville watering hole, appropriately called The Watering Hole, before leaving for the airport. They also were sharing the new developments with one of their few confidantes, Pam Klein, the director of the Rape and Sexual Abuse Care Center at Southern Illinois University at Edwardsville. While working on a number of cases involving sex offenses, Weber and Klein had become friends as well as colleagues who shared the same dedication to justice for victimized females.

As Weber and Rushing told her about the newspaper

clipping mysteriously sent to Dwayne Conway, Klein grinned sheepishly. Weber should have known; Klein did it. She knew about John Douglas's suggestion, and took it upon herself to send the story to the suspect at the top of the list. She was a tough-minded activist investigator, too, and she had no more hesitation than Weber when it came to such tactics. Weber laughed. "Close, but no cigar, Pam."

While they were still chuckling, Chief Don Greer surprised them by sitting down at their table. He had a strange, self-conscious look on his face. "I'm booked on the same flight you guys are on."

Rushing snapped, "What?"

"I called your office and your secretary told me which flight you were taking to see Levine. I booked a seat on the flight, too. I'm going; I've got to be in on this."

Rushing clearly was annoyed, and Weber pulled him aside to discuss it. Rushing was insistent that Greer was not going; Rushing still harbored some hard feelings over what he thought was the withholding of reports and other information by the Wood River police. But Weber argued that it was time to put that behind them.

"Randy, he's the chief. We have to let him go. He's going."

Rushing shrugged. "Okay, but he's paying for the rental car."

By the time the trio reached New York, the hostilities had faded; they got a motel and agreed to Weber's choice of beer and pizza for dinner.

The drive to Dr. Lowell Levine's home in Huntington Station on Long Island was pleasant and the subdivision was lovely. Levine's impressive, two-story house sat along one of the gently curving streets. The doctor met his guests at the door, then treated them to bagels, orange juice, and coffee before they got down to business.

Randy Rushing unsnapped his attaché case and took out three small cardboard boxes, which were packed tightly with paper. Rushing carefully withdrew from each one a plaster model of a set of teeth. He set the casts on the kitchen table as the men pulled their chairs closer.

Only the three investigators knew which set belonged to which suspect—John Prante, Dwayne Conway, or Jack Meyers. Levine labeled each cast with his initials, the date, and the number 1, 2, or 3.

The doctor laid a life-sized photograph of the bite marks on the table and picked up number 3. He set the teeth on top of the marks in the photo, turned the cast back and forth, and shook his head.

"Nope, this isn't the guy."

The three men looked at each other and shrugged. Two sets left.

Levine picked up number 1 and repeated the comparison to the photo. He set the cast aside quickly.

"Not him."

The visitors looked at each other again and fidgeted in their chairs.

Levine took the last set of teeth, marked number 2, and turned it around on the photo. Then he did it again. He looked up and mumbled, "Where are my calipers?" He disappeared from the room, returning quickly with the shiny silver instrument.

The expert measured the teeth in the cast and then the marks in the photo. He measured Karla's tooth, visible in the upper end of the picture, and then measured the cast again.

He set the cast down, tapped it on the top with his finger, and grinned.

"That's the guy," he said drolly.

Weber had never seen three broader smiles as he told Levine, "That's John Prante's teeth, the guy all the evidence points to."

Greer looked across the table at Levine and thought about what had just happened. The guy who helped nail Ted Bundy had just helped nail John Prante. Fantastic.

Levine explained that he could not offer a conclusive opinion; he couldn't testify "to a reasonable degree of scientific certainty" that only Prante's teeth could have made those marks. But he could say Prante's teeth were "consistent" with the marks, and the others definitely were not.

Weber would take that. With the other primary suspects eliminated and all the other evidence collected against Prante, "consistent" was good enough. And anyway, it had to be.

A productive day on Long Island ended with a tour guided by Levine. Greer was thrilled to see the corner where rock singer Billy Joel had his motorcycle accident. An early dinner of swordfish steaks at Levine's favorite seafood restaurant was accompanied by fascinating stories from the expert about some of the cases in which he was involved.

Levine had been cross-examined by Ted Bundy as he conducted his own unsuccessful defense at his murder trial in Florida. Levine said Bundy wasn't as smart as he thought he was, or as crafty as some of the news reports suggested. Levine also offered stories from his work on the "Looking for Mr. Goodbar" case, the murder that led to a book and movie about the very proper schoolteacher who spent her evenings prowling the bars and picking up men, until one of them butchered her.

Levine described helping the police look for a body at a landfill, getting laughs from his guests by explaining how the authorities had used "a delicate, forensic instrument called a bulldozer" to aid in the search.

Weber also had Levine go into some detail explaining the geometry of bite marks—how each set of teeth would leave its own distinctive pattern and shapes. Using a napkin to make a sketch, Levine drew out Prante's design as rectangle-space-rectangle-space-triangle. It was distinctive enough to provide damning evidence against Prante.

Dr. Levine ended the afternoon by offering to have a friend in the Buffalo police department use his expertise in photography to improve the bite-mark photos for the trial.

Before boarding the return flight home, Rushing called from the airport to tell Larry Trent to put Prante under surveillance. A decision to arrest him would be made soon, and Rushing wanted to be sure they could find him when the time came.

After the exciting day in New York, the flight was relaxing and Weber thought a lot about the trial ahead. After Ted Bundy, this would be only the third or fourth case in the country to involve bite marks. Weber was thrilled to be on the cutting edge, and he could see it shaping up as a battle between experts. The prosecutors would produce their experts, whose testimony would link Prante to the murdered body of Karla Brown. The defense would have their experts, doing everything they could to diminish the value of the bite marks, perhaps even attacking the whole emerging science of bite marks and forensic odontology.

During the flight the team also discussed strategy in arresting Prante. There was no question they had the goods, more than enough to arrest him. But were they ready? Weber cautioned that an arrest started the clock on the state's speedy-trial rule. Unless the defendant caused delays, he had to be tried within 120 days if he was in jail or 160 days if he was free on bond.

They finally decided to keep Prante under surveillance and delay the arrest to leave time for everyone to write their reports, reevaluate the evidence, transcribe tapes, and conduct any necessary follow-up interviews. A longer wait might even increase the stress on Prante, making him more vulnerable to the interrogation tactics John Douglas recommended. Perhaps the arrest could be made on the fourth anniversary of the murder, some two weeks away. That would be jolting to Prante, maybe enough to get incriminating admissions, if not a full confession.

Back at Weber's office about 6 o'clock, Rushing got a call from Wayne Watson informing him that Prante had been found in the Brighton area. No one knew why he was there, so Rushing sent Watson to Dwayne Conway's house to see if Prante had paid a visit. It would be worse than Rushing could have imagined.

Conway stunned Watson by describing a four-hour visit

from Prante on Sunday, which convinced Conway his pal
had not killed Karla Brown. Conway announced that everything he told O'Connor and Rushing on Saturday was
false, except that Prante was at Conway's house from
noon to 1 o'clock on the day of the murder. Conway told
the other things to the agents because they confused and
upset him.

Watson feared that Conway never would talk to another
cop, so the agent tried everything to reverse the damage
to the case he knew so little about. He filed back through
his memory of the interview from Saturday and raised all
of those details with Conway. But the nervous little man
said he realized, after talking to Prante, that he had been
wrong on all counts on Saturday.

Conway now remembered that Prante was not at his
house late on the afternoon of the murder or after the police arrived; Conway had been thinking about Prante's
visit the evening before. It had been then that Prante's
face and shirt were wet, but that was from sweat; Prante
always sweated profusely in warm weather. And Conway
denied his earlier recollection about Prante's comments as
the coroner's van arrived. No one ever said anything like
"that the good-looking chick must be dead." Nor had
Prante parked his car at the Laundromat. Conway quoted
Prante as saying he was going to tell the cops from then
on that he was confused about what happened on which
day.

It was obvious to Watson that Conway and Prante had
reached an agreement on a simple story they would stick
to, come hell or high water. Watson now had to report to
the agents who had taken seven hours to extract such
great information from Conway, and explain how he had
destroyed it all in ten minutes. Great, he thought, as he
called Rushing again.

Rushing repeated the news for Weber; the men looked
at each other in amazement that soon turned to raw anger.

"You can't even rest on Sunday," Weber stormed.
"What could Prante have said to Conway to get him to

recant? And what else is Prante doing? Who else is he getting to? That has to stop."

Rushing was nodding. "We'll keep him under surveillance."

"Right. And don't worry about being covert. I don't care if he sees us. Camp on him."

Rushing's anger was unrestrained. "I want to bring in Conway right now for obstructing justice. I'll have Watson arrest him and bring him right here. Let's find out what the hell he is saying."

Weber felt a whole new tide of anger rising inside; part of it was a feeling that he should have seen this coming. In the conversation with Bond, Prante said he was going to try to contact Conway. And Prante called Bond before the second eavesdrop. They should have realized that Prante was becoming more active, driven by the investigators' own tactics designed to make the killer nervous and anxious to find out what was happening. They were squeezing him and they should have seen this coming.

It was Conway's turn to be surprised when Watson reappeared within minutes with Chief Jay Wooldridge as backup, and announced that Conway was under arrest for obstructing justice. Dwayne was shocked to the bottom of his feet; it was clear to Watson that Conway assumed he would be in the clear if he just stuck to his new story. As Watson slipped the handcuffs on him, and Patty Conway began to cry, Dwayne asked why he was being arrested. Watson said he would get the details when he got to Madison County. Conway had little to say during the forty-minute drive.

The team assembled in Weber's office about 7:30 that evening in what was more like a war council than a strategy session. Weber couldn't remember seeing such seasoned cops so angry and frustrated. An incredible investigation powered by daring innovation and a new level of professionalism had been flawed by one mope who was sneaking around fixing witnesses while the cops were flying around consulting experts.

"Well, I've had it with Prante," Weber announced. "We can't let him do anything else like this; no more Mr. Nice Guy. An investigation can drag on so long that it begins to unravel. Once that happens, it can come apart so fast you can't stop it. But this is your case, Randy. I think the final decision should be up to you. What do you want to do?"

That compliment from Don Weber meant a lot to Rushing. He knew Weber's tenacity and leadership had a lot to do with breaking the case. It made Rushing feel good about his own role in this for the state's attorney to defer to him on such a decision.

"I don't think the case is going to get any better," Rushing said.

He stabbed his index finger forcefully into the desk and said, "Let's go get the son of a bitch!"

A new sense of purpose filled the team members as they scurried to complete their assignments for the arrest of John Noble Prante that night. Weber drafted the document he would sign formally charging Prante with murder and burglary—written in a way to support another decision he reached some time ago: Weber would seek the death penalty for Prante for Karla Brown's murder.

O'Connor and Trent filled out the application for a search warrant that would be signed by a judge, allowing the police to look for evidence in Prante's house after he was arrested.

Rick White and Bill Redfern embarked on an urgent version of scavenger hunt to come up with items the killer might recognize from Karla Brown's basement. The room where Prante would be interviewed at Weber's office would be decorated with those items, another ploy suggested by John Douglas. Redfern took it on himself to open an account in the city of Wood River's name at a hardware store. He bought a Mr. Coffee carafe and a set of TV trays like the ones used as a weapon against Karla. In a quick trip to David Hart's house, Redfern and White retrieved one of the silver barrels. Redfern also dropped by a dentist's office to borrow a bridge that could pass for Karla's. By the time they stuck tags and evidence tape across all the objects, even the cops would have sworn they came from Karla's basement.

When Weber completed the charges, John Prante faced three counts of murder and two counts of burglary with intent to commit rape. Under the law, multiple counts of a charge could be filed to allege different legal theories, even if referring only to one act. Weber added burglary to invoke the death penalty law that covered a murder during the commission of another felony.

The charges and application for a search warrant were delivered to Judge Calvo at his home at 9:24 P.M. He watched the progress of the case the last few days as he signed the eavesdrop orders. He nodded when the murder charges were placed before him. "I knew you were going to get this guy," he said. He approved Weber's request that John Prante be held in jail without bond.

The room at the end of the hallway in the state's attorney's office had taken on an eerie atmosphere in anticipation of John Prante's arrival. The lighting was low; items placed carefully in strategic locations offered grim reminders of Karla Brown's death—the TV trays, the coffeepot, the dental bridge, the barrel. Weber found the room spooky.

But it would be a while before the guest of honor arrived. Weber decided to use the room early, for Dwayne Conway's interview—his chance to recant his recantation. If Conway had been at the murder scene, the conspicuous reminders in that room might rattle him enough to get the truth.

Weber was in his office in the corner of the long hallway when Watson and Wooldridge escorted Conway past the door. Weber was joined by Larry Trent, Rick White, and Don Greer to await this strange interview where Conway would face O'Connor and Rushing, the agents he claimed pressured him into a phony statement on Saturday.

O'Connor hoped to revive the relationship he and Conway had established, drawing on some goodwill he had banked with Conway two days ago. Perhaps he could get Conway to confirm the story he gave before his memory was mysteriously altered by a face-to-face meeting with John Prante.

Instead, O'Connor found an unexpectedly defiant Dwayne Conway. He sat there with an incredibly dull look on his face and denied everything with bald-faced lies that infuriated O'Connor. Conway responded to none of O'Connor's attempts to reestablish a rapport, and spurned all suggestions that his earlier story to the police was true. He didn't care whether the cops knew he was lying; he was denying everything and refusing even to admit something had happened to change his mind. It was insulting.

Rushing decided it was time for "good cop, bad cop," and launched into a tirade, threatening to make sure that Conway spent many long years in prison for obstructing justice if he didn't come clean. O'Connor stayed calm, urging Conway in sincere terms to tell the truth. But Conway was adamant and irritatingly defiant.

Finally O'Connor cracked and joined Rushing in long and loud ranting at Conway. O'Connor was violating the most important principle he taught in interrogation courses—never lose your temper. But, by God, O'Connor had fooled around long enough with this clown. There was no chance Conway was going to come around, and it felt good to let off some steam. O'Connor even allowed himself the luxury of the foulest language imaginable to describe the intimate encounters Conway was going to experience with any number of perverse inmates in prison.

Conway was unfazed. He sat there with the same blank look on his face while Rushing and O'Connor went off like Roman candles.

Down the hall, Weber and the others were watching the plaques on the wall vibrate from the shock waves rolling out of the interview room. Greer never would forget the raw edge and the sheer force of O'Connor's angry voice. Weber wondered if these two fine cops actually were going to beat a statement out of this suspect. Weber was sure he could hear objects being thrown around the room; he had never heard anything like it.

Trent could see the combination of shock and amazement on Weber's face. "It's okay, Don, they know what they're doing."

Rushing and O'Connor came out of the room within a few minutes and Weber hurried to meet them, expecting to have to calm them down. Instead, he found the two cops laughing almost hysterically in the hallway.

As much as Weber hated to insult the agents, he had to ask.

"Did you guys hit him?"

Rushing laughed harder. "Nah, we're just banging some stuff around. Don, this has to be the dumbest guy I've ever talked to."

O'Connor added, "It doesn't do any good to use psychological tactics on him. He's too stupid to get them."

They went back in and picked up where they left off. But Conway was rock-solid. Rushing couldn't yell any louder, despite his anger at Conway for recanting his statement. As Conway insisted again that he never said the things the agents recalled, Rushing screamed, "Do you expect us to believe that? What do you think, that we just fell off the truck?"

Conway looked up in all innocence and said blankly, "I didn't even know you came in a truck."

O'Connor yelled, "If none of that statement was true, why did you sign it and swear that it WAS true?"

"I don't know, man. I must have been in the Twilight Zone."

The Twilight Zone, indeed.

That was it. The agents told Weber they were not going to get anything else out of Conway. But Rushing still was angry. "He's not going home, Don. I don't care what happens later, but he's going to jail tonight."

Weber agreed and signed a single count charging that

Conway obstructed justice by furnishing false information to the police with the intent of preventing the prosecution of John Prante.

Dwayne Conway went directly to jail.

A long line of cops formed to arrest John Prante. Chief Don Greer just had to be there after all this time. Randy Rushing had invested more of his soul into this case than any other he could remember. Tom O'Connor was dying to be the one who snapped the cuffs around Prante's wrists and then led him into an interrogation room to begin the real contest. Larry Trent remembered how badly he wanted into this case four years ago, and nothing could keep him from being there when the payoff came tonight.

It was 10:30 when Prante opened his door at 198 Goulding Avenue to greet DCI Agents Rushing and O'Connor, backed up by Greer and Trent. O'Connor felt the reaction in his chest. That was the face of the guy he had been looking for all along.

"Are you John Prante?" Rushing asked.

"Yes, I am," Prante said calmly.

"We're agents from the Illinois Division of Criminal Investigation. We'd like to speak with you about the murder of Karla Brown. May we come in?"

Rushing handed Prante a department form setting out his Miranda rights and then read them to him, one at a time. Prante signed the form as O'Connor thought again how much he hated that ritual. For an interrogator like O'Connor, it was a curse. With all due respect to everyone's constitutional rights, O'Connor still felt the form may as well order the suspect to shut up.

But Prante was willing to talk. He said he already called Don Weber to offer his cooperation, as long as he wasn't a suspect. That was one of the things the cops wanted to hear; Weber told them to get that on the record to create more witnesses and insulate Weber from the risk of being bounced off the case.

And then Prante explained that he had some trouble re-

membering things because of the trauma he suffered in
Vietnam. O'Connor and Trent felt the anger pound in
their temples. They had been there, too, in real combat.
O'Connor was a marine; Trent was in the Army. The last
thing they wanted to hear was whining by some creep trying to blame his crimes on the trauma he suffered in a
war they had fought. The excuse rankled the cops even
more when Prante added that he served aboard the USS
Enterprise while the aircraft carrier was anchored off the
shore of 'Nam.

Yeah, real tough duty, the two cops thought.

Prante said he was at Conway's house the night of
Karla's moving party. "She was a good-looking blonde,"
he recalled. But he didn't remember being at Conway's
the day she was killed; in fact, he couldn't remember any
of his activities that day. He couldn't even remember filing the job applications.

When O'Connor asked how Prante could remember the
night before, but not that day, Prante said he had been reminded of the events when he visited Dwayne Conway on
Sunday.

Prante denied claiming that he had known Karla Brown
from school. He saw her working in her garden in front
of the house once, but had never been inside the house.
Asked if he had been at her house on the day of the murder, he curiously answered, "I never said I wasn't at
Karla Brown's house that day."

That registered with O'Connor. It was less than an unequivocal denial, and that often was a clue that the suspect could be broken in a long interrogation. But Prante
then insisted, "Irregardless of what other witnesses said,
I wasn't at her house that day."

He also wanted to recant a statement he made to Weber
on the phone. Prante was mistaken when he admitted being at Conway's house early on the morning of the murder. He now wanted to make it clear he never was at
Conway's house that day; he was thinking of the day before when he talked to Weber.

Prante also was sure that he never owned an orange

T-shirt with "Big Bamboo" on the front. He had two yellow caps, both of them now stashed in his seabag.

He said he never used the Laundromat across the side street from Conway's. He used a different one about two blocks farther away—the one right next to the Pancake Ranch, he said, surely unaware that Karla Brown had been a waitress there.

Finally, the time came for Rushing to give Prante the word.

"John, I have to tell you that an information has been signed by the state's attorney's office charging you with murder and burglary in the death of Karla Brown. You're under arrest and we'll be taking you directly to jail."

"Oh," Prante said calmly, "I guess I'll have to talk to an attorney before I say anything else."

That was it, O'Connor knew. In a calm, emotionless voice, Prante just ended any chance they had at getting a confession.

As Rushing read each of the counts to Prante, O'Connor snapped the handcuffs on the suspect, relishing the satisfying click.

Prante looked back and forth between the cops, and O'Connor thought a somewhat pale Prante knew he was looking at the faces of the men who might be putting him in prison for good. O'Connor saw resignation under the surface of Prante's calm, as if he realized his crime had caught up with him after four good years on the outside. As they escorted Prante to their car outside, O'Connor saw him looking around the neighborhood. O'Connor thought he could read the guy's mind and he couldn't resist the opening.

"That's right, John. Take a deep breath. It's the last breath of free air you'll ever breathe."

Prante didn't respond.

Rushing ushered him into the backseat, locked him in, and climbed behind the wheel next to O'Connor. Prante was silent for a long time as they headed toward the county jail in Edwardsville. Finally, he said, "You know, my God knows I'm innocent."

Rushing chuckled, but O'Connor decided not to let that kind of blasphemy pass.

"That's odd, John. My God knows you're guilty. He's the one who sent me here to arrest you. We must be talking about different gods."

When Prante was booked at the jail—photographed and fingerprinted—he remained excessively cool, calm, and controlled. He was overly cooperative and polite to the point of being obnoxious. He didn't wear the smirk cops see so often; instead, his face was just blank, expressionless. O'Connor read that as acceptance of his fate. He was displaying the guilty-man syndrome all the way. An innocent man stunned by his false arrest and humiliated by booking would be damned angry by now, and he would be letting his captors know it. Prante was just too cool.

The search of Prante's home turned up little of value. Trent hoped John Douglas's suggestion that killers often take a memento from the murder scene would prove true this time. But nothing was found. Trent knew locating that matching length of white electrical cord or its severed ends would be too much to hope for. No orange "Big Bamboo" T-shirt could be located.

But two yellow ball caps were found, both of them bearing the words "Petroleum Helicopters." A length of rope with several knots was found in the kitchen. Two photo albums were taken—one contained some pictures of a woman sunbathing and the other offered some pictures of nude women at some kind of party. An envelope containing a passport application in Prante's name was seized, along with some personal papers and an address book.

Four girlie magazines beside the telephone were taken, too, since they showed a marked preference by Mr. Prante for women with big breasts. Two eight-by-ten photos in black and white were picked up because the unidentified girl with short, blond hair and large breasts bore a vague resemblance to Karla Brown.

Prante's red Volkswagen station wagon was parked in front of the house, and Trent could see a length of white electrical cord in the rear storage area. But the cops couldn't search it because it was not included on the warrant signed by the judge. So they sealed the doors with evidence tape, securing it until they could get a warrant. In a search the next week, they got the electrical cord and a towrope that had an interesting knot in the end. But the electrical cord never would be matched to the wire used to bind Karla Brown.

When Weber went to Prante's house later, he thought it appeared perfectly typical for a burned out, pot-smoking hippie from the 1960s. It wasn't as messy as Weber would have expected, but it was decorated with exactly the lack of taste and oddball posters he would have predicted. Even the bicycle leaning against one wall in the bedroom seemed appropriate.

Another member of the Conway family was being interviewed late Monday night, too. Wayne Watson, Rick White, and Chief Jay Wooldridge found Patty Conway at her parents' house in Brighton and she agreed to go to the police station to talk about Prante's visit on Sunday. She was convinced that Prante caused the change in her husband's statement. During the four-hour conversation, Prante insistently repeated over and over that he was at Conway's house the entire day of the killing. Dwayne disagreed; he thought their long visit was a day or two earlier, and that Prante was there for only an hour on the day the girl was murdered. They got a sheet of paper and tried to figure out the date and day of the week the murder occurred, but couldn't do it.

It was apparent to Patty Conway that Prante was trying to get her husband to change his mind or remember differently. And she knew that, if someone said something to her husband long enough, he might believe it was true.

She described a chain-smoking John Prante sitting in the trailer. She and her husband were sweating from the heat, but Prante was not. Wayne Watson liked that—it directly contradicted Dwayne Conway's comment that Prante always sweated profusely.

Prante and Conway talked at length about their conversations with Spencer Bond. Patty asked if they thought Bond was working for the police, and the men said they didn't know. Prante thought Bond was mad because Prante had made some passes at his wife years ago.

Prante and Dwayne Conway went over the events surrounding the murder repeatedly, even when Patty's parents stopped by to visit. Prante denied having anything to do with Karla Brown's death and even implied that Conway was trying to send him to jail. Conway swore that was not true, saying all he did was tell the police the truth on Saturday. Another contradiction in Conway's stories, Watson thought.

The visit ended with the two old friends spending a long time chatting and laughing about old times. Before Prante left, he told Dwayne Conway they probably would see each other in court. After he was gone, Dwayne had started talking about getting an attorney to stop the police harassment, something he had not even complained about before. Dwayne made an appointment on Monday morning to see an attorney later, and Watson was glad things had broken open before that happened. Conway may never have talked to another cop once he talked to an attorney.

Patty also deflated the idea that Dwayne was upset and confused by the agents on Saturday. She said, in fact, that he was relaxed and relieved after the long interview; he said he had told the truth. Dwayne was so happy that Patty fixed him his favorite meal—ham and beans with maple syrup—which he ate gladly.

Watson shuddered at that recipe and realized it was something no one could ever accuse the cops of making up. Who else would even think of that culinary combination?

Then Patty Conway remembered one more comment from Prante. He told Dwayne that Karla Brown's murder was no "little thing," and added, "Murder is a capital offense in Illinois and one of us is going to the gas chamber."

Watson thought he had found the key to Conway's change of heart. Prante had explained things very neatly. His deadly message was clear, and included the implication that, since Prante was the smarter of the two, it wouldn't be him who took a long walk down a prison hallway some distant midnight.

The Watering Hole in Edwardsville was the scene of a lively party for the cops that night. After four long years, the man they believed killed Karla Brown was in jail, charged on evidence assembled by a skilled team of investigators and prosecutors using every tool and bit of new technology they could find. The man who might be an accomplice was in another cell; he might flip over on his pal, and if it was learned that he had played a role in Karla's death, the charge always could be increased to murder later.

It wasn't the end of the battle, but it was a triumphant moment that had been too long in coming.

Don Weber was determined that John Prante would face the state's new method of execution—lethal injection—for murdering Karla. Weber would demand it, but it had not been his choice. As Virginia Rulison, Weber's fiancée and office administrator, said, "It was John Prante who chose the way of death in this case."

PART THREE

"... Depression, Rage, and the Calm After the Storm"

Chapter 12

The telephone rang at the country club in Hayfield, Minnesota, where Donna Judson was playing bridge with some friends after golf on Wednesday morning, June 9. She was surprised that the call was for her, and even more surprised when the voice on the other end belonged to Don Greer.

"It's done, Donna. He's in jail. It's over. We arrested a man named John Prante for Karla's murder."

Donna was stunned. "Who the hell is John Prante?" she sputtered.

"He was visiting at a house next door to Karla's. He sat on the porch all day with Dwayne Conway and we think he slipped over there and killed her then."

"What happened to Dwayne Conway? We thought he was the prime suspect."

"He was, but we uncovered new evidence that pointed at Prante. We've arrested Conway, too, for obstructing justice."

Donna Judson and Greer were quiet for a minute and, in the silence, the tears started for both of them.

When Donna went back to her table, her friends could tell she was upset. It was an odd mixture of relief and something approaching joy, and all tempered with tears. Donna ordered wine for everyone, and began to explain. It wasn't long before her husband, Terry, appeared. Greer had called him at home first, and Terry had told Greer how to reach Donna; it was Greer's right to break the news.

The Judsons had stayed in close contact with Greer and

he had kept them well informed. They had become friends, and the Judsons trusted the chief. They worried for a while that they had become too jaded to be optimistic about solving Karla's murder; they had lost confidence in law enforcement. But Greer had told them a little about the bite marks and why Don Weber was pumping the case so hard in the press. Weber even sent them a videotape of the TV newscasts so they knew what was hitting the streets at home.

On a trip to Wood River the week before the exhumation, the Judsons were visiting Greer for an update when he inadvertently named Dwayne Conway as a suspect. Greer had refused to provide names before, and the Judsons knew he had slipped; they pretended not to notice. When they left, they rushed to the library to see if they could find anything in the city directory or phone book, only to be frustrated when the name was nowhere to be found.

Now, barely two weeks later, his name wasn't even important to them. Now the question was, "Who was John Prante?"

When she saw the first picture of Prante in the newspaper, Donna shuddered. The jowly face covered by the thick, full beard; the black hair so shaggy and frizzy. It was painful to accept the sexual assault of her sister by someone Donna found so creepy. Why did the last person Karla saw have to look like that?

Don Greer's next visit that day was to the bar where Jo Ellen Brown worked as a waitress. As he walked toward her with such purpose, her first thought was, Oh hell, did I serve a minor? But she soon realized the grin on his face clearly meant something entirely different. After four years, the day had come. She was thrilled. But, just as she couldn't stop the tears, she couldn't suppress the anger over how long it took to solve her daughter's murder.

As Jo Ellen learned more about Prante in the coming days, she realized it was more than likely she had served him at the tavern. She didn't recognize his picture in the paper, but others said they were sure he had been in the place. What a horrible coincidence.

After Greer left, Jo Ellen called her oldest daughter, Connie Dykstra. Connie was thrilled, too, but just as confused by the arrest of a man she never had heard of before. She finally had started living a little easier again, getting past the long period of fear and grief that stretched halfway across the continent. Now that there was an arrest, she was anxious to see how all the pieces would complete the puzzle.

The bittersweet joy over the arrest was tempered by the new evidence of brutality and the ugliness of the bite marks—new kinds of violation inflicted on Karla. Everyone hoped Karla suffered little, falling unconscious before the assault really got started. That thought had lent some comfort. Now they wondered, and it was painful.

But at least they had a name now, after all these years. John Prante.

Don Weber called a press conference for 2 P.M. on Wednesday, June 9, to announce the arrest of John Prante. Greer thought it should be held at his police station; Weber decided it would be at the county jail, which had a large room that could accommodate the crowd of reporters and TV cameras.

But that morning, word of the arrest was spreading like wildfire. A reporter for the *Alton Telegraph* got a tip and called Terry Hillig, the reporter covering the case. Hillig had heard Prante's name kicked around earlier among some sources, so he called the jail and asked if Prante was in custody and on what charges. Hillig had his story.

The news was spellbinding to the people who had known and loved Karla. Her longtime friends, Kathi Goode Hawkins and Debbie LaTempt Davis, felt great relief and they prayed the police had the real killer. Debbie Davis wanted retribution for the man who had taken the friend who could never be replaced; he should die a thousand deaths.

Jamie Hale had been heartbroken over the exhumation;

another cruel blow to Karla, Jamie felt. And now they had arrested someone she never heard of. She remained convinced that Jack Meyers was the best suspect, and now this John Prante suddenly was charged. But if he really did it, she gladly would shoot him herself.

Jim Nicosia had never heard of Prante, either. But Jim wanted the severest punishment for whoever killed the girl with the little voice that always made him feel so tall. If it was this John Prante, then fry the SOB.

One person who was expecting the announcement was Spencer Bond. After taping those conversations, Bond was convinced that old John was the killer. Since then, Spencer had wondered what the cops were waiting for. He was sad that his friend appeared to be guilty, but Spencer felt no remorse for his role in the case. John had made his own bed, and it wasn't Spencer's fault.

His wife, Roxanne, had resisted the idea that the man who sat calmly in their home so many times was capable of such a cold-blooded murder. But with his arrest, she was resigned to it.

For the cops who had been involved in the initial investigation, the arrest brought mixed emotions. Sergeant Eldon McEuen, on disability leave after injuring his back in a fall on duty, resented being shut out of the investigation by his own department. Only Weber had talked to McEuen about the new efforts, usually seeking information the prosecutor felt was being withheld by the department. McEuen respected Weber and his tenacity, and was convinced he would get the guy if it could be done. McEuen, a lifelong Democrat, even supported Weber in the election two years earlier.

McEuen wasn't surprised when the arm of the law reached for Prante, even though Meyers had remained the cop's hunch. He had no problem seeing Prante as the killer. But most of the people McEuen talked to on the street disagreed; almost everyone thought the whole bitemark thing was bull. That skepticism about Prante's guilt would remain for a long, long time.

Ralph Skinner still was a shift commander, and Chief

Greer had discussed the new evidence with him a few times. But it hurt that he, like McEuen, was not involved at the end. Skinner felt some resentment about Weber and the DCI taking over and, perhaps, projecting the idea that the Wood River cops were bozos who had to be led around.

But, when the arrest came, all of that faded and Skinner simply was glad it was done. He remembered seeing two men on Conway's porch that night, and thought again about sitting across the table from Prante at the first interview. Skinner always had felt uncomfortable about Prante after that.

Sergeant Chuck Nunn wasn't part of the new investigation, either, and he was perhaps the most surprised of the cops when Prante was arrested. Nunn remembered seeing Prante on Conway's porch that night. There he was, right there the whole time, Nunn thought. He was standing there watching all of us run around like Chinese firemen.

Nunn had the most reason to be surprised because he knew Prante. In 1972, when Nunn joined the force, he roomed with two buddies, and Prante often visited a neighbor. The whole group got together several times for beer and barbecue. Prante, then only twenty-three, seemed bright and intelligent, though a little odd. A "semi-philosopher," and certainly not threatening.

When Nunn saw him standing on the porch that night, the two men nodded at each other in recognition. Nunn thought he knew Prante well enough that he never considered him a suspect.

Don Weber prepared a one-page statement that set out the basic facts about the arrest and credited Rushing, O'Connor, and Greer, and the various agencies involved for breaking the case. He gave special notice to the FBI, as well as the patient families of the officers who spent so many long hours on the case.

But he did not disclose the arrest of Dwayne Conway. There still was a chance he would come clean after he sat in jail for a while. If he gave Weber a good reason, there still was time to drop the charge before his credibility was destroyed. He still could be a valuable witness at trial.

At the news conference that afternoon, Weber distributed copies of his statement and Prante's mug shot from the night before—the beard and bushy hair set off by the wire-rimmed glasses. The reporters clamored for more details. Were the bite marks the key to the arrest? Did the experts get what they needed at the exhumation? What did the second autopsy show? Was Prante a suspect in 1978? Was there some relationship between the killer and the victim? Had he been the target of the FBI profile and Weber's unusual comments?

Weber deflected nearly all of the questions, explaining almost sheepishly that he couldn't release much more information now that an arrest had been made. After playing the case so broadly for the media before, Weber felt almost embarrassed at refusing to answer questions now. He had been playing cat-and-mouse, with the press as the bait. But to some reporters and others, Weber's actions seemed more self-serving than that. As he expected, there was snide criticism that he was grandstanding all along. There was little he could do to dispel the gossip.

The next day—Thursday, June 10—Agents Randy Rushing and Tom O'Connor went before the grand jury to lay out the evidence against John Prante so that Weber could seek an indictment. That would avoid the need for a preliminary hearing for a judge to determine if there was enough evidence to maintain the charge—a valuable check on the state's authority. An indictment required approval by twelve of the twenty-three citizen members, balance enough against any prosecutor's power.

Avoiding the public hearing also meant no more disclosure of evidence to the press; Weber already worried that a judge might decide to move the trial out of the county because of the publicity.

The grand jury readily indicted Prante on the charges Weber issued two days earlier, and added a new count of burglary, alleging that Prante committed an aggravated battery after breaking into Karla's house; that was an extra factor exacerbating the crime.

Later that day, Prante was brought to the courthouse in Edwardsville for his first appearance as an accused killer. Weber was gratified when the handcuffed and shackled Prante—escorted by deputies and wearing the baggy orange jumpsuit that passed for high fashion at the jail—shuffled out of the elevator and across the hallway into the courtroom. Prante listened calmly as Circuit Judge Andy Matoesian read the charges and announced that the state's attorney would seek the death penalty. Prante didn't even react to that potentially fatal news; he spoke only to say he was trying to hire his own attorney. The hearing ended after just a few minutes, and Prante shuffled back to jail.

About that time, Rushing was conducting an interesting interview with Prante's dentist, Dr. Ronald Mullen. He had pulled one of Prante's molars in a 1980 emergency procedure, and remembered that Prante refused to allow X-rays of his teeth. Was that as transparent as it seemed? Was Prante avoiding dental evidence that could link him to a past crime?

Dr. Mullen remembered the visit well because it was one of only two times that a patient came into his office carrying an alcoholic drink; Prante arrived with a paper cup full of beer. What a mope, Rushing thought as he collected a copy of Prante's dental records under subpoena. Rushing thought the dentist would make an interesting witness later.

While such details were being handled, the press was digging into the case with all of its resources, and sources. Weber's phone began ringing on Thursday with reporters' questions about Dwayne Conway; Weber's hope of keeping that quiet vanished, and he decided to file the charge against Conway with the circuit clerk's office. To support the allegation that Conway had contradicted his earlier statement to police, Weber attached a copy of Conway's signed statement. That brought another round of stories as the reporters gleaned the tantalizing tidbits Conway had offered the cops during that long Saturday session.

Don Weber returned to an office in shambles from neglect during the intensity of the Prante investigation. Although Weber was dedicated to his campaign promise to lead by example as an active prosecutor in the courtroom, one of the costs was some inattention to administrative details. His predecessor, Nick Byron, was an able administrator, and Weber admired his former boss for that. It was a trade-off he knew was justified and supported by the citizens who elected him to be the chief prosecutor.

It would take about a month to get his office back in shape, and he still would have to squeeze out some time to keep the Karla Brown case moving along. The state and Wood River police hadn't filed their reports yet, and that paper blizzard would be blowing into his office before long. He also would have to sit down and read the older portions of the case file. So much had blown past him in the rush of information that he knew some important details must have been lost in the storm.

After a few quiet days, Weber was called by the sheriff's department on June 14 with a message from Dwayne Conway; he wanted to talk again. It was obvious he was not enjoying his stay as a guest of the county. Surely Prante had promised Conway he would be okay if he stuck with their story, and he had to be less than pleased with the unexpected turn that took him to jail. Bail was set at $75,000, meaning he stayed put unless he came up with $7,500 in cash; slim chance. Conway knew he was looking at a long time behind bars before his trial; the cops hoped Conway realized he had backed the wrong horse and would be straight with them now.

But Conway still was waffling when Rushing met with him. He was looking for some middle ground where he might buy his way out of trouble without completely dumping on Prante. Conway now remembered Prante wearing an orange T-shirt the day of the murder, but it didn't carry the "Big Bamboo" logo; maybe it was a moon design. In the Twilight Zone again? Rushing wondered.

Conway regained his memory of a wet and out-of-breath Prante coming out of Conway's house that afternoon. Prante suggested they go for a beer, but Conway thought the cops would want to talk to him about what was going on next door. Prante responded, "If they want me, they'll come and get me." Prante stayed five or ten minutes more, and was gone before the coroner's van arrived. He never said anything like "the good-looking chick next door must be dead." Rushing asked why Conway remembered that line before.

"I must have dreamed it. Or maybe I just said it to myself."

Another visit to the Twilight Zone for Dwayne, Rushing thought, chuckling.

Conway said he thought Prante wanted to tell him something that day, but just hadn't been able to come out with it. Prante didn't say he was doing his laundry; Conway just assumed that because Prante said he parked his car at the Laundromat.

And, in a surprise to Rushing, Conway now offered his own theory on how Karla Brown met her death: Prante, or whoever killed her, went to her house early that morning, which could explain why Prante was at Conway's so early. The killer raped her and tied her up before leaving. She probably was tied up when her friend stopped by and got no answer at the door. But, after the killer thought about it for a while, he feared that Karla would identify him to the police; he returned and killed her.

Rushing wasn't sure what to make of that scenario. But it was rather detailed to be just wild speculation.

To support his claim that he was telling the truth now, Conway offered to take a polygraph and to submit to hypnosis. Weber arranged for master polygrapher Clinton Cook of the State Police to administer the test; Weber wanted no more mediocrity in this investigation. Prante had slipped by the first test, and Weber wanted to avoid any more slips.

Weber and Rushing told Cook they were sure that Prante killed Karla, and Conway knew more about it than he was admitting. Cook hooked him to the box, and Conway denied that he was in Karla's house that day, that he had killed her, that he knew who killed her, or that he was withholding information.

This time, the result was unequivocal. Conway was not truthful; he had blown the test again. Cook told Weber and Rushing that his expert opinion echoed their hunches; Conway was not the killer but could have been an accomplice. He, indeed, seemed to know more than he was telling.

Conway underwent hypnosis on June 30. Weber's only experience with that had been an unproductive session with Edna Moses in March to see if she remembered more about the two people she and her grandson saw in Karla's driveway. But Weber was willing to give it another try with Conway. And, this time it would be done by Tom O'Connor's brother, Dan; in addition to being a police officer in St. Louis, he was a hypnotherapist.

The session in an interview room at the county jail was videotaped. Conway slumped in a chair as Dan O'Connor took him through a long, slow process of relaxation and regression, guiding him back to June 21, 1978. With his head tipped to one side and his eyes closed, Conway offered a vague description of Prante's arrival about 11 A.M. and their session smoking marijuana and drinking beer on the porch. Conway offered few details, except that Prante mentioned the girl next door was "looooo-kiiiing goooood;" Conway drew the words out slowly. Prante left before the police arrived; he said he was going to Harold Pollard's house.

Weber watched the videotape and shrugged; nothing of any value. In fact, Weber doubted Conway really had been "under." Despite the O'Connor brothers' assurances that Conway was hypnotized, Weber never really bought it. It was too difficult to tell when Conway was conscious under normal circumstances.

But Weber did wonder about this Harold Pollard who

Conway mentioned. That was a new name, and Weber made a mental note to look for the police interview from 1978. If Prante went to his house that night, Pollard may have remembered something useful. Surely the cops had talked to him.

Dwayne Conway's twisted trail of statements and recantations left Weber confused and made it unlikely that Conway would be a useful witness. He had restored parts of his account, such as Prante's wet face and shirt, and his car parked at the Laundromat; those were incredibly incriminating details. But Conway's repeated flip-flops blew huge holes in his credibility, and Weber wondered how he could put such a man on the stand at trial. He had performed badly on two polygraphs and a psychological stress evaluation, and hypnosis had pulled nothing from the vast wasteland of his memory.

And, on top of all of that, the prosecutor himself had charged Conway with lying to the police. A defense attorney would have so many ways to impeach Conway on cross-examination that the jury could end up angry at a prosecutor who would present such a witness.

Conway might even be involved deeply in Karla's murder, and the prosecutor didn't want to cut him some kind of deal for his testimony until he could rehabilitate his credibility. Deciding whether to use Conway in Prante's trial would be a very tough call, and Weber wasn't looking forward to making that decision. Weber allowed himself to hold out a small hope that Conway someday would come forward with the details that would fit the evidence and sound like the true story.

Weber suspected a bit of the truth had been wrung from Conway when Rushing interviewed him at the jail. Conway slipped into the "theory mode" and offered speculation about what happened during the crime. Weber's experience was that such hypotheses often contained more truth than guess. Was Conway's odd theory of how the crime went down something close to the real story?

If it were some version of reality, it jolted Weber. He and the cops and Karla's family decided long ago that she

had suffered little, which made this tragedy a little easier
to handle for those left behind. If Conway was right,
however, Karla suffered a beating and a sexual assault,
and then spent hours bound helplessly in fear, only to
face death when her attacker reappeared.

A most unlikely witness with a fascinating story came
forward on June 29. Captain John Browning of the East
Alton police passed along a report he picked up during an
unrelated investigation; the next day, Tom O'Connor interviewed Sherry Dalton, a chunky blonde who claimed
to be intimately acquainted with John Prante. They met
over drinks in a bar in November 1981, and the conversation included Prante's laments about how tough it was
to find a job and how much killing there had been during
his service in Vietnam. "I had to use my machine gun a
lot," he recalled ruefully. Since coming home, he had suffered from some unspecified problems.

They ran into each other a couple more times at various bars. After such an encounter during the first week of
December, they went to Prante's house, popped a couple
"speed" tablets, and hit another bar. Back at Prante's
house later, they had sex, although he had difficulty
achieving and maintaining an erection. He attributed the
problem to a back injury suffered in 'Nam, and said he
took a prescription with codeine for the pain. He was able
to complete intercourse, however, and Sherry spent the
night with him.

O'Connor thought back to John Douglas's profile
again. One more time, he was precisely on target. How
could Douglas predict that the killer had sexual problems
that included impotence?

Sherry Dalton's infrequent dates with Prante after that
usually included sex. One night in January 1982, Prante
experienced a violent nightmare that awoke Sherry. He
was tossing, turning, and mumbling, and was drenched
with sweat; he was having a bad dream "about a lot of
things." The next month, after Prante had been unable to
get an erection, he pulled back a flag on the wall to reveal

a machine gun hanging underneath. He warned her not to tell anyone because the gun was illegal.

On a couple of occasions, Prante mentioned leaving town because he had been in trouble; he said there was no need to be more specific. When he mentioned it again later, Sherry decided it was time to inform him that she was pregnant with his child and was weary of his discussions of leaving. Prante became angry, pushed her, grabbed her by the arms, pulled her to her car, and took her home. She later aborted the pregnancy.

The agent thought all of this was mildly interesting and told a lot about Prante's character. But he saw nothing of much use until Sherry's next revelation.

While she was having sex with Prante for what would be the last time—sometime between February and April—Prante whispered in her ear, "I killed somebody." It was a strange thing to hear from your partner during the sex act, Sherry said.

"What?" she asked.

"I killed somebody."

"Who?"

"I can't say who."

The next morning, Sherry Dalton asked if he really killed someone. "I can't tell you, because I'll lose my freedom," he replied. She didn't believe any of it.

O'Connor was amazed. Could this witness swear to a confession?

Then Sherry upped the ante again.

"I think that, during the entire time I knew John, I had sexual intercourse with him about fifteen times. On about three of those times, John bit me pretty hard on my left neck and shoulder. I complained to him about biting me so hard. He apologized. He said, 'I'm sorry. I didn't mean to hurt you.'"

Had Prante not only admitted being a killer, but revealed that he was a killer who bit women on the neck?

Two weeks later, Sherry Dalton called back to fine-tune her memory; her improved version was even more incriminating. His "coitus interruptus" recollection had not been just that he had killed someone. He actually had said, "I killed a woman."

"Why would you kill a woman?" Sherry had whispered.

"I was mad."

"How could you get so mad?"

"I was just mad."

Weber and Rushing now had devastating testimony from a woman who had no obvious reason to lie and, in fact, was so frank that she openly discussed drug use, casual sex, and abortions. But Weber and the cops were cautious about the new evidence. They were willing to accept ninety percent of her story as the truth—how she and Prante met, their drinking and drugs, their sexual activities. But would John Prante, who had worked so hard to protect his dark secret, admit it to this woman?

Sherry Dalton's memory got a little unexpected verification later when Prante's medical records showed he had been taking Tylenol with codeine under a doctor's supervision.

Other demands on Don Weber kept him from getting deeply involved in the old Karla Brown files until Wednesday, July 21. He set aside two days for a meticulous review of an intimidating stack of papers—about a foot thick from Wood River, and another four-inch pile from DCI. It was Weber's style to cull through police reports ruthlessly with a prosecutor's eye and twenty-twenty hindsight—separating the wheat from the chaff, he thought of it. He usually tossed out half or more of the reports as useless. In this case, however, the percentage was higher, and Weber kept only twenty pages or so from the Wood River investigation. Most of the documents he would rely on had been produced later by DCI, with Wood River's assistance.

But the one report he kept looking for hadn't shown up. Where was the Harold Pollard interview? Weber couldn't believe that no one had talked to Pollard, this guy who lived on Hamilton Avenue and was the host of a meeting between Prante and Conway an hour or so after the murder was discovered. After another careful run through the file in vain, Weber closed the folder and picked up the phone.

"Randy, where's the Harold Pollard interview?"

"Who?"

"Harold Pollard—the guy Prante said he was going to see when he left Conway's house the day of the murder. Remember? Prante said back in '78 that he was at a house on Hamilton that evening when Conway came over and told him the good-lookin' girl next door had been murdered; that was Harold Pollard's house. Prante probably had the same clothes on when he went to Pollard's that he had been wearing when he killed Karla."

"We'll do it right now."

Harold Pollard—a tall, slim young man—opened the door at 547 Hamilton Avenue. After O'Connor and Detective Rick White identified themselves, Pollard smiled broadly.

"I was wondering when you guys were going to come talk to me."

Harold Pollard had waited more than four years to tell the police his story of the visit by his strange friend on the day Karla Brown was murdered: a sweating, nervous Prante—wearing a yellow "Big Bamboo" T-shirt— arrived at Pollard's in the late afternoon or early evening, and parked his red Volkswagen out front. Pollard never saw Prante in that condition before. He got a paper towel to wipe his face, and then sat down in the living room with Pollard and his mother. Prante seemed extremely shaken, explaining that he had just come from Dwayne Conway's house, where there was all sorts of "law" around. The girl next door to Conway had been murdered or killed; Pollard couldn't be sure which word Prante used. Prante and Conway had been drinking beer and smoking pot all morning, and Prante had to get away from the scene because the cops made him so nervous.

Pollard commented, "They're not after you," and Prante responded, "I just get nervous around cops." He even asked Pollard if he had any tranquilizers, and Pollard said no. Pollard suggested a good psychiatrist if Prante was that nervous, but Prante mumbled, "No, no, no."

Prante went on about the girl and described how she was found on the floor with her hands tied behind her. Prante and Conway got a glimpse of the body.

Pollard remembered that, a couple of days before the murder, Prante mentioned the girl moving next door to Conway and called her Karla Brown. Pollard quoted Prante as saying, "She's a good-lookin' girl," and then lapsing into gutter language to describe what he would like to "get off of her." He kept talking about how he would like to get to know her.

Pollard never saw Prante as nervous as he was that night; he left town soon after that for the Houston area. Pollard saw Prante around Wood River several times since then, but Prante never again mentioned Karla Brown's murder.

O'Connor and White knew they had hit pay dirt one more time. The T-shirt matched Conway's original description, and Prante's behavior screamed, "Guilty." Prante's statements to Pollard completely contradicted Prante's statements to the police.

Harold Pollard explained that he knew Prante rather well. They met in 1973, when Pollard was a returning Army vet and Prante was coming back from the Navy. They had taken a class together at Lewis and Clark Community College and became good friends. In 1975, they shared a mobile home in a small town called New Delhi just a few miles north of Wood River.

Pollard described Prante as a devout atheist with no conscience. Prante once threatened to kill Pollard with a survival rifle because Pollard let Prante's dog out of the trailer.

And Prante was very bitter toward women, probably because of a painful divorce; he could not stand rejection. "Whenever Prante was brushed off by a female, he would withdraw into himself and become very quiet; he would not communicate. I have never seen a man get so torn up about rejection by a female in my whole life."

Bingo, O'Connor thought. A man with the capacity for explosive violence and an intolerance for rejection by a woman he wanted sexually. What a profile for this killer! A man who was sweating profusely and was more nervous than a former roommate had ever seen him, and was worried about all the cops around Karla Brown's house. How much guiltier could he have acted? The motherload of circumstantial evidence, O'Connor thought.

Later, Don Weber could see by O'Connor's impish Irish grin that the cop had heard something special. After his report, Weber was grinning, too. Harold Pollard's portrait of Prante was devastating. This John Prante fit the profile drawn by John Douglas and knew details of the crime he shouldn't have known.

But Weber suddenly felt anger, too. For four years, a man with vital information about Karla Brown's killer waited patiently for the police to knock on his door, but the police never looked for him. Were there other witnesses with important stories to tell who hadn't been interviewed? What else had been missed?

Chapter 13

Neil Hawkins was twenty-seven years old and had been an assistant public defender in Madison County for about eighteen months. He had handled the routine burglaries and thefts, robberies and assaults. And among the six or seven cases he had taken to a jury trial there were two murders—one conviction and one acquittal. That was a pretty good record for a public defender in Madison County. The other full-time assistant in the office, Tyler Bateman, had tried the last two capital cases against prosecutor Don Weber, and both murderers were sentenced to death. When a new capital case came into the defender's office in June 1982, Neil Hawkins—a thick, compact man with pointed features, black hair, and a thick, bristly mustache—decided it was his turn. He went to his boss and volunteered to take his first death penalty case. He would defend John Prante.

One of Hawkins's first thoughts after reading the file was that the death penalty was not applicable. He was convinced that Prante's lack of a prior criminal record eliminated the death penalty from consideration. His research found several cases that clearly supported his conclusion.

He had been fascinated by the investigation that led to Prante's arrest, and wondered about the man he would meet at the first attorney-client interview. What he found was a very calm, controlled man who seemed about twenty years out of date. To his new lawyer, Prante seemed like a laid back throwback to the 1960s. He was even-tempered and easy to get along with; he would not be one of those clients who tried to run the case his own way, ignoring his lawyer's advice and pounding him with demands.

And Hawkins was sure of one more thing after that first interview: this case would go to trial. John Prante showed no interest in a plea-bargain; he said he was innocent, pure and simple.

Don Weber was somewhat surprised when he heard Neil Hawkins had volunteered for the case. Hawkins hadn't seemed quite that forceful, unlike so many other young attorneys looking to make a name for themselves. As a trial lawyer, Hawkins was often referred to as a "bricklayer." He built his cases slowly, brick by brick, course by course. Nothing flashy or flamboyant. He filed motions by the pound, challenging every possible fact and witness, and attacking the case from every angle. To his opponents, Hawkins's style could seem plodding and irritating. But Weber knew Hawkins made the prosecutors work harder to build their own cases and prepare better for trial.

And, with Hawkins on the other side, Weber assumed he would get the "kitchen sink" defense; Hawkins would throw everything at the prosecution. He was a stickler for details, would push Weber incessantly for all of the discovery material on the prosecution's case, and would try to suppress every bit of evidence.

One of the gambits Weber expected was an attempt to get him removed as prosecutor; that was the most worrisome aspect of the coming battle. Hawkins would argue that Weber was a potential witness because of his telephone conversation with Prante, and that should exclude Weber as prosecutor. Keeping himself on this case was a top priority for Weber in the early rounds. This was his case and he wasn't about to let someone else try it.

He had covered himself on that count, even before he picked up his telephone for that amazing call from Prante. Weber made sure there were options for a judge to consider before taking the extreme measure of removing the elected state's attorney. He hoped there would be enough choices for a judge to keep Weber at the helm while protecting Prante's right to explore that facet of the evidence. Weber could handle just about anything else that could happen, but he couldn't face the prospect of someone else standing before a jury to seek justice for Karla Brown.

Although not much was brewing officially on the case during the summer and fall of 1982, John Prante's name came up often around Weber's office. In early July, Weber learned that Prante was getting religion at the county jail. A friend of Weber's, Greg Thomas, was active in the jail-ministry program and told Weber that Prante was attending all of the services and taking part in the worship. Another jailhouse conversation, and yet another hit for John Douglas; he had predicted the killer would turn to religion for solace if he wasn't drinking or using drugs.

Some other mentions of John Prante came in a more irreverent way. As part of the entertainment at a party to be attended by DCI agents and other cops, Weber sponsored a contest to name the best—or worst—line uttered about criminal cases in the last year. Prante's "I don't mind being a witness, but I don't want to be a suspect," won the dubious honor. That had to be the most ironic statement any suspect ever offered to Weber.

What early activity there was in the official Prante file was relatively routine. Neil Hawkins filed a motion in August exercising the defendant's automatic right to one substitution of judge, taking a change from Circuit Judge Edward C. Ferguson. Weber was pleased when Circuit Judge Philip J. Rarick was assigned, even though the judge was a Democrat. Weber had appeared in Rarick's court many times, dating back five or six years to Weber's service in the juvenile division as an assistant prosecutor. Weber considered Rarick a tough, law-and-order judge who was fair to both sides, but countenanced none of the tactics Weber often saw as foolishness by the defense.

The arrest in the Karla Brown case certainly didn't put

an end to serious crime in Madison County. In September 1982, Don Weber won his second death penalty case against Larry Joe Adams for the execution-style murder of a pharmacist in his store in Alton. One problem with the case would help shape Weber's approach to a bit of evidence in the Karla Brown case. A thumbprint from the pharmacy cash register failed to match anyone, including Adams. Weber feared that defense attorney Tyler Bateman would dwell enough on that one chink in the armor to raise doubt in the jurors' minds. So Weber dismissed it as unimportant and hoped the jury would agree. It was one of those unanswerable questions that often arose, but proved or disproved nothing. Weber glossed over it, and so did the jurors. They sentenced Adams to death.

Weber decided that was how he would handle the fingerprint on the handle of the coffee carafe in Karla's basement. The FBI's green-laser had indeed produced a print adequate for comparison. But it matched no one—especially not the guy the cops believed filled the coffeepot with water to douse Karla in a vain attempt to revive her. Weber feared that Neil Hawkins would hammer away at the failure to match the print to Prante and everyone else known to be in the house. Weber would defuse that be arguing it really proved nothing, so it should be ignored. He wondered if that tactic would work again, in another death penalty case.

Neil Hawkins, as expected, flooded Weber with standard motions for disclosure of evidence and other matters. But the one Weber dreaded was filed, too. On November 12, Hawkins demanded the removal of Weber and his assistants from Prante's case. Weber and Keith Jensen were potential witnesses because of the telephone conversation with Prante, and the conflict extended to the entire office. Weber would have to be ready to refute that proposition.

The first hearing was held on December 20, and dealt with a characteristically odd situation in this very odd case. Weber and Hawkins wanted a record on the fact that

the public defender's investigator on the case, Gloria
Jellen, had been dating Sergeant Mike Urban of the East
Alton police. The potential conflict already had caused
Jellen's boss to fire her, but the attorneys decided they
needed a waiver in court from Prante. He agreed.

But during the hearing, Hawkins mentioned that Jellen
had been serving subpoenas on reporters for copies of
press releases and newspaper stories. That set off the
alarm in Weber's head; Hawkins was pursuing the publicity angle. He could go in three directions with that. First,
Hawkins could claim some of the information Prante divulged to his friends came from the media. Second,
Hawkins could try to get the charges dismissed by arguing that Weber's public comments had been so inflamma-
tory that Prante could not get a fair trial. And last,
Hawkins could try to get the trial moved out of Madison
County because of the publicity.

As happened so often at such hearings, Weber had
gleaned a tidbit about defense strategy, and he knew that
Hawkins was working hard. To avoid a prolonged
battle—and to stop the reporters' complaints about the
subpoenas—Weber furnished Hawkins with copies of all
the newspaper stories Weber had clipped. Nothing there
would support a claim that Prante's information came
from the public domain; it had come only from his memory of his crime.

After Prante waived the conflict, Hawkins began his
assault on the prosecution experts; he wanted written reports from Lowell Levine and Homer Campbell. Weber
said he had already given Hawkins what little written
documentation he had, and would forward any more documents that came in. He knew there wouldn't be many,
because the experts preferred not to submit their opinions
in writing.

Hawkins also asked for a written copy of John Douglas's psychological profile—a transcript from the cops'
interview with the agent. It was cited in police affidavits
for the search warrant at Prante's home; that made the
profile an issue in the case. But Weber could not stand for

that. Douglas was part of the investigatory process, and would not be a witness. In that role, Douglas's discussions with authorities were part of what the lawyers called their "work product"—the confidential communications all lawyers are allowed with clients and some other sources. He was a secret weapon that the cops and prosecutors thought they had a right to keep secret.

Judge Rarick read the Douglas transcript later and turned it over to Hawkins, who decided it was little more than mumbo-jumbo really aimed at Dwayne Conway. It was mere happenstance that so much of Douglas's description could fit Conway and Prante—two guys Hawkins thought were cut from the same mold. He saw no role for the profile in the defense case.

But Hawkins then turned his guns toward Weber at the hearing, calling for debate on the motion to exclude the prosecutor. Weber was more than ready, and he pounced. He certainly would not call himself to the stand, and probably not even Keith Jensen. All of the evidence from the phone conversation with Prante was available from other sources; Prante confirmed almost everything in his conversations with Spencer Bond and in his interview the night he was arrested. Weber suggested that a protective order from the judge, barring Weber from testifying would protect Prante's interests. And it would put a stop to a threat to the interests of the citizens in the county. After all, if would be a dangerous precedent to allow any criminal to exclude the prosecutor by ringing him up.

Hawkins accepted Weber's proposal if it included a copy of the prosecution's notes on the phone conversation; Weber had no problem with that and was relieved that the issue was resolved, at least for now.

During the winter and early spring of 1983, there were occasional discussions about a plea-bargain between Weber and Hawkins, but they never were close to agreement. Weber insisted on a guilty plea to murder in exchange for dropping the death penalty in favor of a life sentence. Weber later "softened" his offer to "only" eighty years. But Hawkins wanted a cap of twenty-five or thirty years, and Weber wouldn't consider that. This was a good case, and Weber knew it could be a great trial. Although taking it before a jury would be fraught with dangers to the prosecution, Weber had to admit that he looked forward to the challenge of a fabulous trial built on the most innovative investigation in Madison County history.

As time for the trial drew near, Judge Rarick called another group of Hawkins's motions for hearings on May 10 and 11. The judge denied Hawkins's attempts to suppress the two recordings Spencer Bond made with Prante. Weber was relieved to save such critical evidence. But the judge gave Hawkins victories by barring use of a few of the items seized from Prante's house and car—some of the photo albums, some of Prante's personal papers and books, and the four magazines full of photos of naked women with large breasts.

The judge also looked askance at Weber's defense of the publicity campaign when Hawkins asked to move the trial out of Madison County. Because of all the coverage by newspapers and television, potential jurors had heard a great deal about the case and probably had formed opinions on Prante's innocence or guilt.

Weber responded with a novel argument he expected to play better to the public than to the judge. The publicity was a special tactic designed to put psychological pressure on the killer and force him to make an error. As an investigative tool, Weber argued, the publicity was appropriate; it had, in fact, brought forward key witnesses who focused the case on Prante.

With that explanation, the prosecutor then turned to the legal argument; Hawkins's motion simply was premature. Jurors seldom remember facts from publicity about cases and, if picking a fair jury became difficult in this case, the motion to move out of county could be refiled then.

Weber hoped the judge wouldn't move the trial, forcing the prosecution to lose a home-grown jury panel and haul evidence and witnesses all over the state. To Weber's delight, the judge ruled that the proper time for such a motion was after there had been a demonstrated problem picking a jury. Weber was relieved. He was sure that picking a jury in Madison County would not be too difficult. The famous cartoon showing the panel of jurors asking in unison, "Lee Harvey Who?" was not that farfetched.

But Hawkins wasn't finished yet. He surprised Weber by withdrawing a motion to suppress the statements Prante made to O'Connor and Rushing when they arrested him. That move concerned Weber; it could be an attempt to keep Prante off the stand. Was Hawkins hoping that having the prosecution witnesses testify to Prante's denials would allow the defense to avoid the always risky business of testimony by the defendant?

Judge Rarick set the trial date for June 20, and then stepped down from the case for health reasons. He had been experiencing some heart problems and was facing another hospitalization for tests and treatment. That set up another interesting situation. The case was reassigned to Associate Judge Charles V. Romani, Jr., who had been appointed to the bench only five months earlier; he had never conducted a trial. He was about to be baptized by fire, because not only was his first trial a felony case, it was a sensational murder. Not only was it a murder, it was a death penalty case. Welcome to the big leagues, Judge.

To Weber, Romani was an unknown commodity on the bench. But Weber was comforted by the fact that Romani, who was thirty-three and went by "Chuck," had been the state's attorney in adjacent Bond County for six years. Perhaps that prosecutorial background would stay with the tall, slim young judge who had just shouldered one of the toughest trials to go before a jury in the county.

Hawkins looked at the new judge differently. The defender knew the judge would be fair, and it was unlikely he would use his first trial to impose the death penalty on a man with no other criminal record.

Both lawyers were pleased with one of the judge's first decisions. In casual discussions about the impending trial, they all agreed that the inadequate facilities at the county's old courthouse in Edwardsville would be taxed seriously by the kind of trial this case promised. There was little room in the hallways outside the courtrooms for waiting crowds of spectators, dozens of witnesses, and an unusually high number of reporters. There were no good places to isolate jurors from the rest of the crowd.

So, Romani decided to move the trial to the satellite courtroom at the Government Center in nearby East Alton. It was a larger, more modern courtroom and no jury trials were held there during the summer. There would be plenty of room for all the parties and the expected crowd, many of whom would be from East Alton and adjacent Wood River.

About a month before the trial date, Weber got a list of potential defense witnesses. Among them were Jerry Gibson and Tom Lawson, the former cellmates of Tony Garza—the serial sex offender and onetime suspect in Karla Brown's murder. The cellmates had claimed that Garza admitted killing Karla, which Hawkins hoped would plant a seed of doubt in the jurors' minds. Garza was perhaps the most logical suspect after Prante and Dwayne Conway. After all, if Weber had considered Garza that seriously, shouldn't the jury wonder, too? Was that enough to free Prante?

Weber had to counteract that and leave absolutely no doubt for the jurors. And the best way to do that was by getting Garza's dental impressions. On May 18, Agent Tom O'Connor and Weber drove seventy miles south to the Menard Correctional Center at Chester, the current home of Tony Garza. It was a warm, sunny day, and O'Connor kept Weber enthralled with stories from his days as a big-city cop and a member of the St. Louis P.D. bomb and arson squad. How to disarm bombs, which types of detonators were the most dangerous, how to investigate arson, how to look for burn patterns from flammable liquids. Weber learned a lot and enjoyed the drive.

But when he arrived at the gates of the old stone prison on the Mississippi riverfront, he suddenly realized that he had never been to the place where he had sent so many others. Menard was a 1930s prison, a Jimmy Cagney prison. Even nestled picturesquely between the bluffs and the river, it was an intimidating, foreboding bastille surrounded by high fences topped by merciless coils of razor wire. When the doors clanged shut behind him, the eerie sound wasn't muffled much by the knowledge that he would be leaving in a much shorter time than the others behind those walls.

Garza was anxious to talk as the men got settled in a small interview room. He was relatively friendly, considering the fact that he was sitting across the table from the man who put him there for twenty-two years. Garza, whose upper-body bulk showed hours spent pumping iron, explained that he was willing to do his time for what he had done. But he was tired of bogus accusations that he killed Karla Brown—a girl he never even met. And his mother was getting a lot of grief from people in Wood River who had heard those same accusations.

Garza said Jerry Gibson and Tom Lawson had been in a cell with him at the Madison County jail. Some of the inmates accused Garza of stealing their cigarettes and, despite his denials, they beat the hell out of him. Perhaps that beef was behind these lies about his supposed confession.

Garza gladly agreed to provide his dental impressions and, as he hopped into the chair in the prison infirmary, O'Conner was more than satisfied that Garza was not Karla's killer; he was way too anxious to have his teeth checked. And Weber noticed the lack of spaces between Garza's teeth, unlike the pattern in the bite marks.

Weber also learned something about prison life that day. When Garza asked for a pizza, Weber happily peeled off a few dollars and pushed them across the table. But Garza nearly exploded in panic and hastily explained that it was a major offense for a convict to have cash inside the joint. Weber had to pay at the commissary, and Garza enjoyed the snack while being interviewed. Every part of society has its special rules, Weber thought.

*   *   *

Neil Hawkins won approval from Judge Romani on June 14 to hire experts to assist the defense at county expense. That was fair, Weber knew, given the heavyweight experts he had backing him up. Hawkins called in Dr. Edward J. Pavlik, a forensic dentist from Chicago and chief consultant on dentistry for the Cook County medical examiner; Pavlik recommended a second expert—Dr. Norman D. Sperber of San Diego, another forensic dentist. Pavlik was one of the experts who used dental records to identify the twenty-four victims of mass murderer John Wayne Gacy and the 270 victims of the 1979 DC-10 crash in Chicago. Pavlik and Sperber usually worked for the police, and they knew of the prosecution's experts.

Neither defense expert offered any opinion or guidance up front. Hawkins sent them the photos, dental impressions, and everything else on the bite-mark evidence. And then he told them he wanted only the truth—nothing custom-designed for the defense.

Weber called his hired gun, Dr. Lowell Levine, and ran the names past him; he was familiar with both of them. Levine knew enough about Sperber to believe it was unlikely he would challenge the credibility of the bite marks. Levine would be surprised if Sperber actually testified for the defense at all.

Weber hoped Levine was right. What would a shoot-out among experts do to Weber's case and all that wonderful, exciting evidence about bite marks? Weber just hoped to convince the jury there were bite marks and that Dwayne Conway, Tony Garza, and Jack Meyers hadn't made them. That would leave just Prante.

As the rapid slide toward trial continued, Weber immersed himself in preparation; there always were dozens of details to check and something new seemed to spring up almost daily. He was reviewing the police reports from 1978 when he came across the one-paragraph reference to Edna Vancil, the woman who lived directly across the street from Karla Brown. Mrs. Vancil had seen a car, but her clue led only to the knife salesman working the neighborhood that day. With the Harold Pollard incident fresh in his mind, Weber wondered if Edna Vancil knew anything else she hadn't told the police.

By June 15, she had been tracked down to a new address in Wood River. When Weber and Agent Larry Trent sat down in her living room, she was reluctant to discuss the case with them. She finally admitted being worried about her safety if she provided incriminating evidence.

"Will John Prante ever get out?" she asked timidly. "I don't want to say anything without a subpoena; that way, I won't have any choice and it won't be my fault."

Weber obliged her with a subpoena on the spot, and she began to offer new details about the day Karla was killed. At her old house, her television was in front of the living room window. As she watched TV, she looked directly out of the big window toward Dwayne Conway's house. Dwayne was her nephew and, in fact, his twin sister, Annie Tweed, had been visiting Mrs. Vancil that same morning.

Conway has a twin sister? Weber shuddered at the thought.

And then Edna Vancil gave Weber the payoff.

Annie Tweed got a ride to the house from John Prante, who arrived at Dwayne's between 9 and 10 o'clock that morning. Prante and Dwayne sat on the porch, smoking marijuana and drinking beer, until they disappeared between 11 o'clock and noon.

Great, Weber thought. That's probably the best evidence yet on a time of death.

Mrs. Vancil watched the boys across the street return to their perch on the porch about noon and sit there until Prante left about 3 o'clock.

Mrs. Vancil had some trouble at first with the timing of the events. As the investigators questioned her, however, she began to relate the times of the soap operas she watched to the happenings she watched from the window. Soon she was giving fairly precise times.

Weber shook his head. "Why didn't you tell the police about John Prante in 1978?"

"They didn't ask me about John Prante then. They just asked if I had seen any strangers or strange cars in the neighborhood. And I didn't want to volunteer any information until I got a subpoena."

Weber shook his head again. She was the sixth witness with key information to wait years, until the cops knocked on her door.

After some quick checks, it was determined that Dwayne Conway's sister was living in Franklin, Louisiana. Weber had to send someone to talk to her and to drop in on Lee Barns, also a resident of the bayou state. Would the guy who sat on the porch with Conway and Prante also know more than he told the police in 1978?

Early on June 17, Agents Tom O'Connor and Wayne Watson flew to Louisiana and began a hectic day visiting small police and sheriff's departments in several parishes. The interstate subpoenas from Madison County had to be presented to the police, then a prosecutor, and then a judge in the parishes. The judge then issued a local subpoena and an order to return to Illinois. The slow procedure seemed even more complicated as the agents worked the telephones to line up the proper assistance and local officers to track down Lee Barns and Annie Tweed.

By 1:45 P.M., O'Connor and Watson were sitting in Barns's stuffy mobile home out in the boonies at Gibson, Louisiana, as he explained that he had known Karla Brown since high school in Roxana, and recognized her when he visited Dwayne Conway's house. Barns thought Prante had given him a ride to Conway's that evening, but he wasn't sure. He was sure, however, that he smoked marijuana and drank beer on the porch with Conway and Prante until after dark.

Barns called to Karla as she and some others moved in her furniture. After they exchanged some general comments and Karla walked away, there was some talk among the three men on the porch about how good Karla looked. Prante suggested that they go over and join Karla's party, but Barns balked at barging in uninvited.

After the men went inside Conway's house, there was some more discussion about good-looking Karla. Prante, who was driving a red Volkswagen station wagon, gave Barns a ride home later. And Prante mentioned again how Karla had such "nice, big boobs." A recurring theme for Prante, the agents mused.

Barns added, "John has never seemed to have much of an interest in women, but he seemed very interested and even excited about Karla Brown. I used to be with Prante two or three times a week, and he never talked about any other women the way he carried on about Karla."

More good stuff the cops didn't get four years earlier, and reluctant witness Number Seven.

Six hours later, O'Connor and Watson were looking at Annie Tweed—Dwayne Conway with a wig and no mustache. In her little house near the swamp, she told them about visiting her aunt, Edna Vancil, between 9 and 10 o'clock that morning. But Annie contradicted her aunt on one point. Annie had driven herself; she had not caught a ride with Prante.

Conway had been painting a neighbor's house until Prante arrived in his red Volkswagen and parked in front. Annie even hollered a greeting to Prante and he waved back. He was wearing a yellow cap and a yellow T-shirt. She didn't notice the writing on it that day, but she knew Prante well enough to know that the yellow shirt he always wore had the word "bamboo" across the front of it.

Prante left after perhaps thirty minutes, about 12:30 P.M. She still was at her aunt's when Karla Brown's boyfriend pulled up at the house with another guy in a pickup truck and unloaded a doghouse. It wasn't long before the police and the coroner arrived. The police talked briefly to Tweed and the others at Edna Vancil's. Just after that, Tweed noticed John Prante standing in Dwayne Conway's front yard while Dwayne sat on the porch. Tweed didn't see Prante's red Volkswagen parked out front, as she had earlier. Prante still was wearing the yellow hat and shirt.

Dwayne told his sister later that Prante had left his car at the Laundromat nearby.

Conway's sister was corroborating major parts of her brother's recanted statement to the agents that Saturday in Brighton.

Annie Tweed claimed she had seen Prante smoke marijuana, opium, and hashish, and knew that he had taken speed and LSD. She also charged that John Prante had sold drugs to his friends.

Toward the end of the interview, Annie Tweed asked if it would take much longer. Her favorite TV show, *The Dukes of Hazard*, was about to start and she didn't want to miss it. The agents laughed later—her twin brother likes *Star Trek* and she's watching *Dukes of Hazard*. Dwayne was in jail, implicated in a homicide case, but Annie would prefer to end an interview that might help him so she could watch two hillbillies skid down a dirt road in an orange car.

Chapter 14

The almost childlike printing across the bottom of the page jolted Don Weber. He read the words again, and felt a chill along his spine from this sudden, unexpected flash of illumination into the inner workings of John Prante's mind. Weber knew he had just read the secret, unguarded thoughts of a killer reflecting on the kill. In these few lines, John Prante had tried to be profound. But he had tried too hard, and opened the gate into his dark thoughts just a bit too wide. He had let the truth slip out while the door was ajar.

"I truely [*sic*] understand hardships, depressions, rage, and the calm after a storm," John Prante had written on February 26, 1979.

Weber read the words again and again. " . . . depressions, rage, and the calm after a storm."

The depressions, the rage, and then the calm.

For the first time, Weber had a window into the processes working behind those cool eyes. The serenity was only a veneer. Life as a loser was a series of rejections and depressions. As Weber read those words, he could almost feel Prante's fury when Karla Brown rejected him—another in a long line of rejections by women, reminding him again what a loser he was. Weber could see the rage in Prante's face when yet another "good-lookin'" girl scorned him, perhaps even taunted him.

And then the storm—the explosive, battering forces Prante couldn't control.

Much later, the calm—as he altered the scene and sat back to watch the police.

Just eight months after Karla Brown's murder, John Prante had written those words on a job application at the Madison County Juvenile Detention Center, the facility where kids in trouble were held. Weber was paging through the form when five hand-printed lines at the bottom of the last sheet leaped out at him. The lettering was curious, an odd combination of printing and cursive styles mixed within words. In the word "and," the "a" and "d" were cursive, and the "n" was printed squarely. The punctuation was wrong, often using commas where periods were needed. Capital letters were sprinkled carelessly through the lines. One word was misspelled "truely."

Then Weber read what Prante had written in response to the question, "Why do you want to be employed here?"

"I closely relate to People, whereas I too am Disadvantaged, being a veteran, I truely understand hardships, depressions, rage, and the calm after a storm. I may be able to bring a Gleam of sanity into someones life, within a world gone insane."

The strange, awkward prose left Weber shaken. After the horror of what happened in Karla Brown's basement, Weber could understand why Prante might perceive "a world gone insane."

But the other phrase still haunted Weber. " . . . depressions, rage, and the calm after a storm." It was the criminal's code again; Weber had seen it so many times. There almost always were clues left by the criminal—sometimes purposefully, sometimes subconsciously—that could be used to solve a crime. But to unscramble the code, the prosecutor had to get inside the criminal's head. The clues had to be interpreted from the criminal's perspective; break the code, break the crime.

In this one paragraph, Weber decided, Prante accidentally let too much of his feelings out. He revealed the pain from rejection after rejection—the depression. He defined the murder of Karla Brown—the rage. And he described how he coped with what he had done—the calm after a storm.

Who was this man?

* * *

John Noble Prante was born on August 19, 1949, to George and Eleanor Prante in Alton, Illinois. His father was a pipefitter for the Amoco Oil Co. at its refinery at Wood River. John had one sister, Jo Ellen, who was two years older. John later remembered his parents as loving, and recalled a good relationship with both of them. But his sister remembered it somewhat differently; her brother and mother got along well, but John and his father argued almost constantly. Their father was strict and abused John verbally, always putting him down.

In 1956 the family moved to Saudi Arabia for eight years while George Prante worked for Amoco's operations there. After the Prantes returned to the Wood River area in 1964, John talked a lot about his life in the Middle East—so much that some of his friends became bored with the stories. He often mentioned the Saudis' "eye for an eye" justice system; he had been taken with that for some reason. There was talk among his friends that he had collected films of public punishments, such as the amputation of a thief's hand, and perhaps even had some movies of executions. His friends thought he really got off on that kind of stuff.

John spent two years in the Western Military Academy for boys in Alton before enrolling in Civic Memorial High School in Bethalto in 1966. He was a poor student, piling up D's and F's. He was quiet and reserved, and seemed rather strange to some schoolmates. Others found him friendly and enjoyed talking to him. He dropped out in 1969 just before the start of his senior year. That October, he earned his general equivalency degree from a program in a nearby school district.

In 1968 and 1969, he worked for the McDonnell-Douglas aircraft plant and the Chevrolet assembly plant, both in St. Louis, and was a booking agent for an entertainment company, earning $3 an hour. He was being trained to operate data-processing equipment for an insurance company when he enlisted in the Navy in October

1970. He was trained in basic electricity and electronics before being shipped to Vietnam aboard the aircraft carrier, the U.S.S. *Enterprise*, in April 1971. He was honorably discharged in October 1972, with the National Defense Service Medal, the Republic of Vietnam Campaign Medal, and the Vietnam Service Medal with two stars.

Although his military record showed no evidence of it later, Prante often claimed that he endured a traumatic event aboard ship that started as a fairly minor discipline problem. Prante told friends he got thirty days in the brig where, he claimed, he was beaten repeatedly and sadistically by Marine guards. He called it a horrible experience that left him emotionally scarred.

He moved back to the Alton area and went to work for the Chrysler Corp. in St. Louis in December 1972; he described the job as a field representative and auditor. He started taking classes at Lewis and Clark Community College in Godfrey, and quit his job in April 1973 to attend school full-time on the G.I. bill.

It was during this period that Prante, studying geology, met Spencer Bond, an accounting student; they became good friends. Bond wasn't sure what drew him to Prante—the strange, off-the-wall fellow with such long, stringy hair. A beard one day, shaved the next. Round, John Lennon glasses. Perhaps it was his calm manner, or the voice in that smooth, soothing monotone. He could be very entertaining and fun to listen to, at least in small doses.

Maybe it just had something to do with the times—the psychedelic seventies. Black lights, strobe lights, wild posters, Jimi Hendrix, long hair, bell-bottom jeans, fringed vests, and lots and lots of drugs. Their social group smoked tons of marijuana at the frequent parties, and Prante usually brought a bottle of cheap "kiddie wine" such as Lancer's or Boone Farm.

Most of his friends never saw Prante get violent, but Weber knew the combination of wine and pot could be explosive. Some of the most violent, brutal crimes Weber had seen had erupted under those influences.

Whatever it was that Bond saw in Prante, it seemed to offset the things about him that were so irritating—and there were several. Prante considered himself an authority on everything and obviously thought he was smarter than everyone else in the crowd. He often used big words that others in the group might not even understand; he seemed to think that proved he was the ruling intellectual among them.

Years later, a court bailiff from Wood River would peg Prante perfectly on that count. Mike Donohoo said Prante probably seemed like an intellectual because he hung out with people who would argue over what started World War II, and would be impressed when Prante condescended to explain that it started when the Germans bombed Pearl Harbor. "Oh, yeah. John's right again."

Prante enjoyed being the center of attention, holding forth from his elevated position. Prante's pedestal, Bond thought. When someone argued with Prante, he would stick calmly to his view, no matter how hostile or loud the opponent got. Bond was impressed by that—a real inner calm, it seemed.

Prante talked about Saudi Arabia a lot; he had liked living there. He talked about it so much, in fact, that Bond eventually learned to let the stories go in one ear and out the other.

Bond's wife, Roxanne, noticed that the one subject Prante didn't like was religion. He got very upset when anyone mentioned the Bible—"fairy tales," he called it. Spencer thought Prante rejected the idea of a deity on an intellectual basis.

After the Bonds and Prante had been friends for a while, it was almost a daily experience to see Prante drive up in front of their house in his beat-up orange Honda CVCC. His car always was messy and dirty, the floor full of trash he had just tossed there. He always drove junky cars, and seemed rather frugal all the way around. The only extravagance the Bonds noticed was Prante's penchant for bringing Roxanne stuffed animals; he even gave her some pins he said belonged to his mother, who died in 1976.

Prante was at the Bonds' all the time it seemed, even when Spencer wasn't there. That bothered Roxanne Bond, because Prante never tried to hide his roving eyes. He leered at every woman in sight, no matter what she looked like. He would let his eyes roam across her body—probing—and then offer her a slight smile that seemed to suggest they both knew what he was thinking. Sometimes he would pursue the unspoken suggestion with a quick grab, even if her boyfriend was in the next room. Roxanne thought Prante must be a certified sex maniac. The boyfriends of many of the girls hated having Prante around because of that kind of conduct, and he had been invited rudely to leave more than once by a jealous boyfriend.

Spencer knew Prante spoke rather coarsely about women in private. Prante's comments weren't exactly vulgar, but he often mentioned that this girl had "a nice butt" or that one had "nice boobs." Prante liked big breasts, but any woman was fair game. His house was littered with *Playboy, Penthouse,* and *Hustler* magazines. At dinner with the Bonds one night, Prante unexpectedly hauled out some of those magazines and showed them to his hosts.

Once, in early 1977, Spencer was asleep on the floor when Prante leaned over and put his hand on Roxanne's leg. She quickly slapped it away and told him to keep his hands off. He never touched her again, but he never stopped ogling. Roxanne told her husband about the pass by Prante; Bond didn't mention it then, but he didn't forget it. When it came up out of the blue in a tape conversation years later, no one was more surprised than Bond.

Prante's carnivorous attitude toward women left the Bonds even more amazed one day after they had known Prante for about a year. He asked if he could bring his wife by the house sometime. Wife? They were speechless. There never had been any suggestion that he was married; he had dated women, but never for more than a month or so. There had been no long-term relationship, let alone any indication of a marriage. Bizarre, the Bonds thought.

They learned he had married a girl from California named Karen in 1972, but Prante explained nothing else. When they met her later at Prante's basement apartment behind the Kentucky Fried Chicken restaurant, she seemed almost as strange as her husband. She was a big woman with reddish-blond hair. There seemed to be no real affection between the Prantes. They seemed less like husband and wife than roommates who just happened to be married.

The Bonds were given no explanations, either, when Karen Prante left in 1975. Spencer had the impression she returned to California. John showed no sign that he was upset by the divorce.

Eventually, Prante moved to a small house just across the alley and down the block from the Bonds. It was close enough that the friends began a little game using flashlights to signal each other.

In September 1975, Prante was suspended from Lewis and Clark College because of poor grades. He transferred to Southern Illinois University at Edwardsville. But in June 1977, John Prante left the area to go to work in Galveston, Texas, loading materials for offshore drilling operations. He worked there for a month and then moved to Lafayette, Louisiana, to take a job with Petroleum Helicopter Inc. In addition to picking up a couple of yellow ball caps with the company logo on them, Prante worked in fuel-loading operations and performed other maintenance jobs. He quit after five months.

He moved back to his father's home in Bethalto in December 1977, and returned to classes at Southern Illinois University. He stayed in school until March 1979.

The police investigation had found several job applications filed by John Prante in June 1978—including a couple on the twenty-first, the day Karla died. But Don Weber found little else in the files to document Prante's activities during that period. Applying John Douglas's analysis, Prante probably was lying low, nervously trying to recover from the trauma, and hoping the police weren't smart enough to put things together.

The next record was the job application at the county's Detention Center in February 1979. Read in 1983 with the distinct advantage of hindsight from the long investigation, this was a most interesting document.

Prante had puffed the descriptions of his jobs almost laughably. At Petroleum Helicopters, Prante said, he was a flight line chief and his duties were "to coordinate fuel services to terminal, transit and visiting flights. Maintained a fuel depot, all pertaining maintenance, parts, offshore transfer storage tanks, truck/tanker transport operation; capacity—20,000 U.S. gallons. In addition, my responsibilities included base cosmetics and aircraft corrosion control."

He was paid $3 an hour. Weber figured Prante had gassed up the helicopters, kept the storage tanks full, cleaned up the grounds, and washed the copters.

Under a section of the job application called "Data," Prante told his prospective employer at the county, "I read extensively and attend seminars and some conference courses. Occasionally I do home research in a variety of subjects. World politics interest me more on the whole than national policy, there seems to be more need of help internationally. We as Americans know."

What strange drivel, Weber thought. But the passage that really grabbed Weber's attention was Prante's list under the heading of "Recreations."

"Automotives, aviation, hang gliding, Sailing [*sic*], tennis, pool, swimming, floattripping, camping, geology, cycling, and women."

" . . . and women," Weber read again. Gosh. Prante had started to sound like a real Renaissance man, a man of varied and cultured interests. But he had spoiled it so suddenly by explaining that women were part of his recreational activities. Tacky, Weber thought. No class.

Had Karla Brown been "recreation"?

Through Manpower, a federally founded jobs program, Prante was hired to guard juveniles at the Detention Center in March 1979, helped no doubt by letters of reference from two friends—Spencer Bond and Harold Pollard. Pollard's letter was brief and to the point. He had known Prante for five years and found him to be "a person of outstanding character" who accepted responsibility well.

Bond's letter was longer and somewhat different in tone. It started by describing Prante as a conscientious worker who had taken valuable courses such as philosophy, psychology, and sociology. He was from a good Bethalto family. But then Bond warned that Prante soon would think he knew everything about the Detention Center. "He does have a know-it-all attitude, which you will surely observe," Bond advised.

And then Prante's old friend offered a last piece of advice, from personal experience and observation. "Watch him around the female wards."

Bond's caution that Prante soon would think he knew it all proved accurate. Prante was a problem from the day he was hired; it was obvious to his supervisors that he was incapable of getting along with his coworkers or following procedures. In less than two months, Prante was taking exception to the Center's policies and complaining that the supervisors were picking on him. On May 22, he was fired after his most serious offense—violating a supervisor's instructions not to tell the juveniles how one of them had injured a staff member during a disturbance.

John Prante left town again and, in October 1980, went to work as a deckhand for a barge line in Morgan City, Louisiana. The manager told the police later that Prante was fired in March 1981, for "lack of proper interest in his job." Prante claimed he was fired because he refused to join the Ku Klux Klan.

He eventually returned to East Alton and rented a small house on Goulding Avenue. He had no visible means of support; friends thought he was living on the inheritance from his father's death in 1980. Prante and the Bonds saw each other only a few times after that; when they were together, Roxanne thought John seemed much more nervous than he was before. He would get up repeatedly and look out the window.

Weber flipped shut the file on John Prante and leaned back. " . . . depressions, rage, and the calm after a storm."

Chapter 15

Don Weber was perplexed when he learned what the experts for the defense had to say about the dramatic bite marks that formed such a key part of the prosecution's case. Not only would the experts dispute the conclusion that the marks were consistent with John Prante's teeth, they would challenge the idea that what appeared in those photographs were bite marks at all. The photographs were so poor, these experts concluded, that they offered no value as evidence. The pictures hadn't been taken properly for bite-mark analysis and were so grainy that there was no way of knowing what those dark spots were. They could be bruises or abrasions, but they could just as well be "artifacts"—unexplained marks, patches of dried blood, or imperfections in the photos.

If they were bite marks, there were no scientifically accepted grounds on which to link them to a suspect. There was no ruler in the photos and they had not been taken at ninety-degree angles to the wounds. The body had been moved, changing the position in which the marks were inflicted. The skin was stretched, distorting the marks and perhaps altering the spacing of the teeth or the shape of the dental arch.

A linchpin of Weber's case was facing a serious assault. This would, indeed, be a contest between the experts, and Weber was much less sure about the outcome now. He had hoped the defense experts would concede the existence of the bite marks, perhaps just challenging how solidly they could be linked to Prante. But the conflict would go well beyond that now. Neil Hawkins apparently had done his homework, and he had come up with hired guns of his own. Could they shoot fatal holes in Weber's case?

The new attack on the bite-mark evidence seemed ironic, given the way the upcoming trial was being played in the press. The reporters didn't know the details Weber had just learned, and all of the newspapers were running stories about the "battle of the experts," stressing that the prosecution's consultants had testified in the Ted Bundy trial and the "Looking for Mr. Goodbar" case. The defense experts were involved in the investigation of serial killer John Wayne Gacy and the identification of victims in the DC-10 crash in Chicago. Would they disagree on the controversial bite-mark testimony in this case? Tune in and see.

The stories also said the trial was shaping up to be the longest criminal case in Madison County history. Some estimates placed it at five weeks. It was obvious the reporters were anticipating a good show.

As the stories hit, Weber was conducting a major re-evaluation of trial strategy, forced on him partly by the new information from the defense experts. He already had been leaning toward making the key to the case the testimony by Prante's friends about his knowledge of the evidence—including the bite marks—right after the murder. If the bite marks were to be challenged so strongly, perhaps a shift in tactics was the best move.

He sat down with a notepad and began diagnosing the weaknesses of his case.

First, the bite marks. Now, at least, he knew what he was facing from the defense; he just hoped his experts could counteract the assault. Bite-mark analysis as a forensic science still was in its infancy, and Weber wondered whether jurors in Madison County would give it much credence when brought to them for the first time.

The second problem still was good old Dwayne Conway. Weber really felt Conway was involved in the crime, and the prosecutor was reluctant to offer him any kind of deal to obtain his testimony against Prante. Trying the case without Conway would be difficult, but he had huge credibility problems if he took the stand. Who knew what he might say under pressure? If Conway testified, Weber had to be able to explain why Conway was the prime suspect for so long, and the explanation had to avoid giving the jury cause to wonder if Conway really killed Karla.

The third problem also related to witnesses—there were too many whose testimony was essential. Each of them would offer details that varied slightly, and the defense could use that to confuse the jury and attack the prosecution's theories. It always was that way in trials, but it was worse in this case because the memories were four years old. There even were confusing sets of witnesses—cops from the first investigation in 1978; cops from the second investigation in 1980; cops from the third investigation in 1982; friends and relatives of Karla; different pathologists; different dental experts; and, finally, the group so essential to the case—the Whites, the Bonds, Harold Pollard, and Sherry Dalton.

Establishing a time of death was the fourth problem. Weber would have to create a time zone that could be matched to Prante's presence at Conway's house, giving Prante the opportunity to commit the crime. Edna Vancil would be of great help there.

Fifth—the cause of death. Dr. Harry Parks ruled strangulation by garroting. But Weber knew Dr. Mary Case was reevaluating the evidence; he would learn more about that soon.

And, last, the prosecution's case was almost entirely circumstantial. Weber had loads of evidence that should lead reasonable people to the conclusion that John Prante killed Karla Brown. But there was no indisputable eyewitness and no smoking gun. The winding trail led ultimately to John Prante's door, but everything was circumstantial. That was the kind of evidence that, at best, was hard to understand and, at worst, could evaporate quickly.

Weber wondered about his case. Was it the kind that

seemed wobbly to the prosecutor, but played so well to a jury? Or was it the kind that looked great on paper, but fell apart hopelessly in the courtroom?

Two floors below Weber's office, Neil Hawkins was analyzing the case from a different perspective. The bite marks, under the flood of conflicting information from several experts, probably would be a washout with the jury. There were enough questions about the photographs for valid doubts about the whole issue. The Whites and the Bonds had waited a long time to talk to the police, making their stories susceptible to criticisms and credibility questions. The 1978 investigation had been poor, and reconstructing a case after so many years left room for more mistakes. Dwayne Conway continued to be a wild card of little or no real value to either side. Prante had no criminal record or background of physical violence.

All of that should be enough to raise a reasonable doubt, Hawkins thought; John Prante had a fifty-fifty chance of acquittal.

With less than a week before the start of trial, Neil Hawkins renewed his motion to have Don Weber thrown off the case. Weber hoped that meant Hawkins was getting jumpy after serious analysis of all of the evidence. Maybe Hawkins just decided to try his previously unsuccessful tactic with the new, and less experienced, judge. On Thursday, June 16, Hawkins went before Judge Romani to make the same argument that Weber and his staff should be removed because of the phone conversation. Weber explained once again that he and his assistant would not be witnesses, and that Hawkins already had seen the notes from the conversation. Judge Romani said he would rule later.

The next day, for his own very personal reasons, Weber decided not to wait any longer. Weber explained to the judge that, if the prosecutor was going to handle the trial on Monday, he needed the weekend to prepare. And besides, Weber explained, he didn't want this question hanging over his head for the weekend. Romani seemed to shrug, and then said he would deny Hawkins's motion for the second time; Weber stayed on the case.

Relief again, Weber thought. But this time, the decision freed his mind for another, especially important event.

That afternoon, Don Weber and Virginia Rulison boarded a plane for Reno, Nevada—and eloped. As they waited to board their plane in St. Louis, Weber was approached by a reporter from one of the biweekly newspapers in Madison County who also was on the flight. Weber couldn't believe it; he hadn't even made it onto the plane before he was tagged.

On the flight home on Sunday, Don Weber bumped into Ben Allen, another lawyer from Madison County. Weber had to laugh. At least it proved that anyone's careful plans could fall apart because they couldn't foresee those kinds of fateful coincidences.

Before the lawyers could get to the serious business of picking a jury on Monday, June 20, 1983, they met in the courtroom to hash out the rest of the motions. Hawkins argued that the death-penalty statute in Illinois was unconstitutional; it denied defendants equal protection and put too much arbitrary power into the hands of the state's attorney, who had the sole right to decide who would face death. And, Hawkins added, Weber's offer of a plea-bargain for prison time voided his right to seek death for Prante.

Weber rejected Hawkins's claims completely. No deal had been made for jail time and the death penalty had been ruled constitutional many times already.

Judge Romani agreed and denied the motion. He also rejected Hawkins's requests to move the trial out of the county or sequester the jury; proper admonitions to the jury to avoid reading or listening to the news would protect Prante's rights.

Hawkins then asked for a "gag order" to prohibit the prosecution and the defense from making any comments to the press during the trial. Weber shrugged; he wasn't particularly in favor of it, but he wouldn't oppose it. In fact, it eliminated one more distraction during the trial. The judge granted Hawkin's wish.

Weber had one more motion. The three-year statute of limitations on all charges but murder had expired between June 1978, and Prante's arrest in June 1982. Although Weber might argue that Prante's time in Texas and Louisiana extended the limitation, Weber asked the judge to dismiss the burglary counts anyway. Weber would go all-or-nothing on the murder charges, giving the jury no room for compromise. The judge agreed, leaving three counts of murder—a crime on which there was no time limit for justice.

Donna and Terry Judson met Don Weber for the first time on the day jury selection began. Weber was struck by how much Donna looked like his image of Karla—the same size; the same short blond hair; the same feisty attitude. He liked the Judsons immediately. They were good people, like the rest of this family, and they all were living victims of this murder. Weber remembered why he was dedicated to this case and the mission of being a prosecutor.

The Judsons were impressed by Weber, too. He was open and informative on his strategy. He asked for their thoughts on some issues, and that pleased the Judsons immensely; they were thankful to be part of this team.

Donna's sister, Connie Dykstra, came for the start of the trial. But she decided she would attend only the opening statements; the trial and the details of her little sister's death would be more than Connie could handle.

Jo Ellen Brown decided not to go to court until the end of the trial. She would be satisfied by updates from Donna and Terry, as she had been throughout the investigation. And her need for justice would be satisfied by being there at the end, when she hoped to hear the jury say that John Prante was guilty.

Everyone in the family hoped for that, and for one more thing—they all wanted John Prante to confess on the witness stand. They weren't sure the police finally had the killer; they wanted to hear it from his lips.

Don Weber was looking for twelve normal, typical citizens when he began picking the jury on Monday morning. As he scanned the dozens of people in the pool, the prosecutor felt sure he could find the "twelve good and true" among them.

Two things were most important as he began to select his third death-penalty jury. First, he needed people without quirks and hidden hang-ups that would get in the way of common sense. He wanted people smart enough to understand circumstantial evidence and appreciate the new science of bite marks, and alert enough to catch the difference between the investigations in 1978 and 1982. He wanted people who could grasp the sometimes subtle contradictions among Prante's various stories. Weber needed all of that while making sure he didn't get people who thought they were so smart they would overanalyze the evidence to look for every possible explanation, no matter how unlikely. Weber wanted two or three leaders; the rest should be followers. Gender made no difference—this murder was so brutal and heinous that everyone would be outraged.

The second qualification was a bit tougher—he needed jurors with the will to impose the ultimate punishment on a cold-blooded murderer. That ability was assessed in one simple question as Weber spoke personally with jurors in the selection process (called voir dire) to see what they would say. Weber would look each juror in the eye, point directly to John Prante, and ask, "If I prove to you beyond a reasonable doubt that he murdered Karla Brown, will you sentence that man, right there, to death?"

It was a tough, head-on question that forced each juror to look the man and the reality of the situation right in the face. The only acceptable answer was a firm, unwavering unequivocal yes. Anything less, any hesitation or wavering or explanation, and Weber disqualified the person.

Jury selection was held in the courthouse in Edwardsville, even though the trial would be in East Alton. The process went about as Weber expected; not many jurors had heard of the case, and almost none remembered any details.

Jury selection was fascinating for the Judsons, who sat in on every minute. It helped that Larry Trent, their old high school friend, was there. His calm assurance as an experienced DCI agent was vital to their peace of mind. He was assisting Weber with the details of the trial, and he always was there to urge the Judsons to keep the faith.

Donna kept a daily journal throughout the trial. She was frightened by the limit of twenty exclusions each attorney had to "strike" unwanted jurors; she wondered if Weber might be forced to accept some he didn't want once he had used up his challenges. The procedure struck her as a game between the lawyers, with each one trying to get jurors he favored past the objections of his opponent; that was precisely the point.

Donna studied each juror's face for clues. One man was getting married the next week, but he still had difficulty saying things that might get him disqualified. One woman was accepted on Monday, but came back the next day, saying she decided she never could impose the death sentence on anyone. As the juror was excused, Donna thought it was ironic that the juror would make that decision on June 21, 1983, the fifth anniversary of Karla's murder.

Donna was disappointed when she saw John Prante for the first time in the courtroom that Monday morning—he seemed so normal. He wore a light blue suit and had shaved his beard, leaving only a mustache. He didn't looked depraved or maniacal, or even very peculiar. He made eye contact with the Judsons and smiled slightly as he entered the room, escorted closely by Deputy Bob Henke. Donna wondered if Prante somehow knew who she was; Weber thought it was just Prante's roving eyes. Either way, Prante may have learned who she was; because within a few days, he stopped looking at her.

* * *

In Wood River, another ironic situation occurred on June 21, 1983; Sergeant Eldon McEuen was nearly murdered. Still on leave from a back injury, McEuen was sitting with friends at an outdoor table at a tavern when a stranger walked up and interrupted their conversation with some odd and hostile comments. Sergeant Chuck Nunn was among the group and chased the man away. Later, he was seen near McEuen's truck, and McEuen went over to check him out again. The guy suddenly stabbed the sergeant in the side and fled. He was caught and eventually served eight years in prison. McEuen wondered if something from one of his old cases had caught up with him, but it turned out to be only the unpredictable actions of a disturbed man.

On Wednesday, Hawkins brought in a surprise offer from Prante to consider a plea-bargain. Weber called a summit conference of the team, including Virginia Weber and the Judsons. Everyone agreed that the prosecution was strong enough that little should be given up. Weber was willing to accept a murder plea and withdraw the demand for death; Prante's lack of a prior criminal record would make it difficult to get the highest penalty, anyway. Prante rejected the half-hearted offer of eighty years in prison, sending everyone back to jury selection.

The process held Donna Judson's interest for four days. She was surprised when Judge Romani refused to exclude a juror who had been a friend of Prante's father; Weber used one of his challenges to disqualify the man. With such odd situations occurring, Donna finally decided she would have to trust that Weber knew what he was doing.

By Thursday, June 23, the nine women and three men who would decide whether John Prante was guilty had been chosen, together with four alternate jurors. Sixty-four people had been questioned; the judge excused fourteen, Hawkins disqualified fifteen, and Weber bounced nineteen (he always saved the last one for a screwball).

Weber and Hawkins—as well as the Judsons—were pleased with the panel.

Romani decided to start the trial the next Monday.

On Friday, June 24, Weber and Randy Rushing visited Dr. Mary Case for a final interview before trial. Weber was planning a very detailed opening statement on Monday, and he wanted to know precisely what Dr. Case would say in her testimony. What he heard stunned him, and infused him with an anger that would sustain him throughout the long trial ahead.

Dr. Case said it was obvious that Karla Brown was sexually assaulted; the doctor would enter that medical finding, despite the inconclusive evidence from the gynecological examination at the first autopsy. She used additional factors in a case like this—medical evidence did not have to be viewed in a vacuum. The nudity and the removal of the tampon certainly were sexually motivated. The bite marks were inflicted from close range, when the killer was on top of the victim in a frontal and obviously sexual position. Those considerations, and the lack of any other motive, meant Karla Brown had been sexually assaulted in the medical and legal definitions of the term.

Then Dr. Case gave Weber another shock.

Karla had drowned in that barrel of water. The "cone of foam" around her mouth and nose, clearly visible in the photos, was a medical certainty of drowning. She was breathing when she went into the water, even though no water was inhaled into her lungs. The foam meant Karla was breathing in and out for some time; it could not be caused by the release of air trapped in her lungs.

Karla suffered damage from being choked by hands or perhaps the socks around her neck, but that was not what killed her. Dr. Case said it takes one or two minutes to strangle someone into unconsciousness, and another two or three minutes of strangulation to cause death. Attackers often assume their victims have been strangled fatally when they are, in fact, still alive.

Karla Brown was choked, but the cause of death was drowning.

That significantly changed the scenario of the crime Weber had developed, and it made him so angry he almost shook. Did that shatter the hope he shared with everyone who knew Karla that the violent explosion of the attack quickly rendered her dead or unconscious before she was plunged into the water? He developed that theory based partly on the evidence, and partly because the alternative was unbearable to him.

My God, he thought, had she known what was happening all along? Had she drowned after suffering all that had gone before?

Weber asked if Karla would have been aware of the final moments, and the doctor was able to give him some comfort. The foam occurred during shallow breathing, but Karla could have been unconscious or semiconscious; she probably was not aware of what was happening.

Dr. Case gave Weber a written report and he headed back to Edwardsville. As horrible as these details were, he thought, they really had little impact on the trial. The murder was "a black box" case—what really happened at the scene was unknown, as if locked inside a box no one could open. The exact details and sequence of the murderous events really had little to do with the verdict. The question for the trial was "who."

If Prante were convicted, the doctor's conclusions could be important at the sentencing. Weber could use them as aggravating factors that supported his plea for the death penalty. It was a portrayal of the events that certainly was "brutal and heinous," to use the words from the death-penalty law.

And, Weber thought, delivering a copy of the doctor's report at this late date might rattle the hell out of John Prante.

It certainly surprised his attorney, and Hawkins wasted no time in challenging the new evidence. Before opening statements in East Alton on Monday morning, June 27, Hawkins asked Judge Romani to suppress Dr. Case's conclusion that there was a sexual assault. In a closed hearing in Romani's chambers, Hawkins complained about getting the report just three days before trial and argued that the question of a sexual assault was for the jury to decide on the evidence. He certainly didn't want Weber waving that red flag in front of the jury in his opening statement.

Weber had to smile; Hawkins knew how Weber's philosophy on opening statements had evolved over the years. Weber originally applied the style he learned from Bob Trone, the master prosecutor in Madison County. Trone gave sparse openings that described the case in general and vague terms. Trone wanted the jurors to hear the case unfold through the witnesses. Weber later saw the opposite style from Morris Chapman, one of the region's leading lawyers on personal-injury cases. Chapman laid out every detail so the jury would understand how complicated the case would be and would have a realistic expectation of what the evidence would reveal. Weber had gravitated toward the latter style, and planned an opening in the Prante case that would be very long on details.

Weber was pacing in the small room as he responded to Hawkins. The prosecutor looked at the defendant and said, "Well, Judge, I think that, from the evidence of the crime scene of what Prante did, it is obvious that this was a sexual assault."

Unexpectedly, Prante interrupted from his chair in front of the judge's desk. "It wasn't," he said sternly.

Weber was taken aback; few defendants would argue with the prosecutor this way. Weber pulled Prante's chain again and spoke to him directly.

"It wasn't? Well, what was your purpose?"

"I wasn't there," Prante said slowly.

Weber turned away from the defendant, but rattled his cage some more. Weber told the judge that Prante's comments to Lee Barns about Karla's body the night before and the condition of the body certainly supported a conclusion that this was a sexual assault.

And then Weber decided to let Prante know his manhood would not escape without insult, either. "There will be no clinical evidence of rape, for one or more reasons, which Sherry Dalton may explain at a later time—no actual penetration." Weber wondered what Prante thought of testimony exposing his impotence in a case that focused on his violent nature.

Weber argued that Dr. Case had enough experience to offer her medical conclusion of a sexual assault and be cross-examined by Hawkins. Judge Romani permitted Weber to discuss the doctor's conclusion; and Hawkins could cross-examine her on it.

Hawkins then objected to Dr. Case's conclusion on the drowning, since Weber repeatedly had mentioned strangulation as the cause of death during jury selection. Weber responded that the doctor's report just was submitted on Friday, and Hawkins certainly could have interviewed her. The judge ruled for Weber again.

But Weber lost the next motions. The judge prohibited him from using physical evidence or a blackboard during his opening statement. Weber protested; he planned to display the barrel and some other items, and draw the pattern of the bite mark on the blackboard. But the judge ruled for Hawkins.

Hawkins also asked that Weber be prevented from using the statements of Dwayne or Patty Conway. Her account of the conversation between Prante and her husband was prohibited as hearsay evidence. Weber disagreed; Patty Conway's recollection of Prante's attempt to sway Dwayne would be an admission by Prante against his own interest, an exception to the hearsay rule. Her account of Dwayne's response was admissible, not for the truth of what he said, but just to report his answer.

Romani agreed; Weber could call Patty Conway as a witness.

When Hawkins turned to Dwayne Conway, even Weber agreed with the defense. Weber still didn't know whether he would call Dwayne as a witness, and it would be improper to refer to his statements in opening statements.

As the lawyers headed toward the courtroom for the long-awaited start of the trial, one last deal was struck for two exceptions to the rule excluding witnesses from the courtroom. Agent Randy Rushing would be allowed to sit at the table with Weber in return for Prante's sister, Jo Ellen Brady, being allowed in the courtroom.

Now it was time for Karla Brown to get her day in court.

PART FOUR

Beyond a
Reasonable Doubt

Chapter 16

As the jurors raised their right hands and took the oath, Don Weber felt the familiar tightness. Legal jeopardy had just attached to the murder trial of John Prante. If there was a foul-up now, the prosecution didn't get another chance. You get just one bite of the apple.

Weber scanned the packed courtroom. So many people had turned out to see the long-awaited finale to this tragic tale. Moving the trial to the East Alton Municipal Center clearly had been a good idea. None of the courtrooms in the Edwardsville courthouse could have accommodated the crowd. The ten rows of benches on each side of the main aisle seated the audience comfortably. And the modern courtroom—paneled, carpeted, and softly lighted— was a welcome change from the sometimes harsh atmosphere of the old courtrooms in Edwardsville.

He felt nervous as he stepped before the jurors to make his opening statement. It would mark the last turn in a long road he prayed would lead to justice for Karla Brown—and for John Prante. A lot of people had a lot riding on how well Weber did his job pulling together five years of investigation—some incredibly innovative techniques, some bumbled leads, thousands of hours of hard work, and a dizzying series of details and characters.

The prosecutor opened by explaining that he would present 150 pieces of evidence and dozens of witnesses, all converging to prove one thing: "That on June 21, 1978, about two miles from this courtroom, that person— right there—murdered Karla Brown."

Weber pointed at John Prante again, taking this trial up

close and personal right from the start. It was not about legal theories anymore; it was about real people and real pain and real crimes and real violence. And the man who was responsible was sitting right there. He was cleaned up now. He had shaved the mangy beard and trimmed a little off the frizzy hair. He was wearing a light blue three-piece suit, not a "Big Bamboo" T-shirt and a ball cap. But he was the killer nonetheless, and Weber would prove it.

The prosecutor looked for a reaction to his personal allegations against the defendant. Instead, he got the calm gaze that was Prante's trademark. There was no anger, no resentment. Not even the smirk Weber had seen so many times on the guys who thought they were so tough. Weber had a hard time reading Prante. There wasn't much light in those eyes, and that made them less useful as windows into what was going on behind them.

Weber turned back to the jury to explain that Prante's own mistakes had helped bring him to trial. And then Weber linked the two major pieces of evidence.

"Three days after the killing, that person—right in that chair—was talking about bite marks on the shoulder of the victim. The evidence will show that the police didn't know about the bite marks; that the pathologist who did the autopsy didn't know about the bite marks; and in fact, it wasn't until two years later that the law enforcement community learned that there were bite marks on the body of the victim."

He stroked the jurors by explaining that he had placed a premium on intelligence as he chose them. He hoped to plant the idea that anyone who wasn't convinced Prante was guilty at the end of the trial was a blockhead.

He also sent the jurors a message that most of the physical evidence and the witnesses who weren't pivotal would be presented by his assistant, Keith Jensen. That let the jurors know they could ease back a little at those times, and then listen up when Weber took over. It would be a long trial, and Weber and the jurors would need an occasional break while the drudgery continued.

That was an advantage the prosecution had over Hawkins, who was doing a solo in front of the jury. He was assisted by Vicky Hackett, a secretary from the public defender's office who was helping with the files and other details. But Hawkins was on his own in front of the jury, and that would be wearying.

Then Weber began a long, detailed description of his case, telling almost the whole story from the moment John Prante first saw Karla Brown. Weber used every opportunity to personalize the evidence, linking the victim and killer as directly as possible.

"There will be a ten-gallon barrel that Prante stuffed Karla Brown's head and shoulders into after he filled it with water. There will be the cords that Prante used to tie up her hands. We will present the blouse that she had on, and the socks that were tied around her neck. We will present photographs of the crime scene, and we will present sketches demonstrating the relationship between Karla Brown's house, Dwayne Conway's house, and the Laundromat where Prante parked his car in the afternoon."

Not only were those items important for the jurors, but Weber knew it would play on Prante's mind to know the trappings of his crime would be hauled into court for everyone to see.

Weber explained that there would be no innocent way for Prante to know what he knew, when he knew it. The cops allowed no one—especially "some bum off the streets"—into the house after Karla's body was found. The press reported only a few details, not the specific facts Prante knew. Prante's use of those explanations was preposterous.

The prosecutor ticked off his evidence, point by point, going over some facts in great detail and beginning to offer his interpretations. Some of it clearly was argumentative, and Weber was surprised when it failed to draw the expected objections from Hawkins. Maybe he was anxious to hear as much as possible about the prosecution's strategy. The more Weber pushed the limits without objection, the more latitude he decided to take. Before long, Weber was making most of his argumentative points that were supposed to be reserved for final statements.

Weber explained the motive for this murder through Lee Barns's memory that Prante "was particularly impressed with Karla Brown, and he was particularly impressed with a certain part of her, which I will let Barns describe to you. Prante was more than impressed; he was obsessed with Karla Brown's beauty."

There was the essence, Weber thought. The reporters packed into the front row recognized that, too, and scribbled furiously to catch that last phrase.

Weber then focused on how Prante was caught, naming Alva Busch and Spencer Bond as real heroes, and nodding toward the expertise of Lowell Levine, Homer Campbell, and an FBI expert who helped formulate a new plan of attack.

Weber even explained that he had not decided whether to make a deal on Dwayne Conway's criminal charge so he could be called as a witness. Again, no objection from Hawkins. Weber told the jury how Patty Conway listened to the gabfest in her trailer, and heard Prante utter the immortal line, "One of us is going to the gas chamber."

As Weber began to wrap the statement, he offered his own theory; "Prante went over around 11, murdered her, came back and sat on the porch between 12 and 1 to see if her boyfriend was going to come home for lunch. When the boyfriend didn't come home for lunch, Prante moved his car to a getaway place, went back into the house, and cleaned up the crime scene.

"Prante says he was at Karla Brown's house at a time when we know she was dead. And he knows about the bite marks. And he knows about her being strangled. And he knows about her hands being tied up. Those facts are inconsistent with any conclusion other than the fact that he is a vicious murderer."

This was a murder that didn't have to happen, Weber told the jurors, "except for Prante's feelings of inadequacy with women and except for the fact that he couldn't control his own lust for a girl who wouldn't invite him over to a party."

Weber added one last nod toward the death penalty by telling the jury he was confident they would agree the evidence proved Prante guilty of "this very vicious and heinous crime."

Weber felt drained as he returned to his seat after almost ninety minutes before the jury. The prosecutor was anxious to hear how Hawkins would defend his client. Weber was quite surprised when Hawkins said, "At this time, I will reserve my opening statement, Your Honor."

Weber questioned that tactic. The jury had heard an incredible amount of incriminating details about Prante, but not a word from the defense to rebut it or put it into some less damning perspective. If that was Hawkins's strategy, however, Weber certainly wouldn't disagree.

Hawkins had decided some time ago to save his opening until just before the start of his evidence, to help the jury keep track of the defense case. And Hawkins hadn't heard anything in Weber's statement that was unexpected or required a change in plans.

Hawkins looked at his client. Prante obviously was a little more nervous than he had been before. But he still was calm for a man facing such an ordeal.

The prosecution's first witness was Bill Redfern from the Wood River police, who testified at great length about the scene in the basement of Karla's house. He explained that the swinging saloon doors obscured the view into the laundry room where Karla's body was found; no one could have glimpsed the scene. No civilians had been allowed into the house, anyway. This first witness had eliminated one source of the details Prante knew.

Weber had learned long ago from Bob Trone that it was best to get the physical evidence introduced at the beginning. The evidence process was relatively boring, and best done early so the jurors wouldn't be put to sleep later in the case. With that in mind, Weber had Jensen put Redfern through a long series of questions and answers to introduce more than ninety photographs—one by one—showing the evidence in the basement, the interior and exterior of the house, the spot of blood on the doorjamb, the neighborhood as seen from Karla's, and the aerial views of the houses of Karla Brown and Dwayne Conway sitting so close together.

Redfern produced the photo of Karla with her bowling buddies; she was wearing the sweater found on her body. Weber wanted the jurors to see this shot so they would associate that sweater with a smiling, happy, pretty blonde—alive.

All of the photos were admitted without objections from Hawkins.

To Donna and Terry Judson, the testimony seemed rather tedious until Redfern described photograph number 3-48 as "a tampon which was on the coffee table." Donna was stunned; she had not yet heard about that intimate detail and the implication sickened her. Had Karla suffered that degradation, too? Terry felt revulsion and wondered, who are we dealing with here? What kind of man is this?

Redfern then produced the photos of Karla's body, including the close-ups of the injuries and the way she was tied. Hawkins came alive now; he objected to several of them as redundant and too gruesome, and Judge Romani called a recess to confer with the lawyers in his chambers. Romani admitted some of the pictures over Hawkins's objections, and the defender withdrew challenges to some others as the prosecutors explained what they portrayed and why they were essential.

The judge then turned to three prints of the photo Redfern took at the first autopsy. It showed the right side of Karla's neck and chin, with Dr. Parks's fingertips visible as he pulled Karla's chin back to exhibit the bruises from the strangulation. Redfern hadn't know it at the time, but that difficult shot was recording evidence that would help solve the case.

As the judge reviewed the photos, Weber began to get nervous; he didn't like the direction this was going. Judge

Romani wondered if those shots weren't repetitive and cumulative.

"These are the famous bite-mark photos," Jensen explained.

"The famous bite-mark photos?" the judge asked with a good-natured hint of mocking.

"*The* famous," Jensen responded with a smile. "These are the photos Dr. Parks is going to be shown. In the photos, he is indicating wounds on the head to the photographer, and the wounds to the chin area. But he misses the bite marks."

Weber couldn't restrain himself. The judge didn't seem to be taking Jensen seriously. Weber looked intensely at the judge.

"This is crucial. This is *the* picture in this case," Weber explained. He wondered if losing that shot as evidence might not be *the* ball game.

Hawkins objected again to three versions of the same photo, and the judge added, "They are the same photo."

Weber was beginning to sweat as he saw this vital evidence start slipping away. "Well, no, they're not." He pointed to the first in the series. "This one is the way the cops saw it in 1978; that's all they did with it."

He pointed to an enlarged shot showing the bite marks more clearly, and explained that the experts had used that one to establish the existence of the bite marks. Then he showed the photo that was the largest blow-up that could be produced without any loss of detail.

"We didn't do this on any of the other photos. But these are the ones where the process of the bite-mark technology gets to be important. We are not just doing it to duplicate this photo, but to show the jury how you go from one picture to another, and finally to the one that you really want."

The judge deferred; he would decide on those photos when the experts testified. As the crucial pictures were put on hold, Weber swallowed hard. He hated having that dangling over his head while he presented the rest of the case. Losing those photos as evidence would weaken the bite-mark testimony dramatically, and would be damned frustrating after all that hard work. The pictures were essential for the jury to understand how the marks were missed in 1978—when only John Prante knew about them—and then discovered by Dr. Campbell in 1982.

Back in the courtroom, Redfern narrated the videotape taken at Karla's house by the police. The camera led the jury through the upstairs and down to the basement, where it panned across the couch, the TV trays, the blood spatters, and other important bits of evidence. The jurors were led into the laundry room and shown the barrel. But, just as the camera turned to where the body lay, the screen went blank. Redfern explained that the batteries failed; Weber shook his head at the first stumble in 1978.

Redfern also had prepared a chart of the neighborhood and the distances between the buildings, demonstrating the proximity between the important landmarks. From Karla's back gate to the rear of Conway's house was only thirty-six feet—a quick dash for a man in a hurry. From Conway's front porch to the Laundromat around the corner was a mere 232 feet, an easy walk but far enough away to stash the killer's car out of sight.

Hawkins's cross-examination provided a quick tip to Weber that the defender had been counseled well by his experts. Hawkins wanted to know about the camera and the film Redfern used to photograph the neck wounds. Then Hawkins asked, "The main focus of these pictures is the wounds of Karla Brown, is it not? That's what you were focusing on?"

"On the closer photographs, yes, sir."

"You were looking to show the nature of the wounds and the extent of the wounds, is that correct?"

"Yes, sir."

"Okay. The wounds to the head?"

"Yes, sir."

Weber felt a little deflated as the attack on the photos and bite marks began. Hawkins was setting up his experts so they could argue that the bite-mark images were inconclusive because the camera was focused on the gash on

Karla's chin—not on her neck and collarbone. That would force the "battle of the experts" Weber hoped might be avoided. The defense was not going to roll over and play dead on the bite marks.

Crime Scene Technician Alva W. Busch was the second witness. Weber was surprised when Busch told the jury that, in addition to handling hundreds of burglaries and other crimes, he had investigated more than 200 homicides. Alva has been a busy boy the last five years, Weber thought.

Busch had just started a detailed account of his investigation at Karla's house on the night of the murder when Judge Romani recessed for the day. First thing on Tuesday, June 28, Busch was back to introduce some of the props Weber hoped to put to good use.

The blood- and water-soaked cushion from the couch, where Weber still believed Karla had struggled for her life.

The blue jeans found near Karla's body.

The scrapings from under her fingernails that Busch said showed she had fought her assailant.

The vial of blood drawn from her body.

The sweater that was all Karla wore, and was buttoned tight around her neck.

The white electrical cord that bound her hands.

The Mr. Coffee carafe that carried water in the vain attempt to revive Karla.

And finally, the ten-gallon barrel.

As Busch identified each item, Weber carefully stacked it on a table right next to the defense table—and next to John Prante. It was another sign to the jury that the residue from this vicious crime belonged to this man. Every juror who looked at the evidence could see John Prante right behind it—literally and symbolically.

Weber placed the barrel there very deliberately and then folded Karla's sweater dramatically over the edge, a bit of showmanship to remind the jury of the grotesque way Karla's body was found.

The time had come for a special demonstration, unlike

anything else Weber had presented in a case. He still wasn't sure what it meant, but he found it interesting enough to let the jury see it, especially since Al Busch had worked so long and hard on it.

Busch demonstrated his theory of how Prante had cut the cords around Karla's wrists to produce the leftover sections of wire Busch found on the couch. To help with the demonstration, Busch enlisted bailiff Michael Donohoo, another touch Weber enjoyed. Donohoo was a fascinating character so appropriate for the Madison County courthouse. He was thirty-one and the son of a Democratic Party leader from Wood River. Donohoo's solid streak of conservatism often placed him and the Republican Weber on the same side of the issues, such as capital punishment. Donohoo also was amazingly well read in history, military campaigns, music, and films. He was particularly fond of Cajun culture and food, and traveled so often to Louisiana that he had made friends with some well-known musicians in that area. Donohoo was quite the connoisseur, Weber thought.

But Donohoo's duties were simple here. In the center of the courtroom, he stood with his hands behind his back as Alva Busch tied him with white electrical cord. Busch cut off the ends of the cord and split it down the middle to produce separate lengths virtually identical to what had bound Karla.

As he tied up the compliant Democrat, Busch explained, "I feel that the killer, at one time, tied a slip knot, like this, in one end, placed it over the victim's wrist, and for some reason decided it was not secure enough, or wanted to tie it again. He put the knife through in this fashion, and pulled it through."

As Busch cut through the cord, the two pieces fell into his other hand. One straight piece, the other with a simple loop in the middle.

Interesting, Weber thought again, but what the hell did it mean?

The demonstration was having a profound effect on Donna Judson, however. It was terribly difficult to watch;

for the first time, she began to see these things happening to Karla. The attack on her sister was becoming a more visual experience, and it was painful to witness through her mind's eye.

Donna thought again about her role in the trial. She was a silent witness as a stand-in for Karla, another pretty blonde about Karla's size; the jurors could look at Donna and put her in the place of the 200-pound bailiff Busch was tying up. Donna also hoped the jurors could see, by her presence, that Karla was a real person who was loved and missed by her family.

Weber handled the next several witnesses to be sure the jury understood a couple of vital points. Commander Ralph Skinner and the other officers at the crime scene confirmed that no one knew there were bite marks then, and never heard them mentioned prior to 1980, when the expert's opinion came down. The cops backed up Redfern's testimony that no civilians were in that house, and Skinner explained that details Prante told his friends had not been released to the media then.

Weber was anxious to call the next witness for the jurors. Sergeant Chuck Nunn was the first eyewitness to place Prante at the scene; Nunn identified his old barbecuing acquaintance as the man standing in Dwayne Conway's yard when the police arrived at Karla's house. Prante was wearing a cap, had longer hair and probably some growth of beard. Weber was glad to get a description of a shabbier-looking defendant than the one sitting there in the suit.

On cross-examination, Hawkins tried to weaken Nunn's testimony by pointing out that he never mentioned Prante in the police reports. It was a valid criticism, Weber thought, showing some oversights by the police. On redirect, Nunn explained that he didn't think Prante's presence was important until quite some time later. After all, Nunn had been one of the detectives on the case, so it wasn't like the cops didn't know Prante was there.

Weber reminded the jury that the body in the basement

had been a real person by calling Jamie Hale to talk about how happy and excited Karla was as she worked on her new house. Weber also used Jamie to explain what Karla would have done if confronted by an assailant. "She definitely would have put up a fight," Jamie said.

She described her phone conversation with Karla about 9:30 that morning, and how she got no answer when she called Karla that afternoon. And then Weber stumbled; without knowing Jamie's answer, he asked who had told her about Karla's death.

"Jack Meyers."

Damn, Weber thought. That was not a name he wanted invoked in this trial. Weber ended his questioning quickly, but Hawkins repeated Meyers's name by asking what time he had told Jamie about Karla; about 9 that evening was the answer.

Weber focused attention back on Prante with a simple comparison from Jamie Hale in a rapid-fire series of questions on redirect examination.

"Did Jack Meyers give you a lot of details about the crime, or did he just say she was murdered?"

"He just said she was murdered."

"Did he tell you she had been strangled?"

"No. I asked him how he knew."

"What did he say?"

"He said he called her house."

"Okay. Did he say she had bite marks on her collarbone or on her shoulder?"

"No."

"Did he say that her pants were pulled down around her ankles?"

"No."

"Did he say she was found curled up in the basement?"

"No."

That ought to close that door. Meyers didn't know the details, but Prante did.

Weber called Debbie LaTempt Davis, whose grief still was obvious as she described how close she and Karla were—"She was like a sister to me." Debbie identified

Karla's sweater and explained that she never wore it in warm weather or while she was working around the house.

Debbie found it hard to look at Prante. She felt such rage toward him, but she also felt intense fear. She wondered if he was watching from the basement when she knocked on Karla's door that morning. She found it hard to look in his eyes, knowing that they might have watched her that day.

As Debbie told the jury about her call from Karla "on the day that she died," Weber was struck by her choice of words. Debbie probably could not say "murdered" or "killed"; those words hurt too much. It was almost unbearable that Karla had died, and thinking about how was beyond the limit.

Weber felt even more sympathy for Debbie as she described stopping by Karla's about 11 o'clock, and being surprised that no one answered her knocks at the front or rear doors. Debbie told the jury, "I called her all afternoon, but she never answered." Weber shuddered at hearing the words of Karla's dear friend again. He almost could feel her pain as a terrifying image flashed through his mind. The phone was ringing upstairs, and Karla's body was submerged in the barrel in the basement.

Neil Hawkins had no questions for Debbie Davis. That was the only way for the defense to handle that witness.

David Hart's parents, Evelyn and Robert, were next. Evelyn Hart spoke softly in a voice that still carried the grief as she described calling Karla between 10 and 11 A.M. They talked for less than a minute when Karla said she wanted to ask her soon-to-be-mother-in-law a question.

"And, with that, she said, 'Evelyn, someone is at the door. I'll call you back.'"

Weber was struck by the poignancy in Evelyn Hart's voice as she remembered those last words.

And then she wounded Weber again as she said she went to David's later on the day "the accident happened."

Just like Debbie Davis, Weber thought; Evelyn Hart couldn't speak the words, either.

Evelyn and Robert Hart told the jury that, as they arrived at their son's new house that night, they saw two men on the porch next door. The Harts couldn't identify the men, but Weber knew the inference was clear for everyone.

The defense attorney let all of these witnesses off with few questions or none at all.

Then Weber called a witness who would be a big surprise in a little package. Eric Moses, who was six years old when he saw a man and woman in front of Karla Brown's house that morning, was now a confident and articulate young man of eleven. He took the stand coolly and had no trouble using an aerial photograph to locate the house where he had lived before it was sold to David Hart and Karla Brown. Eric and his grandmother, Edna Moses, were driving to a nearby dentist's office that morning when they turned around in Eric's old driveway. He had unshakable memories of the woman and man he saw standing in that driveway about 10:45 P.M.

"She was about five-one and was wearing a shirt, sort of a short-sleeve shirt with flowers on it." Eric was sure the shirt wasn't the striped sweater Weber showed him.

The man was "sort of heavy weight," and five-eleven, maybe six-feet tall. He had a mustache and short beard, and was wearing glasses, a white T-shirt, and blue jeans.

Good descriptions, Weber thought, and certainly within the tolerance of a child's memory of the appearances of Karla Brown and John Prante.

Then Eric added something that surprised Weber.

"They were sort of talking. And then a yellow dog—sort of yellow, goldish dog or whatever—came out. And then the man yelled at the dog. And then the girl sort of got mad at him."

"Mad at who?"

"The man."

"Okay."

" 'Cause I think that was her dog, and I guess she sort of yelled at the man."

Had that been another factor in the deadly tension that morning? Was Prante such a total loser that he would yell at a woman's dog while he was trying to hit on her for sex?

With Eric offering such details and specific recollections, Weber took a chance.

"I want you to look around the courtroom and tell me if you see the person that you saw in the driveway."

"Well, not really."

Weber pushed. "Do you see anyone who resembles him?"

Eric pointed across the room toward the table where John Prante and Neil Hawkins sat. "Well, let's see. He does and he does."

Prante and Hawkins. Not bad, Weber thought. But then Eric sent the courtroom into laughter by pointing at Weber.

"And you, sort of do, if you were a little taller."

And then at Agent Randy Rushing.

"And so does he."

Even Weber chuckled as the laughs echoed through the courtroom. Four guys with dark hair and mustaches who, Eric added gently, were "kind of heavy weight." It wasn't the answer Weber would have chosen, but it would do.

Hawkins laughed, too; he had seen it coming. As soon as Weber asked Eric for the identification, Hawkins remembered a photograph of Prante that Hawkins thought resembled Don Weber.

But when Weber ended his questioning, Hawkins knew he had to act. He requested a closed session in the judge's chambers to challenge Eric's testimony. Hawkins wanted it stricken because of the boy's age and the prosecution's failure to establish him as a competent witness. Weber disagreed sharply; Eric had been competent beyond any doubt with specific and complete recollections.

Judge Romani agreed with Weber. Under the law, a witness fourteen or older was presumed competent, and one younger than that could be proved competent by his conduct and recollections on the stand. Romani ruled that Hawkins could argue to the jury about young Eric's competency and the weight due his testimony, but the motion to strike it was denied.

On cross, Hawkins asked only a few questions to check some details. There wasn't much he could do with this witness, either.

Eric was followed to the stand by his grandmother, Edna Moses. She told the jury that the man and woman were standing back in the driveway, close to the garage at the rear of the house. Their descriptions matched Karla and Prante pretty well, and Mrs. Moses had another interesting recollection.

"The girl turned completely around and started walking toward the house. The man started to turn around, and that's when I lost them. I don't know what happened after that because I was backing out of the driveway."

"He started to turn around and go which way?"

"Oh, I figure he was following the girl."

That supported the new testimony from Eric. Weber wondered again if Karla stormed back into the house after some confrontation in the driveway, only to be followed into her home by the killer. Had the brutal clash begun with an exchange of words over the dog?

Edna Moses also offered Weber a comment on her grandson's ability to recall.

"He has a fantastic memory."

Hawkins had her describe the man again—almost six feet tall, wearing a light, perhaps white, T-shirt. She couldn't see whether anything was written on the shirt. Hawkins could do little more than challenge the accuracy of the descriptions in the face of such solid testimony.

Weber called another Edna—Edna Vancil—to the stand next to tell her story about watching John Prante at Dwayne Conway's house on the day of the murder. She was Conway's aunt, and Weber hoped that would establish immediate credibility which would overcome slight contradictions. Mrs. Vancil said Annie Tweed—her niece and Conway's sister—got a ride to Mrs. Vancil's with Prante that morning, and stayed until about 3:30 in the afternoon. But Weber expected Annie Tweed to testify later that she drove her car there and stayed until after the police had arrived much later. She saw Prante there after the police arrived, and well after the time her aunt thought Prante had left.

Weber hoped those small details would not cause the jurors to doubt the rest of Mrs. Vancil's story about Prante and Dwayne Conway smoking pot and drinking on the porch, and then disappearing between 11 and noon. They returned to the porch about noon, and stayed there until Prante left about 3 o'clock.

Weber thought her explanation for knowing the times for the various events that day by linking them to the schedule for her soap operas would ring true for the jurors. There was a certain all-American charm in the image of this large woman sitting in her living room watching TV soap operas while keeping track of activities in the neighborhood through the window. It was too natural to be anything but perfectly believable.

Hawkins asked Mrs. Vancil why she hadn't given the information about Prante to Sergeant Eldon McEuen when he interviewed her on the night of the murder. He hadn't asked about Prante, she said.

Hawkins also asked about Prante's car, and she remembered the red Volkswagen. Hawkins pressed, asking if she was positive; she said yes. Those questions surprised Weber and suggested that he should watch for something to come up about the car later.

Weber recalled Ralph Skinner to offer the first testimony about an incriminating statement from John Prante's own mouth. Three days after the killing, Prante said he had been at Conway's only briefly at 8:30 that morning. Prante claimed he had not seen Conway again until 6 o'clock that evening at Harold Pollard's house, when Conway informed Prante of Karla's death. For the first time, Weber thought, the jury heard Prante lying to cover his tracks.

Hawkins stressed that it had been five years since the interview, and that Skinner couldn't remember all of the details without checking his report. The defender also had Skinner say he did not remember Sergeant Nunn mentioning that Prante was at Conway's house that evening.

That was one of the problems with this case, Weber thought. It had been five years, and the witnesses' memories hadn't improved with age. If Hawkins drilled in on such lapses, he might damage the prosecution's witnesses significantly.

The day ended with two experts from the state's crime lab. Larry Lorsbach, the lab director, testified as an expert in tool marks; he concluded that the electrical cord binding Karla was one length that someone split in two. He matched the ends through microscopic examination, which showed that a single-edged instrument, such as a knife, had been used. A tool such as snips was ruled out because the ends of the cuts were not pinched.

Dennis Aubuchon, a forensic serologist at the lab, testified that his tests showed Karla Brown had Type A blood, and all of the blood found at the scene was consistent with hers. The samples taken from the smudges on the frame of the back door and the gate were too small to get a test result. And he was unable to find any evidence of semen on the couch cushion.

After two days of testimony, Weber felt relatively comfortable with the way the case was shaping up. But he had a vague sense of uneasiness over what was coming. Hawkins was doing his homework, and Weber was beginning to fear that the showdown between the experts could go the wrong way. Would all of that fabulous bite-mark evidence go for naught because it had been missed at the beginning?

Chapter 17

David Hart appeared nervous as he walked across the courtroom to take the stand as the first witness on Wednesday, June 29. Don Weber watched Hart closely, and saw the glance he shot at John Prante. The glare in the "if looks could kill" manner made it more than apparent that David Hart hated the man sitting calmly at the defense table. And Weber certainly couldn't blame David for that.

Weber had talked to David for the first time the week before the trial, and sized him up as a complex young man. He was tall, slim, and muscled, quite good-looking in an almost classic way. Sandy hair and fine features. Weber had met David's lovely fiancée. She had to be the most understanding woman in the world; she accepted David's decision to delay a wedding until this trial was over, and showed no jealousy over Karla's memory or the relationship that had existed between David and Karla.

Weber pegged David as a strong man, physically and emotionally. He was a Vietnam veteran and had seen some ghastly things during the war. He probably still carried a lot of that with him. And it was obvious he still carried the pain from the vicious murder of his first fiancée; Weber could see it in David's eyes. Weber wondered if David ever allowed himself a final, cleansing explosion of grief; if he hadn't experienced that release, he still was a volcano. That could make him unpredictable under the emotional trauma he was about to endure on the witness stand, and Weber wasn't sure how David would do.

He provided Weber with some valuable information during their interview. Because of his experiences in Vietnam, David could offer an estimate on how long Karla had been dead by the state of rigor mortis; David put it at six or seven hours. That placed the time of death at sometime between 11 o'clock and noon, and was the most reliable information yet on that point. Weber could use that information to help the medical experts with their testimony and, more important, it fell within the time set by Edna Vancil.

As the third day of trial started, David sat down in the witness chair and folded his hands nervously in front of him; the tension was evident in his eyes as Weber took the questioning directly to the night before the murder. Weber handed People's Exhibit 36—a photograph—to David and asked him to describe it.

"We had just moved into that bedroom, and that was the bed we slept in the night before . . ." His voice trailed off.

There it was again, Weber thought. David couldn't say the words, either.

Weber showed David the colorful, short-sleeved sweater, and he said sadly, "That's Karla's." Weber handed him a picture of Karla in the sweater and asked if he knew when it was taken. David looked at it for a few seconds, and then tilted his head back. The tears began to roll down his cheeks as he said, "I don't remember." He continued to cry as he explained that Karla wore that sweater only in the winter, and that she never worked around the house in it.

David still was struggling to maintain his composure as he began to describe the events leading to the discovery of her body.

"I took Tom downstairs, and when I got to the foot of the stairs, I noticed—I noticed blood all over the floor."

David had begun to sob, and the words were hard to push out.

"I really didn't notice the disarray of the rest of the room until I entered the room and looked up, and I just saw that there was blood all over the couch and there was—everything was—just kind of strewn all over, you know."

David was crying harder and Weber knew the heart-breaking scene would have a great impact on the jury. Once again, this case was becoming very personal. The jurors would see the real results of a murder like this. It wasn't just about the body and the evidence and the murder scene—it was about the end of a young life, and the grief and loss left behind.

Donna and Terry Judson could feel the pain as they watched the young man who had been so close to joining their family.

"And I knew something had happened, but I didn't know what. So, I—I remember I said, 'God, what's happened?' I thought maybe Karla had cut herself and that's why she wasn't home. So I turned around and was going to run upstairs, and when I did—we got a little, like a little laundry room to the left there—and I glanced in the room—and I saw her."

As the last words erupted from him, David buried his face in his hands and began to sob uncontrollably. Weber called for a recess and, after a few seconds, David stood up slowly and hitched up his slacks. Donna Judson thought he looked emotionally drained. But Weber saw David flash an even angrier glare at Prante through the tears. As David left the witness stand—his eyes still fixed on Prante—Weber wondered if he would have to step in front of David to prevent a very understandable mistake. But David walked past Prante and left the courtroom. The defendant returned David's stare, but showed no reaction.

David had regained his composure when he returned to the stand twenty minutes later, but the anger and grief still were evident in his face. He recounted the rest of the scene—even the way he found Karla's body in the barrel—with a steady voice and a resolution to get through this for her sake. He was able to describe the stiffness in the joints of Karla's body as he laid her on the floor. Weber knew that description was hard for David,

but it would help set the time of death later. Weber
showed him the picture that included the bite marks, and
asked if Karla had any bruises or abrasions on her body
before that.

"No, she had—her skin was real clean. She had a real
good complexion. She didn't have any scratches. She
didn't have any complexion problems or marks on her at
all ... She never had a bruise, nothing, on her."

Weber was struck by the poignancy once again. David
almost seemed to be an artist talking about a work of art.
Karla was indeed loved by these people, and especially
by this man who remembered her so perfectly.

There were two more points that would make Karla
real for the jury. Weber asked about her dental bridge
with the false teeth.

"She wore that plate twenty-four hours a day, three-
hundred and sixty-five days a year," David recalled. "She
wouldn't hardly take it out, even for me. I remember one
time, we were going to a party and she broke one of the
teeth off. We had to stop and get some Crazy Glue and
glue it back on. Otherwise, she wouldn't go. She just
would not be seen without the partial plate."

That was new information for Weber, too. He asked if
Karla might have taken out the plate while she was working around the house.

"No. She slept in it. She wore it constantly."

There was no innocent explanation for it to be in the
cup.

Point two. Weber asked, "If Karla had been in a confrontation with someone bigger than her in the basement,
how do you think she would have reacted?"

With an air of defiance, David responded, "She would
have fought. She would have fought and tried to get
away."

Weber drew the testimony to a close by having David
explain that he learned about the bite marks from newspaper stories just before the exhumation.

Then Weber pointed at Prante and asked, "Did that

man, sitting right there in the blue suit, get in your house from the time you got home until you left?"

"No, no," David said angrily as he looked at Prante.

Neil Hawkins had no cross-examination for David Hart; it would have been counterproductive to question him at all. David was a very effective witness for the prosecution. He was believable and his pain was heart-rending. That kind of testimony got to jurors, and Hawkins knew questions by the defense would only make it worse.

The primary purpose for calling Tom Fiegenbaum as a witness was to establish that he was wearing sunglasses that afternoon. In the conversation with Spencer Bond, Prante described watching David and another guy wearing glasses pull into the driveway. If Fiegenbaum wore glasses, it was another point proving Prante had been at Conway's house at 5:30. In an earlier interview with Weber, Fiegenbaum hadn't remembered wearing glasses until Weber asked if it was sunny that day. When Fiegenbaum took the stand after David Hart, he still didn't offer the recollection about the sunglasses; Weber had to prod him again. Sometimes such small points were very difficult to get into the record.

But Weber also had Fiegenbaum add to the growing evidence that no one, especially Prante, was in the house after the police arrived, and that no one mentioned bite marks that night.

Lee Barns had been brought up from Louisiana on Tuesday to testify about John Prante's instantaneous and lustful obsession with Karla Brown—damaging and incriminating testimony. Barns was put up at the Lewis & Clark Motel in Wood River and given $100 in expense money—four days at the standard per diem of $25. Before he testified on Wednesday, he told Weber he had blown all of the money buying rounds in a tavern the night before. Weber couldn't believe it, but reluctantly gave Barns enough money to tide him over until he could be dispatched back to Louisiana.

And Barns then asked, "What do you want me to say on the stand?" Weber caught the implication, but shook his head and answered sharply, "Just tell the truth, Lee. Just tell the truth."

On the stand, Barns explained that he knew Karla from high school, and then drew Prante right into the fray by recounting the conversation with Karla in front of Conway's house on the night of the moving party.

"Did Prante talk to her?"

"Yeah. I believe I introduced him to her."

All right, Weber thought. Prante talking to Karla during an evening of smoking marijuana and drinking with his buddies. The incriminating circumstances were beginning to accumulate.

"How did he react in the state he was in that day?"

"Normal."

Weber couldn't let a straight line like that pass.

"Okay. What's normal for John Prante?"

Hawkins's objection was sustained, but Weber enjoyed a potshot the jury was sure to catch.

"What did Prante say about Karla?"

"How good she looked."

"What in particular was he impressed with?"

Hawkins objected again. Overruled, this time.

"Her body."

"What part of her body?"

"Specifically?"

"Right. Use the words Prante used."

Hawkins objected again on relevance. Overruled again.

"Her chest."

"Did he make more than one comment about it?"

"I believe so."

"Had you been out with John when he was around other good-looking girls?"

Hawkins objected. "That has no basis, Your Honor."

Weber responded, "Judge, the basis is going to show that Prante was more taken with her than other girls."

Hawkins snapped, "Your Honor, I don't want Mr. Weber making a speech."

The judge invited the lawyers into his chambers to argue without the jury. Hawkins complained that Weber was attempting to prejudice the jury against Prante by bringing in facts that had no relevance to the case.

"I think the defendant's main objection here is that it's too relevant and too important," Weber shot back indignantly. "You talk about prejudice. In one sense, every piece of evidence we have presented in this case is prejudiced against the defendant because it shows that he's a murderer."

Weber explained that the point of Barns's testimony was that Prante got more excited about Karla than other women; it went right to the motive for this killing. Weber assured the judge there would be no discussions of other incidents with other women. Judge Romani overruled Hawkins again, but reminded Weber of the limit on the testimony.

Before returning to the courtroom, Hawkins fired one more shot and asked Romani to prohibit Weber from stacking evidence directly in front of Prante. "I don't think the court theatrics are necessary."

The judge was surprised. "In front of the defendant? Be careful with placing the exhibits in front of the defendant, Mr. Weber."

Weber resisted the urge to respond with a mock, "Moi?" and just said through a grin, "Do I do that?"

Back in the courtroom, Weber drew from Barns that Prante never got too excited about women he had just met.

"How about on this occasion?"

"It was different."

"Was he excited about Karla Brown?"

"He seemed to be so."

Prante made repeated comments about Karla throughout the evening and on the ride home. Weber tried to get Barns to quote Prante's despicable description of Karla's "nice, big boobs," but Barns wasn't willing to say it in court.

"Was he talking about a part of her body?"

"Her whole body."

Barns said Prante was "upset, irritated, something like that," when an invitation to the moving party failed to materialize.

Then Weber drew out something Barns revealed in an interview a few minutes before he took the stand.

"Were you ever at a party at Spencer Bond's with Prante?"

"Yeah, all the time."

"Did he talk about the murder?"

"Yeah."

The lawyers were back in Judge Romani's chambers as quickly as Hawkins could raise his objection to the surprise testimony. This conversation between Barns and Prante had not been disclosed and should be barred, Hawkins insisted. Weber explained that the evidence came from Barns just fifteen minutes earlier. While being questioned by Weber during a recess, Barns said he was at a party at Bond's with Prante after the murder, and Prante said Karla Brown's body had bite marks on it. The new evidence was corroborated by the Whites and the Bonds. Weber said Barns's comment should not be suppressed as "intentional nondisclosure" because the prosecution just learned about it. The defense had the same opportunity to interview the witness, Weber pointed out.

The judge wanted a few minutes to reflect on the situation and gave Hawkins that time to interview Barns.

When they met again in chambers a few minutes later, Judge Romani struck Barns's new statement as "a direct admission by the defendant and taking the defendant by surprise." The judge said Weber could use the statement as rebuttal evidence after the defense case, but not now.

Hawkins wasted no time on cross-examination, zeroing in immediately on Barns's conviction and probation for selling drugs in Florida a year earlier. Weber knew that would hurt his witness's credibility somewhat, but the testimony had been worth the chance. Anyway, Barns was Prante's friend, and birds of a feather . . .

Then the defense began to pick at contradictions, including Barns's statement in 1978 that he was walking by Dwayne Conway's that night and his report in 1982 that he got a ride there with Prante. Barns said he was sure now that Prante gave him a ride.

Hawkins also hammered at other points from 1978. Hadn't he told the police he talked to Karla in her driveway first, and then went to Conway's house?

"Well, the houses were so close together you could have been standing in one driveway and be next door."

Hawkins's next point was damaging, too, as he quoted Barns in 1978 as saying he talked to Karla, then talked to Conway on his porch for a while, and then John Prante arrived.

"Is that, possibly, what you told Officer Nunn back in 1978?"

"Possible."

Hadn't Barns said he was the one who wanted to join the party next door, not Prante?

"No."

"Do you remember telling the police that?"

"No."

Hawkins asked about Prante's car; Barns remembered the red Volkswagen. Hawkins asked if he was positive; he was. Weber wondered again where the questions on the car were going. But Hawkins was on a roll, and Weber didn't have much time to think about that. As Hawkins continued to pick away, Weber finally objected unless Barns was allowed to read the old report the defense was quoting. Romani agreed and Barns read the one-paragraph statement recorded by Chuck Nunn.

Hawkins returned to the attack. "Are you saying your memory is better today than it was five years ago, or just a week after the incident?"

"No. I'm just saying that I'm being asked things more specific and to the point than what I was asked in that interview right there. I was asked basically, then, where I was at and what time I was there, and that was it."

Weber hoped that forceful answer might rehabilitate his witness a bit; it pointed out one of the problems with the first investigation. Too many witnesses with valuable information were asked too few questions.

On redirect, Weber introduced the four-page signed statement Barns gave O'Connor and Watson. Weber pointed out that Barns never saw or signed the paragraph filed by Nunn.

"In 1978, they didn't ask you about John Prante, did they?"

"No, sir."

"They didn't ask you if Prante was excited about Karla Brown that day?"

"No, they just asked me about my whereabouts."

"They just wanted to know about you and Karla Brown, and that's what you told them. Right?"

"Yes, sir."

"And when was the first time you were asked specifically about the events following Prante meeting Karla Brown?"

"When the detectives came to Louisiana."

"Twelve days ago?"

"Yes, sir."

"Why do you remember that day at Conway's?"

"Well, because it was the day before Karla got killed."

"And you knew her?"

"Yeah, and I had seen her the day before."

That should repair some of the damage Hawkins's effective cross-examination had inflicted, while stressing the difference between the investigation that went nowhere in 1978 and the one that led to John Prante's arrest in 1982. For the first time, Prante's defense had made some points with the jury. And Weber could only hope he had returned the volley effectively.

He went back to the attack, zeroing in on Prante's alibi for the morning of the murder. Harvey Birmingham, from personnel at the Shell Oil Company refinery at Roxana, told the jury that Prante filed a job application sometime between 8 A.M. and noon on June 21, 1978; there was no way to set the time exactly. Birmingham told Hawkins the application took fifteen to thirty minutes to fill out.

Prante had been there the day Karla was killed, but it didn't provide an alibi. That usually was the case with that kind of defense; close scrutiny of the critical times involved shot them down.

Debra Clifford, a clerk at Airco Industrial Gases, said Prante's application was filed there on June 19, 1978, not the day of the killing. And, she added, one of Prante's references had been Spencer Bond.

Another hole in the alibi.

Records keepers from Rockwell International and McDonnell-Douglas Corp. showed the jury the difficulties in a case this old; their companies didn't keep records that long, so there was no way to know if Prante was there. Weber shook his head again. All of that information should have been gathered in 1978.

Weber recalled Alva Busch to explain briefly how he renewed the investigation in 1980 with his interest in green lasers and his meeting with Dr. Homer Campbell on computer image enhancement of photographs. Busch was the bridge as the prosecution shifted into the new technology that turned this case around.

Weber introduced the TV trays and stand into evidence, and former chief Duke Gorris came on to describe how Dr. Campbell concluded that the stand made the injuries on Karla's face.

Then Gorris described Campbell's startling discovery of the bite marks in 1980. Had anyone known about the bite marks before that?

"Absolutely not," Gorris said firmly. "I was just floored. We had no indication that she had ever been bitten before."

Gorris had set up the momentum for the new effort well, although Weber felt himself chafe as Gorris kept describing all the things "we" had done; the editorial "we" seemed to refer only to the Duke's police.

So, the next witness was even more important for the prosecutor. Agent Randy Rushing, now a lieutenant, explained his appointment as special investigator for the grand jury in 1982 "to assume the responsibility for the investigation into the Karla Brown murder case." Things were in perspective now, and the jury knew which agency was in charge. It was time for a chronological account of what led the team to John Prante.

Rushing explained that the investigation had focused on Dwayne Conway, not Prante. Over Hawkins's objection, Rushing recounted how FBI Agent John Douglas supplied a psychological profile and other invaluable assistance just before the body was exhumed. Douglas recommended a high profile for the investigation to make the killer nervous and shake him from the complacency he developed in the four years since the murder.

"And what specific actions were taken to promote that plan?"

"A high amount of coverage, a high profile by the media was generated."

Weber was surprised, but grateful, that the last line did not draw an objection. The jury and the public now could see why things were done as they were, and why Weber had been so anxious to talk to the press.

Rushing described the exhumation before Weber halted the story. It was another technique he learned from Bob Trone—always use several witnesses to tell the story and call them back time and time again to keep the events in perspective.

On cross-examination, Hawkins surprised Don Weber by focusing on Don Weber.

"When you say 'we decided to make all of these decisions,' was that in consultation with Mr. Weber and his office?"

"There was a lot of consultation done, but I had the ultimate decision as to what was going to be done in the investigation."

"Did you discuss that with Mr. Weber usually?"

"I talk to Mr. Weber about many things, yes, sir."

Weber wondered where that was going, but he knew Hawkins was pulling the prosecutor deeper and deeper into the heart of the case, and it made him a little nervous.

As Weber prepared to call Dr. Harry Parks, a note arrived that Weber thought was almost too indicative of this case from Day One. He shared the note with the court to request a brief delay.

"Your Honor, we have just got a note that Dr. Parks went to Edwardsville instead of East Alton. So, he's going to be a little late."

Dr. Parks would have to fend for himself before the jury. The bite marks and skull fracture had been missed at the first autopsy, and there would be a significant dispute over the cause of death. In an interview with Dr. Parks a week before trial, Weber had told him about the results of Dr. Mary Case's autopsy. At least none of that would be a surprise to him now.

Weber also told Dr. Parks what David Hart said about the state of rigor mortis. On the witness stand, Parks used that to offer a better estimate of the time of death—probably six hours before the body was found, and as long as eight or nine hours. At the latest, Karla died about 11:45 that morning. That was close enough, Weber thought, since Edna Vancil said Prante and Conway were off the porch between 11 and noon.

As the doctor described the injuries to Karla's face, he mentioned that her jaw was broken so badly at the point of her chin that the pieces could be moved apart easily. Weber couldn't help but glare at Prante. That fragile jaw had been shattered by that oaf, and Weber couldn't hide his anger as he thought about the blows to the flawless skin David Hart remembered so well.

Dr. Parks explained that he had not felt a skull fracture when he examined the head with his fingers, and the X-ray report indicated none. He reaffirmed his conclusion of strangulation by garroting as the cause of death. He found no water in her lungs to suggest drowning, and that indicated she was not breathing then.

Weber decided to cross-examine his own witness, and showed Dr. Parks the picture of the foam around Karla's nose and mouth. But the doctor was insistent; the foam was from air forced out of her lungs while her head was submerged, probably after she was dead. The lack of water in the lungs was more important than the photo of the foam.

The prosecutor waded into another topic that pointed out the difference between pathologists from different eras; he hoped the jurors were listening carefully. When he asked whether Karla Brown had been sexually assaulted, Dr. Parks called the evidence inconclusive and referred to the lack of clinical findings—no injuries associated with violent rape and an unusually small amount of sperm cells. Weber knew Dr. Mary Case would present the jury with a more dramatic view from a pathologist trained in "proactive" techniques considering much more evidence than what came off a cotton swab.

When Weber mentioned the bite marks, Dr. Parks said simply that he had not noticed any. He concentrated mostly on the bruises and other abrasions from the garroting. Looking at the photograph, however, Parks agreed that the marks were "consistent with a human bite mark." The doctor added that he knew little about bite marks in 1978. He received his first formal training on their evidentiary use in 1982 and read some articles about them in forensic literature since then.

Weber also used the opportunity to start building resistance to the attacks he expected from defense experts.

"Those marks which you are saying could be bite marks—are they artifacts or are they actual bite marks?"

"No, they are not artifacts. They are actual bite marks."

On cross-examination, Hawkins had Dr. Parks reiterate his conclusion on strangulation and his opinion that the foam probably occurred when David Hart lifted the body out of the barrel. It was obvious to Weber that Hawkins was negotiating over the death penalty. If Prante were convicted, a jury might be less revolted by a strangulation

than a drowning—a fine point important only to the lawyers.

Detective Richard White of Wood River took the stand
next to renew the attack on Prante's alibi. White had
driven the route Prante claimed he followed on his job
search the morning of the murder. White explained that
he departed from Conway's at 8:31 A.M., as Prante
claimed in 1978, and drove to the personnel office at
McDonnell-Douglas in St. Louis. White stayed five minutes, then drove to the office at Rockwell International.
After waiting five more minutes, White drove back to Illinois and went to the Airco office. He waited five minutes again and then drove back to Conway's house,
arriving at 9:59 A.M. The trip took eighty-eight minutes
and would have allowed Prante to make the route—if he
really did all of that—and be back in plenty of time to kill
Karla between 11 and noon.

Hawkins pointed out that White had not taken the time
to go into each office and fill out applications, and had
not driven to any other location along the way, as Prante
might have.

As Agent Tom O'Connor took the stand, Weber hoped
to demonstrate the quality of the officers in the 1982 investigation. O'Connor mentioned he was a homicide and
arson detective in St. Louis for thirteen years and had
taught courses in interrogation for police officers for six
or seven years.

O'Connor then explained how he and Detective White
had interviewed Vicky and Mark White, and Spencer and
Roxanne Bond. Weber wanted the jury to understand that
the interviews were separate and that the cops furnished
no details to the witnesses. O'Connor said each of them
offered independent recollections and signed written
statements.

When O'Connor finished, Weber hoped the jurors realized they had just seen a "super cop" in action. Solving
the Karla Brown murder had taken the best from the
fields of prosecution, police, and forensics.

By the time court recessed for the day, Weber had run

through an incredible list of sixteen witnesses. The testimony moved faster than expected because Neil Hawkins was taking much less time with cross-examination than Weber anticipated. That probably was a good tactic for the defense; Hawkins slipped in and out with quick strafing runs and had made some points, especially against Lee Barns. And Hawkins had done it without boring or alienating the jury.

Still, Weber felt fairly pleased with the case so far, and he knew his best stuff was still to come. He had shown the jurors why the case wasn't solved in 1978, and now he would show them why it was in 1982.

Chapter 18

Before key testimony could be presented on Thursday, June 30, Don Weber had a prickly situation to discuss with the defense attorney and judge in chambers. He had decided not to call Annie Tweed, Dwayne Conway's twin, even though she was mentioned in Weber's opening statement. He interviewed her the evening before and was convinced she was mistaken about some details that contradicted testimony by Edna Vancil. Tweed might be offering her honest recollections, but Weber's hunch was that she thought anything she could do to trip up the prosecution somehow would assist her brother. Either way, Weber couldn't vouch for Tweed's credibility, and he certainly didn't want her casting doubt on the more important testimony by Edna Vancil.

The biggest problem was Annie Tweed's insistence that Edna Vancil's daughter was visiting Edna on the day of the murder. The cops checked that out after the "Dukes of Hazard" interview in Louisiana. Edna's daughter had delivered a baby a few days before Karla was murdered, and there was no way the woman could have been at her mother's house on June 21.

Weber had expected Tweed to testify that Prante was at Conway's after the police arrived. But, Weber told the judge, Prante had admitted that on the tapes with Spencer Bond, and Detective Nunn already had testified that he saw Prante there. Since that was proven from other sources, Weber's failure to call a witness he mentioned in his opening was not an error fatal to the trial.

Weber tried to put Hawkins in a trick box by offering

to let him call Tweed before she was sent back to Louisiana; Weber hoped that would protect the trial record on appeal. But Hawkins wasn't biting; he simply told the judge, "I have nothing to say." He was protecting his appeal record, too.

Judge Romani then took up a new motion by Hawkins to prevent testimony from Spencer Bond that Dwayne Conway named Prante as the killer. Weber agreed for that statement to be barred as hearsay. But he warned that Bond's reference to the accusation from Conway was contained on a tape, and the prosecutor was certain that was admissible. The judge said he would rule on that point later.

Weber still hadn't decided what to do with Dwayne Conway. Should he call him as a witness? There were plenty of reasons for a decision either way, but nothing in the trial so far had pushed Weber one direction or the other. He found himself, for once, terribly undecided. So, he decided not to decide until later.

Weber was excited as he began to call the witnesses he prayed would shoot down John Prante in flames. The Whites, the Bonds, Sherry Dalton, and Harold Pollard would tell the jury how Prante had known things the cops didn't know, things only the killer could have known. The fact that there were bite marks was about to become more important than the scientific analysis of them.

But these witnesses had two weaknesses, and Hawkins was sure to probe them. First, they had not come forward in 1978, sitting on this devastating information until the police found them in 1982. Weber thought he could explain that, but he knew it still might be difficult for the jurors to accept.

Second, these witnesses were now saying that the party was only two or three days after the murder, probably Friday night. They told the police last year that it was a week or ten days later. It was a small contradiction that a good defense attorney would beat like a drum.

Vicky White was first. As she told the jury how she repeatedly turned down Prante for dates, Weber was struck by the realization that she was one of many girls—perhaps forty or fifty—whose rejections had contributed to the rage that erupted on Karla Brown that morning. Prante hadn't beaten and molested and killed and degraded Karla alone. She bore the burden for every woman who ever recoiled at his approach or emasculated him with rejection.

Vicky White also caught Weber's attention when she recalled Prante saying he was at Karla's house before she was killed, but she was all right when he left. That was the criminal's code again; Weber couldn't figure out what Prante meant by that, but the prosecutor filed it for later.

Another detail was that Prante was wearing the "Big Bamboo" T-shirt at the party. Weber liked that; it would make a denial that Prante ever owned such a shirt even more incriminating.

Vicky White also mentioned telling coworkers she thought she knew who killed Karla Brown. She was referring to Prante, of course, and Weber hoped the jury caught the easy inference that anyone who knew those details was the killer.

When Vicky told the jury that Prante mentioned teeth marks on the body, she instinctively brought her left hand up to her left shoulder. That had to be a powerful gesture for the jurors to see for the first time; it still gave Weber shivers.

As Weber expected, Hawkins's cross-examination focused on the delay in reporting these incriminating statements. He pointed out that the memories of Prante's comments came only after considerable publicity about the new investigation and the exhumation, all containing details about bite marks. Valid points for the defense, Weber thought.

Weber asked the definitive question again. "In 1978, when you heard this conversation, were you aware of its significance with respect to this investigation?"

"No, I was not."

Roxanne Bond testified that all she heard was Prante

saying he had to get his "story straight." That was plenty; it fit what everyone else had heard and showed that these witnesses were not getting their "stories straight" or exaggerating what they heard to frame Prante.

Mark White was the toughest of the group to question. For some reason, the prosecutor had difficulty pulling the desired answers out of him. It took several rounds of questions before Mark recalled Prante saying he was the last one to see Karla alive and he was going to leave town because of her murder. It was so labored that Hawkins was able to object successfully about Weber repeating questions. But it was worth it.

Weber went fishing for the sex line.

"Did Prante indicate to you why he was over at Karla Brown's house that day?"

"No, huh-uh."

Great. Another chase.

"Was there anything in the conversation about why he might have been over there?"

"I felt it was probably to go over there to have sex with her."

"Why do you feel that?"

"I don't know. Just one of them feelings, I guess."

Thanks again.

On cross, Hawkins hammered on the date of the party, and the four-year delay in statements to the cops. Weber wondered just how effective that criticism would be with the jurors.

Finally, it was time for Weber's star—Spencer Bond. Weber was confident this forthright, public-minded, and likable citizen would do well on the stand, and he did. Spencer tagged all the bases, never forgetting an important element of the story, and telling it all with unquestionable sincerity. His gesture as Prante indicated the bite marks on the left collarbone was dynamite, even though Weber wished it had been the right side.

Because Spencer was doing so well, Weber decided to try a preemptive strike; he had Spencer explain why he had waited so long to talk to the cops.

"I didn't think I knew anything," he replied with an honesty that rang true with Weber.

Bond's next answer sounded right, too, when Weber asked why he agreed to record conversations with his old friend.

"To either prove his innocence, or guilt."

Hawkins hammered Spencer Bond on the date of the party and then brought up another contradiction. Bond just testified that he was unaware of Karla's murder until Prante mentioned it at the party; but Bond told the police in 1982 that he initiated the conversation about the killing. Which one was it? Bond said he still wasn't sure who brought it up, but had tried to remember as best he could.

Hawkins had applied those points effectively. So Weber used redirect examination to give Bond free rein to explain that he was a little excited when he first talked to the police, and had thought about the details a lot since then. His best memory now was that the party was no more than three days after the murder, and could have been the same night Karla was killed because Bond thought Prante mentioned coming from the home of a mutual friend, Harold Pollard.

Weber's next trump card was the recording of Spencer Bond's first conversation with Prante. Huge speakers were set up in the courtroom; transcripts were provided to the jurors and the press, and Weber slipped one to the Judsons. But Weber's attempt to draw testimony from Bond about the key points in the conversation was blocked by a sustained objection from Hawkins. Judge Romani said the tape had to speak for itself.

Listening to the scratchy tape for eighty minutes was difficult, but most of the jurors seemed to keep up. Throughout the courtroom there was a collective "swish" when it was time to turn a page of the transcript. But Weber was worried; the astute agents hadn't caught all the contradictions in Prante's statements the night the tape was made. Could the jurors find them amid the blizzard of gibberish?

Weber then began a long series of appearances and reappearances by witnesses with crucial parts of the story to tell. O'Connor described Prante's arrest and statement to police that night. The agent drew a chuckle when he quoted Prante as saying "he had contacted a Mr. Don Weber at the state's attorney's office." But the next line was becoming a running gag between the cops and Weber; it had, after all, won the best-line contest.

"He told Mr. Weber that he did not want to be considered a suspect," O'Connor said with a straight face and a twinkle in his eye. The line would pop up for the rest of the trial, and Weber and the cops would have to squelch the smiles.

Prante also had claimed that he had been in error when he admitted to Weber that he had been at Karla's house the day of the murder; when he got busted, Prante said he never had been at Karla's.

Hawkins asked if Prante hadn't said he was confused when he made the call to Weber. O'Connor was bulldog certain Prante never claimed to be confused.

On redirect, Weber asked if Prante had done something that changed his mind about being at Karla's. Hawkins objected, but the judge ruled the defense attorney had opened the door on cross. O'Connor was only too happy to explain that Prante's story changed after he talked to Dwayne Conway, who insisted that Prante's visit was on the day before the killing. More on the meeting at the trailer later, Weber thought.

Day Four of the trial ended, and Weber was more than satisfied with the way the evidence sounded from the Whites and Bonds. Had the jurors listened closely enough to hear Prante's own words slamming the door to death row behind him?

The recording of Bond's second conversation with Prante was scheduled to be played Friday morning, but Weber changed his mind and his tactics. He didn't like the way the first one came off in the courtroom, and decided not to play the second one. Instead, Bond testified about the conversation, allowing Weber to draw out the specific points he wanted the jury to absorb—no gibberish, just brass tacks.

In rapid order, Bond told the jurors that Prante admitted being at Conway's house on the day of the murder, from 10 or 11 in the morning until five, six, or seven that evening. He never went inside Karla's house, but talked to her on the walkway between the houses—just as Eric Moses remembered. Prante said the cops sealed off Karla's place, and no one could have gotten onto the property. Prante left after the coroner's wagon arrived and he said, "Wow, that girl over there must be dead." He claimed he didn't know the victim's name until he saw it a few days later in the newspaper, which directly contradicted Lee Barns's testimony. Prante later contradicted himself by saying he didn't even now about the murder until the police interviewed him at his father's house.

Weber hoped the jury really was hearing this. Prante's own words eliminated any chance that he learned the details about Karla's body with a peek while the cops were there. And it should be getting clearer that Prante remembered too many details to be confused; you don't remember details you didn't see. If John Prante started the trial protected by a wall of reasonable doubt, Weber hoped he was knocking down the bricks pretty quickly now.

Hawkins went after Bond on Prante's memory of his telephone call to Weber making the prosecutor wonder again why that was of such interest.

"Did Prante tell you what their conversation concerned?"

"About John's innocence and how he shouldn't be considered a suspect in this murder case."

Now, even Spencer Bond was using the line. He was in on the joke, too.

"Do you recall whether or not he said Mr. Weber told him he was a low-level suspect?"

"Yes, he did."

Bond said that Prante quoted Weber as saying their top suspects were Dwayne Conway and Jack Meyers; Weber wondered if the jury realized he was just stringing Prante

along. Hawkins had Bond read the section of the transcript where Prante recalled Weber's description of
Meyers's violent activities with women: ". . . sticking
their heads down toilets and flushing them, and beating
up on chicks. And he knew Karla Brown. He's our chief
suspect." Weber said the cops already had taken Meyers's
dental impressions.

Pretty slick, Weber thought. Now he knew why that
conversation was so important to the defense. Hawkins
had just informed the jury that Jack Meyers was a major
suspect with a strange way of courting women.

Hawkins wasn't finished with Bond.

"Throughout the course of this conversation, Mr. Bond,
did Mr. Prante again profess to you his innocence in this
regard?"

"Yes, he did."

"In fact, did he, at that time when you were asking him
those questions say for the two of you to call Don Weber
that night and talk to him about it?"

"Yes, he said we could."

"And he said he wanted to talk to Mr. Weber because
he was not guilty of this?"

"That's what he said, yes."

For good measure, and to establish some bias against
Prante, Hawkins even asked if Spencer hadn't accused
Prante of making a pass at Spencer's wife.

"I sure did." Bond nodded. Still some resentment,
Weber thought.

As Hawkins sat down, Weber leaned over and whispered to Keith Jensen. It would be better for him to handle the redirect since Weber was the focus of much of the
cross. Bond explained again that Prante had asked if he
was working for the police. That put Prante's protesta-
tions of innocence in perspective; if Bond was a suspected informant, after all, would Prante confess to
murder or would he insist he was innocent?

"When Mr. Prante indicated to you that Mr. Weber had
said he was a low-level suspect, is that what Mr. Prante
said?"

"Yes."

"Did he indicate whether low-level meant the type of person he was, or where he stood on the degree of suspects?"

The comment drew a sustained objection, and a few chuckles.

Randy Rushing returned to explain that the authorities told Bond to use phony cover stories and other lines to elicit as much information as possible from Prante and Conway. Weber hoped that would counteract Hawkins's suggestion that Bond had lied for some evil purpose.

Rushing also made it clear why the cops went to Dwayne Conway's right after the second wiretap of Prante. "We felt that time was of the essence to get to Dwayne Conway before John Prante did."

Tom O'Connor bounced back to pave the way in case Dwayne Conway testified. Because of the hearsay evidence rules, O'Connor was barred from quoting Dwayne Conway's statements from that long interview at the Brighton police station. But O'Connor was able to explain that he talked to Conway for six or seven hours and that he signed a written statement. Obviously, the inference should be, Conway gave the cops some good stuff on Prante.

Weber even had O'Connor explain that the interview was conducted in comfortable surroundings and without undue pressure. It wasn't like TV; a confession wasn't beaten out of the suspect.

Weber brought in Dr. Warren Waters—the dentist who took Prante's dental impressions—to describe the process and add that Prante's teeth were very distinctive. Most people did not find the procedure particularly humiliating, unlike Prante.

With a real edge in his voice, Weber asked, "Dr. Waters, this procedure is not as unpleasant or humiliating as being drowned, is it?"

"No," the doctor said quietly.

It was a good way to end the morning session.

* * *

Just before lunch, Weber informed Neil Hawkins that Dwayne Conway would not be called as a witness. Weber just couldn't swallow hard enough to cut a deal with this guy; Weber had too many suspicions that Conway was involved in the crime to let him walk away from the charge with a sweet deal.

Weber then called Patty Conway to testify about her observations. The judge reminded Weber that testimony about what Dwayne Conway said to his wife still was prohibited as hearsay.

Patty Conway told the jury her husband was "relieved and hungry" after the long interview with the police; she fixed him his favorite meal of ham and beans, cornbread, and maple syrup. Weber gulped again; he was glad he'd had lunch already.

The next day, a nervous John Prante visited the Conways' trailer; he didn't want any trouble, but needed to know about Spencer Bond and the events the day of the murder. Prante sat on the edge of the couch and chain-smoked as he talked to Dwayne Conway.

"He told my husband that he and my husband had partied all day that day."

"Okay. And what was Dwayne's response to that?"

It was a good try, but Hawkins was listening too closely and his objection to hearsay comments was sustained. Weber had second thoughts about that ruling, and it struck him that the complicated hearsay rules left a loophole for this situation. At a conference at the judge's bench, Weber argued that Dwayne Conway's statements were made in the presence of the defendant, one of the exceptions to hearsay; Patty Conway could report what she heard her husband say to the defendant. Hawkins disagreed, but the judge took Weber's view.

He stepped back to the witness, a small victory in hand.

"Okay, what was Dwayne Conway's response to Prante's statement?"

"He said that they had not partied that day; that it had

been the day before or a couple of days before. Dwayne said he had painted all day that day."

"Describe to the jury what happened next."

"They talked at some length about the day of the murder. They tried to figure out what day of the week it was. At one point, John Prante talked about the fact that Karla Brown's murder was a capital offense and was punishable by death, and that one of them would go to the gas chamber for it."

There was the devastating line Weber was waiting for. Now the jurors had heard Prante's own realization that his crime was catching up with him, and he was facing the punishment he deserved. Weber repeated it for the jury, to let it sink in.

"Who was he talking to when he said, 'One of us will go to the gas chamber for this'?"

"My husband, Dwayne Conway."

"What was your impression that Prante was trying to do that day?"

"I felt he was trying to influence my husband."

The conversation went on for hours, she said, and she even left to play a game of badminton with a neighbor. Weber never ceased to be amazed at what some people would do in the midst of crisis. When Patty Conway returned, John Prante and her husband were laughing about old times. As Prante left, he laughed and said, "We'll probably see each other in court."

Hawkins asked a few questions on cross just to remind the jurors that Patty Conway did not hear all of the conversation.

Randy Rushing came back to describe Dr. Lowell Levine's analysis of the dental impressions of Prante, Conway, and Meyers. Rushing explained that Meyers had not been a serious suspect for some time, and that he and Conway were eliminated completely by Levine's comparison of their teeth and the bite marks.

Rushing described how the police learned of Prante's visit to Conway and of Conway's disclaimer of his statements from Saturday. The arrests followed quickly, Rushing added.

Hawkins returned to his practice of drawing Weber into the testimony, having Rushing explain that Weber issued the charges against the defendant. Weber responded on redirect by having Rushing add that Weber issued all the charges in Madison County for the last three years.

Weber had to offer the judge an excuse for a delay in producing the next witness. Sherry Dalton, Weber explained, had transportation problems and would appear soon. Actually, Weber had just sent her home to change clothes after she arrived wearing something resembling a pair of bib overalls—with no blouse underneath. Rick White was ordered to take Dalton on a quick trip home to change into something suitable for court.

She reappeared in an off-the-shoulder sundress that hugged her much too tightly—still not right for court, but better.

She took the stand to offer ruinous testimony against her old lover and add the insult to his manhood. Sherry's candor was refreshing, Weber thought, as she calmly recounted first meeting Prante in the tavern called Why Not? and how he gave her some "speed" pills later. She was unaffected by Weber's admittedly odd inquiry of how many times she and Prante had sex.

"Around twelve, fifteen. I don't know; somewhere around there," she answered without a hint of embarrassment, but with the suggestion that it was difficult to keep track.

Weber moved in for the line that would not only humiliate Prante but offer some explanation for his attitude toward women.

"Were there ever any problems?"

"Yeah."

"Describe to the jury the problems."

"Oh Jesus. Well, there were a few times that he couldn't, you know—he couldn't do it."

Weber glanced at Prante. He still showed no reaction,

even though it had to be infuriating to have his sexual problems announced in the courtroom.

Sherry Dalton described Prante's anger at the news she was pregnant with his child, and then recounted the bizarre pillow talk the night when he whispered that he had killed a woman because he was really mad.

"Were there ever any other problems, other than just his failure to be able to perform properly?" Weber asked in another assault on Prante's dignity.

"Well, there were a couple of times he bit me on the neck, and it made me mad."

"What happened then?"

"Nothing. he said he was sorry; he didn't mean to hurt me."

"What area did he bite you on?"

"My left shoulder."

Hawkins had to raise doubts about Sherry Dalton's credibility; he began by focusing on her pregnancy and abortion. When was it?

"February of '81, I think."

"February of '81?"

"Yeah, it had to have been that long ago, or '82. I don't know. I have had three abortions."

Weber sighed; what a way to keep track of dates in your life.

Hawkins brought up the delay in reporting to the police again. In her typical candor, Sherry explained that she hadn't realized Prante was a suspect in the Karla Brown murder until she repeated his comments to Captain Browning from East Alton. The captain was interviewing her while she was in the hospital after a fight. Good enough, Hawkins thought.

As Sherry left the stand and crossed the courtroom, one of her thongs flipped off her foot. She giggled, "How embarrassing," and bent over to pick it up, proving to the jury behind her that she wore nothing under the tight dress. She carried her shoe out of the room as a ripple of laughter rolled through the audience. At the prosecutor's table, Weber dropped his chin into his hands and shook his head.

But he hoped following Sherry Dalton with testimony from Harold Pollard would be like delivering a left jab followed by a right cross. Pollard—a tall, thin, nervous man—recalled his days as Prante's roommate and explained how rejection by women sent his friend into "depression and withdrawal."

"I believe John would let it get to him more than most people would."

Pollard described Prante's arrival in his red VW between 6:30 and 7 the night of the murder, wearing the now-famous "Big Bamboo" T-shirt, a yellow cap, and jeans. He was agitated and anxious, and asked for tranquilizers. When Pollard asked what was wrong, Prante replied, "A little bit of everything." He had just come from Dwayne Conway's—barely ten minutes away by car— where he had been smoking and drinking all day. Prante said the girl next door to Conway had been killed. A lot of police officers had arrived and that made Prante very nervous.

Pollard quoted Prante as saying he had got a look at the girl's body over the shoulder of an officer who was standing in the doorway, and she was curled up on the floor with her hands tied behind her.

A nervous Dwayne Conway arrived at Pollard's shortly after Prante, and the two men discussed what was happening back on Acton Avenue. But the witness was certain Prante already had given him the details about the murder before Conway arrived.

Weber had Pollard recall Prante's comment a day or two before the killing about the girl moving in next to Conway.

"He said she was a really nice-looking girl, you know, and he wouldn't mind, you know, having relations with her."

"Are those the words he used?"

"Well, no sir. As near as I can come to recalling it, he

said that a nice-looking blond chick had moved in next door, and that he wouldn't mind getting some off her."

Weber looked at Prante again; no reaction. But Weber thought, That's right, John, stay calm. Just keep telling us in your own words what a creep you are.

Prante was usually pretty cool and collected, and it was unusual to see him as agitated as he was that night. He stayed for about an hour and then said he was going over to Spencer Bond's. More corroboration for Bond, Weber thought.

Prante said a week or two later that he was leaving for Houston.

Hawkins went after Pollard from the first word.

"Mr. Pollard, when was the first time you contacted the police about this?"

"Well, sir, the first time I had been notified by the police or contacted by the police is when the DCI agents came by."

"And they contacted you?"

"Yes, sir, they did."

"You said at this time you were taking tranquilizers. Is that true?"

"Yes, sir, for my nervous condition."

"What were you taking?"

"Valium."

"Are you still taking those?"

"No, sir. I cut my dosage pretty low."

"Have you ever been a drug addict?"

"Well, sir, I have had problems with drugs in the past, but I haven't had any problems for three years—four or five years."

Hawkins asked if he was sure about Prante's car; again, Weber mused. What was the point? So far, everyone who knew Prante had put him in the same doggone red VW.

Randy Rushing testified again about Prante's arrest, quoting the defendant as saying he didn't care what all the other witnesses said, or what he had said on the tape recordings; he had never been at Karla's house or Conway's house the day of the killing. Weber wanted the jury to hear Prante's pat story. Even if he took the stand, he would have to stick with that story at all costs. Weber just hoped the costs would be plenty high.

Weber thought the first week of trial ended well. The jurors had seen a murderous version of the "what did he know and when did he know it" scenario.

Hawkins's cross-examination had been appropriately short and sweet. He had made a few points that worried Weber, especially about the failure of the crucial witnesses to go to the police with their information. Was it possible for average citizens to believe that these people didn't realize they knew something very important about a vicious murder?

Chapter 19

Don Weber eagerly anticipated the second week of the trial, when he finally would get a chance to introduce his bite-mark experts. He was anxious to see how the evidence he found so exciting would play in the courtroom, with the media, and before the jury.

Dr. Homer Campbell flew into St. Louis on the morning of Monday, July 4. Weber feted the doctor at a barbecue at Weber's home and took him to the annual fireworks extravaganza under the Gateway Arch in St. Louis that evening. Later, Weber popped the videotapes from the Bundy trial into the VCR and discussed the serial killer's case with the expert who had been such an important witness. During their discussions, Weber learned that Campbell's wife, an anthropologist, had been the one to link the injuries on Karla's face to the TV-tray stand.

Weber even had his teeth checked by Campbell that night, since little Eric Moses testified that Weber looked like the man talking to Karla in the driveway. Campbell laughed as he ruled out Weber as the one who made the bite marks. But the lark gave Weber another idea that might be fun in court.

Sergeant Eldon McEuen, still weak and hurting from his nearly fatal encounter with a deranged man's knife blade just two weeks earlier, was Weber's first witness on Tuesday, July 5. The pain in his side was obvious as he gingerly took the witness stand.

McEuen described his interview with Prante that was,

coincidentally, five years ago to the day. As McEuen recounted Prante's claims about the job applications, Weber hoped the previous evidence already had destroyed that alibi. The sergeant stressed that Prante claimed to be unsure whether he had returned to Conway's house that morning. How could Prante's memory improve several years later? Weber wondered.

McEuen's last statement was that Prante went to a friend's house on Hamilton Avenue that evening, and Dwayne Conway showed up to announce the murder of the girl next door. Weber winced; the police might have found the key if they had followed that one, seemingly innocent statement. Harold Pollard could have put them on the right track to Prante, and the case might have been solved in less than a week.

Weber almost felt like rubbing his hands together. The time had come to begin the parade of experts, and Dr. Mary Case was first. Weber suggested that Donna Judson leave the courtroom; but she wanted the facts, no matter how painful they were to hear.

Weber hoped the jury would be as impressed with Dr. Case as he was; she started by describing her positions as deputy chief medical examiner for the city of St. Louis and full-time associate professor of pathology at St. Louis University. She listed her degrees and memberships in various medical and pathology societies. And Hawkins didn't even challenge Weber's request to certify her as an expert in medical pathology. The doctor explained that she had performed several thousand autopsies, searching for clues that would tell her why, how, and when a person died. She performed the second autopsy on Karla Brown as a courtesy to Madison County.

She turned her attention first to the facial injuries. The blow that split open Karla's chin also broke the jaw underneath in two places—the effect of blunt trauma from a heavy object delivered with significant force. The image of the TV stand held above Prante's head flashed through Weber's mind.

The neck organs had been removed during the first autopsy and were missing, so Dr. Case could not confirm the damage to them. The hyoid bone connected to the tongue was intact, even though it often is broken during manual strangulation. And there were no marks showing that the victim had bitten her own tongue, another common occurrence during strangulation.

Then, for the first time publicly, it was disclosed that Karla suffered three head injuries, including a skull fracture, that were missed in the first autopsy. Dr. Case found three injuries to the scalp from blows to the back of the head. One of them caused a hemorrhage over the left side of the brain at the base of the skull, and there was a fracture there about three inches long; it ran in a vertical line into the opening for the spinal column. The injuries could not have been caused by falling backward to the concrete floor, and Weber had a different scenario in mind.

"Could that have been caused by someone, after the victim was on the floor, hitting her head on the floor?"

"That is a possibility, yes."

Weber wanted to know how that kind of injury would have affected Karla.

"Conceivably, it could have been lethal. It could have produced unconsciousness very shortly following the time it was done. It would have been very painful and, at least, caused dizziness and concussion. Not immediate death, but over a period of several days, there is a possibility that it could have been a lethal injury."

Weber moved to the first expert opinion on the bite marks. Dr. Case could see bluish faded marks on Karla's neck that indicated hemorrhaging under the skin. Microscopic examination of tissue from those marks confirmed the bleeding was fresh.

"That means, first of all, that this injury was not inflicted two days prior to her death. It was not inflicted one day, or six hours prior to her death. It was not inflicted one hour prior to her death because there was no inflammation. This was, in fact, done very, very shortly before she died—at or about the time of her death, during the rest of her injuries. She was alive, secondly, when this was done. It was not done after she died. She was alive when this wound was inflicted because there was bleeding, and that requires a certain degree of blood pressure."

"Do you have an opinion, after having made this examination and reviewed these photographs, whether or not this was a sexual assault?"

"Yes, I do."

"And what is that opinion?"

"That this was a sexual assault, that she was sexually assaulted in the course of all the other things that were done to her."

Weber wanted the jury to understand how the new breed of forensic pathologists worked; there was more than clinical evidence to consider.

"And why do you feel that?"

"This is a female in a state of partial undress. The clothes, at least, have been moved, if not entirely removed from the body. She was killed in a manner in which close body contact was made with her. A number of things were done to her. She was menstruating at that time; a tampon was removed and was found at the site of the initial encounter. All of these facts, to me, very strongly indicate that this was a sexual assault."

Facts like these, especially including bite marks, usually mean one attacker, not two, the doctor told Weber.

Then she offered her startling conclusion that Karla drowned. She may have been unconscious from the head injury or strangulation, but the foam around her nose and mouth meant she had been breathing in and out, and drowned.

"There are few certainties in medicine, but that's one that is a certainty. If you get an individual out of a body of water and you want to know whether they were dead or alive when they went in, if they have this foam coming out, then we know they were alive when they went into that water."

Weber wondered if the jurors were feeling the same anger he did as he heard these very graphic, very gruesome details.

Hawkins had not enjoyed the doctor's testimony, but he didn't think she actually added much to the state's case. The cause of death had no real impact on the trial. If Prante was convicted, it might count against him at sentencing if the victim suffered longer. Hawkins took that approach on cross-examination, asking for more analysis of the possibility of strangulation.

Dr. Case explained that, while the strangling was significant, that kind of assault takes quite some time to cause death. Not much help to the defense. Hawkins asked about the foam, but the doctor was steadfast.

"The one meaning of that is that the individual was alive when the individual went into the water."

"Was there any water in the lungs, Doctor?"

"The original autopsy described no water in the lungs. But it is totally irrelevant to a diagnosis of drowning, and I did not even consider that in making an opinion."

"Okay, thank you very much. I have no other questions of this witness."

Weber almost grinned. I guess not, he thought.

Donna Judson sighed under the weight of what she had just heard. Those details made the attack and the violence so much more real. Karla had, indeed, suffered. There was no way to know for how long; but Donna now knew that it had been intense.

Donna and Terry took Dr. Case's testimony as gospel; she had an air that exuded confidence and competence. They thought she brought a fresh and needed bit of class to the trial amid witnesses who talked about wine and pot parties and hours in honky-tonks.

Dr. Homer Campbell strode into the courtroom in cowboy boots and a string tie, and an ease that brought this expert down to earth for everyone.

He listed his pedigree as a forensic odontologist and a clinical associate professor at the University of New Mexico School of Medicine. He was grandfathered into the American Academy of Forensic Odontology without taking the certification exams. He described his expertise in bite marks and computer image enhancement of injury patterns. He had examined more than 200 cases. He was qualified as an expert witness in ten states and had testified twenty-nine times—including the Ted Bundy case. About a fourth of his trial work was for the defense, a point Weber thought spoke well for the doctor's credibility as a scientist.

Hawkins asked a few cursory questions, but Judge Romani didn't hesitate to qualify the doctor as an expert.

And Weber didn't waste any time in getting to the facts. Campbell identified the TV-tray stand as the weapon that put the gashes in Karla's face, and he stood before the jury to compare the photos of the injuries to the bottom of the stand.

On a blackboard, Campbell drew the shapes of different teeth and the dental arch to show class characteristics. On the upper row, bite marks left two, wide rectangles for the front, central teeth. The laterals on each side of the centrals were smaller rectangles. The canine, or eye, teeth usually made round or triangular marks. On the bottom, the four central incisors left about the same size rectangular marks, with the round or triangular marks on each end for the canines.

Individual characteristics included spacing between the teeth and whether any of them sat out of line. More details could be left by fillings or teeth that were broken, chipped, cracked, or worn.

Bite-mark comparisons were made by taking casts of a subject's teeth and then pressing them into wax to reproduce a pattern that could be checked for class and individual characteristics. But there were no published standards for making comparisons or preserving bitemark evidence.

Campbell explained that bite marks were overlooked quite frequently, and often were seen in photographs taken for other purposes. Weber glanced at the jury to suggest, Gee, just like in this case.

Although bite marks were photographed best at right angles with a ruler in the photograph, it certainly was possible to analyze them as evidence in less than ideal conditions.

It was time to get down to the case at hand. Weber gave Campbell the photograph of the marks on Karla's neck and had him stand before the jurors to describe it. There were two, perhaps three bites superimposed on each other. The arch was flattened out somewhat because of the camera angle, but it was there and some individual class-characteristics could be seen.

Weber handed Campbell the cast of Prante's teeth and asked for a description.

"The front teeth are rather large; the ones to each side are smaller; the eye teeth are worn off rather flat and blunt in this case. The lower teeth show the four wide front teeth, all relatively the same size, and the two eye teeth adjacent. On the lower model, the teeth are relatively straight, as far as arch form."

Still holding up the cast, Dr. Campbell pointed out the unusual spacing between each of the upper teeth.

"Do you have an opinion as to whether or not those teeth are consistent with the injury wounds in the photograph?"

"Yes, I do."

"And what is that opinion?"

"That they are consistent. You see a wide tooth and a wide tooth, and a more narrow tooth and a more narrow tooth, with spacing in between the teeth. In other words, there is a space between each tooth across the front. That's why I say they are consistent."

It had been a Homeric journey, but Weber finally had told a jury that John Prante's teeth could have made the bite marks on Karla Brown's neck. Weber wondered if it sounded as good to the jurors as it did to the prosecutor.

Dwayne Conway's teeth, however, were something else.

"These teeth are severely crowded. You notice the lateral incisors are sitting back toward the tongue from the arch, so that there is not a consistency here, and there is no spacing in between them at all. They are very crowded and actually folded together."

Dwayne Conway's teeth could not have made the bite marks on Karla Brown, Campbell said. "He absolutely could not have."

The mold of Jack Meyers's teeth showed good alignment among teeth of rather regular size. Only one tooth was spaced oddly. They didn't make those bite marks, either.

"Dr. Campbell, when did you arrive here in St. Louis?"

"Last evening."

"Did you have occasion to look at my teeth and Mr. Rushing's teeth?"

"Yes, I did."

"Could either of us have made the injury patterns?"

"No, sir, you could not."

The jurors grinned and the reporters in the front row chuckled. It was an amusing maneuver, and he would try it with a twist again later.

Campbell turned to the image-enhancement procedure and the computer that performed the magic. He showed the jurors the photos he took of the enhanced images of the bite marks. One of the original photos had been of no use in comparisons because the marks had been made in a fold of skin. But another photograph yielded an improved image Campbell analyzed as the mark of a set of lower teeth; the identity of the owner of the teeth troubled Weber. He hoped the jurors would catch the complete explanation.

"Whose lower jaw is that particular photograph consistent with?"

"The marks on this photograph are consistent with the models Number 56 and Number 66."

"Sixty-six would be Jack Meyers?"

"Yes, sir."

Weber looked at the jurors, thankful he could perceive

no looks of concern or confusion. They were waiting for the rest of the explanation.

"Now, with respect to Jack Meyers, could his mouth have made the bite marks that you see in that picture?"

"Absolutely not, because the upper teeth are not consistent with the upper marks, which show the spacing in between every tooth. So, they could not."

The jurors seemed to accept that.

"But Mr. Prante's upper jaw and lower jaw are both consistent with the marks you have seen in the photograph?"

"Yes, sir."

Not so bad, Weber thought.

He ended on a high note designed to counteract the defense experts. The battle should be joined now.

"Do these bite marks all appear to be actual bite marks rather than artifacts or pooled blood or anything of that nature?"

"It is my opinion that these are bite injuries. These areas appear to have been clean, so that there is not pooled blood, for instance, or dirt on anything else."

Hawkins immediately attacked the quality of the photographs, having Campbell describe the ideal way to take pictures of bite marks. When Campbell mentioned that he preferred to have color photos, Weber thought back to Alva Busch's camera calamity—another incident from five years ago was haunting Weber today.

The defense also set up another attack for later by asking Campbell if the skin was a good medium for retaining bite marks. Campbell knew where that was headed, and explained that ten years earlier, the experts had serious questions about retention of bite marks in skin. Since then, however, so much had been learned that the skin now was considered "a very, very accurate medium."

Hawkins gave Campbell a pointer and asked him to step over to the easel holding one of his enhanced enlargements to show the jurors how some of the bite marks overlapped. The doctor traced the different arches and patterns as they crossed each other, and then concluded, "So this is not just one, single bite, but a multiple-type aggravation bite."

Weber was taken slightly aback by the new term. It sounded as if Prante almost had been trying to devour his victim.

Campbell added that there was one bite mark, however, that was separate and distinct, and could be used for a valid comparison.

Hawkins asked if more than one set of teeth could make the same bite mark. Campbell replied that each person's teeth were individual; but his comparison of the teeth in question to the bite marks was based on the gross characteristics being consistent.

Hawkins asked for a definition of the term "consistent" when comparing Prante's teeth to the marks on Karla's neck; the defense attorney got whacked with the response.

"That's just a very high degree of probability that you never find another set of teeth that would make the same marks. I would say it would be virtually impossible."

Those words were sweet music to Weber's ears. He looked over at Prante, who sat calmly with his cool gaze fixed on the witness.

Weber was glad when Hawkins turned and sat down; it was not a strong way to end a challenge to this expert's testimony. Weber had several points to make on redirect; he started by having the doctor explain again that the lack of color photos and ideal conditions did not weaken his finding of "consistent." Then Weber asked if it would be possible for a layman to have looked over a police officer's shoulder at the murder scene and recognized bite marks on Karla Brown's neck as she lay on the floor, the sweater buttoned up and the socks around her neck.

"No, sir. They are covered up."

How often were the evidence and photographs taken under ideal conditions? Weber wondered.

Campbell had only seen one that he did not handle personally from the start.

"Particularly, in the Ted Bundy case in Florida, were those bite marks taken under the ideal situations?"

"Absolutely not."

"And was a positive identification made anyway?"

"Yes, it was."

"And was Mr. Bundy convicted?"

"Yes, sir."

"No further questions."

Hawkins had no re-cross, and Dr. Homer Campbell stepped down. That ended Weber's evidence for the day and brought him within three witnesses of closing his case.

Dr. Lowell Levine arrived Tuesday night with his friend and photography expert, Detective Lieutenant Michael Melton of the Amherst, New York, police department—as promised. Weber met with them that night to prepare for the next day. Early Wednesday morning, July 6, Weber guided Levine down the hallway behind the courtroom in search of the defense attorney. Weber introduced Levine to Hawkins and took extra care to engage them in conversation for a few minutes. Hawkins didn't notice anything peculiar underway.

Back in the courtroom, Weber's assistant called Lieutenant Melton to the stand; Weber was reserving his strength and concentration for Levine. Melton explained that he was in charge of the department's first-rate technical-services unit and laboratory.

The witness testified that the limit on enlarging photos was the point where the detail was lost because the picture became too grainy. To increase the contrast of the bite-mark images in the black-and-white photos in this case, Melton used a high-contrast film to take pictures of the pictures; and then the new pictures were enlarged as much as possible. Melton added that he also took photos of wax impressions of bite marks provided by Dr. Lowell Levine, and enlarged them to six times life-size.

Melton produced an enlarged photo of Karla's neck and shoulder developed to contrast the dark markings he pointed out to the jurors. In his opinion those dark spots were bite marks.

Hawkins took over to ask Melton what he was looking for when he changed the contrast. Melton compared the images in the original photo he received to black chalk used on a blackboard. The information was there; it just was hard to see. He increased the contrast to highlight the information that was there.

Only one point was stressed on redirect. Was the information there in the original photo?

"It does contain information, yes."

Don Weber felt his engines revving as Lieutenant Melton left the stand and Weber rose to call his next witness. A lot was riding on the testimony of Dr. Lowell Levine.

The slim bearded man looked perfect for the role of scientist and expert witness. Weber had studied the tapes of Levine's testimony in Bundy's trial; if only this went as well. As Levine began to list his education, experience, and credentials, Weber hoped the doctor's slightly aloof style and trace of a New York accent wouldn't alienate these good jurors from middle America.

Levine, too, was an associate professor of forensic medicine, teaching at the New York University School of Medicine. He was a consultant to the Nassau County medical examiner's office and, like Campbell, was a member of the American Board of Forensic Odontology. Levine was a past president and vice president of the American Academy of Forensic Odontology; Dr. Campbell was the current vice president.

Weber found particularly impressive Levine's service as a consultant to the U.S. House Select Committee on Assassinations in the investigation of the murder of President John F. Kennedy. Levine mentioned he was a consultant in body identification in the DC-10 crash in Chicago, which meant he had worked with Dr. Edward Pavlik, a defense expert the jury would see later. Levine had testified as an expert in fourteen states, the District of

Columbia, before an Army board of court marshal, and Congress. He was qualified as an expert again, with no objection from the defense.

Levine established a professional attitude immediately when Weber asked him to discuss forensic odontology. The doctor explained that the word derived from the Greek for dentistry and was, simply, the application of dental evidence in the interest of justice. Levine said forensic odontologists were called in to help identify remains in crimes or disasters, and to analyze bite-mark evidence found so commonly in sexual activity around the time of death in murder cases.

He went over the same ground covered by Campbell on how photos of bite marks should be taken and how experts compared the marks to teeth. In a matter-of-fact voice, Levine described testifying about a bite injury in a bloody area on a woman's breast in a case in Texas—the verdict was guilty—and said it was no different from using a fingerprint to identify a suspect. Levine agreed with Campbell that the pictures in the Bundy case were less than ideal; Weber hoped the repeated references to the famous case were helping to convince the jurors that these men were heavy-hitters.

Finally, Weber had Levine offer his opinion that the photo on the easel from Melton's testimony showed bite marks. Weber gave a lengthy description of Karla's murder, the crime scene, and the condition of the body, and then asked if any of those facts changed the doctor's opinion about the images in the picture.

"Well, it speaks for itself. There's information there."

Levine displayed the three dental molds as he described his comparison of them of the photos. He agreed with Campbell that Dwayne Conway and Jack Meyers absolutely could not have left the marks. Levine then stood in front of the jurors to show them on the enlarged photo why the marks of Prante's upper teeth, with the spaces between them, "could have caused that injury pattern."

During his comments about the shapes left by teeth, Levine said that anyone could study them by biting into a Styrofoam cup. Someone in the crowd was getting an idea for later.

Weber closed his questioning by referring to Eric Moses's identification of four men in court—Prante, Hawkins, Rushing, and Weber—who looked like the man seen talking to Karla Brown.

"You already have talked about Mr. Prante's teeth. Have you had an occasion to observe the teeth of the other three people involved?"

"Yes, sir."

That explained the chatty meeting earlier with Hawkins that set up Weber's next question.

"Could any of those other three people possibly have made those impressions on Karla Brown's shoulder?"

"No. They don't have that spacing pattern in their teeth."

"No further questions."

Hawkins was ready again, and had Levine describe the ideal conditions for preserving bite-mark evidence. And then the defense attorney moved in for the challenge.

"You talked briefly, Doctor, about human tissue. Would you consider that a good medium or a bad medium?"

Levine had faced this question before, even in the Bundy trial.

"Ten or twelve years ago, I, personally, and the staff of the medical examiner, considered it a very suspect medium. But, over the years, dealing with cases where the identity of the perpetrator of the bite was not at issue, we have found that skin can capture the unique and individual characteristics of the teeth with excellent fidelity."

"But, it was your opinion years ago that it was not an excellent medium?"

"It was very suspect as a medium, yes, sir."

"You recorded that in an article, I believe?"

"Yes, we were warning about that, to be careful about making positive identifications—in the '72 *FBI Law Enforcement Bulletin*—until we had more data to really be certain of what we were talking about."

Levine had been challenged with his previous opinion

before. The article he wrote more than ten years ago, before so much bite-mark investigation was conducted, had been used to try to impeach his credibility in the Bundy trial, too. All he could do when that article was brought up was smile and explain that things had changed.

Hawkins asked if the photos of bite marks in the Bundy case had been taken specifically to record the marks. As Levine answered, Weber thought that was another "thanks" he owed the defense.

"I don't believe they were. In fact, I believe that the pathologist who did the postmortem had his film not go through the camera, and I believe only one photograph, which was serendipitously taken by a police officer, was adequate for comparison purposes."

Even more like this case, Weber thought as he remembered Alva Busch's camera again.

Hawkins brought up a case from the 1970s in Illinois in which Levine testified for the defense. Levine concluded that a man charged with murder could not have left the bite mark on the body. Several years later, a man who had all of his teeth pulled for no dental reason was arrested in another case not far away. When his dental X-rays were obtained, they showed some unique characteristics that linked him to the first murder, too. The man confessed to both crimes, proving Levine's testimony correct.

Hawkins noted that three prosecution experts were wrong in the first case when they testified the man had left the bite marks. Levine dismissed their expertise, because one was an orthodontist and one was a forensic pathologist. The third, a forensic odontologist, Levine said sheepishly, had been contradicted every time he testified.

On redirect, Weber decided to get the expert's opinion at its most basic level. Assuming the bite mark on Karla Brown's shoulder had to have been made by Dwayne Conway or John Prante, who did it?

"If you are telling me that those are the only two people in the world who could have left that bite mark, then I would have to say it had to be left by Mr. Prante."

After all of that, the last question for these experts had been the definitive one. A year ago, Weber knew that making this an "either/or" case could be the key. With Levine's last answer, Weber thought he heard the click of a key to a cell on death row.

The last witness for Weber was Dr. Ronald Mullen, Prante's former dentist. He had seen between 6,000 and 7,000 patients, and fewer than one percent of them had the kind of spacing Prante did between the upper, front, six teeth.

Hawkins tried to widen the field, but got blindsided instead.

"Doctor, do you have a number of how many times you have seen that spacing?"

"I would say less than fifteen."

"I have no other questions."

Judge Romani looked at Don Weber.

"Your Honor, at this time, subject to the admission of the exhibits, the People would rest."

The judge admitted all of Weber's evidence, including the photos of the bite marks. First thing the next morning, the defense would begin its efforts to show why John Prante should not be convicted as Karla's killer.

In the first row behind Don Weber, Donna and Terry Judson had just been won over completely by the prosecution. Under the weight of all the witnesses and the experts, the reluctant Judsons were convinced that John Prante killed Karla. In fact, Terry thought he could hear a door slam shut when Dr. Mullen said that only one percent had spacing like Prante's teeth. To Donna, that sounded more like a 100 percent chance it was Prante. The Judsons thought Weber had moved beyond reasonable doubt with his evidence, and they knew they had been demanding jurors in their own right. Now, they wondered, what were those other twelve, stone-faced people in the jury box thinking?

Chapter 20

When John Prante sat down at the defense table on Thursday, July 7, a special item had been left there for him. In front of his seat was a Styrofoam cup, with a gaping hole where someone had bitten a piece out of the rim. Prante calmly swatted the cup aside, knocking it off the table.

No one else seemed to notice the episode, except the culprit whose bite mark in the cup would have been easy to trace for anyone who had listened to the evidence over the last two days.

Deputy Sheriff Bob Henke chuckled to himself as he watched his prisoner's cool reaction to the subtle, but pointed, taunt. Henke had applied the testimony of Dr. Levine to an unintended purpose, turning the Styrofoam-cup idea into a prank. Henke thought it was so humorous, in fact, that he left an identical memento on the desk of Neil Hawkins's assistant, Vicky Hackett. Over the next few days, Henke would add to his repertoire by knotting Hackett's extension cord with slip knots and drawing little bite-mark patterns on her notepads. She knew who the phantom was, of course, and thought the gags were almost as funny as Henke did.

Henke—a husky, mischievous, cherubic-faced man—was the official guard for John Prante, escorting him each day on the twenty-minute drive between the county jail in Edwardsville and the courtroom in East Alton. Henke was Prante's constant companion, watching him every minute and staying with him in a small conference room during recesses. Prante seldom discussed the case, although he occasionally asked Henke how he thought the trial was going; Henke would shrug.

Prante talked quite a bit to Vicky Hackett, quoting Bible verses and urging her to read specific passages and the Psalms. She read some of them, looking in vain for a clue she thought he might be trying to pass along.

Prante was most relaxed in the company of his sister, Jo Ellen Brady. Vicky Hackett and others could tell it helped Prante to have her behind him in the courtroom. The siblings seldom talked about the case when they sat together in the conference room at recesses. They chatted about relatives, old times—anything but the trial.

Neil Hawkins's first official act in the defense case that morning was a motion for a mistrial. Weber actually was pleased, because defense lawyers didn't try to abort cases going their way. In Judge Romani's chambers, Hawkins argued that Weber's broken promises to play both eavesdrop tapes and, more important, to call Conway's sister as a witness damaged the trial and prejudiced the jury with false predictions. But Weber responded that Annie Tweed's testimony was proven by several other witnesses, making her as unnecessary as Weber thought she was unreliable. And Spencer Bond had provided ample testimony for the jury on the second tape.

Romani ruled that Weber's explanations were acceptable and there was no substantial prejudice to the defendant; motion denied.

There was one more issue; at the end of court the day before, Weber was subpoenaed as a defense witness. He wasn't sure what Hawkins had in mind, but it was the kind of fuzzy attack that made the prosecutor nervous. Weber wanted the subpoena quashed.

Hawkins explained that he wanted Weber on the stand to confirm his statements to the press over the years about other suspects, the bite marks, chances for a quick solution, and the quality of the investigation by the Wood River police. Weber argued that everything he knew was available through other witnesses, and it was highly improper to get the prosecutor on the stand and to squeeze evidence and opinion out of him.

The judged sided with Weber; there were other witnesses to provide the desired testimony without forcing the prosecutor to the stand.

As Hawkins poised to start the defense, he was disappointed by his own analysis that Weber's case played a little better in court than it looked on paper. Spencer Bond was relatively credible and likable, in a rather hokey way. The stories by the Bonds and especially the Whites held together better than Hawkins expected; he hadn't shaken them as much on cross-examination as he had hoped. But the wiretap recordings were innocuous and certainly contained no blatant admissions that damaged Prante.

David Hart probably was the most effective witness, just because of his credibility and his emotional impact on the jurors. But Hawkins thought that Dr. Levine came across as an arrogant, East Coast know-it-all whose testimony wouldn't play well with the jurors. The Wood River police obviously slipped up during the initial investigation, and that could raise doubts about the police work all along the way.

But the defense's best hope was to prove that the so-called bite marks were nothing of the sort. Hawkins was confident he could establish reasonable doubt on that point with his experts, and that would destroy the prosecution's only physical evidence.

There still was a good shot at acquittal.

Weber was anxious for Neil Hawkins to outline his plan of attack. Surely his opening statement would be a detailed rebuttal to Weber's case, explaining to the jurors how defense experts would demolish the bite-mark evidence. Would Hawkins tip his hand on whether John Prante would take the stand? The prosecutor sensed the tension in the courtroom as Hawkins stepped before the jury.

"I have a few brief preparatory remarks to make."

Hawkins must be understating his plans.

The defender explained that difficulty in scheduling his expert witnesses would draw the trial out until the next Wednesday; he apologized for the circumstances beyond his control. Then he began to hit the points the defense would make with its evidence; Weber edged forward in his chair.

First, the proof would show that Prante had not fled the area in a panic after the murder, as prosecution witnesses suggested. In fact, he didn't leave for almost two years.

Second, Hawkins would prove that Prante was not driving the red, squareback Volkswagen that everyone remembered. Prante's father had strict control of that car; John was allowed to drive only a blue VW. Weber finally had his answer on that point.

There would be character witnesses, friends of Prante who would describe the man they knew. "I will let you listen to them yourselves."

And finally, Hawkins named his three experts. But he mystified Weber by saying, "I will not go into that. I will let them explain it to you and show you what they have to elicit in this case. Listen to the evidence on the bite marks."

Hawkins finished with a request for the jurors to listen to the evidence carefully and with an open mind. When the trial was over, he would ask them for a verdict "consistent with common sense, logic, and justice."

That was it? No explanation of his witnesses' testimony? No curiosity-piquing predictions of sparks between the experts? Once over, less than lightly, was a new tactic for Weber, and it certainly caught him off guard.

But Weber thought Hawkins was smart and direct in attacking with his first witness—Jerry Gibson. Hawkins would offer the jury another suspect—a convict who had confessed to the murder the prosecution was trying to pin on Prante.

Gibson—the rough-looking cellmate of Tony Garza from 1978—promptly detailed a criminal record that included a shooting in 1977 and marijuana convictions in 1977, 1978, and 1982. He got right to the point, however, and offered his version of Garza's confession to killing Karla Brown. He had beaten her, sexually assaulted her, and strangled her with a scarf or pantyhose.

Weber went after this witness with a howitzer.

"Mr. Gibson, judging from your extensive record, I take it you really don't think too much of the law enforcement authorities, is that correct?"

"Yes, I do. I think it's a great system."

Weber let the sarcasm drip. "And how many times has this great system sent you to prison?"

"Twice."

Weber hit hard at details from Gibson that failed to match the events—breaking in through a basement window; evening instead of morning; and using a scarf or pantyhose, rather than socks. Then Weber drew testimony that Gibson and others in the cellblock had beaten Garza—a motive for Gibson to lie about him.

"And you didn't like Garza?"

"After he said he killed Karla Brown, no. I don't like murderers."

Weber suggested that Gibson made his allegations in 1978 strictly to get a break on the charges pending against him.

"The police were looking for a suspect, and you had a problem?"

"You're interpreting the whole thing the wrong way," Gibson lectured. And then he surprised Weber and almost drew a laugh by protesting, "I refuse to answer that. I'll take the fifth on that."

Witnesses never realized how conniving it sounded to throw that around carelessly. Weber kept the pressure on.

"You did this just as a public service, coming forward on Garza?"

"I hate to see somebody burned that didn't do something."

"You're just doing this as a public service, right?"

"Right."

"And because you're so public-minded and peaceful and law-abiding, right?"

Hawkins's quick objection was quickly sustained.

"You testified on direct examination that the reason you came forward was that, quote, I was trying to make a deal at the time."

"That was at the time. So, why didn't you use me as a witness?"

Weber couldn't let a great straight line like that pass.

"Because your testimony is completely unbelievable," the prosecutor snapped.

As Hawkins objected, Weber turned and strode back to his seat, confident he had eradicated that little problem.

The defense called records keepers from Lewis and Clark Community College and Southern Illinois University at Edwardsville to testify that Prante had attended college at irregular intervals between the summer of 1973 and the winter of 1982, including the fall and winter quarters of 1978 just after the murder. That proved Prante did not flee the area quickly in June 1978.

On cross, Weber took just enough time to point out that Prante wasn't a student at either school that June, and that both schools showed Prante attending at times in 1982 when he was a full-time guest at the county jail. Weber also pointed out the oddity that Prante was not seeking a degree at the university.

Hawkins turned toward the proof on the red Volkswagen with testimony from Elda Laatsch, who was married to Prante's father from October 1978, until he died in 1980. She said "Johnny" always drove an older, blue Volkswagen, not his father's red squareback. Johnny was not allowed to drive the red car until his father gave it to him in September 1978. Weber was amused, however, at the answer to Hawkins's question of why John Prante was barred from the red car.

"Well, I sort of got the impression that he didn't take care of things like George would have liked him to take care of them."

A slob, just like Agent John Douglas predicted.

On cross, Weber simply established that Elda Laatsch did not know which car either man had driven on June 21, 1978.

John Prante's sister, Jo Ellen Brady, was the next witness in the car wars. She agreed that her brother drove the blue Beetle because he didn't take care of the cars; he drove his father's cars to drag races and damaged one in a wreck. "My dad said never again," she explained.

She also remembered talking to her brother about the Karla Brown case in 1978, probably before the police questioned him; Hawkins steered clear of details, but he sprung from that to her description of Prante as a nervous person.

"He had this habit of constantly shaking his foot or shaking his leg, and I would move off the couch next to him because the couch always was shaking. He was always just moving; he wouldn't sit still."

That portrayed John Prante as a volcano waiting to erupt, Weber thought. It played into Weber's plan, assisted by John Douglas, for cross-examining Prante if he had the guts to take the stand. Weber started laying the groundwork with cross-examination of Prante's sister.

"Now, you described your brother as a nervous person. Has he ever talked to you about being in a rage?"

"No, not talked about it to me, no."

"Have you ever known him to be in a rage?"

"I have known him to be very angry."

Weber started to ask if she knew why he would have written those amazing words on his application for the job at the county juvenile center, but drew a sustained objection from Hawkins. Weber pursued the point in a different way, however, and Jo Ellen Brady said her brother would leave if he got mad.

"Calm on the outside and bubbling on the inside?" Weber asked.

"You could tell if he was angry."

"How would he express his anger to you?"

"He would yell at me."

Okay, Weber thought, we've established the rage. Falling back on Prante's application again, Weber probed for depression. Jo Ellen said her brother was terribly hurt by his divorce, another factor that fit. But she didn't know whether he had trouble handling rejection by women.

"After he would get real mad at you, would he have the ability then to come back and act rather calmly?"

"Yeah, the next day or so, yeah."

Weber remembered again. ". . . depressions, rage, and the calm after a storm."

Seven character witnesses for John Prante took their turns on the stand, wrapping up Thursday afternoon and providing all of the testimony Friday to conclude the second week of the trial. Most of the four women and three men were rougher-than-average around the edges. Most of them had friendships with Prante that were anchored in taverns, like the places where two of the women worked. One man wore a denim vest that led Weber to ask if he belonged to a "motorcycle organization"; he said no, but Weber didn't buy it.

But that was the same reaction Donna Judson was having to this group. In fact, she had never seen a collection quite like these witnesses. It was a real education for her.

They described John Prante as a calm, easygoing, polite guy. He opened doors for women. He was quiet, even-tempered, intelligent. Never saw him get violent. One woman knew Prante for seventeen years and went to church with him. She was so surprised by his arrest, "You could have knocked me over with a feather."

Weber asked the first witness if she ever saw Prante alone with a woman half his size who had rejected his advances. Of course, she hadn't. But Weber had to bring the jury back to the crime and the real circumstances. The John Prante on trial here was not the one people saw in a bar or a church; he was the one Karla Brown saw in her basement that morning.

But Weber saved his harshest cross-examination for the last man in the group Friday morning. Leonard Chairney gave Weber several openings among his answers to

Hawkins's questions. Prante once argued in a bar with a man who owed him money; but there was no violence. Prante walked out after loudly telling the guy to pay up. Chairney also mentioned that Prante was paranoid around cops, and talked about the Karla Brown murder just before he was arrested.

"I asked John if he did it. John said he didn't do it. He was scared. He said he had talked to Mr. Weber."

Mr. Weber pushed harder on that, asking if Prante was nervous.

"John wasn't nervous at all until after he had talked to you."

I'll bet, Weber thought. He adopted that sarcastic tone again as he asked, "Do you think someone is paranoid because they are scared the police are going to catch them for a murder they did? Is that 'paranoid' to you?"

"John had a bad experience when he was in the service. I don't know what it was over, but he told me he had a bad experience one time, and I know the man is scared to death around policemen. So am I. So are a lot of people."

Weber asked if the man Prante walked away from in the bar was bigger than four feet eleven and 100 pounds. When Chairney said he hadn't seen the other man, Weber pushed so hard that he drew an objection from Hawkins. The judge agreed and admonished Weber, "No arguing with the witness."

Several more questions drew sustained objections, too, but Weber knew he was having an impact. It was clear that Prante had lied to his friends about being at Dwayne Conway's house on the day of the murder, and Weber wanted the jury to wonder why.

His caustic attack was not sitting well with some other friends of Chairney and Prante in the courtroom, and their mumbled insults could be heard as the confrontation at the witness stand ended. Romani warned the crowd not to make any more comments or, as judges love to say, "I'm going to clear this courtroom." Weber had never seen it happen, but it still sounded intimidating.

* * *

The near-capacity crowd that attended every day so far swelled to standing room only for the special session held on Saturday to accommodate two of the defense's expert witnesses. The spectators jammed into the rows of benches and, when they were full, stood along all the walls. Don Weber's parents and his wife's uncle even showed up to watch the spectacle. Weber almost felt like a gladiator marching into the arena. Everyone seemed to understand that the trial had reached critical mass on the bite marks. It was make or break time for both sides.

Weber was unsure what Hawkins had accomplished with his witnesses so far. Had the jury found as little in the defense as the prosecutor had? But Weber tried to compensate for his bias by asking other observers for their opinions; most of them thought things were going well for the prosecution. That helped a little, but Weber still worried how the case looked from the jury box. He knew the testimony by the defense experts could tell the story of the verdict. Hawkins surely would score points when his consultants criticized the bite-mark photos and disagreed with the prosecution experts over their value.

But Weber's job today was more than just damage control. He had a big point to make; he couldn't let the defense experts say the spots on Karla's neck were not human bite marks. He could live with experts minimizing the marks as links to Prante or anyone else. But he could not let them say they weren't bite marks.

On the other side of the aisle, Hawkins and John Prante had been disappointed by some of the testimony from the character witnesses Prante recommended as his best friends. They waffled a bit on his character, and Weber got to Chairney significantly. But Prante still thought the trial was going fairly well. As Hawkins called his first expert, he figured the day of reckoning had arrived.

Dr. Donald E. Ore was a pediatric dentist and an associate professor of pediatric dentistry at the University of Illinois College of Dentistry at Chicago. He had been trained as a forensic dentist and worked on many bite-

mark cases, although that soon would become an issue.
He was a consultant to the Cook County medical examiner's office and Dr. Edward Pavlik, who headed the office's dental team and would be Hawkins's next witness.
Ore was part of the team in the final identification of the victims of the DC-10 crash in Chicago. His specialty was photographing dental evidence and bite marks.

To test the doctor's qualifications, Weber applied advice from his experts, Campbell and Levine. They said Ore identified remains through dental evidence; he didn't analyze bite marks and should not be qualified as an expert in them. Limiting him that way would leave little for him to say. So Weber drew testimony from Dr. Ore that his work in the DC-10 crash did not involve bite marks, and he had not performed any computer image-enhancement work, either. Ore had seen enhancements done and had read articles by Dr. Homer Campbell. My expert, Weber thought, is your instructor. Good.

The judge qualified Dr. Ore as an expert only in photography, and Hawkins led him immediately through his description of the proper way to take photos of bite marks. But his language seemed stilted and his vocabulary was quite technical, Weber thought. Dr. Ore might be aiming his testimony well over the jurors' heads.

When Ore started to discuss how bite marks were inflicted, Weber objected that the doctor was not an expert in bite marks. The judge sustained the objection; Weber hoped he had made an important point for the jurors.

When Hawkins showed the photos in this case to the doctor, he said he saw some injuries. But when he started to explain what was wrong with the photos, Weber made a sustained objection again.

Weber began to apply a technique he learned in the first case he tried involving an expert witness. Weber could wreak havoc on experts by dropping objections at the end of the other attorney's lengthy, hypothetical questions setting out the facts. It always befuddled, frustrated, and confused the experts marvelously.

Dr. Ore eventually was allowed to explain that the photos lacked a ruler to indicate the size of the person or the wounds, or how much the picture had been enlarged. Photos enlarged too much suffered breakdown of the grain and distortion of details.

On cross, Weber put all of the doctor's technical explanations into perspective for the jurors.

"What's a photograph supposed to do?"

Ore looked confused. "When you ask that question, sir, are you asking in relationship to the forensic area we develop, or a photograph?"

"Well, let's put it this way. A picture is supposed to record what is viewed through the lens, right?"

"Correct."

Okay, Weber thought. Basic enough. There was information in the pictures, but Ore didn't like the quality. Was that it?

Dr. Ore was more precise. "I have no idea of the magnitude of the enlargement of these pictures. Consequently, they impart to me no meaningful information."

"Well, they impart some meaningful information." Weber held up an enlargement of the bite on Karla's neck. "You can tell that's part of a shoulder, can't you?"

"No, sir. I don't know which is up. There is no orientation as to superior, inferior . . ."

Orientation, superior, inferior. Weber almost laughed. Everyone in the courtroom knew what that picture showed, but Dr. Ore was worried about orientation, superior, and inferior—and which way was up. He didn't know how to give a simple answer.

Weber held up the photo from which the enlargement was made, and got Dr. Ore to agree that he could compare both of them to determine what was shown in the enlargement. Weber pointed to the various shapes in the enlargement and asked if the doctor could recognize them as the neck and shoulders.

"Yes, sir."

When Weber sat down, he hoped the jurors understood that a good photo was just one that showed you something.

* * *

Dr. Edward Pavlik introduced himself to the jury as an orthodontist, explaining his specialty as "the study of the bite." Even Weber thought that was a classy touch—certainly appropriate in this case. Pavlik was a guest lecturer at several well-known schools in the Chicago area; had been the chief of forensic dentistry and head of identification teams for the Cook County coroner's office; and was a consultant to quite a number of police agencies and prosecutors. He belonged to professional groups with Campbell and Levine, too, but was the only expert in Illinois certified by the American Board of Forensic Dentistry.

Hawkins asked if Pavlik wrote articles. The doctor smiled knowingly toward Weber and said, "I don't write too many articles. There are some people in the field who like to write articles. I just try to stay in my county and do what I'm called for, rather than pursuing that." Weber recognized the slap at Dr. Levine. Pavlik and the prosecutor smiled slightly at each other.

Pavlik was in charge of identifying the bodies from two of the worst—and most dissimilar—disasters in Chicago history. He led teams that matched names to the thirty-three victims of John Wayne Gacy—the serial killer in a clown suit who buried his victims under his house—and 270 victims of the DC-10 crash.

Weber questioned him on his qualifications with the same approach he used before. Pavlik agreed there had been no bite marks in either of the tragedies he cited.

The doctor was qualified as an expert in forensic odontology and described the protocol for taking proper photos of bite marks. He mentioned that he always had photos taken by three cameras because one of them invariably failed to work or the film went bad. Weber chuckled; he could relate to that, especially in this case.

Dr. Pavlik showed the jurors a series of proper bitemark photos. And then he described a procedure Weber hadn't heard before but thought was excellent. A mold of a suspect's teeth was used to make a bite mark in wax.

The wax impression was photographed and enlarged to life-sized. The bite mark was traced on a clear plastic overlay, which was then placed on top of a life-sized photo of the bite mark on the victim. All points should match, Pavlik said.

Weber agreed that would be devastating evidence—in a perfect world.

Hawkins handed Pavlik the photos in this case—in the real world—for his analysis. The expert saw a hint of a wound on the neck, but the skin was stretched by someone pulling the chin back. Pavlik compared the effect to writing on a balloon and then squeezing the balloon into different shapes that distorted the writing.

The doctor produced a paper plate on which he had drawn an arched bite-mark pattern along the edge. He showed it to the jury, tilting it slowly to show how the angle changed the shape of the arch. Weber thought it was a cheesy prop, but it was effective.

As Pavlik looked at the enlarged photo, he unexpectedly handed Weber an important concession.

"If someone were to ask me if I see a bite mark—there are abrasions on the neck that can be consistent with a bite mark. When I say consistent, there are patterns there. They are a bruise pattern. Bite marks are usually a bruise pattern, and this could be a bite mark."

He qualified that by describing cases in which similar marks were made by strangulation, by a woman falling on top of a pendant, and by heel marks left when the victim was kicked.

The injuries in the enlarged photo also appeared in a straight line, lacking a dental arch common to bite marks. The only way that could happen was for the skin to be stretched, and that would distort the spacing between the teeth. The larger, high-contrast pictures lacked anything that would tell him what he was looking at and which end was up.

"I find very little evidence here, number one, to even substantiate we have a bite mark. If we do have a bite mark, I have many points that I can't answer. Why would it take a straight-line configuration? And, if that is the case, if these happen to be teeth, I can't measure the teeth because there is no ruler in the picture."

Pavlik explained that adolescents have spaces between their upper front teeth that close as they age. But some adults—he guessed the numbers at five to ten percent—retain spaces between those teeth. He stood at a blackboard to draw the shapes of the front teeth, and to explain how variables can affect the marks they leave. Lighter pressure alters the shape and the spacing, since a shorter tooth might not imprint the skin; that would suggest a space where there really was a tooth.

It was time for Hawkins to move on. "Doctor, for comparison purposes, how would you classify these pictures?"

"For comparison, I would probably qualify them one step above useless."

The comment made Weber wince and sent the reporters in the front row scribbling furiously with one of the best lines so far.

Pavlik called them "dirty pictures" because the wounds had not been cleaned. He couldn't tell whether he was looking at dried blood or other material that would wash off later. Image enhancement would only pick up what was on the photo, so that process would not be definitive.

The doctor was unwilling to assume that the photo showed teeth marks and spaces. But, if it did, "... it might be two front teeth and one off a little bit, with some spacing." He still was bothered by the straight-line appearance, and noted that none of the suspects' dental molds had teeth lined up that way.

"So, Doctor, is it your opinion this evidence is not valuable for comparison purposes?"

"Absolutely. Not valuable."

Weber was pumped for cross-examination. This was an important point in the trial, and he had to be in top form. His experts had drilled him on the proper way to cross Pavlik. But first, Weber wanted to establish who the experts really were.

Dr. Pavlik refused to speculate on whether Dr. Homer Campbell would vote for written standards on bite-mark analysis by the American Academy of Forensic Sciences—the group for which Campbell was national secretary, Levine was a past president, and Pavlik was a member. And, when Weber asked if Dr. Lowell Levine was recognized as an expert in forensic odontology, Pavlik tensed and responded, "I would just as soon not get into personalities because I have personal feelings on these men, and I certainly don't want to put those into this testimony here."

With some sarcasm, Weber asked, "Can I see your plate?" He hoped the jury detected his skepticism about the value of a paper plate in such technical testimony.

Weber and Pavlik sparred for some time over how much the dental arch on the plate would flatten out as the angle of view changed. Weber tilted the plate for the jurors' eyes, trying to show them that an arch could flatten almost to a straight line if the camera angle in a photo was low enough. Pavlik agreed it might "flatten out," but he was resolute that an arch never would become a straight line.

Weber tried a slippery maneuver.

"In these pictures here, describe to the jury what, to you, could be bite marks."

"Could be bite marks?"

"Right."

He was surprised when Dr. Pavlik pointed to the area along Karla's neck and responded, "Oh, I think you could say any of this could be. You could say part of this could be. Bite marks don't have to be a full arch. They could be a number of teeth. This certainly looks like an arch."

That sounded like a major point—perhaps a touch-down—to Weber. He led Pavlik carefully through several questions that had him describing the shape particular teeth left in bite marks. The four front teeth left rectangles and the canines left triangles, Pavlik said.

Weber picked up the enlargement of the bite-mark photo and asked Dr. Pavlik to identify the general shapes in the pattern, one by one. As a sarcastic, in-your-face exchange began, Weber pointed to the first shape.

"What's this darkened area right in here? Describe that in geometric terms."

Pavlik paused, and said, "That has the shape of a rectangle."

"What else have we talked about today that also has the form of a rectangle when it bites?" Sarcasm dripped again.

"Upper front tooth or lower front tooth."

"What's this that's right next to it here?"

"It's another rectangle."

"What's this in between those two rectangles?"

"It's a space."

"Now, if you've got two rectangles and a space, what is it that we talked about this morning that, if bitten into a shoulder, would make two rectangles and a space?"

"Upper two teeth or two lower teeth."

Weber kept pushing.

"So, what we have got then that you will agree on is, we've got a rectangle?"

"Right."

"A space?"

"Right."

"A rectangle?"

"Right."

"A space?"

"Right."

"And what could be the beginning of another rectangle?"

"Agreed."

Weber was on a roll now.

"Could this be a mark left by a canine tooth? I don't want to know, 'Is it?' I don't want to know, 'Are you happy with it?' I don't want to know, 'Will you stake your reputation on it?' I just want to know, 'Could that be the mark left by a canine tooth and the resultant pattern with these?' "

The question drew some grins in the audience, but Dr.

Pavlik wasn't biting. He wouldn't call the mark a triangle from a canine tooth because he couldn't find the lower teeth marks.

Close enough, Weber thought.

He picked up the mold from Prante's teeth—following the instructions from his own experts—and began pointing to the upper teeth.

"What we have here is this tooth, and a space. Right?"

"Right."

"We've got a space there, and a space there. Right?"

"Right."

Weber picked up the picture of the bite marks and held it close to the mold.

"Assume that this is a bite mark. Are these teeth consistent with leaving that bite mark?"

"Yes."

Weber had what he wanted from Pavlik, and he wanted to shout. But he kept plugging.

"They could have left that mark, but you don't want to say if they did or not?"

"Consistent," Pavlik said firmly as he looked at the mold and the photo. "Could be consistent, yes."

Weber had made his point and then some; every expert so far said consistent.

"Dr. Pavlik, how many bite-mark cases have you testified in, in court?"

"One."

Weber ended with a rocket.

"Could John Prante's teeth have left the mark in Karla Brown's shoulder, in your opinion?"

"Could they?"

"Could, yes."

"Yes."

As the judge called a recess, Weber felt victorious. He had exceeded his goal when the defense's own expert pronounced the mark consistent with Prante's teeth and agreed they could have left it on Karla's neck.

When Dr. Pavlik returned to stand for redirect examination, it looked like the defense had completed its picnic set. First it was a paper plate. Now they had a Styrofoam cup.

Pavlik explained that he taken the "rather superficial" step of making bite marks in the cup with the dental molds of Prante, Conway, and Meyers. The doctor's conclusion from the test was that Meyers's and Prante's bite marks were similar enough to be indistinguishable.

"To my opinion, they are so very close I can't tell them apart."

Weber charged again on re-cross. He held up the molds of Prante and Meyers. "Well, these two are very different though, aren't they?"

"Yes. That's the whole point." The very different teeth had made similar bite marks.

Pavlik was willing to rule out Dwayne Conway's teeth, however. They had no spaces between them.

Weber got one more concession before Dr. Edward Pavlik was done.

"In your opinion, are there bite marks in that picture anywhere on Karla Brown, or in any of the pictures you have seen?"

"Bite marks would have to be considered as the primary trauma in the neck area."

The trial was recessed until the next Wednesday, July 13, for the testimony of Hawkins's final expert. Weber wondered if John Prante would step up to the plate that day, too.

Chapter 21

Reasonable doubt. The phrase kept echoing in Neil Hawkins's mind during the four-day break in the trial. He was sure his first two experts had implanted at least a reasonable doubt in the minds of the jurors. Surely it was reasonable to doubt, as those experts did, that the blurs in these photographs absolutely had to be bite marks. Surely the jurors saw at least some chance that they were something else. Perhaps the third expert would tip the scale well beyond reasonable doubt—that elusive and unquantifiable commodity so essential to the defense.

Dr. Norman D. Sperber carried himself with confidence and authority as he took the stand on Wednesday, July 13; Don Weber assumed immediately the expert would be formidable on cross-examination. Sperber was a forensic odontologist who had been a consultant for the San Diego police and sheriff's departments, the district attorney, the coroner, and other law enforcement agencies. He had been appointed by Congress as the national dental consultant to the FBI National Crime Information Center, and had drawn up the form used to record children's dental information in case of an emergency. He was a member of all the proper boards and societies, was certified by the prestigious American Board of Forensic Odontology, and was a member of its committee drawing up standards for bite-mark analysis. He had published five articles in the *FBI Bulletin,* the same magazine that long ago featured Dr. Levine's article on the unreliability of skin for retaining bite marks.

Sperber had been an expert witness in six states and

two court marshals. He had testified in twenty-four bite-mark cases—twenty of those as a prosecution witness—and had been a consultant on more than 150 others for both sides.

There wasn't much Weber could do to challenge this man's qualifications, so Weber tweaked him with special information provided, again, by the prosecution experts. With a couple of simple questions, Weber drew from Dr. Sperber that he was a defense witness in a well-known case in Texas, and the defendant was convicted. In other words, a jury had rejected this expert's testimony for the defense before.

The doctor wasted little time before offering his opinion that the original photo of the bite marks was so "dirty" as to be "unsuitable for comparisons of any sort by anybody." The enlargements were such poor quality that it was difficult to say what they portrayed. The camera angle built in gross distortion.

"I'm not sure that there are any bite marks shown and, if there are bite marks, I wouldn't deem them at all satisfactory for analysis."

Dr. Sperber showed the jury a circular label he applied near bite marks. When taking the picture, he kept the camera at the angle in which the label retained its circular shape, indicating the proper angle to record the mark accurately. But Weber thought that proved his point; the bite mark on Karla showed up flat in the picture because of the camera angle.

The doctor's next demonstration was a slide show featuring two problems with "dirty" pictures—bite marks that really were just dried blood that washed off, or bite marks that did not appear until after the area was cleaned. More slides showed apparent bite marks that turned out to be the result of blood settling in the body after death—postmortem lividity. What looked like bite marks in other photos turned out to be injuries from strangulation. That could be the case in the photo of Karla Brown's neck, Dr. Sperber warned.

Slides of bite marks on the corpse of a little boy

showed how proper photography enabled Sperber to link them to the boy's mother and her boyfriend. In another case, Sperber traced the suspect's teeth on a transparency and applied it to the bite mark on a child, implicating one of five suspects and leading to a confession.

Some of the photos were fuzzy, he said, but they still contained enough information for a valid analysis because they were taken correctly.

After the show, Dr. Sperber renewed his criticism of the photos in evidence. The marks resembled bites, but could be old bruises or scars. The pattern was a straight line, which bite marks never were. How bad were the photos? "They're unusable."

"So, there's no way you can make an analysis of any type, is that correct, Doctor?"

"There's no way the vast majority of forensic odontologists who are skilled in bite-mark evidence would attempt to make analysis."

Hawkins had produced a tough witness, indeed.

As Weber approached the doctor to begin cross, the prosecutor knew this could be "winner take all" on the bite-mark issue.

"Dr. Sperber, concerning that last statement. I guess that's just your opinion. I mean, you don't have any authority for saying that; you haven't been appointed their spokesman."

"No, Mr. Weber." The tone was combative and the use of the name hinted at disdain. "I haven't been appointed anybody's spokesperson. But in just about every case of bite-mark evidence that I have ever seen or been involved in or given an opinion on, there is some kind of identification on the photograph. If you don't have that, you are not dealing with the science, Mr. Weber. You are dealing with witchcraft or opinion."

As the doctor offered a few more comments in that vein, Weber realized the witness knew what he was doing; Sperber was taking control of the questioning from the prosecutor. But that would not happen here; Weber interrupted to complain that the response was wide of the question. He asked again if Sperber was appointed to speak for the vast majority of forensic odontologists. Sperber replied that he was a member of the committee on bite-mark standards, and began to list them again. Weber had heard enough. "I think we are going to get this cross-examination done a lot quicker if you try to limit yourself to the question I ask, please."

The retort was sharp. "I thought I had, counselor."

So sharp that the judge added, "Just answer the question."

That would help rein in the witness, Weber knew.

Weber showed Sperber the photo of Karla's neck.

"Now, I'm not asking you whether or not we have a distorted bite mark in that picture. I'm just asking you whether or not those lines and spaces could be a bite mark."

"I have never seen anything like that before in my life. I guess it could be, because anything is possible. But I have never seen anything like that."

That was enough of a concession to get started. Weber led Dr. Sperber down the same path he had taken Dr. Pavlik, getting the witness to agree that the marks in the photograph appeared to be rectangles.

Weber picked up the mold of Prante's teeth and asked if those upper, central incisors could have made the rectangular marks. Sperber said no, because the teeth showed a slight curve that he did not see in the photo.

Weber pounced. "So, you are picking up an individual, characteristic detail—out of this photograph you said was useless—to rule out this man. Is that what you're doing?"

There was no response. Weber let the silence hang in the air for a moment before asking if the camera angle could have caused the curve of a tooth to flatten out.

"I guess that's possible."

"So, what you're saying then, is that one of these teeth could have made that rectangle?"

"With all the possible distortion, yes, I suppose it's possible."

That much done, Weber got the doctor to agree the adjacent shapes could be rectangles and spaces, too.

"Okay. So this could be a bite mark right here?"

"Yes, sir."

"And the bite mark could have been made by the defendant's teeth?"

"By that defendant's teeth; it's possible."

Another bingo.

Dr. Sperber scored some points by sketching on the blackboard how cracked or broken teeth leave marks that seem to suggest a space where there really was a tooth. Weber couldn't do much against that, so he introduced one of his favorite arguments, stolen years ago from his brother, Philip. Weber asked the doctor to list the features of a bite mark. "You know. A duck has a bill, and webbed feet, and feathers, and wings. What does a bite mark have?"

First, a curved pattern, an arch.

"In any of these photographs, are there curved areas in the general area of the collarbone?"

"Yes, sir."

Second, spacings.

"Are there spacings in some of those curved areas in that picture?"

"There appear to be interruptions in the general dark marks, whatever they are."

The third and fourth characteristics were size and human bite. The prosecutor and the expert dueled a while, but finally agreed that the curved, spaced area had a size consistent with a human bite mark.

Fifth? Symmetry. "Those marks appear to be symmetrical."

"So," Weber drawled, "that's five things and so far all five things are consistent with the fact that we have a bite mark."

Dr. Sperber paused for what seemed a long time, and then reluctantly nodded yes.

Weber ran through the list of characteristics again. "So,

we have all of those things that tell us we have got a duck here, and they are all present in your opinion?"

"Uh-huh. You betcha'."

With that answer, Weber tried to wrap it up by asking if Prante's teeth could have made those wounds on Karla's shoulder. The doctor would not give in that easily; he wanted to go through each of his complaints about the photos again.

"I don't feel comfortable with any of these pictures, Mr. Weber, which is why I flew out here."

Weber tried again. "Okay. Now, I understand that this isn't the way that you would do things in San Diego, California. But what I'm asking you, in this courtroom in East Alton, Illinois, is could—not did they—could the defendant's teeth have caused the injury to Karla Brown's shoulder?"

"If we apply the reasoning you have said, it's possible that his teeth might have made those marks as seen on the shoulder."

The doctor was adamant that he could not say whether or not John Prante made the mark. Weber would settle for less.

"Okay. Could have? Could have done it?"

"Could have done it."

"And the six characteristics that you listed, that you look for in bite marks, are all there?"

"Yes, sir."

As Weber sat down, he wondered if it had sounded as good out there as it did to him.

Hawkins was anxious to get Dr. Sperber back on track with redirect. What were the reasons he would say those weren't bite marks? Sperber returned to the dirty picture idea, adding that any number of objects could have made those marks. There was no way to know if the picture showed old marks that were there for years. They were consistent with a bite mark; but, with a photo that failed to meet reasonable and scientific standards, an analysis of bite marks would set a dangerous precedent that threatened to weaken the science of forensic odontology.

Weber came back on re-cross to explain Dr. Case's examination of the tissue samples and bruising. Sperber agreed that could establish the marks as made about the time of death.

Everything considered, could Prante have made the bite marks?

"Yes, sir, anything is possible."

Hawkins got one more try. "That's just possible, Doctor? Is it not probable?"

"Oh, that's possible. Definitely not probable."

As Dr. Sperber left the stand, both attorneys felt they had made their points. Not a bad morning's work.

Weber thought he had won the debate, but he conceded that Dr. Sperber had been more adept at fencing than the previous witnesses. He had changed subjects on the prosecutor and derailed his train of thought several times. And Weber respected Sperber's honesty and dedication to his science.

As Weber headed for lunch, he still didn't know whether he had to face John Prante on the witness stand that afternoon. The match with Dr. Sperber had been tiring; how much did Weber have left if he had to take on Prante, too? Surely, Prante would testify; he had to explain a myriad of contradictions and wobbly stories and incriminating details. He remembered too many specifics, too many times; he knew things he couldn't know if he was innocent. Surely he had spent the last year—perhaps the last five—working up a good story for this day. He had to be ready to explain why he got confused and how other people misinterpreted his comments.

John Prante on the stand presented Weber with problems, too. Jurors expected the defendant to explode under withering cross-examination, perhaps even to burst into a dramatic confession before the last commercial. Those confessions never really happened in court, and the only way for a prosecutor to get much in the way of fireworks was to be mean; that carried the risk of alienating the jurors. Weber had to tread a fine line, but he couldn't let

Prante look so meek and mild that jurors would have difficulty believing he would hurt a fly.

Weber had a secret course well charted by FBI Agent John Douglas. Douglas had coached the prosecutor in the trial of Wayne Williams, the serial killer of twenty-seven children in Atlanta. Douglas told the prosecutor to wear down Williams with a long, arduous cross-examination, and then use some special techniques to make the witness show the anger and power that killed the victims. It worked when Williams exploded furiously on the stand, calling the prosecutor a fool and the FBI goons. Williams was convicted.

Weber wondered if he would get a chance to use the weapons John Douglas had provided for this part of the case.

The prosecutor thought his experts and cross-examination of the defense experts should have proven to a number of the jurors that Prante's teeth made those bite marks. But there probably were some others who remained unsure. So Weber planned an end run for them. He would increase his emphasis on the evidence from Prante's friends—looking more toward the words from Prante's mouth than the teeth in that mouth.

It was awfully late in the trial, and Weber still wondered where he stood. What was the jury hearing? Did he have Prante yet, or was he wiggling out of it? Weber still had no opinion on the outcome of this tough trial.

At lunch, Weber was congratulated by his colleagues, the cops, and his parents for his cross-examination of the experts. Donna and Terry Judson were so impressed with Weber's "duck" routine that they began quacking in its honor. It was picked up by the prosecution's team and became a running gag.

When the attorneys met in chambers after lunch, Neil Hawkins asked Judge Romani to allow the introduction of a newspaper article as evidence; Hawkins wanted to use the *Globe-Democrat* "cheerleader" story that proposed an explanation for Weber's obsession with the case. Weber had vowed he would solve the crime. "He has picked a defendant, and he picked Mr. Prante," Hawkins charged.

Weber objected strenuously. Injecting a prosecutor's opinion was improper and the story added the irrelevant issue of his personal feelings. Hawkins was preparing an accusation for closing arguments that Weber would be satisfied to get someone, anyone.

Romani agreed with Weber and barred the story.

Back in the courtroom, Hawkins addressed the judge. "At this time, I would call the defendant, John Prante."

For Hawkins and Prante, there never was a question about whether he would testify. He wanted to tell his story, and they knew it was mandatory that he explain his actions and the testimony of the other witnesses. Hawkins had not coached him; the defender knew what his client would say and where his story would go.

Weber watched Prante closely as he took the stand to fight for his freedom, and perhaps his life. Dressed in the light blue suit, he still looked perfectly relaxed. But Weber thought he detected some anxiety in the eyes. As Hawkins guided Prante slowly through an account of his years living and going to school in the area, Prante's voice was even calmer than it had sounded on tape.

The comparison slipping into Weber's mind was Norman Bates dressed as his mother, sitting so calmly in the padded cell at the end of the movie *Psycho*. The deluded Norman was thinking, "I'll show them. I wouldn't even hurt a fly."

Donna Judson, hearing Prante speak for the first time, was surprised that his voice wasn't lower and stronger. She hadn't expected such a soft, moderate sound from this coarse-looking man.

The voice was so low that many of those crowded into the rear of the courtroom couldn't hear well. They spent much of Prante's time on the stand straining to hear, or asking their neighbors if they heard the last bit of testimony.

Weber was listening intently to Prante, but the prosecutor also was using this time to get ready for cross-examination.

Files were being pulled and transcripts were being readied. It was time to go for broke.

Hawkins moved immediately to one of the cornerstones of John Prante's view of himself and how he fit into this world. Hawkins asked about Prante's traumatic experience in the Navy, and he launched into an elaborate description of how staying overnight in the Philippines had put him on fifteen days of "ship's restriction," and how he ended up before the captain after he failed to report as often as required on restriction. Even there, Prante explained, he had been victimized by a cruel mistake. He misunderstood his commander's intentions and, out of fear, threw himself on the captain's mercy before the commander could intercede on his behalf. The result was thirty days in the brig.

"The first thing that happened there was, 'Hit the floor. I want to see how many pushups you can do.' I think I knocked off about forty, fifty."

He said the Marine guards forced him to do so many pushups that he eventually could do 200 at a time easily. As he described abuse and cruelty, his voice began to quiver.

"They would wake you up at 2 o'clock in the morning sometimes; drop a billy club on your head. 'Get down and give me two hundred.' We got down and gave them two hundred."

Prante started to cry and put his hand over his face.

"Excuse me. It's—I still remember it like it was yesterday, and it hurts."

Weber looked at the jurors. They were watching Prante intently, but Weber couldn't read their faces. He thought Prante's whimpers were insultingly phony and manipulative, and that they played horribly in the courtroom.

From the other side of the room, Hawkins glanced over and thought the jurors were rapt by the wounded man they were seeing.

Prante described continued beatings by the Marines that finally pushed him over the edge. "I commenced to beat my head on the wall. I wanted to end it. I didn't want to live anymore."

Fighting back tears with every word, Prante recounted how he ended up in sick bay, and how word of his distraught condition went up the chain of command, all the way to the admiral. He cried again as he remembered being too nervous to serve on the flight deck anymore; he was given a transfer.

Hawkins had Prante explain that the Marines were the equivalent of the police aboard ship, and how that left him fearful of any police officer he saw anywhere. "I didn't want them to be near me. If I were out driving around, and I saw one in the mirror, I would freak out."

But it was worse than that. "I always felt that if I were busted for something small, I'd probably run. I would make them kill me because I wouldn't go behind bars again."

Tough luck, Weber thought. Better get used to the idea, John.

Hawkins asked Prante to go back to the evening of June 20, 1978. "Can you recall that evening?"

"Only through what I have read, and what I have heard, and come to believe myself."

That was the code, Weber thought. Prante would remember only what fit into his story without making himself look bad.

Prante described smoking pot and drinking on the porch with Dwayne Conway and Lee Barns, and watching the people arrive at "Karla's house next door."

Weber was struck by Prante's familiar use of her name.

Barns had stepped into the driveway and spoken to Karla briefly. Prante didn't know anyone at Karla's party, nothing else happened, and Prante took Barns home.

Prante was giving soft, slippery answers, Weber noticed. Everything was qualified with "I believe" or "to the best of my knowledge." Prante was phrasing everything to give him room to wiggle when the inescapable contradictions were raised later.

Prante said he was driving the blue Volkswagen in

1978. He normally would wear a decent shirt and wouldn't go out in just a T-shirt. He was wearing a red and white ball cap, or one of the caps from Petroleum Helicopter; he didn't mention the color.

On the morning of the murder, Prante put in job applications and arrived at Conway's between 10 and noon. They sat around the front porch and got high again. How long was he there?

"I keep having this feeling that I was there all day, that I stayed the entire day. That just keeps coming to mind."

Too soft, too vague, Weber thought. If this was Prante's plan for defending himself, it should fail miserably.

Nothing else happened until the police began arriving at "Karla's house." Since Prante and Conway were smoking marijuana, and because of Prante's distaste for the cops now crawling all over the neighborhood, Prante suggested moving inside.

"Do you recall where you went after you left Dwayne Conway's house that evening?"

"It keeps feeling right to say that I went to Harold's, mostly because I can recall going to Harold's, and I can recall at that time, that Dwayne came over. This stuck in my mind that Dwayne showed up, and he was shook to some degree, and he went on to explain more about what was going on there at Karla's."

The next time Prante heard about the murder was at Spencer Bond's, when Spencer was joking about it. "He was pointing fingers and stuff. He was saying, 'Well, maybe you did it.' No man, no way. No way."

Prante took a quick shot at Bond in the middle of the description, mentioning that "Spencer was in business back then." Weber wondered if the jury caught the drug-sales implication.

The defendant remembered being interviewed by then-chief Ralph Skinner, who wanted to know what Prante saw that day. But Prante couldn't recall much more about the discussion; he had been nervous and had a hard time remembering things from that period because he was partying a lot with booze and pot.

"I remember one time going for a lie detector test," Prante added. He slipped in that inadmissible tidbit smoothly, Weber mused.

Prante produced the title to the red, 1974 Volkswagen, showing it was transferred to him by his father on September 25, 1978. Before that, Prante said, he always drove the blue Beetle. His father wouldn't let him drive the other cars because he had wrecked one in 1976 when he was "wasted, I mean really blowed away" one night. "Somewhere I have this feeling that I did a complete flip and landed back on the wheels, but I'm not sure on that."

Hawkins pulled Dwayne Conway into the story, and Prante described him as a good friend who had been a troubled teenager. Prante had taken Dwayne under his wing to help straighten him out, letting him run and party with Prante's group. "He turned out to be relatively a good person," Prante vouched.

He recalled an incident after he returned from Louisiana in 1980. He was at Spencer Bond's when Dwayne Conway came in, nervous and desperate for a beer. The police had just taken his dental impressions because they had learned Karla Brown was bitten.

" 'And there's another thing, John,' " Prante quoted Conway as saying. " 'Do you realize we never said the same thing on our statements?' And I said, 'No. We still haven't gotten our stories straight?' We never took the time."

Weber thought Prante was setting up his old pal, Dwayne, as the stooge; it was Conway who was worried about getting the stories straight. Prante was suggesting he really wasn't concerned that much about their stories until 1980, contradicting the recollections from the Whites and Bonds.

In 1982, the publicity in the newspapers and on television began about the new investigation and the exhumation; and then Spencer Bond showed up with all of his questions.

"That started making me a little more paranoid and a

lot more curious to find out what was going on," Prante said.

Of course it did, Weber thought, just as John Douglas predicted.

Prante was stunned by Bond's accusations; Prante never said the things his old friend was remembering, and it set off Prante's special, internal alarm.

"I always have this thing, whether it is my subconscious or self-conscious, but when something isn't right, I can either hear a negative-type bell that starts ringing—a feeling of paranoia in me—or if something is right, I can feel a positive-type bell. Something he was saying just didn't sound right. And he's saying things that I had never known before."

Weber rocked back in his chair and looked at the jurors. Did Prante really want these adults to believe this drivel? They were listening, but Weber couldn't tell what they were thinking.

Bite marks, buckets of water. Prante never heard of these things that Spencer Bond was remembering. It went on for hours, finally giving Prante a headache. In the days after that, Prante talked with several other people because Bond had made him so paranoid.

"I even called up a lawyer and then, against his better judgment, I talked to Mr. Weber."

That got a chuckle from the crowd, and Weber grinned as he remembered what the real effect of that call had been.

Prante said he offered his help to Weber, who said there were other people under suspicion and denied that Spencer Bond was working for the police.

"And the next thing I know, I'm the prime suspect."

Amazing how that worked, wasn't it? Weber thought.

"Did Mr. Weber tell you whether or not you were a suspect at that time?"

"He said I was a low-level suspect and I was not to worry about things, because I would be excluded very shortly. He wanted to know a lot more about Dwayne Conway."

Prante went to Conway's that Sunday afternoon to try to find out exactly what happened at Dwayne's house four years earlier.

"After three or four years, now we were going to finally get our stories straight and find out what he had said and what I had said on the statement, compare what it was supposed to look like, and just basically figure out what was going on, because we had no idea."

Weber winced. Had Prante meant to admit that he and Conway were trying to "get their stories straight"? The prosecutor thought that wouldn't sound too good to the jurors.

Prante and Conway had trouble remembering which day the party was and what happened the day the police arrived. They were worried about what Spencer Bond was up to, since he had made such surprise visits to both of them.

Hawkins asked about the "gas chamber" line, and Weber had to admit Prante's response was pretty clever. He said the two men were afraid Bond was trying to put both of them over the barrel, figuratively, and Prante said, " 'Whatever he's trying to do, he's going to put one of us in the gas chamber.' It wasn't, 'One of us two is going to the gas chamber.' It was, 'If he can do it and, for one reason or another, he's doing it.' "

Prante said Conway accused the police of harassing him into making a phony statement the day before, putting false words in his mouth and haranguing him to sign the statement even though he was about to fall out of the chair from lack of sleep.

Judge Romani sustained an objection from Weber that the testimony was hearsay because Conway was not available to testify.

Hawkins turned to Sherry Dalton. "Did you ever tell her, at any time, that you killed anybody?"

"As a matter of fact, I told her that I had never killed anybody."

Weber was somewhat surprised when Hawkins asked only one question about her testimony before moving to the day Prante was arrested. He was questioned for some time by Randy Rushing and Tom O'Connor, with O'Connor suggesting Prante had gone into a rage or had a flashback to Vietnam. Prante finally said he wanted a lawyer, and it only was then that they announced he was under arrest and read his rights. Prante was flabbergasted. In the car, O'Connor kept telling Prante how much time before he arrived at the jail, urging him to offer the rage or flashback lines. O'Connor even mentioned Prante's trouble in the Navy, shocking Prante that the cop knew that. When Prante was booked at the jail, O'Connor told him, "I don't ever want to hear you say nothing about a Marine again, or I'm going to hit you, man."

That was the first word Weber believed; he doubted that O'Conner the Marine would listen to any corpsbashing by Prante the swabbie.

Prante denied owning a "Big Bamboo" T-shirt, but said he once borrowed one from Harold Pollard to wear on a date because all of Prante's clothes were dirty. Must of been some date, Weber thought.

Prante explained the wires found in his car were used to hook up the taillights when he towed the Volkswagen behind the Lincoln, which he had sold shortly before his arrest.

"John, is this all you know about the investigation of the death of Karla Brown?"

"Yes, sir. This is it."

"Did you know Karla Brown?"

"No, sir," he said softly.

"Did you ever tell anyone you killed Karla Brown?"

"No, sir, I haven't."

"You, yourself, did not commit the murder of Karla Brown, or know anything about it?"

"No, sir."

At a recess after Prante's direct testimony, he looked at his lawyer and asked, "How'd it go?" Hawkins shrugged. "Okay. It could have been better, but it could have been worse."

When Don Weber approached Prante for cross, the prosecutor could see apprehension in the man's eyes. Weber was anxious to try to show him to be a liar and killer, but the process would be slow and drawn out and difficult. Weber wondered how Prante would stand up.

First, Weber set the ground rules by having Prante agree that he had read all the police reports and statements from other witnesses in the file. Some of his answers were so soft that Weber asked him to speak up.

Next, Weber addressed Prante's police phobia, getting him to agree that he wasn't nervous when Chief Skinner interviewed him. He agreed he probably told Spencer Bond later that the police could ask anything; he was not worried. Yes, he even said several times he might go in and talk to the police and, in fact, called Weber.

The prosecutor recalled Prante reporting a burglary to the police, noting that there were fingerprints on a window. "You know a little about fingerprints?"

"I only know that when you see a ridge, that is a fingerprint."

"You know about wiping fingerprints off?"

"No."

Weber mentioned the legal advice warning Prante not to talk to the authorities anymore. Despite that, Prante called Weber and gave a statement to Rushing and O'Connor.

"I made a mistake and I thought I knew it all. I thought—"

"You thought you could talk your way out of it, and it turns out you couldn't?"

"If I thought that, I would have had an attorney."

Weber was hammering at Prante with his own statements. What about Prante's vow to get involved in this investigation? Would someone so paranoid about the police get involved in an investigation that didn't concern him? Prante shrugged. He had been worried about what Spencer Bond was doing; that was all.

Weber reminded Prante that he denied being at

Conway's house on the day of the killing when he was interviewed by Chief Skinner.

"Now, explain to the jury why you said that."

"Well, it's—I don't know. Memory problem."

"What?"

"Memory or confusion."

There was the whole defense, Weber thought. He pressed the attack by ticking off the things Prante mentioned to Spencer Bond about the events the afternoon of the murder. Three or four cop cars. The guy in the pickup truck wore glasses and had brown hair. He was heavier than Prante. An ambulance arrived.

Prante piped up, "I don't recall seeing an ambulance."

"Well, tell the jury how it is that, three days after the killing, you couldn't even remember if you were there that day, but five years after the killing you remember that the guy who pulled in the driveway had glasses on?"

"Well, it's a strong probability that I was either hung over, or hadn't been awake more than a half-hour. Something of that nature."

The judge had to tell Prante to speak up again. As he fought to retain control, his voice had dropped even lower.

Prante couldn't remember the interview with Sergeant McEuen on July 5, just something about a photograph that day. That brought Weber to Prante's second phobia. Weber picked up Prante's photo album, asking if he always disliked being photographed.

He saw Weber pick up the album. "No, 'cause there's some photographs in my albums on that."

"Which albums are you talking about?"

"Photo albums. There's photos of me in there. Not many. There's a couple. And it did apply to them."

"In fact, there are sixteen pictures of you in these photo albums, aren't there?"

Had Prante's phobia about having his picture taken come up after McEuen told him about Eric and Edna Moses seeing someone talking to Karla in the driveway?

"I guess. I don't know."

That should put that to rest, Weber thought.

"Do you remember telling McEuen that there was a party over there, and there were good-looking girls there, and the gal living there was beautiful, and you had hoped you would be invited over there?"

"No, I don't remember saying that."

"Could you have said that?"

"No, I couldn't have said that."

"You did not say that to McEuen?"

"What I'm getting to is that, in the truth of the day in '78 . . ."

Weber wasn't going to let that revealing comment slide by.

"Well, what do you mean, 'the truth of the day'? Is there a different truth in '78 than there is now?"

"What I'm saying is, that there's massive confusion here. I have been told to believe a bunch of things by your people."

"Who told you to believe things?"

"Didn't Spencer? He tried to convince me of all kinds of things that I knew I had never said. What I'm saying is, that I really don't know what I'm saying. Run that past me again."

Prante looked foolish; Weber asked again about wanting to go to the party. Prante didn't remember saying it, and wouldn't have meant it if he did.

"Okay, what do you mean you wouldn't have meant it?"

"I had no interest in the girl."

"You hadn't talked about her prior to her being killed?"

"No, I hadn't."

"You hadn't met her that night of the party?"

"No. I never met her."

"Didn't know her name prior to the killing?"

"No. No, I didn't."

Prante thought he first learned of Karla's death when Conway arrived at Harold Pollard's house.

Did Prante remember telling Detective Rick White that

he had seen Karla puttering around in her front yard the day of the killing?

"I don't remember ever talking to Rick White, but I do remember the incident of seeing Karla out in the front yard, puttering around the yard. It had to be morning or mid-afternoon, early afternoon. The clothes were different than what you have showed in display here, though. The clothes that I remember seeing her in was white shorts and a white, flowered top."

Weber was stung by the significance of that admission, and he believed it was absolutely true. The killer remembered the clothes his victim wore because, if John Douglas was right, the killer probably took them as a souvenir. Weber pressed hard.

"Uh-huh. Just like the Moseses saw, right?"

"I believe so."

Weber hoped the jury would catch the implication about a killer and his mementos, even though he didn't expect Prante to fall for something so transparent.

"Where are those shorts and white, flowered top now?"

Hawkins's objection was sustained, but Prante responded, "I have no idea."

Weber went back to Dwayne Conway, mixing the questions to keep Prante off balance. Prante agreed that he and Conway differed about the events on the day of the killing when they talked at Conway's trailer. Weber saw a chance to slip in part of Conway's statement.

"Okay. Dwayne Conway wasn't going to alibi you for sitting on the porch all day, from 10 until the police arrived, was he?"

"You're right."

The challenger was not so slick, nor was his story so polished. Weber attacked the essence of Prante's defense.

"Did you tell Rushing and O'Connor, 'Regardless of what the witnesses say, I was not at Karla Brown's residence the day of the murder'?"

"Yes."

Weber returned to Prante's claim about borrowing Pollard's "Big Bamboo" T-shirt. After all, Prante, who said he weighed 180 pounds, was a pretty big guy.

"Did you really do 200 push-ups at one time?"

"Sure."

"Have a lot of upper-body strength?"

"Back then, yeah, in '71."

"Did you, on June 21, 1978, have a lot of power in your arms and hands?"

Prante caught the implication. "No more than anybody else."

"Harold testified that you were very bitter toward females and you couldn't stand rejection. Do you want to explain that to the jury—your bitterness and your rejection?"

"I don't think I have been bitter towards women. That's that man's opinion."

With that groundwork laid, it was time to kick in the power and make the last turn toward the clubhouse. Weber listed the details from the Whites, the Bonds, Harold Pollard, Lee Barns, and Sherry Dalton. He dredged up each secret fact that should have been known only to the victim, the killer, and in some cases the police. And Prante denied that he revealed any of those things to his friends; he hadn't even known about them.

As Weber went through the statement of each witness, and Prante issued his denials in rapid fire, Weber slapped the files onto the table. The "splat" from each report echoed through the courtroom as the files—and the irrefutable evidence—piled up.

"Did you tell Harold that Karla Brown had been found on the floor?"

"No."

"Did you tell Harold that she had been found with her hands tied behind her?"

"No."

"Did you tell Harold that she had been beaten up pretty bad?"

"No."

"Did you tell Harold that she had been strangled, tied up, and beaten?"

"No."

"Is there any way you could have known that . . ."

"No."

". . . when Harold Pollard testified that you knew it?"

"Nope."

"Did you tell Harold that you got inside the house and got a look at the body on the floor with the hands tied behind her?"

"No."

"Is there any way you could have?"

"Huh-uh. No way."

And Prante especially did not mention bite marks on Karla's shoulder to Spencer Bond or Vicky White, nor had he bitten Sherry Dalton. He never was in a rage, as described by Sherry.

Weber handed Prante his job application with those stunning words in it.

"Well, how do you understand 'depression, rage, and the calm after a storm'?"

" 'Cause—one of them—I'm a sailor. And, two, the rage part and the depressions—you would not believe how many times I have had to bolster Dwayne back after defeat with a woman, how many times he'd almost committed suicide."

Weber had Prante read the last item he wrote under "recreation."

"Oh, I list 'and women.' Uh-huh," Prante said calmly. He tried to make it sound matter-of-fact, but Weber was sure the jurors could read the implication.

Prante denied that Lee Barns had introduced him to Karla.

"So, I guess you are telling the jury he got up here and lied?"

"Yes, he did."

Weber pointed to the stack of files on the table. "And that goes for Pollard, Bond, Vicky White, Mark White?"

"Harold was confused. Spencer—I'm not sure why he

did it. And I have known the Whites—that if Spencer says, 'Let's do this,' they will say, 'Yep, yep. yep.' "

"So they're framing you because they are real good friends with Spencer Bond?"

"I'm not sure why all of this is coming down. I have my hunch, but . . ."

"Could it be because you actually told them that, and you actually killed Karla Brown on June 21, 1978?"

"No, no. There's no way. I couldn't have done it, and I didn't."

It was time to play the trump card dealt by John Douglas. It was time to take the truth about the horror in Karla Brown's basement right into the face of her killer in a way only John Douglas could have understood. Weber began a slow march to the witness stand, getting closer and louder with each question.

"Now, you described what Karla had on that day, so you must have seen her, right?"

"I guess I did."

"Well, you were having a conversation with her by the sidewalk . . ."

"No."

". . . when the Moseses pulled in this driveway?"

"No."

Weber was only a few feet from Prante. "Were you having an argument with her?"

"No."

"Did you follow her back downstairs?"

"No."

"Downstairs, did she try to kick you in the knee?"

"No."

Weber's eyes narrowed, and he leaned in close enough to touch the defendant.

"Now, Mr. Prante, you testified about your push-ups . . ."

Weber thrust his hands in front of him, gesturing as if he were strangling someone.

"When you had your hands around her neck . . ."

Prante spat out, "I didn't!"

Weber was almost in Prante's face. ". . . and you were choking the life out of her . . ."

The defense attorney nearly shouted, "I object."

Judge Romani called the attorneys to the bench, and Weber knew his shot at breaking Prante had been lost. The tension and drama of the one and only moment was broken while the judge heard Hawkins's objection to Weber's theatrics. Weber argued that he had to be allowed latitude on cross, but the judge told him to stay back from the witness and avoid theatrics.

Weber wouldn't know for a long time how close he had come to real fireworks. The only person who could gauge that was the court reporter, Alisa Heyen, whose seat near the witness stand put her almost between the two men. Only she could see Prante's feet shifting under his chair and his knuckles turning white as he gripped the arms of the chair with increasing power. She was convinced Prante was about to leap out of his chair at the prosecutor.

Hawkins had seen, however, how close Weber was to scoring significant points with the tactic of getting in the witness's face. The defender knew an objection at the right moment would destroy the tension Weber clearly was building.

When Weber stepped back before the stand, he hoped to reignite Prante's fuse by recalling how Karla had been impertinent enough to bleed on him. But it was obvious from Prante's face that he had regained his composure. Weber tried to pick up where he left off. "Do you remember saying, 'If I thought that somebody did it—like if I thought Dwayne went over there and came back with blood up to his elbows or something, I would have to do something about it?' Do you remember saying that?"

"All right. Okay."

"Is it your opinion that that's what happened? That someone had to come back with blood up to their elbows?"

"No. It was only an assumption. I had no idea what happened that day to anybody, whoever did it."

John Douglas's tactic almost had worked. Douglas said

the killer still would be furious that his victim had the te-
merity to bleed on him, and reminding him of that could
set him off uncontrollably. Weber was sure he had pushed
Prante to the edge of the abyss.

Weber turned and walked back to his seat, hoping the
jurors had seen the real John Prante. A depressed, angry
man capable of explosive violence; a man whose memory
really was carefully selective, not poor. He had been
caught telling stories that contradicted each other—
internally inconsistent—as well as stories that were contradicted by the facts—externally inconsistent. The only
way Prante could know what he knew when he knew it,
was to be the man who killed Karla Brown.

Judge Romani read a series of stipulations to the jurors
that included parts of newspaper stories Hawkins hoped
contained enough details about the murder to give Prante
some basis for his statements. Weber knew the timing
was off, however; the details came out after Prante revealed them to his friends.

Hawkins rested the defense case, and court was recessed.

The next morning—Thursday, July 14—Weber called
his rebuttal witnesses. Rushing and O'Connor testified
they read Prante the Miranda warnings before they questioned him. White and Greer said Prante made voluntary
statements on the day the dental impressions were taken.
Harold Pollard said only Prante had a "Big Bamboo"
T-shirt.

Then Weber called Dr. Homer Campbell, who flew
back from Albuquerque to rebut the suggestion that Tony
Garza was Karla's killer. Weber's team agreed Campbell
had been the best and most credible of all the expert witnesses, and he was the clear choice to rebut the defense.
Besides, Weber's experience suggested that jurors in
southern Illinois preferred the guys in cowboy boots.

Weber handed Campbell Tony Garza's dental impressions and asked if those teeth could have made the bites
on Karla's neck. The doctor said flatly, "They could not

have," then stepped in front of the jury box to point out each contrasting detail. Weber asked if the bite marks were human. Definitely, was the answer—no doubt at all. It was gratifying to have an expert offer such positive, absolute opinions after all the waffling.

Campbell was just as certain when asked if he was looking at dirty pictures. "That's not a dirty photograph as far as I'm concerned. I have seen a lot of dirty photographs, and that isn't one of them."

Weber handed Campbell the Styrofoam cup bearing bite marks of Prante and Jack Meyers. "Can you tell them apart?"

"Oh, absolutely."

"Which are which?"

"The top one is the defendant's, and the bottom one is someone else's."

Weber ended with what he hoped was a big splash.

"With respect to the teeth that you have examined in this case: Tony Garza, Jack Meyers, Dwayne Conway, John Prante—I think you looked at Mr. Rushing's teeth, and my teeth, and Mr. Hawkins's teeth. Of those people, who could have made the mark on Karla Brown's shoulder?"

"The only teeth that are consistent with that particular mark are the defendant's."

Weber took a deep breath; the jurors had heard all the evidence in the longest trial of his career. He just hoped all of the effort over five years had not been in vain.

Chapter 22

"I think the evidence has shown in this case that there isn't any question that John Prante killed Karla Brown. I think there is some question as to exactly how he went about it. But I don't think there is any question that he did it."

When Don Weber faced the nine women and three men of the jury for closing arguments that morning, distilling the case to one basic question was simple. The prosecution's witnesses, especially the experts, had proven beyond a reasonable doubt—beyond any doubt in Weber's mind—that John Prante was Karla's killer. Weber thought his experts clearly had outgunned the defense experts. Now he stood before the jury to put it all into perspective.

All of the contradictions they heard from Prante's own mouth could be interpreted. "He had no reaction, and he could give no reason, as to why he intentionally misstated a number of things. There's only one reaction you could have to that, and that's that you are dealing with someone who is guilty, someone who can't tell the truth, because the truth isn't in him."

Weber told the jurors to apply their common sense and experiences in life to what they had heard and seen in the courtroom. There was a perfect example among the witnesses.

"If you are Vicky White and you read in the newspaper that Karla Brown's body is going to be exhumed because the authorities didn't know about bite marks in 1978, and you remember John Prante told you about the bite marks in 1978, then from your own, common experiences in

life, it's very simple to conclude that John Prante is the
murderer. That's what Vicky White did."

Faithful performance of the jurors' duty was essential
to justice, and that meant it was their duty to convict
Prante because there was no reasonable doubt of his guilt.
Some doubt could exist on some details, and the verdict
still should be guilty. Weber explained that a doubt over
whether Prante drove a red car or a blue car was not
enough to acquit him; the facts proved, anyway, that
Prante was driving the red car.

The jurors didn't have to know the sequence of events
to find Prante guilty. They didn't have to know when
Karla was beaten with the TV-tray stand, or whether she
died on the couch or in the barrel of water.

All of the experts—even the reluctant defense experts—agreed there were bite marks on Karla's neck; the
prosecutor's experts concluded the marks were consistent
with John Prante and no one else. In fact, only one percent of the population could have teeth comparable to
Prante's. Who else could it be?

"You don't have to believe there are bite marks on the
shoulder, or that the bite marks are consistent with John
Prante, or that they show you anything. But you have to
believe one thing—that John Prante murdered Karla
Brown. These other things, I think, are clearly proven by
the evidence."

Weber conceded that each juror probably had a different theory of what happened that day, because only two
people really knew.

"One was Karla Brown. And, even though she spoke to
us from the grave, she couldn't testify and she couldn't
tell you exactly how it happened. The other one is the defendant, and he lied about it. So, no one probably will
ever know exactly how John Prante killed Karla Brown."

Weber began to set up the arguments about the death
penalty, explaining that the murder charges alleged that
Prante killed Karla while committing a burglary, and that
the burglary was done with the intent to steal something

or commit a rape. The removal of a tampon certainly was a substantial step toward the rape.

One of the major issues was John Prante's memory. All of the details Prante listed to several witnesses proved he had better recall then than he wanted to have now. Weber cited the memory of Eric Moses, the little boy whose grandmother said had such a fantastic memory, and who proved it by recalling the clothes of the woman he saw in Karla's driveway.

"Well, who else in this case had a memory as fantastic as Eric Moses? There's one person, and that's John Prante. He remembered the blouse and the color of the blouse."

Weber was pointing at the man at the defense table. Among the bits and pieces of this tragic tale, Weber's belief that Prante took Karla's clothes was one that made the prosecutor furious. When he thought about Prante pawing through his souvenirs, Weber's righteous anger rolled out and he had to struggle to control it.

In minute detail, Weber went through all of the contradictions between Prante and the other witnesses. Four people knew specific details of the crime scene in 1978, and said they heard them from Prante. Why would everyone else lie about John Prante? No reason at all. Why would Prante lie? Because he was guilty and he was trying to save himself.

Weber even explained why Neil Hawkins asked so few questions of the Whites, the Bonds, Harold Pollard, Sherry Dalton, and Lee Barns—because there were no prior inconsistent statements or lies, and they had no reason to lie about Prante. Weber recalled Sherry Dalton's admission to three abortions—testimony to her honesty. "Now, someone who would volunteer a statement like that in this courtroom is not going to lie about anything else."

Prante told Sherry about the rage in which he had killed a woman. "It fits into what he said on his employment application, and this is what happened in this case being described in very glib terms, in third-person terms.

'Depression, rage and the calm after the storm.' They are so closely paralleled here. He's almost telling us in writing that that's what happened to him on June 21, 1978. And, because of his rage, Karla Brown is no longer living."

When the calm after the storm set in, the man who admitted knowing about fingerprint ridges cleaned up the scene.

Who became nervous when the publicity and psychological tactics started? Not Dwayne Conway or Jack Meyers or Tony Garza. John Prante called the prosecutor, called a lawyer, called Spencer Bond, and then tracked down Dwayne Conway for a four-hour visit.

Finally, Weber offered the jury an expanded version of the theory he gave them in his opening. Prante visited Conway sometime after 8 o'clock, spent ninety minutes or so putting in job applications, and then returned to Conway's about 10. He spent some time on the porch smoking marijuana and drinking, getting up his moxie to go next door to visit the girl who had made such a lasting impression on him. About 10:45, Prante talked to Karla in the driveway. He somehow followed her into the house, being admitted or sneaking in. By 11 o'clock, Prante's rage had exploded. He had beaten, strangled, and bitten Karla, and then fled to Conway's house, just thirty-six feet from the back door. Prante still had Karla's blood up to his elbows, because he left some on the back door and the gate.

He watched for her boyfriend to come home for lunch. When that didn't happen, Prante moved his car, probably to the nearby Laundromat. He returned to the basement between 2 and 3 o'clock to clean up the scene and stage it to look different from what had happened. He didn't want it to appear the guy next door had done it; he wanted to send the police looking for some "bizarre, maniac killer" who dressed his victim in a sweater she wouldn't have worn then—still buttoned at the top—and then left her in a barrel of water. When Prante put the sweater on her, he had to cut the cords and then retie them—just as Alva Busch had shown the jury.

And, after all, who was the only person who revealed details about the crime scene and never made a mistake? John Prante.

The prosecutor issued a challenge to the defense attorney. "Unless Mr. Hawkins can get up here and explain to you how Prante knew about the evidence at the time he knew it, it's your duty to convict John Prante."

Weber reduced the case to four points that called out for a guilty verdict.

First, Prante told Vicky White and the others about the bite marks in 1978, two years before anyone else knew about them.

Second, he told Spencer Bond he was at Karla's house between 2 and 3 o'clock, when the evidence proved Karla was dead.

Third, he claimed to be the last person to see her alive.

Fourth, he described the crime scene perfectly to Harold Pollard just after 6 o'clock that evening, when he shouldn't have known what he knew.

"What I know and what you should know without any doubt, but certainly without a reasonable doubt, is that John Prante murdered Karla Brown. And you should know one other thing. It's your duty to convict him because we're talking about justice for Karla Brown as well as justice for John Prante. And I trust that her epitaph can be written and completed: Karla Brown, born February 26, 1956. Murdered June 21, 1978. Her killer brought to justice by a Madison County jury, July 15, 1983.

"And there's only one way for her to get justice, and that's for you good people to convict the man who murdered her."

Don Weber was pointing at John Prante again.

Neil Hawkins's position before the jury was simple, too. The prosecution's witnesses not only were four years late, but .they were contradictory and inconclusive. Hawkins started with Lee Barns, who in 1978 never mentioned introducing Prante to Karla, or his supposed interest in her, or that Prante wanted to go to the party, or that Barns had ridden with Prante, or that Prante was driving a red car.

The Whites and the Bonds not only did not come forward in 1978, but they did not come forward in 1982 when they supposedly realized they had important evidence against Prante; they waited for the police to come to them. Their stories were essentially the same, even placing the bite marks on the left shoulder, not the right as seen in the photos. Their claim that Prante said the body was curled up in the basement easily could have come from the press coverage, which included reports three days after the murder that the body was found bent into a barrel—a curled-up position.

And what about this party where Prante was supposed to have divulged this information? "Vicky White seems to think it's Saturday; Mark White thinks it may have been Friday or Saturday; and Spencer Bond even moved it up as far as Wednesday."

Their claims that Prante said he had to get his story straight with Dwayne Conway also failed to withstand scrutiny. The police hadn't even talked to Prante about discrepancies until July 5, 1978, so how would Prante have known earlier that there was any need to get the stories straight?

What about all this talk that Prante was leaving town? "His mother and stepsister testified that he was in this area until 1980, when he went to Louisiana. He did not flee this area, did not make himself hidden or anything. He was a regular resident of these parts. He's not hiding as these witnesses would have you believe. He was here, where anybody could find him."

The jury heard Prante steadfastly deny any involvement in Karla's death and deny making any incriminating statements in 1978, despite Spencer Bond's persistent and tape-recorded accusations.

And Sherry Dalton—she didn't report her information to the police until they were questioning her on another case. Hawkins added, "Mr. Prante, in fact, denied ever telling her that he killed anyone, much less a woman. He denied that he killed anyone in Vietnam. He never told her that. She never had it corroborated that she was ever bitten; she has no proof of that."

Edna Vancil, who watched the same TV programs every day and timed her recollections by that, only put Prante on the porch at specific times; she didn't know where he was at any other time, because she can see only one view from her chair.

Hawkins said Harold Pollard's first "fact" was wrong; he said Prante arrived at 6 o'clock, but there was ample evidence that Prante still was at Conway's house then. Detective Nunn saw him at 6:20 and Robert Hart, David's father, saw a man who surely was Prante at 6:30. And, Robert Hart described a man in a dark T-shirt and jeans, not the yellow shirt seen by Pollard.

Hawkins offered another interesting perspective about Pollard's claim that Prante said the body was found curled up on the floor. Only David Hart saw that position. Pollard learned of that description somewhere else, such as in the newspapers or through local gossip. After all, Pollard's recollections had not been reported to the police until 1982, long after the publicity.

"None of these witnesses came forward or attached any importance to any of this testimony at any time until after 1982. It might be believable in 1978 that they knew bite marks were there. It's not believable in 1982, after it's been in the paper. If they knew before it was published, before all of these facts were in the news, it may be more believable. It's not believable now. It's just repeating what they read or what they heard."

Hawkins then turned toward Weber. The prosecutor made widely reported announcements in 1978, 1980, and 1982 about solving this case, and it was reopened with great fanfare in 1982. Weber admitted to the press then that the exhumation and second autopsy were needed because the enhanced photos were insufficient for his experts' use. And Weber said his prime suspect then was

Dwayne Conway. Suddenly, amid all this publicity, John Prante was arrested.

Boiling it all down, Hawkins said, "The only piece of corroborative evidence they have is the alleged bite marks on Karla Brown. They are the only physical evidence they have even tangling John Prante with this case."

And what did the experts really say about the bite marks? The prosecutor's witnesses said they were consistent with Prante because of some spaces between the teeth. And the defense experts said the photos were next to useless—taken without any standard procedures for scientific use. Sperber said it couldn't be a bite mark because he never had seen a bite pattern in a straight line.

Hawkins also challenged Weber's claim to the number of people with spacing in their teeth comparable to Prante's; Weber claimed one percent, but Dr. Pavlik said it was ten percent.

"So the only physical, corroborative evidence the state has, has been rebutted by the experts I have put on for the defendant, testifying there's no way that anybody can make a judgment based on those bite marks on that neck."

The idea of John Prante as an enraged killer also was debunked by the character witnesses—people who knew Prante best and described him as a peaceful person who never got into fights or talked badly about women. Prante's sister said that, when he did get mad, he simply left; he did not fly into a rage and lash out.

"He's not a violent person, as Mr. Weber would have you believe—a person that goes into a rage and then has a calm after the storm."

Finally, there was the testimony of John Prante. He denied any involvement in this murder, but admitted he was next door "smoking and getting high." He admitted alcohol and drug problems, and credibly claimed a poor memory that left details confused. He cooperated with the police, told them what he remembered, and allowed his picture and fingerprints to be taken. He did not flee; except for a few months in Louisiana, he stayed in Wood River.

He went to see Dwayne Conway that Sunday only because he was confused by Spencer Bond's insistent accusations; the "gas chamber" reference was a reaction to Bond's tactics.

Hawkins dismissed Weber's fingerprint accusation, adding that anyone who watched television knew how to wipe them off.

"Mr. Weber also now is trying to give the killer in this case more credit than he gives trained police officers or trained pathologists. He wants you to believe that the killer in this case knew that those bite marks were traceable. At that time, in 1978, the trained police didn't know that; the trained pathologists didn't know it. How could he expect anyone to know that unless they were an expert in the field, and there weren't very many of those around in 1978."

It was time to close. "Mr. Prante stands here presumed innocent and he is innocent; he did not commit this crime. Mr. Prante's only crime is, he just happened to be next door at the time the crime was committed. Nothing more. He did not implicate himself in this crime, never said he did it, and didn't know anything about this crime."

He reminded the jurors they could not convict on conjecture and speculation, and added, "I will just ask you to remember in cases like this that justice is just as well served when the innocent are acquitted as when the guilty are convicted."

Don Weber was anxious for his rebuttal. First, the somewhat tardy witnesses for the prosecution—they weren't the kind of people who usually gushed to the police about anything. But more important, they didn't realize they knew anything significant until they read about the bite marks in 1982.

What about the bite marks? Weber repeated the familiar refrain: rectangle, space, rectangle, space, triangle. Each expert recognized the pattern as a human bite mark, and the prosecution's experts said it was definitely, without a doubt, a bite mark. No unknown object made that mark accidentally; the object that made it was in John Prante's mouth.

If Prante was innocent, he had the world's worst luck.

"The poor luck this guy has had—all of his friends lying about him; all of the police catching him up in these lies; all the lies he told himself; what his old buddy, Dwayne Conway, told about him. Imagine the bad luck this guy has. The victim has some marks here that just match his teeth. That has got to be the worst luck of anybody I have ever seen. And, it's impossible."

The prosecutor described John Prante as a man who had built up a lot of rage in his life—a divorce, time in the brig, drug abuse, and no invitation to Karla's party. He finally exploded and killed the woman who inflicted one rejection too many.

Weber angrily denied the allegations about publicity. "Is that what we are here for, because we just pulled some guy in because I wanted to get my picture in the paper, or because Randy Rushing wanted to get a promotion, or because the Wood River police wanted to have a bottle of champagne? If that's what you believe, then I guess you can acquit him. But when you do, you better watch out when you go out, because you can't trust the police anymore. They are the only people standing between you and criminals like John Prante. We're proud of the investigation, and we wouldn't be proud and wouldn't be satisfied if we didn't have the right man."

Weber explained that everyone involved in the case had done their duty, and added, "You know, Karla Brown came back literally from the grave in this case, to solve the killing four years after she was buried."

It was time for the jury to do its duty and convict John Prante.

"I will rest and abide in your judgment, as everybody else in the case will, and as will the girl who is in a grave right now, crying out for justice."

The courtroom fell silent as the burden fell to the jury.

* * *

Deliberations began at 11:20 A.M.; Weber checked his watch and decided he wouldn't get nervous until 4:30, allowing the standard time for a murder conviction—four and a half hours—with time for lunch.

When the prosecutor's group gathered for lunch, the Judsons and others chanted, "Rectangle, space, rectangle, space, triangle." Weber smiled, but he felt uneasy. Four of the jurors had seemed to be right with him during the closings; the other eight were inscrutable. This could go either way. It was an old case with some old evidence, and experts who disagreed. But it was as good as it ever would get; Weber and the police had done their best.

Neil Hawkins felt a sense of relief when the case passed to someone else's hands. He had done his best, too, and it was up to the jurors now. They had been stone-faced and Hawkins was unable to detect any reaction while he delivered his closings. He expected deliberations to last at least four to six hours, and quite possibly could go into a second day. John Prante thanked him for a good job, and Hawkins gave Prante a wish for the best.

Just after lunch, the jury sent a note to Judge Romani, asking how Vicky White's testimony was obtained. Weber wanted to explain that someone had told the police about her comments; but Hawkins argued against that. The judge finally sent the standard reply—a note saying only that the jury already had heard the evidence.

The afternoon passed with each group sitting in its separate offices and others milling restlessly about the hallways. About 5:15, Weber felt an unwelcome tightness, a slight uneasiness. He tried to reassure himself, but it was hard to get under control; he was past his comfort zone.

Donna and Terry Judson were handling the wait better, refusing to consider an acquittal. Weber was superb in his closings, and the Judsons couldn't believe any juror would accept the defenses's position that Prante was just some unlucky guy who happened to be sitting next door and whose teeth happened to match the marks on Karla's neck.

Donna Judson finally allowed herself the luxury of hating John Prante when she heard him describe what her sister was wearing minutes before her death. It had been hard to listen to, and it devastated Donna. You creep, Donna had thought as she watched the man on the stand.

Even Terry Judson had allowed the analytical side to move over so the hate could move in. Terry still wanted a confession on the stand; but a conviction would do.

Jo Ellen Brown had sat in for the closing arguments—her first time in the courtroom—but went home to await the verdict. She was surprised by her first look at John Prante; she expected him to have a beard as he did in the newspaper photo. But from her seat in the second row, Jo Ellen still thought his face looked awful—splotchy and coarse. She never visualized what had been done to her daughter. But looking at Prante, and hearing the facts, she couldn't shut out the images anymore; it made her ill.

At 5:45, word came that the jury had reached a verdict. Everyone assembled quickly in the courtroom, and the jurors filed in. Weber, Hawkins, Prante, and the veteran reporters in the first row searched the jurors' faces, waiting to see if they looked at the defendant; they didn't.

Terry Judson slipped his arm around his trembling wife; David Hart was sitting nervously just behind them, leaning forward with his elbows on his knees. Terry anticipated the sound of the verdict, and imagined it as a switch that suddenly would turn the light on again after five long years of darkness.

Those interminable seconds—the period of time Don Weber hated more than anything else—passed as the verdict was handed from the foreman to the bailiff to the young judge. Reading his first trial verdict, Judge Romani said solemnly, "The verdict the court has been handed reads as follows: We, the jury, find the defendant, John Prante, guilty of the offense of murder."

As muted applause and cheers went up across the courtroom, a sobbing David Hart leaned forward and grabbed Terry Judson's arm.

Weber finally let out the breath he had been holding.

At the defense table, John Prante closed his eye
briefly, but showed no other reaction; he was dead calm

Hawkins asked for the jurors to be polled, and each or
affirmed their vote to convict. But Don Weber and Donn
Judson saw more than that. They saw angry, resolute ju
rors who, for the first time, were showing their reaction
to the evidence they heard over thirteen days. Webe
looked into their faces and saw twelve good, decent peo
ple he believed already had decided they would impose
the ultimate penalty upon the man who had imposed th
ultimate injustice on Karla Brown. It would be Weber
job to ask them to take that last drastic step, and orde
John Prante strapped to a gurney while an intravenou
bottle dripped a lethal potion into his veins.

Judge Romani told the jurors to return at 1 o'clock c
Monday to begin the penalty phase, a two-part hearing i
which the jurors would make the life-or-death decisic
for Prante.

The crowd moved into the corridor, where the re
straints on the celebration dissolved. Everyone hugge
and cried and congratulated each other. Weber, usually re
served about displays of affection, happily hugged Donn
Judson and David Hart. Weber could feel the stinging i
his eyes, too; it had been a long odyssey.

Donna called her mother with the news. Through he
tears, Jo Ellen said firmly, "I knew we had him." Sh
turned down Donna's offer of a ride to the victory part
For Jo Ellen, a quiet evening at home was best.

Donna then faced the press to thank Weber, his staf
and the police for allowing her sister to find a final res

David Hart also spoke to the reporters he had avoide
before. His face still wet from tears, Hart thanked Webe
Rushing, and the rest of the team. "Without them, th
never would have been solved. I've been in this since da
one, and these guys did a job above and beyond."

Weber and Hawkins, still under the gag order, cou
not comment.

Hawkins was sure a conviction was coming in whe
the jury returned so quickly; he didn't announce that

Prante as they headed toward the courtroom. Prante took the verdict surprisingly well, Hawkins thought. Although it had been obvious that Prante had real hopes for an acquittal and was disappointed, he had not shown the kind of profound reaction that would have been reasonable.

For Weber, it had been a case he had to win; he couldn't lose it after the hard work and dedication of everyone involved. And he couldn't lose it after putting himself on the line with the publicity and the innovative techniques. When you make that much noise standing out in front, you'd better be able to back it up.

It was the best verdict Rushing ever witnessed, and led him to coin the definitive phrase of the trial—"You can lie through your teeth, but your teeth don't lie."

For Donna Judson, it was the kind of experience denied women who never celebrated an exciting sports win as a team member. It surely was just like the "thrill of victory," the atmosphere in the team locker room after winning the World Series. For her, it was the Super Bowl of her life.

And it brought to an end the five-year mission for the Judsons. The last word was written in an even more dramatic fashion the next morning. Sitting by the swimming pool, Donna completed the journal she kept during the trial. Finally, with the evidence and the verdict in, Donna felt Karla would believe it was over and could rest at last; they had the right man and he would be punished. As Donna wrote her final thoughts in the journal, her pen added the signature, "Karla Brown."

In amazement, Donna called Terry over and asked, "Whose handwriting is that?"

Terry knew instantly; it wasn't Donna's.

"It's Karla's."

Chapter 23

The looks on the jurors' faces hadn't escaped Ne
Hawkins's attention. He had no trouble reading the inter
in their eyes. Early on Monday afternoon, July 18
Hawkins stood before Judge Charles Romani and shifte
a heavy burden onto the shoulders draped in the blac
robe. With John Prante's agreement, Hawkins waived th
jury and placed Prante's fate in the hands of the judge.

Don Weber was somewhat surprised by the defense'
tactic; it was unusual to change horses midstream. But o
second thought, Weber realized it was exactly the rigl
move by Hawkins. Those twelve people had become
hanging jury, and Prante's only chance to escape deat
rested with the judge.

But Weber also knew the man in the robes was a pros
ecutor himself until seven months earlier. He had pre
sided over his first trial, hearing the facts of this bruta
crime and listening to the defendant lie in the judge's ow
courtroom. Under these circumstances, Weber though
there was little chance of Prante escaping the ultima
penalty from Judge Romani.

Hawkins, however, remained just as convinced that n
judge would impose death on John Prante. Despite all c
the evidence that might cry out for death, no judge coul
overlook Prante's lack of a significant criminal record.

The first of the two penalty phases was to determine
Prante was eligible for the death penalty. Weber only ha
to prove that Prante was at least eighteen when he com
mitted the crime, and that the murder happened durin
commission of another felony—a burglary. In the secon

phase, Weber would be required to prove there were no mitigating factors strong enough to preclude the imposition of the death penalty.

Weber told the judge that it was perfectly clear that John Prante was older than eighteen, and did not have the permission of David Hart or Karla Brown to be in their home and do what he did; that established the commission of a burglary and sexual assault.

Hawkins insisted that the state offered little more than innuendo of a burglary. There was no proof, either, that a burglary or sexual assault occurred at the same time as the murder. Those acts could not be assumed to be simultaneous with the killing for the purpose of the sentencing.

Judge Romani deliberated for sixty-five minutes in his chambers, and accepted Weber's arguments right down the line. From the bench, Romani added that it had been proved that only Prante could have killed Karla Brown. Prante was eligible for the death penalty, and the hearing would continue.

Hawkins was surprised; he genuinely believed that more than an innuendo of sexual assault was needed to qualify for death.

But then the judge surprised Weber and delayed the final phase, until September.

Some of the jurors stayed to await the decision they no longer had to make, and Weber and the Judsons talked with several of them. The jurors were pleased to confirm their suspicion that Donna was Karla's sister; they couldn't help but notice how the young woman in the front row favored the young woman in the photographs.

The jurors' analysis of the evidence also proved intriguing. Some of them dismissed the bite marks entirely; with experts on both sides disagreeing so completely, the jurors called it a draw. Instead, they focused on the testimony of the Whites, the Bonds, Harold Pollard, and, of all people, Sherry Dalton.

Although that confirmed Weber's final appraisal of the evidence, he still was disappointed that the bite marks he found so intriguing scored no better with the jurors. It helped a little to hear from some jurors, however, that the bite marks were important to their decisions.

Reporter Charlie Bosworth had covered the new investigation and the trial for the *St. Louis Post-Dispatch*. A few weeks after Prante was convicted, Bosworth was interviewing State's Attorney John Knight of Bond County about a case he was prosecuting. Bosworth knew that Knight was an assistant prosecutor under Chuck Romani, and succeeded Romani when he left to become a judge. Since Romani was only weeks away from a final decision—perhaps very final for Prante—Bosworth sought Knight's opinion on a topic of considerable discussion in Madison County.

"You know Romani better than most people, John. Do you think he's going to give Prante the death penalty?"

"Well, a lot of people who don't know Chuck might think he's too nice of a guy to do that. He's so easygoing and friendly, a lot of people might underestimate how really tough he is. He was a tough prosecutor for years, and that's a pretty brutal murder there. When it comes right down to it"—Knight paused dramatically—"I wouldn't be surprised if Chuck doesn't let John Prante ride the lightning."

It was a jolting line; a new euphemism for the electric chair with a shocking image, even if the chair no longer was the instrument of death in Illinois. In the twenty years since the last execution, the legislature had changed the method to lethal injection, although a condemned defendant could choose either method.

The charges of obstructing justice and conspiracy to obstruct justice against Dwayne Conway seemed like an open-and-shut case to Weber; and a conviction against Conway would eliminate his right not to testify against Prante at the death-sentence hearing.

On September 20—one week before the sentencing for Prante—Keith Jensen took Conway before a jury in the courtroom of Circuit Judge P. J. O'Neill. In a one-day trial, Conway testified that he recanted his statement to the police only because it contained inaccuracies he could not swear to in court; he insisted he was not protecting Prante.

In closing arguments, the jury was urged to convict Conway because he obviously intended to impede the prosecution of Prante by switching stories so late in the game. But Assistant Public Defender Jim Hackett said the state failed to prove that Conway had any intent to obstruct justice. After six hours of deliberations, the jury was hopelessly deadlocked at eight votes for conviction and four for acquittal; the judge declared a hung jury and a mistrial.

Weber was surprised and disappointed; his plan to use Conway at Prante's sentencing hearing was scuttled, and another trial would have to be held for a guy who already had caused an unbelievable amount of trouble in this case.

John Prante faced Associate Judge Charles Romani, Jr., in one of the large, stately courtrooms on the third floor of the Edwardsville courthouse for sentencing on Tuesday, September 27. The Judsons and Jo Ellen Brown were there for the last chapter in the story.

Don Weber believed with all his heart that Prante should pay the supreme cost for the brutality he inflicted on Karla Brown and those she left behind. Not only had Karla suffered in unimaginable ways, but her family and her community were marked forever by the crime. But Weber knew there was one factor weighing heavily in Prante's favor; his lack of a substantial criminal record was quite a shield to Weber's attack.

Another choice for the judge was to invoke the state's "extended term" law. The maximum sentence of forty years could be doubled if the crime was accompanied by "exceptionally brutal and heinous behavior indicative of wanton cruelty."

But Weber was not looking for any mercy for John Prante.

"What we are here for today, Your Honor, is to determine what value society is going to place on the life of Karla Brown, and in the way she was murdered," Weber began.

He had Randy Rushing testify about Conway's charges that Prante shoved a rifle in his face and fired a shot through the ceiling; and had slapped around his wife, Karen. Spencer Bond and Harold Pollard testified that Prante used several kinds of drugs and sold marijuana to fifteen or twenty customers. Prante once threatened to kill Pollard, too. All criminal acts. His record in the Navy showed he failed to report for duty seven times, and served thirty days in the brig.

In closing arguments, Weber hammered at the attack on Karla as "brutal and heinous," two of the key words that elevated criminal acts above standard punishment. Prante stalked her lustfully and assaulted her cold-bloodedly in her own home with violence that could be called "overkill." Then he not only returned later to clean up the basement, but took Karla's clothes as hideous souvenirs. He showed no compassion or remorse for Karla, but cried for himself on the witness stand. Prante's long list of outlaw activities should be enough to overcome the lack of an official criminal record.

"In John Prante dwells a fatal and malignant heart—the type of fatal and malignant heart that deserves only one penalty."

Weber said the judge's duty was "to impose the sanction of death on the man who, for no reason, in a brutal and senseless manner, imposed the sanction of death on a defenseless, twenty-two-year-old girl."

Neil Hawkins attacked the credibility of Bond and Pollard as witnesses to Prante's past; they admitted selling marijuana to just as many customers. Prante's character witnesses at trial, however, described him as a peaceful, passive man. And Prante spent four years after the murder without any record of other crimes.

Hawkins invoked Prante's newfound religious convictions, and rejected Weber's depiction of the inner man.

"The defendant does not have a malignant heart and should not be eliminated from society." Prante had considerable potential for rehabilitation, Hawkins stressed as he called on the judge to reject the call for death, and to send this man to prison.

Weber had one more chance, and he could not let the reference to Prante's religious conversion go unanswered; that troubled the prosecutor. Karla Brown never was given the chance to reflect on her life or repent if there was reason. It was unjust to argue that Prante should be rewarded for a typical jailhouse conversion—prisoners often got closer to God as they got closer to prison and, especially, to a death sentence.

"It was the defendant who chose the way of death all the way down the line," Weber said.

As Weber asked Judge Romani to impose the ultimate sentence as a statement about society's values, Neil Hawkins already knew what was about to happen. When he had stood before the bench to argue for Prante's life, the defense attorney had caught a glimpse of the judge's notepad, and an unmistakable scribble.

Before announcing his decision, the judge gave John Prante a chance to speak for himself. The defendant walked calmly to the middle of the courtroom and unfolded several sheets of paper.

In that quiet, controlled voice, he addressed important parts of the case against him. The evidence proved he was driving a blue car, not a red one. The witnesses quoted him as saying the bite marks were on the left shoulder, when the medical evidence clearly showed they were on the right side. He studied the bite marks in the Styrofoam cup prepared by a defense expert and found them almost identical.

"As Mr. Hawkins said, my only guilt is one of being at the neighbor's house next to the crime scene."

He insisted that Lee Barns lied on the stand. "I don't know why he did, but he did. And I hope God will forgive him."

Prante complained that the jury was not sequestered,

and that his case was damaged by the pretrial publicity generated by Weber. The defendant also complained that Hawkins had not been given enough help by the public defender's office, even though he was up against "the top two prosecutors of the county."

Prante thanked Judge Romani for his handling of the trial, calling him "a very good man." He thanked Hawkins again, adding that he hoped he hadn't offended him with his other statements.

"Mr. Weber, you are extremely persuasive. I believe your calling should have been in the work of a minister, because I think you would have been considerably better in that than the law of man."

Thanks so much for your suggestion, Weber thought.

Prante said he was angry at first at the people who testified against him, but was able to forgive them.

"I suspect that after this, there will always be somebody who will believe that I am guilty of this crime."

Weber shook his head and thought, I'm sure there will be more than a few, John. Weber had never heard anything quite like this.

Then Prante turned to Karla Brown's family, catching them by surprise.

"I want the relatives of Karla Brown to understand; I can't expect you to believe me, but I hope, in your sorrow, you may understand that I want to say I'm sorry for you in your loss of Karla. But I can't accept any responsibility for her death. I believe Jesus and have repented from all my sins. But I cannot repent for something I have not done. I prayed for her often in the hope that Christ will protect her now."

His words left Donna Judson disgusted; Jo Ellen Brown looked at Prante and saw just another liar.

"Judge Romani, at this time I have given you my life, which you can have. But you cannot have my soul and spirit. I pray that you will have mercy upon me so that I may have the time to prove my innocence. I pray that I will not have to give my life for the guilt of another person. Thank you, sir."

The young judge looked down from the bench, and began to speak in a firm, resolute voice.

"The decision of the court in this case is a very difficult decision, Mr. Prante. It involves your life and you do have some rights, which the court has tried to protect throughout this trial. The court also realizes that Karla Brown had some rights—the right to live her life to its fullest, and it was taken away from her at the age of twenty-two."

Romani said he weighed all aspects of the case carefully and applied the proper law to them, including the lack of a significant criminal record.

"The court finds from the evidence, Mr. Prante, that this was an exceptionally brutal and heinous crime. The court feels that the things that were done to this victim before, during, and after her death are brutal and heinous, and are things that should not occur to any human being."

Finally the sentence. As Romani asked Prante to rise and face the bench, Hawkins already knew he had won his fight to save John Prante's life.

"Mitigating factors sufficient to preclude the imposition of the death penalty are present. The court is not going to sentence you to death."

But the crime was heinous enough to invoke the "extended term" provision.

"The court hereby sentences you, John Prante, to the Illinois Department of Corrections for a term of seventy-five years."

That was the number Hawkins has seen written on Romani's pad.

As Deputy Bob Henke cuffed and manacled a solemn Prante to begin the trip to prison, Don Weber shook his head in disappointment. He fully expected Romani to send Prante to his just and deserved death. But Weber knew the sentence was well within reasonable bounds— still a fair end to this long and fascinating case.

Donna Judson was surrounded by reporters as she spoke for those left behind.

"Karla's family believed that Karla's life was a lot more important than seventy-five years of John Prante's. But we feel it was justice, and we can accept that. We were all in favor of the death penalty. We had discussed that as a family, and we decided that it was right for what he did to my sister."

Jo Ellen Brown had opposed the death penalty at first, but finally agreed it would have been a just punishment for Karla's killer. When she heard the prison sentence imposed, however, she thought it was enough; it sounded fair to her.

As Weber, the cops, the Judsons, and the others said their good-byes—in some cases ending unique relationships forged amid this wrenching investigation—Jo Ellen Brown quietly walked out of the courthouse alone. In a bar across the street, she sat down and ordered a drink—the first of many. She drank in solitude all night, her thoughts reaching deep into the memories of the special daughter lost so long ago, and only now avenged. There was grief for some things that had been, and for some things that might have been. There were regrets for words said and unsaid. But mostly, there were warm memories of the good times, and the love between a mother and a daughter that neither death nor time could diminish.

Jo Ellen fanned those embers and basked in the warmth. The memories would last forever; they would have to.

Justice had been done, and the rest had to be put away on this long night. The pain of a sunny morning so long ago. The horror of the uninvited visit. The hate for this cruel visitor. The time to leave all of those behind had come for Jo Ellen and, finally, for Karla Brown.

Epilogue

It soon became clear to John Prante that he would not be welcomed with open arms into the society at the Menard Correctional Center in Chester, Illinois. The harassment by other inmates began immediately. There were persistent rumors that his attempt to pin the murder of Karla Brown on Tony Garza, a resident of Menard for almost five years, was not looked upon kindly by Garza or the other prisoners. At Prante's request, prison officials relocated him to "PC," the Protective Custody unit where prisoners in danger in the general population are kept in segregated cells.

In January 1984, Dwayne Conway pleaded guilty to obstructing justice for impeding the prosecution of John Prante; he stood mute at the hearing. The plea-bargain called for a sentence of 108 days—the time he already served in the county jail—and probation for twenty-five months. The conspiracy charge was dropped and he was freed.

As tough as life in prison was for John Prante, his efforts to overturn his conviction suffered an even worse fate. Judge Romani rejected a posttrial motion in December 1983, when Neil Hawkins argued that his client was denied a fair trial.

Prante hired a private attorney to handle the appeal from there. Lawyer Gage Sherwood was surprised when he met his new client at Menard prison. Instead of the seven-foot, 300-pound monster one would expect in such a terribly violent case, Sherwood was greeted by a quiet, pleasant man who was easy to get along with and so passive that he continued to have problems with other inmates. And, Prante absolutely proclaimed his innocence in a story that never wavered under intense questioning. Sherwood was convinced he had a viable appeal. In a ninety-eight-page brief to the Fifth District Appellate Court, he ripped into Weber's conduct of the case with a vengeance and argued there was not a shred of evidence that John Prante ever was in Karla Brown's house.

In October 1986, the Appellate Court denied the appeal on all points, dwelling on Prante's statements to the Whites, the Bonds, and Harold Pollard—especially about the bite marks and the position of Karla's body. "The defendant not only had the opportunity to commit the crime, but also was privy to information knowable only by one who had participated in the commission of it."

The Illinois Supreme Court later found no grounds to hear a further appeal by Prante.

Weber has never had a case reversed on appeal.

Not long after the trial, Don Weber received a special package from Donna and Terry Judson containing a small plaque on which Donna embroidered a new truism of criminology—"You can lie through your teeth, but your teeth don't lie. John Prante, July 15, 1983."

The border of the plaque was a very special pattern—rectangle, space, rectangle, space, triangle.

The memento still hangs on Weber's office wall.

After a difficult campaign in 1984, Weber lost his bid for reelection to a Democratic candidate by 1,365 votes out of a total of 103,000. Weber opened a private office and renewed an earlier goal of becoming a patent attorney. He practices patent law and, occasionally, does some criminal defense work.

By the late 1980s, Agent John Douglas's operation in the basement of the FBI Academy had become an incredibly successful unit of thirty-five people who analyzed hundreds of crimes each year to assist the police across the country. But he really was propelled into the national limelight after he served as technical adviser to author Thomas Harris for his novels, *Search for the Red Dragon* and *The Silence of the Lambs*. The movie from the second book, which blended three of the worst serial killers from Douglas's files into one terrifying villain, was a blockbuster that won five Academy Awards and featured an FBI expert modeled after Douglas.

His success did not come without cost, however; the strain of his journey into the dark, ugly side of the human mind wounded his own. In 1983—amid his work on the still-unsolved Green River serial killings in the Northwest and the investigation that led to Wayne Williams's conviction in Atlanta—Douglas developed a near-fatal brain lesion. He had sensed disaster was coming; he took out an income-protection insurance policy and, the day it became effective, he collapsed. He spent five months recuperating.

Douglas remembered the Karla Brown case—one of his earliest successes—as a crime less about sex than about anger and power; about a loser finally and violently shouting that no one would reject him again and live to tell about it. This killer would have claimed a female victim at some point—perhaps even a little girl if the opportunity arose; the resentment toward women had to erupt sooner or later. He was an immature, inadequate man who spent more time with pornographic magazines than relating to real people. He spent much of this time depressed over his life.

He had employed that small barrel to pose his victim in the most humiliating way, to degrade and dominate her even more. And to send a message to the police: what happened was her fault because she rejected him so coldly. She made him do it, and she got what was coming to her.

Biting Karla was a kind of cannibalization, a predatory devouring to possess her in a special way. When Karla re-

sisted, he might even have liked it. But Douglas was not
so sure Karla would have fought with the ferocity in
which her friends and family were so confident; Douglas
knew even big men could have the fight knocked from
them with one staggering blow. And the killer had become furious at Karla's rejection; he may not have realized how badly he was injuring her—amid the rage. After
her injuries were apparent, he began to cover his tracks—
the calm after the storm.

But Douglas changed his earlier theory that the killer
may have left the house and returned later to alter the
scene. Douglas now understood that a basement was too
dangerous; once the killer left, he would not have ventured back into a room with only one exit.

After four years, his world collapsed under the news of
the reopened investigation, the bite marks, and the exhumation. Douglas said the televised coverage and Weber's
statements to reporters would have made the killer crazy.
Douglas compared it to the movie *Jaws II*—just when the
killer thought it was safe . . . And he compared Weber to
a bugzapper: Prante was irresistably and fatally drawn to
the flame.

Ten years after Karla Brown was murdered, the way
she touched people still was remembered fondly, not only
by her family, but by the prosecutors and cops who knew
her only in death.

Alva W. Busch remains one of the preeminent crime-
scene technicians in the state and hopes to add true-crime
writing to his repertoire.

Captain Randy Rushing is the assistant to the deputy
director of the Illinois State Police, second in command
over all of the uniformed officers.

Captain Larry Trent is the area commander for the DCI
agents in all of southern Illinois.

Lieutenant Wayne Watson is the zone commander for
the DCI in Collinsville.

Major Tom O'Connor is the assistant chief of police at
Maryland Heights, Missouri, and remains one of the lead-

ers of the St. Louis Major Case Squad. In 1991, he also led the officers trying to control the riot that followed a rock-concert performance by Guns N' Roses.

Don Greer became the administrative assistant for the state's attorney in Madison County, and then moved on to become chief of police in Crestwood, Missouri.

Rick White remains an officer in Wood River.

Neil Hawkins continues to represent clients as an assistant public defender in Madison County.

David Hart is happily married and a father, and is known as one of the finest electricians in the area.

Donna and Terry Judson still live in Minnesota. Jo Ellen Brown, who finally learned to begin living again, moved to Connecticut to live with Connie Dykstra and her family. People still ask Jo Ellen if she really believes John Prante was guilty. "Well, of course I do," she always replies.

Dwayne Conway was last seen by the authorities when he volunteered to paint a mural on a wall at Brighton City Hall—in the same room where he was interviewed by Tom O'Connor and Randy Rushing. Then Conway dropped out of sight. Weber wondered if the man's daydream about being picked up by aliens finally came true.

John N. Prante still serves his time in the "PC" Unit at Menard, overlooking the Mississippi River. He is quiet and considered strange by the other inmates, most of whom leave him alone now. His religious conversion has worn off; he doesn't talk about forgiveness much anymore. His appeals are exhausted and he is scheduled for parole—on December 9, 2019. But he continues to talk to lawyers about further appeals and is suggesting a DNA test of the semen recovered from Karla's body.

And, for the first time, John Prante has been talking to someone else—this time about what really happened in that basement on June 21, 1978. In December 1992, a former cellmate of Prante's told the authors that Prante had made some startling revelations about the murder of Karla Brown—facts the cellmate couldn't possibly have

known were stunningly accurate. Over several months
Prante parceled out tidbits a few at a time; sometimes a
letter from his sister or news about the prosecutor, Don
Weber, prodded Prante into revealing conversations. He
said the years of marijuana use left him with frequent
blackouts. But he seemed to have a pretty good—if
selective—memory of that day.

John Prante, finally, has admitted killing Karla Brown.
But just as Agent Douglas had predicted, Prante blamed
Karla. It was all her fault. He hadn't meant to kill her, but
she made him angry when she rejected and taunted him;
he was innocent.

Prante had, indeed, been attracted by Karla's beauty; he
called her a "little fox," and claimed to have known her
from college. He was "pissed off" when she pretended
not to know him in front of his friends the night of the
moving party.

So he decided to set things right and get what he
wanted. With a length of electrical cord from his car
tucked into his pocket, Prante stole back to Karla's after
he left Conway's that morning. He parked at the
laundromat—just as Weber had guessed—and slipped
through the back door of her house. He confronted her in
the basement, and she demanded to know what he was
doing there. He demanded to know why she had embarrassed him in front of his friends. She recognized him
then, but the reunion was not cordial.

Prante glossed over some of the details, but said Karla
rejected his sexual advances, and he tried to rape her as
they struggled on the couch. He tied her up with the cord.
He even mentioned, crudely, that she was menstruating
and, more important, he admitted that he bit her. In another dramatic reenactment, the cellmate brought his fingertips up to the side of his neck. After all those years,
that gesture still was chilling.

What started as sexual assault became a murder when
Prante's inadequacy became apparent; as Sherry Dalton
had learned, Prante had trouble achieving an erection.
And Karla—as ferocious as others were sure she would

e—taunted him. "You can't even get it up," she sneered. She laughed at him. Fourteen years later in his prison cell, Prante recalled his humiliation, hung his head, and whispered, "It had happened before."

But this time, the ridicule was more than he could take, and years of anger and rejection exploded. "All hell broke loose" was the description by the cellie. Prante said he struck Karla with a table, bloodying her and knocking her unconscious. He claimed he pushed her head into a bucket of water to try to revive her, again shading the truth about what he really was doing. He was leaving out many pertinent, and disgusting, details to minimize his ghastly conduct for his cellmate.

Prante fled Karla's house and returned to Conway's to wash up; he was about to slip out when Conway discovered him, just as Dwayne had told Agent O'Connor. Prante had to offer a weak excuse of stopping by to use the bathroom and get a beer. He hung around to watch the action and remembered seeing a guy drive up in a pickup truck. The cops talked to him, but they didn't catch on.

Soon the investigation faded out and Prante headed south. While he was in Louisiana, his sexual anger flared again—just as Douglas knew it would. Prante picked up a girl and drove to a secluded spot to drink and smoke pot. While they were kissing, he bit her, too; that made her angry and she refused to have sex with him. He beat her into unconsciousness, dragged her into the woods, and drove off. The cellmate never heard what happened to her.

Prante returned to Madison County, assuming it was safe, only to be shocked when Weber announced the case was being reopened. As the investigation intensified, he sought out a number of people to try to persuade them to remember things his way. He said he tracked down one guy who was living in a trailer out in the boonies, an obvious reference to Dwayne Conway. Prante talked for hours, finally getting his friend's mind right. One girl kept remembering that she saw him that day in a yellow T-shirt with writing on it. He tried to convince her she was wrong, but she kept remembering "the damned writing" on the shirt, Prante fumed.

Then came the exhumation. "I liked to shit when I found out they were digging her up again," Prante told his cellie. It was all downhill from there. "That Weber went right for the jugular with all of that stuff about the bite marks and even the kind of knot Prante tied in the cord. Prante was relieved to escape the death sentence, but didn't think he deserved seventy-five years, either. After all, it was all Karla Brown's fault.

So, after all the years, John Prante hoped for a DNA test on which to pin his claims of innocence. Weber had to grin; only a loser like Prante would try to wrangle his freedom by using his own inadequacy. Since he was physically unable to have sex with Karla, of course the DNA test would not link him to the semen. There was a devious, although pitiful, cleverness to Prante's latest ploy.

For Don Weber, the report of Prante's confession was as satisfying confirmation of everything the prosecutor had known in his heart. And finally, the loved ones Karla Brown left behind could get almost everything they wanted to help her rest in peace. They had not heard it from John Prante's mouth, but at least they knew he had confessed that he was Karla's killer.

Make Room For Great Escapes At Hilton International Hotels

Save the coupons in the backs of these Ⓢ Signet and Ⓢ Onyx books and redeem them for special Hilton International Hotels discounts and services.

June

REVERSIBLE ERROR
Robert K. Tanenbaum

RELATIVE SINS
Cynthia Victor

July

GRACE POINT
Anne D. LeClaire

FOREVER
Judith Gould

August

MARILYN: *The Last Take*
Peter Harry Brown &
Patte B. Barham

JUST KILLING TIME
Derek Van Arman

September

DANGEROUS PRACTICES
Francis Roe

SILENT WITNESS:
*The Karla Brown
Murder Case*
Don W. Weber &
Charles Bosworth, Jr.

2 coupons: Save 25% off regular rates at Hilton International Hotels
4 coupons: Save 25% off regular rates, **plus** upgrade to Executive Floor
6 coupons: All the above, **plus** complimentary Fruit Basket
8 coupons: All the above, **plus** a free bottle of wine

(Check *People* Magazine and Signet and Onyx spring titles for Bonus coupons to be used when redeeming three or more coupons)

Disclaimers: Advance reservations and notification of the offer required. May not be used conjunction with any other offer. Discount applies to regular rates only. Subject to availabi and black out dates. Offer may not be used in conjunction with convention, group or an other special offer. Employees and family members of Penguin USA and Hilton Internation are not eligible to participate in GREAT ESCAPES.

- -